Ex-Library: Friends of
Lake County Public Library

The Pacific War

The Pantheon Asia Library

New Approaches to the New Asia

The Pacific War

World War II and the Japanese, 1931-1945

by Saburō Ienaga

Pantheon Books, New York

LAKE COUNTY PUBLIC LIBRARY

10816700

English translation Copyright © 1978 by Random House, Inc.

All rights reserved under International and Pan-American Copyright Conventions. Published in the United States by Pantheon Books, a division of Random House, Inc., New York, and simultaneously in Canada by Random House of Canada Limited, Toronto.

TAIHEIYŌ SENSŌ (Title of the English edition)
by Saburō Ienaga
Copyright © 1968 by Saburō Ienaga
Originally published in Japanese by IWANAMI SHOTEN, Publishers, Tokyo, 1968.

Library of Congress Cataloging in Publication Data

Ienaga, Saburō, 1913–
    The Pacific War.

    (The Pantheon Asia Library)
    Translation of *Taiheiyō sensō*.
    Includes bibliographical references and index.
    1. World War, 1939–1945—Japan. 2. Japan—History
—1912–1945. I. Title.
D767.2.I313 1978   940.53'52   77-88768
ISBN 0-394-49762-7

Manufactured in the United States of America

First American Edition

Contents

Note

Japan's surrender to the Allies on August 15, 1945, ended a disastrous fifteen-year military adventure into China, Southeast Asia, and the Pacific Islands. Contemporary Japan offers a "before-after" contrast rare in the annals of imperialist expansion. The nation ruled by myths of imperial divinity and sacred mission and dominated by generals and "thought police" who indoctrinated a supine public into obedience and militarism is a dim memory. In its place a society informed by more rational and thoroughly secular values has developed. The country's modest military forces are defensive, restricted by legal and fiscal restraints, and threaten no other nation. Japan today has few if any pretensions to Big Power hubris.

Saburō Ienaga's career spans the periods of Japan on the warpath and Japan on the mend. He has made explicit and activist commitments to building and preserving the postwar society of civil liberties, disarmament, and peace. In the turbulent decade after Japan regained its sovereignty in 1952, the new political order was threatened by conservative and rightist forces determined to turn the clock back. Attempts to revise the 1947 Constitution, increase police powers, and revive "patriotic values" were the hallmarks of authoritarian revanchism. But so far the political forces set free after 1945 —liberal and leftist political parties, unions, far-sighted business leaders and intellectuals—have held the line.

Ienaga's concern that Japan might again suffer the stifling pall of censorship and indoctrination has guided his scholarly .

interests and political activities. In the latter realm, his long
battle against the Ministry of Education's authority to certify
textbooks is one of the most celebrated legal battles of the
postwar era. As much a campaign of public education as a bid
to prevent what Ienaga considers an undesirable revival of
central authority over education, the case is at present before
the Supreme Court.

That Japan should not again be a bad neighbor to Korea,
China, and Southeast Asia has been fundamental to Ienaga's
vision of a peaceful international community. Ienaga has dis-
sented, for example, from his government's policy of a military alliance with the United States and support for American
"containment" of China and intervention in Indochina. Many
Japanese, Ienaga included, see unhappy similarities between
Japan's expansionism and America's record in Asia since the
late 1940s.

How can a historian help to prevent collective amnesia? As
the Pacific War fades into the past, young Japanese know less
of its horrors and of the conformist society that spawned
aggression. Many of Ienaga's generation and persuasion fear
that ignorance of the 1930s and the war presages militarism
and an indifference to civil liberties. The next phase may be
to isolate and silence criticism in favor of a neoconservative
national consensus, followed by expanded military forces and
a slide toward the authoritarian past.

Ienaga wrote *The Pacific War* to remind a new generation
that its peace and prosperity have roots in the fascism and
aggression of the 1930s. It was not Ienaga's purpose to revive
war guilt over atrocities or to castigate villains by reciting the
record of stupidity in high places. He sought to rekindle idealism and dedication to a free and peaceful society, to keep
Japan on an even domestic and international keel. That, in his
judgment, could best be done by describing "the horrors of
war." Otherwise, a generation raised on sugar-coated history
would be likely to repeat the errors of the past.

The Pacific War blends analysis of institutions—the Meiji
Constitution, the educational system, and the military—with

a narrative account of the rapid, bizarre escalation of military operations. The author's methodology is deceptively simple. Ienaga asks, How could the Japanese people have prevented the war? The question directs attention away from conventional diplomatic history—although without prejudice to this approach—toward those political and intellectual fetters on a populace that prevent it from influencing national policy. It presumes that an enlightened public may prevent an irrational war regardless of the economic or strategic pressures impelling the elite toward conflict.

Applied to the U.S. intervention in Indochina, for example, Ienaga's approach would focus relatively less on the record of senior policymakers as revealed in the Pentagon Papers and more on the American educational system and the media. The crucial question might be, How could the American people have been made to believe that intervention in a nationalist revolution in a corner of Southeast Asia was any of their business, let alone a major strategic interest worthy of the nation's blood and treasure?

Another aspect of Ienaga's methodology is the use of accounts by Japanese individuals who saw the face of war and were directly affected by the conflict. The author draws widely upon materials by ordinary soldiers, refugees, housewives, schoolchildren, and even enemy prisoners of war. The use of these sources demystifies war. It is no longer a grand test of national honor, a time of reckless heroism and devotion to duty. War is separation, privation, rape, death—the body of a Chinese woman by a road in northern China or a wounded Japanese soldier abandoned along a jungle road in Burma. The Pacific War described by participants bears little resemblance to the version often presented on Japanese television and in the movies. Ienaga's sources are an antidote to this entertaining but insidious pap.

While *The Pacific War* was written for Japanese readers, the book affords an insight into the persistence of pacifism, the antagonism to rearmament, and the reluctance of most Japanese to accept the conventional wisdom that an economic power must inevitably also become a military power. Perhaps that is the cardinal enduring lesson from the war.

Frank Baldwin

Preface to
the English Edition

I wrote this book to show the Japanese people the naked realities of the Pacific War. My objective was to stimulate reflection and self-criticism about the war.

With the development of weapons of indiscriminate mass murder and the real possibility of a nuclear holocaust, Japan's experience of the "horrors of war" may prove a valuable lesson for other countries as well. Our postwar Constitution renounces war and stipulates that war potential is never to be maintained. The Japanese people's efforts to achieve these goals stem from a fervent hope that our country will never again experience such a tragedy. The ideal of "eternal peace" for all mankind has also shaped our attitudes toward war and armaments.

The publication of *The Pacific War* in an English edition now makes the book available to a larger audience. To me the appearance of an English edition is both highly significant and extremely gratifying.

May 1977   Saburō Ienaga

Preface

The title of this book, *The Pacific War,* requires a brief explanation. The term "Pacific War" covers the period from the Manchurian Incident in 1931 to the unconditional surrender in 1945 and encompasses the whole series of Japan's military clashes with other countries. In my view, these events are inseparable, all part of the same war. Precision might be better served by the term "Fifteen-Year War," or by a title which referred to that part of World War II in which Japan was involved. However, such terminology raises other problems. Although some writers use the term "Fifteen-Year War" and it has appeared in book titles, its usage has not yet been accepted by the Japanese public. Furthermore, while from the perspective of world history the decade and a half of fighting in Asia was indisputably a phase of the Second World War, I could not use "World War II" in the title because I cover only Japan's direct involvement in the conflict. Unfortunately, other terminology was even less satisfactory; the term "Greater East Asian War," the official wartime nomenclature, was utterly unacceptable to me.

A one-volume treatment of the conflict posed special problems. To attempt to describe the course of a war of general mobilization that touched upon every aspect of Japanese life would require a comprehensive review of Japanese history since 1931. Similarly, to fix the conflict's broader significance as part of World War II would lead to the history of international relations during the period, as shaped by conditions within the Allied and the neutral nations. Only through such exhaustive research could the totality of the Pacific War be grasped. An accurate, scientific history of the Pacific War must be truly comprehensive: multi-disciplinary and multi-archival. A project of such scale is beyond my limited abilities and resources.

Yet for a historian of Japan, particularly for a researcher on modern Japan, not to attempt an interpretation of the Pacific War would also be irresponsible. This is particularly true for a person like me who was an adult at the time. No one could live through those years without being directly involved in the war. Choices had to be made: To cooperate with the authorities? Opportunistically to make the best deal possible for oneself? To feign obedience and comply? To watch the war from the sidelines? To resist? Everyone confronted these choices in their daily thoughts and actions. Unless we look back at the decisions we made and consider whether we acted properly or not, we cannot lead a serious existence in the postwar world. In other words, I agree that the unexamined life is not worth living, and add that a life lived in wartime demands a special re-examination. That obligation has an additional dimension for a historian of Japan because a rigorous re-evaluation of the war is needed. Despite the vastness of the subject and my inability to write a comprehensive scholarly study of the conflict, I was determined for these personal reasons to write a book on the war.

Practical difficulties and restrictions led me to adopt the following methodology. The scope of the book was limited to areas within my abilities and academic disciplines. For example, I decided at the outset not to treat certain problems beyond my competence: the economic causes of the war, the machinations of the ruling elite, diplomatic negotiations, the details of battles and campaigns, and the war policies of other countries. Instead, I brought my special training to bear upon a few basic issues, trusting that if I stressed these major matters, the most important questions about the war would not be slighted. This rather bold focus enabled me to probe the meaning of the war, which for me includes the question how contemporary Japanese can prevent a reoccurrence of this kind of disaster. I wanted to avoid extraneous matters, however important and fascinating, and to reach the core of the war and its lessons for the Japanese people. In this way, I hope that *The Pacific War* will be unusual, perhaps even unique, in the literature on the war.

This book evolved from four public lectures in May 1965 sponsored by the Shisō no Kagaku Kenkyūkai. The original presentations were amplified in my lectures at Tokyo Kyōiku University from the spring of 1965. Once I had started on the research, it was not long before I realized what an enormous task lay ahead. I felt like a soldier trapped in an endless campaign where victory is unattainable but retreat unthinkable. Readers will have no difficulty in spotting the deficiencies in my strategy.

This work differs from my specialized academic research in another respect. In other scholarly writing my purpose was to present new materials and new facts or to publish an original interpretation. Here my stress is radically different. Aside from the general format of the book, which is original, my treatment of each aspect of the war is overwhelmingly based on generally available historical materials and previously published works. Nonetheless, the accessible documents alone are virtually beyond count, and when one adds in the enormous amount of historical materials in many countries which are not yet available to researchers and the several hundred million participants with something to tell us about the conflict, the attempt to write a scholarly book on the Pacific War after a few years of research seems foolhardy.

Yet with all limitations I had to accept or impose on the project, I was more determined than ever to write my own book on the Pacific War. As a survivor of that outrageous carnage which took the lives of so many of my generation, and as a Japanese citizen who fervently hopes that the "evils of war" will never recur, I had constantly asked myself how I could isolate and analyze the crucial issues of the war. Throughout the research for and the writing of this book I have been relatively unconcerned with the conventional academic approach. For any shortcomings that have resulted from this decision, I assume full responsibility and request the reader's indulgence.

Saburō Ienaga

July 7, 1967
The Thirtieth Anniversary of the Marco Polo Bridge Incident

PART 1

Why Was the
War Not Prevented?

1

Misconceptions About China and Korea

The Pacific War began with the invasion of China in 1931. Widely condemned by the League of Nations and many other countries as a violation of the Kellogg-Briand Non-Aggression Pact and the Nine Power Treaty on China, the attack made Japan more isolated and desperate and ultimately led to war with America and England. In Japan, the few opponents of an imperialistic war against China never had enough popular support to prevent the conflict and were easily silenced. A domestic political force capable of preventing aggression against China just did not exist. An understanding of the reasons for this abject slide into aggression must start with the Japanese view of China formed in the decades before the 1930s and with Japan's policies toward China. And since the prototype for China was Korea, it is to Japan's relations with Korea that we first turn.

Centuries ago, the Japanese imperial court at one period paid tribute to China. Even after the formal tributary relationship ended, China was called the "great country of T'ang," a term of deference, and regarded as a culturally advanced, powerful nation. The Japanese attitude was generally one of deep respect. Contempt for China, the prevalent stance in the twentieth century, was not part of the traditional outlook. The relationship with Korea, however, was always different. A military foray into the peninsula in the fourth century was part of an attempt to form a unified state in Japan.[1] Part of

Korea, Mimana, was directly controlled by Japan; the kingdom of Paekche was a tributary. Culturally, Korea was an advanced country, a bridge across which the glories of Chinese civilization—language, art, religion, a system of government, and ethics—flowed into Japan. But politically Korea was a weak dependency of its great neighbor, China. Because of that weakness, Korea and the Koreans were not given the respect afforded China. Over the centuries, the Japanese occasionally meddled in the peninsula. One unsuccessful invasion took place late in the sixteenth century. Another invasion was seriously debated in the early 1870s. In 1876 Japan used military force to compel Korea to sign the Kanghwa Treaty, which ended the Kingdom's policy of seclusion. The treaty was similar to the unequal treaties imposed by the West on Japan two decades earlier: Korea had to grant Japan extraterritoriality and surrender control over its customs revenue. Japan saw no inconsistency in demanding the abrogation of its own unequal treaties while simultaneously imposing one on its neighbor. The Western Powers had completed the imperialistic division of Asia and Africa when Japan began to modernize. Japanese leaders, looking around for territory to seize, found only Korea. Japan perceived the modern international arena as a dog-eat-dog struggle where the devil and colonialism took the hindmost. The Powers' aggressive designs caused apprehension, but few Japanese considered a Pan-Asian response—cooperation with other Asian nations to resist Western encroachment. On the contrary, the decision to align with the West and become part of the imperialist club by seizing Korea was widely approved.

The Meiji Restoration in 1868 was the start of Japan's modernization, the race to catch up with the West. But there was little change in the rural communities that formed the nation's backbone. Japanese leaders preserved and nurtured the premodern elements that permeated the social system and popular consciousness; in fact, the premodern base was used to launch modernization. But the strength of these traditional values had a restraining effect on conceptions of international affairs. Japanese inevitably tended to regard international relations as tests of strength decided by superior power; concepts of the equality of nations or of international justice were not thought important (efforts to revise the unequal treaties imposed by the West owed little to such idealistic notions). Japan uncritically followed the prevailing amoral code of "might makes right" among nation-states.

Toward the Western Powers, the Japanese response was either servile accommodation or a spirited antagonism. Toward weak countries, it was an arrogant attempt at domination. The latter response lacked any sense of common humanity; the idea that "all men are brothers" was simply missing. The traditional value system, which conceived of other peoples as enemies or objects of plunder, now governed our relations with other countries.[2] For example, early in the nineteenth century, Satō Nobuhiro (1769–1850) asserted an ultranationalism derived from the dictum "Japan is the foundation of the world." In *Kondō hisaku* (A Secret Strategy for Expansion), written in 1823, Satō proposed making the whole world "provinces and districts" of Japan. His grand design began with the conquest of China. The first blow should be at Manchuria, "so easy to attack and hold"; then Japanese forces would occupy all of China. Satō laid out the strategy for conquering China in fine detail. The intellectual links, if any, between this ideology of military aggression shaped in a feudal society and concepts of international relations after the Meiji Restoration have not been fully established. However, there is an eerie similarity between the basic ideas of *A Secret Strategy for Expansion* and the concept of the Greater East Asia Co-Prosperity Sphere. The ideology of military conquest was at least latently linked to the advocacy of an attack on Korea and other expansionist ventures in the early 1870s. I suspect it was the wellspring nourishing the aggressive ideologies that flourished in the 1920s.

During the most vigorous phase of the People's Rights movement in the 1880s, individuals like Ueki Emori (1857–92) envisioned a world without aggression and war.[3] Ueki thought it could be achieved by not following in the steps of the West's rapacious expansion, by reducing or abolishing armaments, and by establishing a world government. Some advocates of small-power status for Japan (Japan was then in fact a small power) urged that establishing democracy at home was the highest priority; Japan should not aspire to become a great power by overseas expansion, especially not by military expansion.[4] They, however, were a minority even within the People's Rights movement. Government leaders and most of the People's Rights advocates fervently desired that Japan become a great power by acquiring new territory. They started the quest for glory by fighting China for hegemony in Korea. Domination of Korea became a national goal shared by successive administrations and the public at large. Victories in the Sino-Japanese War (1894–95) and Russo-Japanese War (1904–05) removed Chinese and Russian influence from the peninsula. Japanese ascendancy was complete, despite impressive Korean resistance, with the annexation of Korea in 1910.[5]

The Sino-Japanese War changed the Japanese image of China as a great center of classical culture, a powerful nation. The writer Naka Kansuke, an elementary school student during the war, recalled the jingoistic mood in his classroom: "After the war started my friends would talk of nothing else but the 'brave Japanese, the cowardly Chinks.' The teachers urged us on like a pack of puppies whelping after a Chinese bone. We repeated it at every chance, 'brave Japanese, cowardly Chinks, brave Japanese, cowardly Chinks.' "[6]

Popular songs of the time fanned hatred of China. A few selections will convey the ugly tone: "Evil Chinamen drop like flies, swatted by our Murata rifles and stuck by our swords. Our troops advance everywhere. We brush the Chinese army aside and cross the Great Wall." "The battle for Asan was fierce; we caught the Chinks by surprise, they're running for Hwangju now, pigtails between their legs." "The Chinese are scared. They run away saying, 'We can't beat the Japanese Imperial Army,' pigtails swinging in the breeze." "As always our troops are victorious, victorious. Chinks lose because they're afraid." "Cowardly Chinese, Chinese. Frightened of our imperial forces, frightened away." "Our troops move ahead, our troops fight away. Chinese soldiers massacred everywhere. What a sight!"[7] These songs not only whipped up hostility to China; the repeated use of the term "Chink" showed a racist contempt.

Formosa (Taiwan) and the Pescadores Islands were ceded to Japan as part of the peace settlement. The Russo-Japanese War brought control over the Kwantung concession and the South Manchurian Railway zone. Ruling over the Chinese in these areas fostered a greater sense of superiority; the seized Russian rights in Manchuria inspired still more ambitious plans; and Western preoccupation during World War I provided the opportunity. The famous Twenty-one Demands forced China to concede Japan special rights in Manchuria and Eastern Mongolia.

The wars for control of Korea exceeded their objective and escalated into a general advance into China. Policies toward Taiwan and Korea became more ruthless as pressure increased on China; resistance to annexation in both areas was mercilessly crushed. I discovered a vivid example of that cruelty among the papers of a military man assigned to Taiwan immediately after the island was ceded to Japan. It was a photograph of Japanese troops beheading two pig-tailed Taiwanese rebels who apparently had been captured in a skirmish. The horrible scene foreshadowed the atrocities committed in every area touched by Japanese forces during the Pacific War.

Koreans and Taiwanese were not represented in the Japanese Diet,[8] their personal rights were severely circumscribed,[9] and they were treated as second-class citizens in their own countries. Economic domination was equally comprehensive; both economies were controlled by Japanese monopoly capital. The contrast between the privileged position of the ruling Japanese and the wretched plight of the indigenous populations was sharp. An enormous amount of Korean land, the titles to which were vague by modern ownership criteria, was confiscated during the land survey from 1910 to 1918 and ended up in Japanese hands. Landless Koreans became laborers, went to Japan, and accepted meager wages in the hope of eking out a living.[10] The odyssey only brought them face to face with racial discrimination and abuse. Chang T'u-sik was a typical victim of anti-Korean discrimination. Born in South Kyongsang province in 1916, Chang was brought to Tokyo six years later. The taunts of Japanese children rang in his ears: "Ugh, a Korean! A Korean!" When Chang opened his lunch in school Japanese students shouted, "Oh, it stinks!" and "Garlic, garlic." After that humiliating experience he never took a lunch to school again. The racist taunting continued into adulthood with remarks like "You Koreans, don't forget what you are."[11]

Resentment at Japanese seizure of land exploded in 1919 as the March First Movement for Korean independence ripped across the peninsula. Japan suppressed the demonstrations with troops; thousands of Koreans were killed and wounded.[12] Koreans were the victims of another outrage after the 1923 Kantō earthquake in Japan. The authorities encouraged false rumors of Korean looting in order to forestall antigovernment violence. Thousands of innocent Koreans were murdered by local "police" squads and vigilante groups in and around Tokyo.[13] Troops were also used to suppress a protest against harsh labor duty by Taiwanese aborigines in Wu-she in 1930. Many of the natives were killed and wounded.[14] The authorities tended to use troops and firearms on Taiwanese and Koreans; similar protests or confrontations were controlled with less force and loss of life when only Japanese were involved.

Ozaki Hidetarō, a reporter for the *Taiwan Nichinichi Shimbun,* was a moderate and cultured person. Yet even such liberal Japanese behaved differently in the colonies. His son Hotsumi recalled his father returning home by jinricksha one day. When the Taiwanese coolie quibbled about the fare, Ozaki beat him with his walking stick.[15] That was standard treatment of Chinese in the Kwantung concession and other places ruled by Japan. Hirano Reiji, a reporter for the *Osaka Mainichi,* was sent to Dairen about the time of the Tsinan Incident. The chief correspondent in the Dairen office met him, and they went to the office in a carriage driven by a Chinese. At their destination, Hirano's superior argued with the driver over the fare, insisting that it was too high. The correspondent finally ended the argument by shouting, "You stupid bastard!" and chasing the Chinese driver down the street.[16]

Manchuria was nominally Chinese territory, but it was rapidly becoming a Japanese colony. The South Manchurian Railway, a pillar of imperialist control in the region, made enormous profits from cheap Chinese labor. For example, in 1926 the average monthly salary for Japanese regular and temporary employees was 7.6 and 4.2 times, respectively, the wages of Chinese temporary employees. Grim statistics show the difference in working conditions and safety by nationality: In the coal mines operated by the railroad, in the period from 1909 to 1930, 3,806 Japanese were killed or injured compared to 114,029 Chinese. Perhaps 40 to 50 million tons of coal were extracted from the Fushun and Yent'ai mines by about 1930, but more than 100,000 Chinese workers died or were injured in the mines.[17]

Japan fought two wars in a decade and expended lives and treasure to get bits of Chinese territory to exploit as colonies or semi-colonies. Those military successes and sacrifices, most Japanese thought, gave Tokyo the right to control and exploit Chinese territory. Their attitude was identical with the European and American conviction that control of colonies in Asia, the Pacific, and Africa was "manifest destiny."[18]

A national consensus approved of an imperialist policy toward China, but there were sharp disagreements and differing emphases over implementation. At one end of the spectrum were the moderates who favored enlarging Japanese interests by peaceful means: investment, opening new markets for Japanese goods, and cooperation with England and America. At the other end were the expansionists and militarists, who were

prepared to go to war if necessary to suppress Chinese nationalism and resistance and drive England and America off the
Asian continent. A variety of views and strategies lay between
these two poles. Japan's policy toward China was not always
asserted with military power. The decade from the early 1920s
was one of "normal parliamentary politics" after the long rule
of the Meiji oligarchs. Shidehara Kijūrō was foreign minister
in the cabinets formed by the Kenseikai party and its successor, the Minseitō. His espousal of international cooperation
and armament reduction was called Shidehara diplomacy. Yet
even Shidehara was explicitly expansionist. In a 1931 meeting
with the Chinese diplomat Ch'en Yu-jen only a month before
the Manchurian Incident, Shidehara justified Japanese control
of the region:

> Chinese seem to think Manchuria is part of China but it
> used to be Russian. There is no doubt that if the situation
> had been left alone, Manchuria would soon have ceased
> to be under Ch'ing authority. The only reason the Man-
> chu regime was able to hold this vast fertile region was
> a Japanese military presence. Since the Russo-Japanese
> War, Manchuria has enjoyed peace and prosperity un-
> paralleled in any other Chinese area. Japanese are con-
> vinced that the development of the northeast region is at
> least partly due to our businesses and investment there.

Shidehara's antipathy to Chinese aspirations was also apparent in a speech at Keio University three years earlier, in
1928. Noting the antiforeign movement in China (a boycott of
foreign goods) to raise national consciousness and end the
unequal treaties, he remarked that Japan had abolished its
unequal treaties not by illegal action but by strengthening
itself. China should follow the Japanese example. Shidehara
called on the Chinese people to show "restraint."[19] Methods
and style aside, the essence of Shidehara diplomacy was the
pursuit of special political and economic concessions in China.

If the leading proponent of a peaceful China policy was at
heart an expansionist, one can imagine the mentality of the

committed jingoists. Ikezaki Tadakata, a writer on military affairs, wrote in 1929: "It is well known that Japan's overpopulation grows more serious every year. Where should we find an outlet for these millions?" The Western Powers had divided up the world: "the only remaining area is the Asian mainland. Moreover, Japan's claim to the region is written in the blood and treasure of two wars." Even if the United States opposed Japan's legitimate expansion in China, "we should resolutely pursue our interests." If the U.S. persisted in blocking Tokyo's plans, Japan should go to war.[20] Ikezaki's views were a sophisticated version of the public attitude toward China.

The expansionist ideology of civilian writers like Ikezaki was not sufficient to propel Japan into war. But when military leaders adopted these views, the impetus toward hostilities gained a fatal momentum. In the same year that Ikezaki's book was published, Lt. Colonel Ishiwara Kanji drafted "A Plan for the Solution of the Manchurian and Mongolian Problems as a Basic Policy to Change Our Country's Destiny." Ishiwara insisted that "Japan's survival depends upon a favorable resolution of the problem of Manchuria and Mongolia"; "Japan must expand overseas to achieve political stability at home"; "The future of Manchuria and Mongolia will only be satisfactorily decided when Japan obtains those areas"; and "Japan must be willing to fight America to achieve our national objectives."[21] Ishiwara's proposal was a remarkable scenario for the Pacific War! He was far more explicit than Ikezaki about "obtaining" Manchuria and Mongolia, although both were agreed that war with the United States might be necessary to accomplish Japan's goals.

Popular contempt for the Chinese supported the advance onto the continent. Shidehara placed the blame for China's ills on the Chinese people: "Unequal treaties are a result of domestic political shortcomings, not their cause. Unless a problem is attacked at its roots, the undesirable consequences will persist."[22] He ignored the debilitating effect of the alliance between the imperialist countries, including Japan, and com-

prador businessmen on China's sovereignty and efforts at reform. He tried to hold the Chinese people responsible for the
imperialism that had made China a semi-colony. Ikezaki con-
temptuously derided China's ability to withstand Japan:
"China may squirm and struggle but it will not slow down the
Japanese army. Three or four divisions and a few river gun-
boats will be quite enough to handle the Chinese bandits."[23]
Ishiwara wrote in 1930: "China is not a unified nation. It is
Japan's divine mission to assist the Chinese people." He
added, "The four races of Japan, China, Korea and Manchuria will share a common prosperity through a division of
responsibilities: Japanese, political leadership and large indus-
try; Chinese, labor and small industry; Koreans, rice; and
Manchus, animal husbandry."[24] Ishiwara's design was a bold
elucidation of the ideal of the Greater East Asia Co-Prosperity
Sphere. It assumed the innate superiority of Japanese over
Chinese and made imperialist Japan the sovereign leader of
Northeast Asia.

Ishiwara was one of the plotters of the Manchurian invasion
and a central figure in the events leading to the Pacific War.
But his aggressive views were no personal idiosyncrasy. He
represents the systematic formulation of an irrational Japanese contempt for their Asian neighbors fostered over several
decades and the imperialist policies sanctioned by that attitude. As long as that mentality and policy were dominant, a
military confrontation was unavoidable with a China which
sought a new national identity and had begun to resist imperialist domination. Why were the Japanese people intolerant of
Chinese and Koreans? Why did they lack the capacity for
critical analysis of imperialist policies and the wars they bred?
I think the answer lies in the state's manipulation of information and values to produce mass conformity and unquestion-
ing obedience.

2

Thought Control and Indoctrination

Internal Security Laws against Intellectual Freedom

In 1868, the new Meiji government moved immediately to control newspapers and publications in order to suppress support for the former regime. A series of internal security laws, starting with the publishing regulations (1869) and the newspaper law (1873), restricted freedom of speech. These laws carried sweeping provisions such as "To publish indiscriminate criticism of laws or to slander individuals is prohibited" or "To add indiscriminately critical comments when describing government actions and laws is forbidden." Officialdom sought immunity from criticism by these regulations.[1] The 1875 libel law and newspaper regulations were extremely severe; there was for a time a reign of terror against journalists.[2]

A vigorous nationwide challenge to the new government, the People's Rights movement, occurred in the 1870s and 1880s. To divide and weaken the movement, authorities dangled the carrot of financial rewards before some of the opposition. Others were harassed, locked up, and silenced. Strict enforcement of ever-tougher internal security laws proved to be the most effective weapon against dissent: regulations on assembly (1880), revision and amendment of the same law in 1882, revision of the newspaper regulation (1883), and a law prohibiting the disclosure of petitions to the throne and the

13

government (1884). Freedom of assembly and association were also severely restricted. The People's Rights movement was destroyed, and political activity of any kind became extremely difficult.[3]

But the People's Rights activists did achieve their immediate objective: the establishment of an elected parliament. The government announced in late 1881 that a constitution providing for an elected assembly would be drafted by 1890. The dissidents had demanded that the new constitution include guaranteed political rights. Draft constitutions prepared by the left wing of the Jiyūtō (Liberal party) contained absolute guarantees of intellectual freedom, academic and educational, and of speech.[4] The People's Rights movement was a bid for a national assembly, a sharing of governmental power, and simultaneously a struggle to establish freedom of expression and basic human rights. Its failure aborted the drive for freedom of speech. After crushing the movement, the government secretly and arbitrarily drafted the constitution and promulgated it on February 11, 1889. There was no popular participation in the process; the emperor presented it to the people as an "imperial gift."

The Meiji Constitution did not guarantee basic human rights. Freedom of expression was recognized only "within the limits of the law." The liberties granted in the constitution could be virtually abolished by subsequent laws. Restrictions soon tumbled from the government's authoritarian cornucopia. Freedom of publication was affected by the Publication Law (1893) and the Newspaper Law (1909); freedom of assembly and association by the Assembly and Political Organization Law (1890) and its successor, the Public Order Police Law of 1900; and intellectual freedom by the lèse majesté provision of the criminal code and by the Peace Preservation Law (1925). Movies and theatrical performances were strictly controlled by administrative rulings rather than by laws passed by the Diet. Thought and expression were so circumscribed that only a small sphere of freedom remained.

The internal security laws were primarily intended to prevent discussion or factual reporting about three areas the authorities deemed sensitive: the monarchical system and public order, the dignity of the imperial family, and public morals. An additional objective was control of information about military and diplomatic affairs. The Peace Preservation Law was enacted to suppress socialist ideas and the socialist movement. Later it was used against other ideas that displeased those who ran the state.

The Meiji political system gagged and blindfolded the populace. Denied the basic facts and a free exchange of opinion on the major issues of state and society, the public could hardly participate in charting Japan's future. The sensitive areas noted above were stated in the law as vague categories; they could be interpreted broadly and stretched to trap the dissident. Any major contemporary issue might fall under one of the dangerous categories. There was always the fear that newspapers, other publications, and public speeches would be prohibited by an arbitrary police ruling. No appeal was possible against police harassment. Scripts of movies and plays were subject to prior censorship and controlled in the same way as publications and public speeches. Furthermore, these internal security laws carried criminal penalties. Under the lèse majesté provision and the Peace Preservation Law, individuals with beliefs repugnant to the government, even if those beliefs were not expressed overtly, could end up in prison.[5]

Of course, not every idea that incurred official wrath was a valuable contribution to Japanese political life. But a healthy political and social consciousness cannot develop in a society where the exchange of vital facts and ideas is fettered. Leaving other deleterious effects aside for the moment, the impossibility of reporting information essential for informed, independent judgments about war and national security left an intellectual vacuum. It was filled by official militarism, and the public, unaware of the truth or of alternatives, automatically came to support the government position.

In 1901, for example, the chief of the Kagurazaka police station in Tokyo discovered that a declaration by the Shakai Minshutō (Social Democratic party) drafted by Abe Isoo advocated abolition of the House of Peers, adoption of popular suffrage, and the reduction and abolition of armaments. The police official demanded removal of the House of Peers item. When Abe refused, the party was banned. *Rōdō sekai* (Labor World) and other publications that printed the declaration were confiscated. Rather severe repression for a political party that consisted of six intellectuals! But the authorities did for a while at least stamp out three dangerous ideas.[6]

There were a few hesitant beginnings of antiwar sentiment in Japan. One strain was represented by the Christian pacifism of Uchimura Kanzō and his followers during the Russo-Japanese War. Another was a humanistic aversion to war, as expressed in Yosano Akiko's poem "Kimishini tamau koto nakare" (My Brother, Don't Waste Your Life in the War). But these currents never coalesced into an organized movement. It was the Socialists who raised the antiwar issue in a systematic way.[7] The inclusion of disarmament ideas in the Shakai Minshutō program was a seminal act in the development of antiwar ideas in Japan. At the time, the government regarded socialism as a hodgepodge of impractical ideas with no effective political following. The authorities were more concerned about radical democratic ideas, such as abolition of the House of Peers and popular suffrage, than about the economic provisions in the party platform. That changed about the time of the Russo-Japanese War, when Kōtoku Shūsui, Kinoshita Naoe, Sakai Toshihiko, and other Socialists published the *Heimin Shimbun* (Commoners Newspaper) and began a full-fledged socialist movement.

Alarmed authorities cracked down hard and continuously harassed the activists. The denouement came when Kōtoku Shūsui, by then an anarchist, and twenty-three others were sentenced to death in the Daigyaku Jiken (conspiracy to assassinate the emperor) in 1910. Twelve were executed, including

Kōtoku, who was falsely implicated; twelve sentences were reduced by imperial pardon. The government used the conspiracy trial as a pretext to prohibit all publications about socialism. Antiwar books like Kōtoku's *Nijū seiki no kaibutsu, teikokushugi* (Imperialism, the Monster of the Twentieth Century, 1901), Yamaguchi Kōken's *Hateikokushugi* (Antiimperialism, 1904), and Kinoshita Naoe's *Hi no hashira* (The Pillar of Fire, 1904) were all banned (*Hi no hashira* was reprinted in the late 1920s but with numerous deletions by the censors).

Antimilitarism gradually gained support during and after World War I. There was also open opposition to Japan's Siberian expedition to intervene in the Russian Revolution. That opposition, however, was due to a sharp cleavage among Japan's leaders about the wisdom of meddling in the confused Russian picture. It was a policy split within the ruling elite; the public at large played no role. Control of information and restrictions on criticism of the Siberian intervention, the military, or Japan's colonial policy continued. Ikeda Kyokugai's *Ku? Raku? Shinpei no seikatsu* (A Recruit's Life: Agony or Pleasure? 1915), a semi-documentary story of barracks life with no ideological overtones, was banned because of its grim depiction of military life. More politically conscious writing met a predictable fate. As the proletarian literature movement spread in the 1920s, works with an explicit class perspective presented antiwar ideas and unflattering descriptions of the military. For example, Kobayashi Takiji's *Kani kōsen* (Cannery Boat, 1929) described troops crushing a strike. Novels like Kuroshima Denji's *Busō seru shigai* (City under Arms) revealed the hardships and suffering of soldiers in the Siberian expedition. Both were proscribed.

Printed materials were controlled by a reporting system under which official action nominally took place after publication; in practice, however, material was submitted before distribution. Officials reviewed the publications and ruled arbitrarily. Motion pictures were subject to prior censorship under Ministry of Home Affairs regulations issued in 1925. The ministry screened films before public release and often banned them altogether or ordered extensive cuts. Foreign films got the same unfriendly welcome. The American film *All Quiet on the Western Front* was shown in Japan in 1930. Although it was about the German army in World War I and had nothing to do with Japan, the antiwar theme was anathema to the government. The most powerful scenes were censored: the beating of the noncommissioned officer who had mistreated the student volunteer soldiers; war-weary troops in the trenches suffering from battle fatigue; the battlefield carnage; soldiers on a rest break bitterly complaining about the war; German soldiers spending a night in a shell crater with French corpses; and a veteran making an antiwar speech to schoolchildren. Not much remained of the classic antiwar message when the censors sheathed their scissors and released it to the theaters.[8]

In the early 1930s, the Communists, with their slogan of Opposition to Imperialistic War, were almost the only group with an analytical position against war. The government cracked down by outlawing the party and imprisoning its leaders. The Communist movement went underground. Antiwar criticism disappeared from the public dialogue; there was no way for critical ideas or opinions to reach the public. Restrictions on intellectual freedom and expression aimed at the Communists went beyond abridging their rights of speech, assembly, and association. Police and prosecutors used their summary powers under police regulations and the Administrative Performance Law to arrest and detain illegally political activists and persons with antigovernment views. Victims were physically abused and held in pretrial detention for long periods. Law enforcement officials broke the law constantly by abusing their legal authority,[9] violating citizens' rights, and frightening the public into silence. The government crushed freedom of expression, pacifism, and antimilitarism by vigorous use and abuse of the internal security laws, the state's first line of defense against overt dissent. The authorities also appreciated that the best defense is a good offense. They therefore created a powerful weapon with which to indoctrinate ideas and values conducive to spontaneous mass support of militarism: the public education system.

Education for National Conformity

The new Meiji government's zealous imposition of controls on freedom of expression was partly an extension of the feudal practice of keeping the people ignorant. The Meiji leaders inherited the Tokugawa government's controls on publication, political activity, and Catholicism. That the government should control education and thereby indoctrinate the population had not yet occurred to the authorities; the notion was conceived only later as an absolutist emperor-centered state was established.

In the beginning, the Meiji government recognized the need to build a modern school system. For many years afterward, during the "enlightenment period" when Japan was absorbing so much from the West, the government wanted the people to have a sense of intellectual openness and inquisitiveness about Western technology and culture. Far from rigidly restricting educational content, government policy allowed the schools to use as textbooks publications full of the political and legal doctrines that underlie Western social concepts, Christian ethics, and modern democracy. Books issued by commercial publishers could be used in the schools without government approval.

But when the People's Rights movement reached a high point in the late 1870s, the policy changed. In 1880 the government compiled a list of books favorable to democracy, including Fukuzawa Yukichi's writings, and prohibited their use as textbooks. It was the first move toward official intervention in the content of education. The government abandoned the policy of encouraging intellectual curiosity and cultural enlightenment, began a revival of Confucian feudal virtues, and started to compile textbooks to inculcate these values.

The government moved step by step—but at a quick pace, one might add—to rein in the educational dragon before it got out of hand. At first a reporting system was set up for textbooks. The schools selected the books and notified the authorities of what texts they were using. Then the government required the schools to obtain approval *before* adopting books. In 1886 a certification system was implemented. Books could not be adopted as texts unless they were certified by the Ministry of Education. The state had acquired the power to control textbooks, a power that increased steadily.[10]

After 1904, elementary-school texts were compiled by the national government; all Japanese children were taught from books produced by the Ministry of Education. In a premodern society, regardless of how powerful the rulers are and how weak vis à vis authority the people may be, it is virtually impossible for the ruling class to indoctrinate the entire populace. The requisite means of communication do not exist. A ruling elite needs a modern school system to get its message across. Modern Japan accomplished a vast quantitative increase in the citizenry's intellectual level by rapidly establishing compulsory education, increasing the compulsory period from three to six years, and attaining an enrollment rate of more than 90 percent by shortly after 1900. Nearly every child received a basic education. However, the standardized educational content stamped a uniform outlook on most Japanese minds. The diversity of ignorance was replaced by the conformity of state-approved knowledge. An impressionistic young child often retains his early education through adulthood despite later experiences. And in prewar Japan, for most people formal education ended with elementary school.

The middle schools were allowed to use certified textbooks until 1943, permitting a modicum of variety. Given the very detailed Ministry of Education curriculum, however, the use of commercially published books made little difference. Furthermore, not many students went on to middle school; the national conformity created by the state textbooks in the early grades was not alleviated at this level. Government control of educational content was notably weak (but not nonexistent) at the higher school (*kōtō gakkō*), technical college (*senmon gakkō*), and university levels. Still fewer students went on to this advanced training, however. Those who did formed a special stratum of intelligentsia. The gap between the intellectuals and the popular consciousness was itself a barrier to ameliorating mass conformity.

What were all Japanese being taught to believe and honor? The policy of standardizing education was a response to the People's Rights movement and naturally accelerated the propagation of antidemocratic, statist values. Instead of the democratic political system and a constitution with guaranteed human rights demanded by the People's Rights movement, an emperor-centered absolutist constitution was imposed from above. No mere head of state, the emperor became a monarch with sacred authority based on the myths of the *Kojiki* and the *Nihon shoki,* an object of worship. In 1890, the year after the constitution was announced, the Imperial Rescript on Education was issued in a bid to inculcate total submissiveness to the political authority presided over by the emperor. The practice of emperor-centered patriotic ceremonies on the opening day of school each year began about the same time. Children were required to venerate the imperial photograph, and there was a solemn ceremonial reading of the education rescript. These rituals were used to instill an awed obedience to the emperor and the state.

The Imperial Rescript on Education's most direct function was as a sacred object in these ritual observances. It also had a noteworthy practical role as the ultimate normative statement on public education until 1945. The contents of ethics textbooks, for example, were based on the values and injunctions of the rescript. The document is a complex ideological blend that reflects the objectives of the men who worked on it.[11] Motoda Nagazane, the Confucian teacher of the Meiji Emperor, wanted to impose Confucianism on the people as a state religion. Itō Hirobumi, one of the leaders of the Restoration and of the new government, and Inoue Kowashi, his intellectual advisor, wanted a political system which, although allowing a degree of constitutionalism, was state-oriented. The sovereign's authority should be paramount. Yamagata Aritomo, another Restoration leader and one of the founders of the modern Japanese military, was a forceful advocate of the rescript. Seven months before it was issued, Yamagata wrote in a "Memorandum on Military Armaments" that "Korea is the vital point within Japan's sphere of national interests" and "the indispensable elements of a foreign policy to protect those interests are first, troops and armaments and second, education. Education should foster and preserve patriotism."[12] The militaristic command in the rescript shows Yamagata's influence: "Should emergency arise, guard and maintain the prosperity of our Imperial throne." There is also the phrase "always respect the Constitution and observe the laws." While nominally acknowledging the constitution as the basis for parliamentary politics, the rescript subverted the basic purpose of modern constitutions: to limit state authority and guarantee human rights. The rescript mentions the constitution only in the context of the people's obligation to obey the law; there is no reference to limits on state power. A spirit of respect for human rights was totally lacking.[13] Naturally enough, and again quite contrary to modern constitutional thought, the public education based on the rescript was slanted toward unconditional obedience to state authority.

Passive acquiescence to the state was not enough. The Meiji authorities wanted education to turn out citizens who spontaneously and enthusiastically supported national policies. A willingness to die for the country in time of war was stressed as "loyalty to the emperor and love of country" *(chūkun aikoku)*. The inculcation of feelings of contempt toward

China in the elementary schools during the Sino-Japanese War in the example given earlier seems to have occurred across the country. The same phenomenon was reported from an elementary school in Takamatsu, Kagawa Prefecture. During the ethics class the teacher "showed pictures and described in exciting detail how our loyal and brave officers and soldiers drive the pig-tailed Chinks to P'yongyang, keep hammering away at them and finally capture the vile enemy's positions." Most of the students "sat with one arm folded over the other on the desk, bend forward, heads thrust out, eyes glued on the teacher and hanging on his every word, totally oblivious to anything but the war story." A "war report" prepared by teachers was displayed on the school bulletin board: "September 22, 1894. Battle report. Japanese troops defeat Chinese at P'yongyang and win a great victory. Chinese corpses were piled up as high as a mountain. Oh, what a grand triumph. Chinka, Chinka, Chinka, Chinka, so stupid and they stinka."

Militarism was systematically inculcated during the Russo-Japanese War. For example, all elementary school principals in Saitama Prefecture were assembled and informed of the "topics that should be taught during the present emergency." The war and patriotism were to be stressed in every subject. In ethics the teachers were to discuss "the meaning of the imperial edict declaring war, the imperial edict on the course of the war, the exploits of valiant Japan and our valiant military men, the special behavior expected of children during the war, and the duty of military service." Japanese language classes were to study "the imperial edicts related to the war, articles about the war situation, letters to and from soldiers at the front." Teachers were to use war-related pictures provided by the government to spark discussion. Arithmetic classes were to do "calculations about military matters." The topics for science were "general information about searchlights, wireless communication, land mines and torpedoes, submarines, military dirigibles, Shimose explosives, military carrier pigeons, heavy cannon, mortars, machine guns, the Arisaka cannon, and military sanitation." Physical education would include "character training and war games." Music classes were to reverberate with war songs. The objective was to militarize the entire curriculum. The impact on the children was soon apparent. Consider a third-grade student's composition: "I will become a soldier and kill Russians and take them prisoner. I will kill more Russians, cut off their heads and bring them back to the Emperor. I will charge into battle again, cut off more Russian heads, kill them all. I will be a great man."[14]

This might be discounted as a transient wartime excess except that there was a war every ten years and the curriculum was called to the colors each time. The national consciousness was markedly affected by these jingoistic booster shots every decade. Furthermore, they left a permanent militaristic tint to the standard curriculum taught during the interwar years. A glance through the pages of the government textbooks brings back the martial ghosts of the past.[15] The elementary-school ethics book for second-grade students published in 1903 contained the following lessons:

Lesson 23. The Emperor attends the annual maneuvers of the army and navy and watches the soldiers and sailors perform their duties. We must appreciate the emperor's royal benevolence.
Lesson 24. Kiguchi Kohei was not the least bit afraid before the enemy. He bravely sounded the call to advance on his bugle three times. Inspired by his brave example, our troops attacked and defeated the enemy, but Kiguchi was hit by a bullet and fell to the ground mortally wounded. Later they found his body with the bugle still at his lips.
Lesson 25. Our torpedo boat sped through the dark night, attacked the enemy fleet and sank four ships.

These three lessons with illustrations appear in one sequence. In *Elementary School Reader No. 8* published the following year, Lesson 7 is entitled "Takeo Joins the Service." Takeo and his father have this exchange:

> *Takeo:* Father, the idea of "joining the service of my country" makes me so proud and happy. I'll be trained and when war comes, I will not be afraid to die. I'll give everything I have to show what a good Japanese fighting man is made of.
> *Father:* That's the spirit! You must be that determined. Don't be afraid to die. Don't worry about us here. And you must always be faithful to the Imperial Precepts to Soldiers and Sailors.

I was fortunate in attending elementary school from before World War I to the mid-1920s, the most liberal educational period until after 1945. The third-edition textbooks then in use had the most material on international cooperation, for example, of the five prewar textbook editions. Nevertheless, we got a strong dose of militarism. The books were only a shade different from those of the earlier period. Our ethics text also had the story about Kiguchi the bugler. The book we used in second grade had an inspiring lesson on loyalty.

> Commander Hirose Takeo set out on a dark night to block the harbor entrance at Port Arthur with a steamship. Braving enemy fire, he completed his preparations and was about to leave the ship. But Chief Warrant Officer Sugino was missing. The commander searched all over the boat three times. Finally, as Commander Hirose left the larger ship and boarded a small boat, he was hit by enemy fire and died a glorious hero's death.

In our Japanese reader there was a story called "A Sailor's Mother":

> A sailor receives a letter from his mother: "You wrote that you did not participate in the battle of Toshima Island. You were in the August 10 attack on Weihaiwei but you didn't distinguish yourself with an individual

exploit. To me this is deplorable. Why have you gone to war? Your life is to be offered up to requit your obligations to our benevolent Emperor." An officer, seeing him reading the letter and crying, comforted the sailor: "Son, there'll surely be another glorious war before long. Let's accomplish great feats of bravery then and bring honor to our ship Takachiho. Explain that to your mother and put her mind at ease."

The modern and contemporary history sections of our *Elementary School Japanese History* consisted of two parts: "Emperor Meiji" and "The Reigning Emperor" (the Taishō emperor). The discussion of domestic politics in the first part ended with a section on "The Promulgation of the Constitution." The rest of it was filled with material about the imperial family, wars, or Japan's increasing international prestige: "The Sino-Japanese War," "Treaty Revision," "The Russo-Japanese War," "Annexation of Korea," and "Death of the Emperor Meiji." The Taishō section also had nothing but events like the coronation of the emperor, Japan's role in World War I, and participation in the Paris Peace Conference and the Washington Conference. There was not one word about domestic social or political developments.

The song textbook had the story of Commander Hirose set to music:

The cannons roar, the shells scream
Standing on the deck awash with waves
The commander's call pierces the darkness
Sugino, where are you? Are you there?
He searches every corner of the boat three times
He calls but gets no answer, looks but finds no trace
The boat gradually sinks beneath the waves
Enemy shells fly thick and fast
The commander moves to the small boat
A flying shell, he is dead.
How tragic his death outside Port Arthur
Heroic Hirose's fame lives on

The military never missed a chance to get their message across. Even ordinary songs like "We're Children of the Sea" *(Ware wa umi no ko)* had an extra passage added:

> Let's go! Aboard the ships and away. We'll gather the treasure of the sea.
> Let's go! Aboard the battleship. We'll defend this nation of the sea.

Whether I was taught them in school or just picked them up on my own is not clear, but the songs for which I know both the melody and the words are usually military songs. I still know "Lt. Colonel Tachibana," with the line "Night wears on at the Liaoyang Fort." And I can still sing the navy battleship march that goes "Defending or attacking, like a floating fortress of steel . . . so dependable."

The ethics, language, and history textbooks, with their written and visual messages, had a significant jingoistic influence. Yet the military songs with their "brave and gallant" melodies hit a deeper emotional level. No amount of rational reexamination of the past and appreciation of postwar democracy can erase those stirring tunes of glory from the memories of the prewar generation.[16]

Military training was brought directly into the schools. Perhaps the army thought that even the khaki-colored curriculum might not produce a sufficiently aggressive mentality. In 1917 the Ad hoc Commission on Education passed this resolution: "Appropriate measures should be quickly implemented . . . to encourage military training in the schools." The reasons included: "To create a strong and healthy people by improving physiques through physical training and to develop knowledge and skills in military matters and thereby cultivate loyalty by moral discipline (national spirit equals martial spirit), and to lay the foundation for future military training is an essential element of education in Japan today that cannot be slighted." Objections such as the following were raised in committee meetings. One critic said, "A defect of our present educational system has been the poor development of children's intellect. They have been forced to think in a certain way. They have no ideas of their own. The students are crammed full of information but never encouraged to think. It is a pedagogy that ignores free will, independent thinking. Will not military training have the baneful effects of making the children still more docile, less able to think for themselves?" Another said, "The fundamental spirit of the military is absolute obedience to authority. However, general education is based on freedom of the mind. I fear there will be a clash of antagonistic priorities. This must be avoided." The criticism was unavailing; the resolution was adopted unanimously.[17]

Starting in 1925, active duty military officers were assigned to every school from the middle school level up (except girls' schools), and military training became part of the regular curriculum. The next year youth training centers were established in every city, town, and village as part of a four-year program of four hundred hours of military instruction for males whose formal education ended at elementary school. The military threw its training net wide to catch everyone: the sons of the middle and upper classes who continued on to higher education and the boys from proletarian families who went out to work after finishing elementary school.

The state had arrayed powerful weapons against the individual. A militaristic education implanted jingoistic ideas in the populace and overwhelmed a critical consciousness toward war. All education was standardized under the centralized control of the Ministry of Education. Neither teacher nor parent could make any educational choices for the children. Academic freedom for teachers in the classroom was not recognized. From nursery school through high school, students were told what they would learn and what they would think.[18] Under these conditions it was all but impossible to train students to think rationally about society, especially to have a critical attitude toward authority.

The whole educational process deserves careful study and analysis for its socializing role, but I must confine my remarks to those parts of the system that overtly and directly implanted militarism in the minds of Japanese schoolchildren. We saw one result of that education in the elementary school child's composition about the time of the Russo-Japanese War. Let's look at the process as reflected in a roundtable discussion sponsored by the *Asahi Gurafu* in 1932, not long after the Manchurian Incident. The participants were fifth- and sixth-grade boys and girls from the Taimei Elementary School in Tokyo.

Interviewer: What is the Manchurian Incident all about?

Katō: The Chinese insulted us and our soldiers are fighting them in Manchuria to avenge it.

Interviewer: The League of Nations has been making quite a fuss recently. What do you think of the League?

Katō: It's a place where the cowards of the world get together to talk.

Interviewer: If you were Foreign Minister, what would you do?

Nakajima: The League of Nations is biased, so I wouldn't have anything to do with it.

Hotta: If I became Foreign Minister, anybody that kept repeating that kind of nonsense would get a real punch in the nose. (laughter)

Interviewer: Do you think there will be a war between Japan and America?

Fukuzawa: Yes, I think so. Americans are so arrogant. I'd like to show them a thing or two.

Katō: They act so big all the time, they need a good beating. I'd annihilate them.

Fukutomi: Oh, I'd like to try that too.

Interviewer: If Japan becomes more and more isolated, what would you do?

Several students: We'll keep trying, we'll keep going, we'll stick at it till we die. (A forceful chorus of voices)

Fukutomi: The end is when you're dead, isn't it? (She meant "I'll keep on to the end," and said it in a steady voice.)

Interviewer: What's most annoying these days?

Fukuzawa: Shidehara's weak-kneed foreign policy.

Fukunaga: The cowardice of the cabinet.

Interviewer: How about the opposite? What has been most delightful?

Nakajima: Our great victory at Machansan.

Katō: It's great to see Japan winning one battle after another.

Fukunaga: I really liked it when Ambassador Yoshizawa told Chairman Briand that the League was stupid and that it should do just what Japan wants.[19]

Of course, young people were not in school twenty-four hours a day. Their minds and values were also shaped by their family life and the reading material they saw outside the classroom (I remember that the youth magazines we read carried jingoistic articles like "The Future War Between Japan and America").[20] While not the only formative influence, public education undoubtedly had a great impact. Kikuchi Kunisaku studied discipline problems in the army for the period from 1915 to 1937. His data were from the statistics on draft dodgers and insubordination, disorderly conduct, suicide, etc., in the *Army Annual Report (Rikugun nenpō)*. Kikuchi found that the problem soldiers labeled by the army as "unpatriotic persons" came largely from two strata of the population. They tended to be either intellectuals from imperial universities and other prestigious elite schools or to be men with little or no formal education.[21] The mass of the population in between had been conditioned by public education to accept military discipline. Any doubts about militarism had been killed by the chilling frost of state indoctrination.

The state could not keep young people in the protective womb of the lower schools forever. Overdosed with submissiveness to authority and glorification of war though they were, some middle-school graduates went on to higher school and the universities, where government control was relatively weak. Or they went to work and discovered the real world of labor-management relations and exploitation. By further intellectual growth and from personal experience, there should have been opportunities to escape from the orthodox ideological spell of the elementary and middle schools. In fact, some people became quite radical or independent minded as a result of exposure to new views and ideas. Yet it was not so easy. Information and political ideas were circumscribed by the internal security laws. The average public-school graduate was so full of approved "facts," myths, and patriotism as to be immune to fresh or radical ideas. Those who had their eyes opened by higher education or later experience still had to contend with the sobering reality that, because of state repression, there was no way for their dissident views to have an effect on society.

I speak from personal experience. I was in elementary school during the most liberal years of the prewar period. Yet through middle school I soaked up jingoistic ideas and never questioned them. When the Manchurian Incident occurred shortly after I entered higher school, I was incapable of understanding its real nature. I was shocked to discover classmates who rejected the orthodox values and ideology I had accepted as gospel truth. They had different views and they acted upon them. The latter part of 1932 was the turning point in my own intellectual and spiritual growth. To escape the snares of my "education," I rejected most of what I had been taught in the public schools. It still took another twenty years to overcome the handicap of that early indoctrination and be able to grapple with fundamental questions.

The prewar state kept the populace in a powerful vise: on one side were the internal security laws with their restrictions on freedom of speech and thought; on the other side was the conformist education that blocked the growth of a free consciousness and purposive activity for political ends. The vise was tightened whenever any individual or popular resistance challenged reckless military action. These laws and public education, used as instruments of coercion and manipulation, were the decisive factors that made it impossible for the Japanese people to stop their country from launching the Pacific War.

3

The Military: Authoritarian and Irrational

The Imperial Army and Navy enjoyed virtually unlimited freedom of action. And their modes of action reflected the remarkably irrational and undemocratic character of the military. It was typical of the Japanese military mind to charge recklessly into an unwinnable war and continue it to the point of national destruction. Two aspects of the armed services and the Pacific War will be discussed: the defense establishment's institutional position in the state, and the internal dynamics of the military.

The Military and the State

In the early Meiji period, the military were placed under the authority of the Council of State; there was no separation of civil and military affairs. After the creation of a general staff in 1878 as an organ independent of the Army Ministry, the military functioned separately from ordinary government administration. This was the famous independence of the supreme command.[1] General staff independence was not abridged by the Meiji Constitution promulgated in 1889. The constitution established a parliamentary system under which elected representatives in the Diet participated in government decisions, but it reserved a very broad area of authority to the emperor. Executive agencies acting for the emperor could function without Diet approval. The right of supreme command and the right to determine the size of military forces were both included in this sweeping executive power. The former was specified by Article XI: "The Emperor has the supreme command of the army and navy." The latter was covered by Article XII: "The Emperor determines the organization and peace standing of the army and navy." A few legal experts tried to restrict the general staff by citing Article LV, which stated: "The respective Ministers of State shall give their advice to the Emperor and be responsible for it." Proponents of civilian authority argued that since the constitution specified no exceptions, under a strict interpretation the right of supreme command should be exercised as a state minister's advice to the throne. This argument would have invalidated the general staff's preconstitutional independence and reduced the chief of the general staff to equal status with other cabinet ministers.[2] This interpretation, however, did not prevail; the supreme command retained its special status after promulgation of the constitution. Thus, from the start of Japan's constitutional era, the military occupied a unique and powerful position in the state structure.[3]

Although the supreme command's independence was accepted, opinion about its scope varied widely. One school of thought regarded the supreme command as an undesirable exception to the principles of parliamentary government because it was not responsible to the Diet.[4] Advocates of this view sought to restrict the jurisdiction of military advisory organs. The generals countered by asserting that security was crucial to national survival and that defense took precedence. They tried to expand the command authority and prevent interference by other government agencies. (A 1930 general staff opinion said: "The military should give the widest possible interpretation to the authority of military command organizations.")[5] The differences in viewpoint and emphasis could hardly have been sharper.

The emperor was the supreme commander. He was supported by advisory organs, the army and navy general staffs (originally the navy general staff was not an independent agency like the army general staff). The general staffs planned and executed command functions entirely independent of the rest of the government. The Army and Navy Ministries were initially part of the government structure; as administrative and not command organs, they did not have special legal status. Nevertheless, the service ministries managed to acquire a supreme command prerogative. When the cabinet system regulations were first promulgated in 1889, Article 7 explicitly stated that "in matters involving military secrecy and command reported by the chief of the general staff to the throne, except those matters on which the emperor himself informs the cabinet, the army and navy minister should report to the prime minister." But at some point the words "by the chief of the general staff" were deleted from the text, blurring the restriction. The service ministers claimed authority to report directly to the emperor without cabinet approval; under this privilege they had only to inform the prime minister of their action. The army and navy ministers thus gained their right of direct access to the throne by an unethical trick.[6]

Their special status was buttressed in other ways. The service ministries remained the special preserve of professional military men. No civilian control was ever allowed. For a time during mid-Meiji, the qualifications for army and navy minister were not specified; a civilian might have been appointed. By custom, however, the positions always went to general officers or admirals. After 1900 the regulations were changed to specify that the army minister must be an active duty general or lieutenant general, and the navy minister must be an admiral or vice-admiral. In 1913 the regulations were revised again to allow the selection of reserve or retired generals or admirals. Another change in 1936 again restricted the position to officers on active duty. The appointment of military officers continued right down to the end of the Pacific War. Even a party cabinet—that is, a cabinet formed by the majority party in the Diet, the pattern from the 1920s on—had to name military men to the service posts. There could be no civilian or Diet-member cabinets. Furthermore, the military could topple cabinets by having an army or navy minister resign or prevent their formation by refusing to provide officers to serve in these positions.

During the Meiji period, civilian leaders like Itō Hirobumi and Inoue Kaoru and military leaders like Yamagata Aritomo shared personal and professional bonds that transcended parochial issues. They had fought together to overthrow the Tokugawa government and they were the dynamic young elite who created the new Japan. There was competition between the men from Satsuma and Chōshū, the two fiefs that led the Restoration. Still, they were the ins, the bureaucrats who held the reins of power, and they stood united against all rivals. They matured into the oligarchs and the senior leaders of the Restoration. As *genrō* or elder statesmen, they were in a position superior to the government and the military. Their advice to the emperor was based on this unique prestige and authority. There were thus few serious conflicts between civil and supreme command policies.

As the *genrō* gradually retired or died and the political parties became an important force in the Diet, the independence of the supreme command frequently caused serious friction. It was an impediment to parliamentary government. The cabinet was responsible to the people for national policies, but events were often decided by the military, who were responsible to neither the people nor the cabinet.

In 1912 Army Minister Uehara Yūsaka insisted upon an increase of two army divisions. When the cabinet refused, Uehara submitted his resignation and the Army Ministry let it be known that no successor was available. The cabinet had no choice but to resign. Control over the appointment of service ministers gave the military the power of life or death over any cabinet.[7]

In 1930 a cabinet headed by Hamaguchi Yuko overrode the stiff opposition of Katō Kanji, chief of the navy general staff, and obtained ratification of the London Naval Treaty. By this treaty, Japan agreed to a 10:6 naval ratio with the United

States. It was a time of "normal constitutional government," when several successive cabinets were formed by the majority party in the Diet. International cooperation was a hopeful trend in the years after World War I. Supported by these favorable winds at home and abroad, the Hamaguchi cabinet sailed into navy waters and boldly insisted that it could decide the nation's armament level, which had been a military prerogative under Article XII of the constitution. The navy general staff and its supporters fought back, arguing that military force levels were a supreme command matter and that the government could not conclude such a treaty without their agreement.[8] A furious controversy erupted, but the Hamaguchi cabinet won, in part because the democratic and antimilitary trend of the 1920s was still strong.

The military did not supinely accept defeat. Pent-up frustration at the armament reduction conferences and the antimilitary mood of the mid-1920s finally exploded in desperate violence. The counterattack by reactionary military officers wrote finis to "normal constitutional government" and forced a sharp turn away from international cooperation toward overseas aggression. The independence of the supreme command was the military's most effective institutional weapon in the revolt against civilian leadership.

An explosion along the main line of the South Manchurian Railway near Mukden on September 18, 1931, started the seizure of Manchuria. The bombing was a planned criminal act by the Kwantung Army. Immediately after the explosion Morishima Morito, the Japanese consul general, rushed to the Mukden Special Service Agency and urged Itagaki Seishirō and other Kwantung Army staff officers to seek a peaceful solution through diplomatic negotiations. Itagaki replied angrily, "The prerogative of supreme command has been invoked, yet you are trying to interfere with a command action?" Hanaya Tadashi whipped out his sword and threatened Morishima with "Anyone who interferes with the authority of the supreme command gets this!"[9] Fifteen years of death and destruction were sparked that night by army officers acting illegally under the cover of the "prerogative of supreme command." One fait accompli followed another, hostilities escalated, and the end was a cataclysmic disaster for Japan.

Japan began full-scale hostilities in China in 1937. Even then, none of the civilian cabinet officials, including Prime Minister Konoe Fumimaro, knew how far the military intended to push into China. The Foreign Ministry had no idea what to tell other countries, and other government agencies were at a loss to plan for the future. Finally Otani Son'yū, minister of colonies, could bear the uncertainty no longer. At a cabinet meeting he asked in what general area the military actions would stop. Army Minister Sugiyama Hajime refused to say a word. Navy Minister Yonai Mitsumasa felt he had to say something. He replied, "The plan is to stop on a line between the Yungting River and Paoting." Sugiyama flushed angrily and stormed at Yonai, "Can you discuss such matters before these civilians?" The situation got so bad that even Premier Konoe, who had a good personal relationship with the military, was reduced to asking the emperor what was going on. The prime minister requested that the emperor inform the cabinet about matters the military reported directly to the throne which he, as prime minister, absolutely had to know for future planning. The emperor told Konoe that the military were unwilling to discuss certain matters at cabinet meetings because civilian politicians were present, and he agreed to pass on essential information to the premier and the foreign minister. The arrangement covered only information *from* the emperor; the premier could not offer his views on these issues.[10]

At an Imperial Headquarters-Cabinet Liaison Conference on August 16, 1941, a military participant said that conference matters should not be discussed in detail at regular cabinet meetings because classified information would be disclosed. Other cabinet ministers should be told only what they absolutely had to know to perform their duties. Foreign Minister Toyoda Teijirō took exception: "The other cabinet ministers are also ministers of state. Why is it wrong to consult with them?" The reply came back, "There's nothing wrong from a legal point of view." The foreign minister rejoined, "Are you denigrating the Constitution?" His adversary retorted, "Theoretically speaking, you are correct, but when it comes to protecting military secrets, we must be practical." The military remained adamantly opposed to sharing information with other cabinet ministers.[11]

The crucial decision to go to war against America and England followed the same pattern. Everything related to Japan's military strength was classified. Cabinet ministers and other senior advisers *(jūshin)** lacked the information to assess Japan's chances for victory. Tōgō Shigenori, foreign minister later in 1941, stated after the war that he had doubted the military's assurances of victory. Yet lacking the information to refute their claims, he had to accept their judgment and agree to hostilities.[12]

The services kept the government ignorant of the military situation after the war began. The army and navy each jealously guarded their autonomy. Not only would they not tell the civilians anything, but each service refused to share information with the other. Although Tōjō Hideki was both prime minister and an active duty general, for example, the navy did not inform him of the defeat at Midway till a month later.[13] Tōjō could not interfere with or dictate to the navy.[14] Shigemitsu Mamoru only learned after the war that the Combined Fleet had been destroyed in the battle of Leyte Gulf.[15]

The military's insistence upon the widest scope for command prerogatives allowed them to run circles around the civilians. The generals and admirals used their leverage and power to bring all government affairs under military control. When the Okada cabinet fell as a result of the military mutiny in Tokyo on February 26, 1936, Hirota Kōki was named to form a new cabinet. The army looked over the tentative list of cabinet appointees and objected to several of the choices. The Seiyūkai and Minseitō went along on the understanding

*The *jūshin* or senior statesmen were an extraconstitutional group of political advisers all of whom had once been premier.

that each party would get two cabinet positions. The army later reneged and demanded that they settle for only one ministerial position each.[16]

In 1937 the army took umbrage at a question asked in the Diet by Hamada Kunimatsu, calling it "proof of the political parties' antimilitary sentiment." The army's price for cooperation was that "the party expel Hamada, reflect upon its errors, and give total support to the government." The Hirota cabinet was finally forced to resign. As a new cabinet was being formed, the Army Ministry's Military Affairs Bureau prepared a proposal that all but dictated the ministerial lineup:

> The following individuals are unacceptable for premier: Ugaki Kazushige, Osumi Mineo, Minami Jirō, Yamamoto Eisuke, Katsuda Kazue, Araki Sadao, etc. 2. Preferred cabinet ministers: Finance: Baba Eiichi, Yūki Toyotarō; Home: Kawada Retsu, Karasawa Toshiki, Yasui Eiji, Yoshida Shigeru [not the diplomat]; Education: Futara Yoshinori; Navy: Suetsugu Nobumasa; Army: Sugiyama Hajime, Itagaki Seishirō; Justice: Obara Naoshi, Shiono Suehiko; Foreign: not to be restricted to a specialist in diplomatic affairs. 3. Party members who will not disaffiliate themselves from their party upon entering the cabinet are unacceptable.[17]

When Ugaki Kazushige was ordered to form a cabinet, the army vice-minister, the chiefs of the military affairs and personnel bureaus, and relevant section chiefs and their subordinates held a conference at the army minister's official residence. They agreed that "The army will not provide a minister to the cabinet. The ministry must refuse to negotiate with premier-designate Ugaki about an appointee. The reason is that no army minister can maintain discipline if Ugaki is premier." The general staff concurred. Military Police Commander Nakajima waited near the Kanagawa Prefecture-Tokyo boundary to intercept Ugaki on his way to the capital. Nakajima got into Ugaki's car and told him, "The younger officers are very upset and the situation is delicate. Therefore, the army minister has asked me to tell you that he wishes you would decline the premiership."

It was a not very subtle attempt to dissuade Ugaki from forming a cabinet. Nakajima even tried to block the new cabinet by arresting Hayashi Yasakichi, a reserve officer, and other supporters of Ugaki, a gross violation of his authority.[18] Uncowed by these threats, Ugaki tried to form a cabinet. But no one would serve as army minister, and finally he had to give up. The army's opposition to Ugaki was nominally because he was involved in the abortive March 1931 plot. If Ugaki became prime minister, it would harm army discipline. But it was ridiculous to say that a civilian premier could have a negative effect on discipline. The real reason was Ugaki's support in the Minseitō. The army had just clashed with the party politicians and toppled the Hirota cabinet. Now Ugaki was building support from a political party. The army would not stand for it.

The practice had been firmly established by this time of the army minister, the chief of the general staff, and the inspector general of military education—the three most powerful officers in the army—recommending the new army minister to the premier designate. In addition, in May 1936, the regulations were revised to restrict appointment of army and navy ministers to active duty officers. A premier designate could no longer outflank the services by tapping a retired officer. Army ability to block any new cabinet was again unassailable. According to one interpretation, this change was agreed to on the condition that subsequent army ministers could be appointed without the approval of the army Big Three.[19] The evidence on this point is ambiguous; the practice continued until the post-surrender Prince Higashikuni cabinet which rejected their choice of Doihara Kenji in favor of Shimomura Sadamu.[20]

In 1940 the army vice-minister and vice-chief of staff agreed that the Yonai Mitsumasa cabinet should be replaced in order to push a military alliance with Germany and Italy. The chief of staff Prince Kan'in concurred: "If a majority of the army regard a cabinet change as necessary, in the interests of the country extraordinary measures would be unavoidable." He sent a memorandum to Army Minister Hata Shunroku which stated in part, "It is essential at this time that a strong national unity cabinet be formed which is capable of resolutely carrying out its obligations. I request that you take appropriate action." The only "appropriate action" for Hata was resignation. When the premier sought a replacement, the three army leaders replied that although they were not refusing the request, the army's situation was "quite difficult." Since this was tantamount to an outright refusal, the Yonai cabinet was forced out.[21]

The military utilized its independent authority as broadly as possible to impose its priorities on the nation. If legal methods and the skillful use of institutional advantages were inadequate, they used their monopoly of force to terrorize and destroy opponents. Kwantung Army staff officer Hanaya's drawn sword against Consul Morishima in Mukden was one vivid example. Conspiracies to seize power began in March 1931, even before the Manchurian Incident, when generals Koiso Kuniaki, Tatekawa Yoshitsugu, and others used their field grade subordinates to plan a coup d'état in collusion with the civilian ultranationalist Okawa Shūmei, a lecturer at the Colonization Academy, and his followers. Army Minister Ugaki was reportedly also involved in the March conspiracy.[22] Colonels Hashimoto Kingorō and Nemoto Hiroshi planned another coup d'état for immediately after the Manchurian Incident, the October plot of 1931. The Kempeitai (military police) learned of the plan and placed Hashimoto, Nemoto, and the others in protective custody before they could strike.[23] It was an open and shut case of criminal conspiracy to commit an insurrection, yet the culprits were neither courtmartialed nor even disciplined. This lax treatment contributed to the military's brazen proclivity to use force.

The May 15 Incident was the next military bid for power. Premier Inukai Tsuyoshi was murdered in his official residence in broad daylight on May 15, 1932, by uniformed naval cadets as part of a plot by navy cadets, army officer candidates, and civilian rightists. The kid gloves treatment of senior conspirators had encouraged young officers to believe they could take direct action and get away with it. Far from being ashamed of these thugs and murderers, most of the officer corps were sympathetic and used the incident to intimidate civilian politicians. They let it be known that "in the event that a party cabinet was formed solely on 'parliamentary principles' (i.e., from the majority party in the Diet) the army would be restive."²⁴ These threats ended party cabinets.

The propensity of senior military leaders to capitalize on the rashness of junior activists recurred after the mutiny of February 26, 1936, the most serious breach of discipline in the history of the Imperial Army. A group of army officers and civilian rightists led troops in an uprising. They murdered Lord Keeper of the Privy Seal Saitō Makoto, Finance Minister Takahashi Korekiyo, Inspector General of Military Education Watanabe Jōtarō, and others and occupied the Nagata-chō area of Tokyo, the site of government offices, for several days. The military then used this flagrant breach of the chain of command as a tacit threat to the civilian authorities.²⁵ As described above, the army designated personnel in the next cabinet.

Intimidation took many forms. Tokyo was full of rumors in December 1935 that young officers were planning to occupy the Diet and stage a coup. On the evening of December 22, several young officers, summoned by Lt. Colonel Mitsui Sakichi, assembled at a restaurant in Shinjuku to discuss a plot. Nothing came of the "planning session." The Ushigome Kempeitai unit commander explained that "This Diet session must pass a military budget that gives the services every *yen* we asked for. That's why we are threatening the politicians that the young officers might 'do something.' A bunch of hot blooded young officers getting together scares the hell out of them." The army staged the scenario to achieve its political objectives.²⁶ Senior army generals refused to punish the conspirators, even in blatant criminal actions like the March and

October plots in 1931, because it would damage "the prestige of the Imperial Army." The generals not only overlooked insubordination but turned the violence to their own ends. A combination of lax discipline plus cynical manipulation was the crucial background factor in the February 26 mutiny.

The Imperial Army and Navy were ostensibly disciplined professional forces obedient to the emperor's will. Numerous plots and coup attempts showed that in fact the services were completely unable to control their own officers and men. The Manchurian Incident was proof positive of a total breakdown in military order. The Kwantung Army staff planned and executed the operation behind the backs of the senior officers in Tokyo. Army leaders at the center were also unable to control the Kwantung Army's subsequent moves. In an effort to rein in the runaway forces in the field, Chief of Staff Kanaya ordered a halt to offensive operations. He took the extraordinary step of obtaining permission to issue orders under his name rather than the usual slower procedure of acting after imperial authorization.[27]

The political zeal of middle-ranking officers was the major impetus for the military's interference in civilian government. The army minister and other senior commanders were supposed to be in charge. It was their job to curb this politicking and maintain order. But they were manipulated by the younger officers, protected them from punishment, and became their spokesmen. It was *gekokujō* or the overthrow of seniors by junior men, a familiar phenomenon in Japanese history.

The 1930s were a decade of pure *gekokujō:* junior officers broke military regulations, overseas units ignored policies made in Tokyo, and the military as a whole had no scruples about disregarding the wishes of their supreme commander, the emperor. Harada Kumao was private secretary to the *genrō* Saionji Kimmochi and a close observer of events at the pinnacle of civilian society. Harada frequently lamented in his diary in 1938–39 that the military had excessive influence at the palace. Harada had learned that the emperor's aide-de-camp made no attempt to convey the emperor's wishes to the military. Instead, he functioned as the military's spokesman at court.[28] In 1940 the emperor received a report from the Board of Audit about discrepancies in the army's accounting and management. The emperor asked the chief of staff about the allegations. He responded that "there was no basis to the report," a barefaced lie. The emperor pressed him, but the chief of staff gave no further reply.[29]

The military used their powerful position to bypass or dominate other government agencies. They insisted upon the widest latitude for command prerogatives, but refused to take any responsibility for mistakes or the undesirable consequences of their actions. They were utterly irresponsible and arrogant. The February 26 mutiny was not immediately crushed because Araki Sadao, a military affairs councilor, and other army leaders gave signs of approval and support. They had Major General Yamashita Tomoyuki deliver a message from the army minister to the rebels to that effect. Although these generals should have been prosecuted as co-conspirators, once the insurrection was under control they blamed everything on the rebellious officers and civilians. The hapless rebel leaders were tried in camera and executed, including Kita Ikki, the civilian rightist theoretician, who was not directly involved in the conspiracy. Senior army leaders escaped scot free.[30]

Occasionally there was a pretense of disciplinary action. In 1940 Army Minister Tōjō Hideki "transferred" several officers for violating orders in the advance into French Indochina. Although instructed to avoid a clash, Japanese units attacked the French. The officers involved were Tominaga Kyōji, chief, First Division, general staff; Satō Kenryō, vice-chief of staff, South China Expeditionary Army; and Nakamura Akihito, commander, Fifth Division. But not long after these "disciplinary transfers," Tominaga became chief of the personnel affairs bureau, Army Ministry; Satō was named chief of the military affairs bureau; and Nakamura turned up as commander of the Kempeitai. Each made a quick comeback to important positions in Tokyo. Even in those rare instances when senior officers were held "responsible" for violating orders, they got off with a very light tap on the wrist until the situation cooled off.[31]

In December 1936 former premier Okada Keisuke reportedly criticized the military: "Hardly any of the middle–ranking officers are capable of objectivity. If they bungle so and so, they say, 'Somebody made a mistake,' and they blame it on somebody else. To allow such military men freedom of action is very dangerous. Unless they are able to make rational assessments of events, they cannot begin to think of taking responsibility for their actions. It's a bad situation."[32] After the war, former colonel Horiba Kazuo wrote a devastating criticism of the senior officer corps: "Most of the officers in responsible positions were incapable of an objective assessment of their own actions . . . individuals prone to vacillation, evading responsibility, and a lack of perspective tended to end up in the important posts," and "to decide government policy but not accept ultimate responsibility is a crime, to ignore previous mistakes and repeat errors of national policy is a crime."[33] Horiba was a career military man, a brilliant general staff section chief. These comments cannot be dismissed as civilian carping. Hayashi Saburō, a colonel during the war, wrote: "When a 'gung ho' type bungled, the personnel people overlooked it. Even when disciplinary action was taken, it was done apologetically. But there was a strong tendency to treat cautious men—those, for example, who opposed escalation—as cowards. Furthermore, if they made a mistake, they usually got hit with a stiff punishment."[34] The irresponsibility of the military and the institutional arrangements that permitted such an imbalance of power in their favor were a major cause of Japan's destruction.

The Military Gestalt: Values and Victims

The Japanese military gestalt was another reason for the abuse of power. And the Pacific War was a mirror image of that gestalt: recklessness, absurd persistence beyond the point of no return, and innumerable acts of savagery. That kind of war did not just happen. It was not the result of accident or loss of control. Japan's modern military replaced the feudal samurai class of hereditary fighting men. The prestige of the feudal warrior (with his sword and warrior's code, *bushidō*) gave way to a new military system patterned after the latest Western models. The Meiji Restoration was not a social revolution from below, a mass political awakening. A small, dynamic elite seized power, crushed the nascent popular reformists who sought a fundamental restructuring of the social order, and created an absolute state around an emperor system. The new military forces were a natural result of that process of change directed from above. They were completely different from the popular conscript army formed in France at the time of the French Revolution. Japan's military were an integral part of the new authority structure. They consisted of two strata: officers who were bureaucrats in the new state and common soldiers, an exploited labor force from the most impoverished level of the farming population. Bureaucrats, intellectuals, persons of property, and others received deferments. Conscription was a corvée on the rural masses; military service fell mainly on the second and third sons of farm families.[35]

No spirit of égalité and fraternité softened differences of rank in the Meiji army. On top were the officers, privileged imperial officials. On the bottom were ordinary soldiers who had been dragooned into a cruel, demeaning labor service. Each group was further subdivided into different ranks and levels. To function, this structure required absolute obedience of subordinates. When the People's Rights movement flourished, the government feared the army might be infected by "dangerous thoughts" and tightened discipline still more. At one point, radical elements in the movement planned an armed uprising. Discussions of how to organize rebel forces included a proposal that the officers be elected.[36] Nothing could have contrasted more with the authoritarian origin and structure of the government forces.

For much the same reasons that a German-style constitution was adopted, the army was organized along German lines. In 1887 the government adopted the Prussian cadet system and established a separate military preparatory school for future officers. The change reduced the liberal arts curriculum; the training became more narrowly focused on military subjects. The result was an officer corps of rigid mentality and limited experience. In 1889 the Army Ministry disbanded the Getsuyōkai (Monday Association), an officers' group, and prohibited all factional groups. Even study groups such as the Artillery and Engineers Association (Hokō kyōdōkai) were broken up. No organizations or associations, except the semiofficial Kaikōsha (Army Officers' Association), were allowed. These restrictions stifled creative research by military men, impoverished strategic thinking and military doctrine, and made the army even more undemocratic.[37]

The military were determined innovators in certain essential spheres of modernization, efficiency, and rationalization. In the early years of Meiji there was much resistance to Western clothing, but the army quickly adopted Western uniforms. Even as late as the early twentieth century, ultranationalists stubbornly opposed the introduction of the metric system. There was even a comic story in the public campaign against alien measurements that equated one meter with one death (*ichi metoru wa ichi mei toru ni tsuzuru.* The pun is on *metoru* [one meter] and *mei toru* [take a life]). Yet the military lost no time in switching to the new system. From the late 1920s on, many Japanese weapons were among the best in the world.[38]

Despite these modernist impulses, the mental outlook of the military was marked by extremely reactionary and irrational views. In 1908 the revision of military codes was begun. The Infantry Manual was adopted in 1909, the Army Education Regulation in 1913, and the Field Regulations the following year. Japanese army strategic doctrine was systematically stated for the first time. A striking feature of the doctrine is its excessive emphasis on "spirit." The literature is full of phrases about "the attack spirit," "confidence in certain victory," "loyalty to the emperor," "love of country," "absolute sincerity," and "sacrifice one's life to the country, absolute obedience to superiors."[39] Primary emphasis on esprit de corps and morale during the Sino-Japanese and Russo-Japanese wars, when hand-to-hand fighting was often decisive, is understandable. But it continued despite fundamental changes in the nature of warfare. Enormous advances in weaponry meant that victory was no longer necessarily determined by the battlefield bravery of soldiers. The military went into the Pacific War still clinging to the concept of fighting spirit as decisive in battle. The result was wanton waste of Japanese lives, particularly in combat with Allied forces whose doctrine was based on scientific rationality.

Consider a few examples. It was absolutely forbidden in the Japanese army to withdraw, surrender, or become a prisoner of war. The 1908 army criminal code contained the following provisions: "A commander who allows his unit to surrender to the enemy without fighting to the last man or who concedes a strategic area to the enemy shall be punishable by death." "If a commander is leading troops in combat and they are captured by the enemy, even if the commander has performed his duty to the utmost, he shall be punishable by up to six months confinement."

The Field Service Code, issued in 1941 over Tōjō Hideki's signature as army minister, contained the injunction "Do not be taken prisoner alive." In Mori Keinan's *Senjin jutsugi,* an easy-to-understand commentary on the regulations, the author cited the case of a Major Kuga. During the fighting in Shanghai he was wounded, lost consciousness, and was captured by the Chinese. Upon release, Kuga committed suicide to atone for his disgrace. Mori wrote: "This act typifies the glorious spirit of the Imperial Army," an admonition that any Japanese fighting man taken prisoner must kill himself. Even a lowly private who was captured but managed to return safely to his unit was expected to commit suicide. Many young Japanese were forced to throw their lives away in adherence to this code.[40]

Army training emphasizing spirit over matter had a certain success in turning out brave soldiers unafraid of death. However, when Japanese forces encountered the superbly rational Allies, the limitations of élan were inevitably exposed. Kamiko Kiyoshi's memoir, *Ware Reite ni shisezu* (I Survived Leyte), described the clash of mind and matter in the Philippines. Kamiko, an NCO in the Kwantung Army, was transferred to the Philippines in late 1944 when the battle was almost over. Kwantung Army soldiers were the epitome of devotion to duty, unflinching courage, and fighting spirit. Kamiko depicts the rapid collapse of morale before the tactics of the American forces. The Americans began their attack at 10 A.M. and ended fighting for the day at 5 P.M. They kept regular fighting hours as if they were working in a government office or a company. "To the Japanese army, with its traditional belief in night marches and night attacks, it was a very strange way to fight a war. I realized after a while that it was much more rational."

Japanese forces were often overextended to the point of exhaustion: they were frequently so fatigued that the soldiers could not throw hand grenades half as far as in training. The Americans would throw grenades from well down on a slope, yet the grenades cleared the ridgeline and exploded on the Japanese side. They could do it because they were not exhausted. The Kwantung Army invested enormous time and energy in training for round-the-clock combat and hand-to-hand fighting. But while the Kwantung Army was charging around Manchuria in the dark shouting "banzai," warfare had become incredibly mechanized. Kamiko's unit was sent into combat and immediately came under long-range artillery fire and took casualties. They did not see an American soldier, let alone get close enough for hand-to-hand fighting.

The U.S. troops got good meals and even received medical supplies by air drop. They wore light metal helmets and fought with light carbines. The Japanese forces got soup dotted with a few grains of floating rice. Although much shorter in stature, they used heavier equipment and weapons. Battlefield effectiveness naturally differed greatly because of these discrepancies. Even brave NCOs highly motivated by "spiritual training" saw that the Imperial Army's strategic doctrine was outdated and stupid.

Military irrationality was also manifested in a despotic authoritarianism. Officers, although subject to restrictions, were still a privileged stratum at the top of the officer-NCO-enlisted man hierarchy. Differences of rank and junior subordination to seniors notwithstanding, the officer class in general had the status and authority of feudal lords. The privates, especially the new recruits, were at the miserable bottom of the pyramid. They had no human rights. They were nonpersons. Military education, training, and the daily routine of barracks life at the squad level was an unending stream of humiliation and rough treatment. It was on the drill field and in the squad room that the unique characteristics of the Japanese military were most visible.

The facts of barracks life were well known before the war, since most able-bodied men had been drafted for compulsory service. They had tasted army life and had told their friends and neighbors about it. Yet there is a surprising paucity of written accounts. Ikeda Kyokugai's *Ku? Raku? Shimpei no seikatsu* (Pain or Pleasure? A Recruit's Life), a detailed description of army life mentioned earlier, was banned. Under the prewar internal security laws it was impossible to publish material that honestly described army life. *Pain or Pleasure? A Recruit's Life* is a valuable historical document because it shows the asinine, inhuman treatment of recruits. After the war many superb accounts were published, including Noma Hiroshi's writings on his war experiences[41] and his realistic work of fiction, *Shinkū chitai* (Zone of Emptiness), and Gomikawa Junpei's *Ningen no jōken* (The Human Condition). These works show that the brutal treatment of recruits continued right down to the end of the war in 1945.

Though officially prohibited, physical abuse of trainees was commonplace. The military and the police were the two bastions of institutionalized illegality. Police abuses of authority in arrests, detention, and torture were notorious. Judges pretended not to know about the police torture rooms and the mistreatment of suspects and prisoners.[42] The army and the police were partners in crime, above and impervious to the law. It is no exaggeration to call the "Greater Japanese Empire" a Kafkaesque state dedicated to the abuse of human rights. On the one hand, the people voluntarily surrendered their rights either because of a largely agrarian, premodern consciousness or because of a conformist, statist education. The state, on the other hand, made sure that most of the people never understood that they had civil rights. Indoctrination was reinforced by police and army swords.

Army draftees were called *issen gorin* (one sen, five rin, or less than a penny, the cost of a draft notice postcard in the 1920s). They were expendable; there was an unlimited supply for the price of the postcards.[43] Weapons and horses were treated with solicitous care, but "no second-class private was as valuable as an animal."[44] After all, a horse costs real money. Privates were only worth *issen gorin.* Soldiers' rights were treated as cheaply as the men themselves.[45] The navy, with its greater reliance on modern technology and a cosmopolitanism acquired from foreign travel and contact with other navies, was relatively more rational than the army. Its harsh treatment of enlisted personnel during training, at shore installations, and aboard ships at sea, however, was identical with that of the army.[46] Cruelty toward subordinates was a psychological technique. It provided an outlet for pressure by allowing each rank to shift the oppression to the one below. The oppression snowballed as it rolled down the ranks, till all the tensions and abuse landed on the recruits. They were the lowest of the low; they had no outlet, no one they could mistreat.

These were the objective group dynamics of military life. Subjectively, however, military leaders believed that stiff discipline was the only way to train troops, and it did appear to be effective. That article of faith was expressed in comments like "If soldiers are treated softly, they get used to it. You have to be tough from the start so the men realize 'They're in the army now.' "[47] Junior officers were cautioned against being lenient: "You don't want to be the kind of officer about whom the men say, 'He's a good guy. He wouldn't order us forward in this heavy enemy fire.' Your troops won't respect you."[48] Enlisted men should hate their officers: "Their resentment is often converted into fighting strength. The repressed anger of the drill field and camp life explodes in wartime as a blood-thirsty desire to slaughter the enemy." The "skillful" commander could "by treating his men with calculated brutality mold them into a fierce fighting unit against the enemy in time of war."[49] (The abuse of recruits involved more than realistic training to prepare men for combat. Apparently, many older enlisted men were able to avoid overseas assignments because of their ability to handle the raw trainees. They had a vested interest in shaping up the new men even if it took fists and kicks to get the desired results.[50]) The inevitable side effects of training to "breed vicious fighters" was a penchant for brutality against enemy prisoners and civilian noncombatants. Men under constant pressure would explode in irrational, destructive behavior. Individuals whose own dignity and man-hood had been so cruelly violated would hardly refrain from doing the same to defenseless persons under their control. After all, they were just applying what they had learned in basic training.[51]

Military life was rough and tough,[52] yet most of the NCOs were volunteers who loved their assignments. They had found a home in the army. They enjoyed the amenities of their position. The drill instructor was a demi-god to the recruits. When training ended for the day, the recruits fought for the privilege of untying the squad leader's puttees. In the bath they held the soap for the NCOs and washed their backs. The noncommissioned officers were flattered and fawned over night and day. Another attraction of army life was a perverse equality found nowhere else in Japanese society. No matter how prestigious or wealthy a man's family, all this was left behind when he entered the service. He was just another recruit. The NCOs were catered to by men who would not have deigned to speak to them in civilian life.

An even greater inducement was the relative ease of military life, strange as that may sound. Compared to the dawn to dark back-breaking toil of the impoverished farm households where they grew up, many NCOs found army life "far easier," and "not very hard work, a lot better than being a farmer."[53] They got enough to eat and a pension if they stayed in till retirement. It is not surprising that second and third sons with no expectation of getting any land of their own should find military life very attractive.[54] Most of the NCOs assigned to the important duties of training and leading troops came from the lower stratum of society. The "toughness" of the Japanese military, which produced an endless supply of good fighting men by these brutal methods, actually came from the poverty of rural Japan, where the struggle for survival was more demanding than even army life. A "toughness" rooted in privation, obedience to authority, and brutality was effective in limited battlefield engagements. What happens when it is locked in a protracted war against a highly rational, democratically organized "enemy"? Was it not absurd to think that Japan could prevail through "toughness"? The military never understood that the "toughness" so effective against the Manchu troops and the tsarist Russian forces, which were more irrational and brutal than Japan at that time, would be a fatal weakness in the Pacific War.

PART 2

The Conduct
of the War
and the Result

4

The Beginning: Aggression in China

Japan and China were on a collision course. To Japanese, the Middle Kingdom was a land of "Chinks," a place to maintain and expand profitable business interests. Contemporary Japanese were oblivious to Chinese aspirations. But China was stirring. Demands to free the country from its semi-colonial humiliation were forming in the collective self-conscious and bursting out on the stage of history. Popular protest and agitation marked the new China. Rejection of Chinese demands at the Paris Peace Conference sparked a protest on May 4, 1919, that grew into a sustained, nationwide demand for reforms, the famous May Fourth Movement. When foreign-officered police killed Chinese demonstrators in Shanghai on May 30, 1925, the country erupted with boycotts, protests, demonstrations, and a great fifteen-month strike.

These mass movements were part of the nationalist and anti-imperialist struggle. They were produced by profound changes in Chinese society: the development of Chinese capital, the formation of a modern working class, the increase in political consciousness of students and intellectuals, and the antifeudal struggle by a part of the peasantry. In retrospect it is clear that these events were an epochal shift in Chinese history, not just disparate explosions of discontent and unrest.[1] But at the time very few Japanese perceived them as anything but the chronic disorder and instability of China.[2]

The First Moves

Against this tumultuous background, the Kuomintang's Northern Expedition to unify China began in 1926, and the Nationalist government was established the following year in Nanking with Chiang Kai-shek as "Generalissimo." No sooner did the Nationalists defeat the warlords than they attacked the Communists, starting a civil war that further complicated China's internal politics. The Chinese Communist party (CCP), led by Mao Tse-tung, set up a base at Chingkangshan in the mountains on the Hunan-Kiangsi border in 1927 and steadily began clearing a liberated zone. A Chinese Soviet Republic was established at Juichin, Kiangsi, in 1931 with Mao Tse-tung as chairman. Despite the Kuomintang-Communist confrontation, the nationalist consciousness of the Chinese masses grew stronger. The anti-imperialist struggle to free China from colonial subjection sought specific goals: the abolition of extraterritoriality, tariff autonomy, and the return of the foreign settlements and leased territories.

If Japan had been a champion of Asian nationalism, had really desired independence and progress for its neighbor, and had joined with China to liberate Asia from Western imperialism, the subsequent history of the region would have been vastly different. Japan would have identified with Chinese nationalism, helped to end foreign domination, and made a real effort to create enduring good relations with the new China. Unfortunately, Japanese leaders chose the opposite course of action. They competed with the West for a place at the imperialist table and a slice of the Chinese melon.

The army in particular was preoccupied with using military force to compel Chinese acquiescence. Of Japan's special rights in China, the army was especially determined to retain the position in Manchuria, acquired at such cost in blood and treasure in two wars. Some army leaders favored direct action, even by illegal methods, to gain control of the whole region. At first Japan appeased and manipulated Chang Tso-lin, the warlord who controlled Manchuria. As conditions in China changed and Chang was in the way, some army officers conceived a plan to kill him and seize all of Manchuria at one stroke.

In 1928 Chang Tso-lin was forced to withdraw from Peking by the approach of Nationalist forces. Kwantung Army staff officer Kawamoto Daisaku and his co-conspirators decided to strike. As Chang's train passed over a crossing on the Chingfeng Railroad and South Manchurian Railway, it was blown up by an explosive charge placed by engineers from the Korea Army, the Japanese force stationed in the colony. As a pretext for dispatching troops and occupying all of Manchuria, bombs were thrown at the Japanese Residents' Association and other places in Mukden. However, the Mukden consulate's insistence that troops were not needed blocked their dispatch. The Kwantung Army plotters blamed three opium-addicted Chinese vagrants for the assassination. They were taken to the explosion site to be executed, but one escaped and told Chang Hsueh-liang, son of the murdered warlord, about the plot.[3]

Chang Tso-lin's death was an act of premeditated murder. The criminals should have been punished to protect the honor of the Japanese state. Premier Tanaka Giichi promised the emperor he would take disciplinary action, but the Army Ministry was opposed, and the plotters could not be punished. Because of the emperor's displeasure, the Tanaka cabinet had to resign.[4] In China, the assassination of Chang backfired; the flames of Chinese resistance burned brighter. Chang Hsuehliang pledged allegiance to the Nationalists and placed his forces under Chiang Kai-shek's banner and moved ahead with a plan to develop Manchuria without Japanese assistance.

The Japanese ruling elite was extremely apprehensive about these events; national interests in Manchuria, the "lifeline" of the nation, were hanging in the balance. Some army officers, mainly in the Kwantung Army, renewed their determination to seize all of Manchuria. In the spring of 1931, a "Proposal Regarding the Problems of Manchuria and Mongolia" was drafted at Kwantung Army headquarters. It called for a "covert operation in the four northeast districts and a fabricated pretext for military action" in order to "overthrow the Chang Hsueh-liang government and occupy Manchuria and Mongolia."[5] On May 29 Kwantung staff officer Itagaki Seishirō argued that making Manchuria and Mongolia Japanese territory was an urgent priority.[6] These plans came to fruition on the evening of September 18, 1931, when Japanese forces blasted the tracks of the South Manchurian Railway outside Mukden. Army units, "in response to the explosion," immediately attacked Chang Hsueh-liang's troops at the North Barracks and occupied the area.

It was widely reported at the time that Chang's troops had set the explosion. The true facts were concealed for many years. After the war Hanaya Tadashi, one of the chief plotters along with Ishiwara Kanji and Itagaki Seishirō, admitted how the incident really occurred. According to Hanaya, the plot included several unit commanders in the Shimamoto Regiment, a Mukden independent guard unit; former Kempeitai captain Amakasu Masahiko, who had murdered the anarchist Osugi Sakae after the 1923 Kantō earthquake; and others. Captain Konda Shintarō arranged the explosion. The Chinese troops were blamed for it, but most of them were still asleep at the North Barracks when the Japanese attacked. They had been unaware of the fracas at the railroad. Mukden was quickly occupied and placed under military administration. In a few hours the Kwantung Army had achieved a fait accompli that was the pretext for seizing all of Manchuria.

The meticulous planning behind the "spontaneous incident" is apparent. The army engineers who placed the explosive charge were told not to derail a train. In fact, they were not to cause any damage to the trains. The charge was to be laid so that even if the track on one side was cut for a distance, a train would still be able to pass over it. They calculated and placed the charge perfectly. A train passed over the site not long after.[7]

The Mukden plot also involved Kanda Masatane, a staff officer, and other officers in the Korea Army. They agreed that the Korea Army would strike in concert with the Kwantung

Army. They were to set off explosions on the South Manchurian Railway in the Chientao area and then send troops across the border into Manchuria. However, there was a mixup over the timing. Because the explosion near Mukden was carried out sooner than originally intended, troops were not sent from Chientao. The Kwantung Army drew up new plans to give the Korea Army a piece of the action. They called for the Kwantung Army Special Service Unit to arrange bombings in Kirin and Harbin to terrorize the Japanese residents as a justification for moving troops. As military operations expanded, the Korea Army would be requested to send troops across the border to reinforce the Kwantung Army.[8] The plans were implemented; troops were sent to Kirin but not to Harbin.[9] Korea Army commander Hayashi Senjurō ignored the general staff. Acting on his own authority, he sent an air squadron and a mixed brigade across the border into Manchuria.[10]

These moves were in blatant violation of the nonaggression treaties and the Nine Power Treaty. They were also criminal acts under domestic law. The army criminal code, Article 35, stated: "A commander who initiates hostilities with a foreign country without provocation shall be punished by death." Article 37 stated: "A commander who, except in an extreme emergency, moves troops beyond his area of jurisdiction shall be punished by death or imprisonment of not less than seven years."

The Japanese state should have punished the individuals who committed the acts in Manchuria. What measures were taken? Foreign Minister Shidehara Kijūrō, who had been informed by the Mukden consulate of what the Kwantung Army was up to, reported the information to the cabinet and checkmated Army Minister Minami Jirō. The cabinet agreed on a policy of limiting the incident. They initially had the support of Chief of Staff Kanaya Hanzō, who disagreed with the "young Turk" officers and wanted to stop the Korea Army from sending troops across the border. Nevertheless, when the troops in the field kept moving and Tokyo was faced with a fait accompli, senior army leaders rather quickly and the cabinet more reluctantly ratified the actions in Manchuria. The emperor belatedly approved the movement of forces from the Korean peninsula, sparing General Hayashi from being accused of the "crime of insubordination."[11] Ishiwara, Itagaki, Hanaya, and the other plotters at some point along the way had gained immunity from prosecution. The assassination of Chang Tso-lin and the first plot to seize Manchuria had ended in a fiasco. This time the officers had hit the mark.

The army had struck under cover of the independence of the supreme command. Yet the government was not without recourse. It should have been able to control the rebellious units after the fact by refusing to provide funds. The Korea Army's unauthorized move into Manchuria was a particularly good opportunity to reassert control because army leaders themselves were divided. Premier Wakatsuki Reijirō proved an unexpected disappointment when he said, "The units have already moved, so what can be done?" No cabinet minister demurred, and the cabinet almost routinely approved the expenditures.[12] If the Wakatsuki cabinet had not avoided a showdown and had persisted with tough measures to control the Kwantung Army and the Korea Army, the course of later events might have been different. The civilian leadership would have had to pay a price, but it still would have been a bargain compared to the bill that fell due shortly.

However, the Mukden Incident was more complicated than just young army officers in the field running amok in defiance of their military and civilian superiors. The cast of characters was not divided into the "bad guys" of the Kwantung Army versus the "good guys" in Tokyo. The Kwantung Army struck without formal orders from headquarters in Tokyo. Yet in fact the subordinate units were just taking the actions long implicit in the aggressive aspirations of key generals at the center. That is obvious from a general staff study in April 1931 entitled a "Solution to the Problem of Manchuria and Mongolia." The study included a three-stage "judgment of the situation." The "third stage" was "a proposal for the occupation of Manchuria and Mongolia."[13] That diffuse complicity is further substantiated by the braggadocio of Koiso Kuniaki, chief, Military Affairs Bureau, Army Ministry, in a mid-August 1931 meeting with Kido Kōichi and Harada Kumao. Koiso "suddenly started talking about the independence of Manchuria" and said, "The Japanese like war. If the guns start firing, they'll all jump in for a good fight."[14] Senior army leaders in Tokyo approved of the troop movements in Manchuria after the fact because they were sympathetic before the fact. The Manchurian Incident actually was a broad criminal conspiracy between a local unit and Tokyo army leaders. Perhaps it was too much to expect a party cabinet lacking the prerogative of the supreme command to forestall such a plot. Thereafter, one by one agencies of the Japanese state, some enthusiastically, others passively, joined the cabal and kept the war going for fifteen years.

The Kwantung Army moved quickly to consolidate and expand control of Manchuria. They extended military operations to northern Manchuria and Liaohsi, and began maneuvering politically to set up a puppet government. As early as September 22, Kwantung Army Chief of Staff Miyake Kōji, along with Doihara Kenji, Itagaki Seishirō, Ishiwara Kanji, Katakura Tadashi, and others had agreed on a plan to establish a Chinese administration headed by Henry Pu-yi, the heir to the Manchu dynasty. It was to be a pure puppet government: "Japan will be responsible for national defense and foreign affairs at the request of the new administration." Japan would also "administer major transportation and communication facilities."[15] Foreign Minister Shidehara attempted a peaceful settlement through negotiation with Chiang Kai-shek, but Tokyo was unable to stop the Kwantung Army from another fait accompli—the establishment of a puppet regime.[16]

Security troops of the Chinese Public Order Bureau in Tientsin were attacked on November 29 in a covert operation run by Doihara. In the confusion, Pu-yi was abducted from the city.[17] On March 1, 1932, the new state of Manchukuo

was proclaimed, with Pu-yi as "provisional president." The
Kwantung Army had paved the way by completing the occupation of Manchuria in January 1932 by taking Chinchow, an
operation delayed by general staff restraints. All of Manchuria
was now effectively severed from China and under the authority of "Manchukuo."

The Wakatsuki cabinet had fallen in December 1931 because of the demands of Home Minister Adachi Kenzō for a
"national unity cabinet." Inukai Tsuyoshi and the Seiyūkai
then formed a cabinet, which on March 12, 1932, decided to
take solicitous care of the waif on its doorstep. Policy toward
Manchukuo included the following provisions: "The mainte-
nance of public order in Manchuria and Mongolia will be
entrusted to the Empire [Japan] . . . Manchuria and Mongolia
are the Empire's first line of defense against Russia and China;
no external interference will be tolerated. In accord with these
obligations, the Imperial Army forces in Manchuria will be
increased appropriately and necessary naval facilities will be
established. Manchuria will not be permitted its own regular
army." The policy continued: "In implementing the above,
efforts will be made to avoid conflicts with international law
or international treaties. In particular, in view of the Nine
Power Treaty, etc., as far as possible actions should be formally the independent proposals of the new state."[18] Manchukuo was placed under army control as a forward base in
Japan's advance to the continent. In order to avoid charges of
playing fast and loose with international agreements, everything was given the window dressing of "the independent acts
of the state."

The last party cabinet in the period of "normal constitutional government" officially recognized, although ex post
facto, the puppet state created by the army's criminal conspiracy. China's legitimate sovereignty over Manchuria was destroyed by Japanese military force. The restoration of good
relations between the two countries became increasingly difficult. In January 1932 the emperor asked the Minister to China
Shigemitsu Mamoru, "Japanese-Chinese amity will be impos-

sible for some time?" Shigemitsu replied, "As long as the Manchurian issue remains, I believe it will be impossible to achieve better relations."[19] The price of the successful seizure of Manchuria was Chinese enmity. Moreover, the army's triumph in Manchuria only whetted its appetite for a piece of China proper. The army attempted to expand military operations from Manchuria, Mongolia, and North China to all of China. Japan was already bogged down in an aggressive war, trapped in the swamp of military intervention and escalation.

Escalation: From Manchuria and Mongolia to All of China

The conquest of Manchuria fanned the fires of Chinese nationalism to a white heat. Japanese goods were boycotted in Shanghai as part of the anti-Japan protest movement, and relations between the two countries grew more tense.

There were always military or nationalist operatives ready to make a bad situation worse. Tanaka Ryūkichi, an aide to the military attaché in Shanghai, planned an incident to divert the Western Powers' attention away from Manchukuo. At his instigation, several Japanese Buddhist priests peacefully strolling along a Shanghai street were set upon by "villainous" Chinese. Tanaka "avenged" the deaths and injuries by an attack on a factory that was a center of anti-Japanese sentiment. Tanaka's plotting caused the first Shanghai Incident of January 1932.[20] The navy had been enviously watching the army show in Manchuria. Now the admirals thought it was time they shared in the glory. A naval brigade was landed to make short shrift of the Chinese, but it was fought to a standstill in fierce street engagements. The Ninth Division was sent from Japan to bail out the marines.

The 19th Route Army commanded by Ts'ai T'ing-k'ai was the main Chinese unit in the battle. Not directly affiliated with Chiang Kai-shek, the officers and men were highly motivated against Japan. Aided by the citizens of Shanghai, they put up

a stiff resistance. Heavy fighting continued until an expeditionary force of the 11th and 14th Divisions under the command
of Shirakawa Yoshinori arrived from Japan and finally forced
the 19th Route Army to withdraw. A British-American proposal led to a truce agreement in May. The fighting did not
expand into a full-scale war.[21]

The Powers criticized Japan's actions in Manchuria, the
sideshow in Shanghai having if anything increased attention
to developments in China. In October 1931 the League of
Nations Council passed a resolution by a vote of 13 to 1 (Japan
opposing) calling for Japan to withdraw its troops from Manchuria. In February 1933, the assembly of the League by a
vote of 42 to 1 (Japan) adopted a resolution disapproving of
Japan's control of Manchuria. Matsuoka Yōsuke promptly
led the Japanese delegation out of the hall in protest. Official
withdrawal became effective in March.

The most vociferous critic of Japan among the Powers was
the United States. Under the leadership of Secretary of State
Henry L. Stimson and with a policy of nonrecognition of
Manchukuo, America insisted upon maintaining the status
quo in China. Yet American opposition was limited by the
staggering effects of the economic depression at home and the
latent intent of some American leaders to make Japan a bulwark against communism in the Far East. America was not
prepared to go beyond expressions of disapproval. England, as
a target of Chinese anti-imperialism, shared common interests
with Japan and made no attempt to get tough with Tokyo.
French and German attitudes were similar. The Powers restrained the smaller countries which took a very strong position against Japan at the League of Nations. The Lytton
Report, the final report of a commission of inquiry sent to
Manchuria by the League, was extremely moderate, a reflection of the Powers' influence.[22] The Soviet Union had just
started its first Five Year Plan and was not ready for a showdown with Tokyo. The USSR chose to avoid a clash when
Japan advanced into northern Manchuria, a Russian sphere of
influence. Instead of challenging the Kwantung Army, Mos-

cow offered to sell the Chinese Eastern Railroad. A transfer agreement was concluded in March 1935, and the Soviet Union withdrew from Manchuria. These were the objective international conditions that contributed to the military's relatively easy conquest of Manchuria.[23]

Manchukuo quickly acquired the outward trappings of a government and an economic development plan. In September 1932, Tokyo formally recognized Manchukuo as an independent country and signed the Japan-Manchukuo Agreement. In March 1934 a monarchical government was established with Henry Pu-yi as emperor. The Chinese, of course, did not recognize the phony state of Manchukuo. Nevertheless, the Nationalist government, giving first priority to the civil war with the Communists, had little enthusiasm for simultaneously attempting to recover Manchuria. In addition, the sense of loss for Manchuria was not as direct or intense as for territory inside the Great Wall. Thus, in July 1935, the Manchukuo-China Transportation Agreement restored regular communication and transportation between the two areas. Japanese aggressors seemed to have realized their dream—control of the vast spaces of Manchuria. Indeed, there is no gainsaying the fact that the Manchurian Incident was a great success for its planners. But they wanted more. They expanded military control to Mongolia and North China and overreached themselves.

In January 1933 the Kwantung Army occupied Shankaikwan, the gateway to North China, and started the campaign against Jehol province, which was soon incorporated into Manchukuo. The Kwantung Army next moved against Inner Mongolia, bought off Li Shou-hsin's forces, and turned them into a puppet army. Next was an alliance with Teh Wang, a young Mongol prince and a descendant of Genghis Khan. Later, in December 1935, Li Shou-hsin's forces, on Japanese orders, successfully attacked the Chinese defenders and occupied Kuyuan. During the campaign, the Kwantung Army ordered Manchurian Airlines to form a special air unit and provide air support for Li's troops.[24] In April 1936, the Inner

Mongolia Military Administration was established in Teh Hua, Chahar province, under Teh Wang with Li Shou-hsin as his second in command. The Kwantung Army also moved against Hopei province, in 1933, launching two attacks inside the Great Wall. In May of that year the Kwantung Army concluded the Tangku Truce agreement and gained a foothold in Hopei. The following month General Umezu Yoshijirō, commander of Japanese forces in China, presented a series of demands to General Ho Ying-chin, head of the Peking military command, which led to the secret Ho-Umezu Agreement. Anti-Japan and anti-Manchukuo elements and troops were required to leave Hopei. The next step was the Doihara-Ch'in Agreement, negotiated by Doihara Kenji, chief, Mukden Special Service Unit, and Ch'in Tech'un, a leader of the Chahar provincial government. Under its terms, the Chinese promised not to impede Japan-Manchukuo operations in Mongolia. The pro-Japan forces of Sung Che-yuan were moved from Chahar to Hopei. By these two agreements, the Kwantung Army established a strong position in Hopei.

The operations section of the army general staff had decided by 1932 that so long as China remained "hostile," Japan was justified in "occupying Tientsin and Peking and helping to establish pro-Japanese administrations in North China."[25] By 1933 the Kwantung Army also desired "the establishment in North China of pro-Japanese and pro-Manchukuo administrations not affiliated with the Kuomintang."[26] According to the Kwantung Army: "The natural resources of Manchuria are far exceeded by those in North China. There are limitless deposits of iron and coal in Shansi province. If we are careless, these resources will end up in English or American hands. Talking about 'international morality' and allowing others to always get the jump on us will give Japan the short end of the stick. In our view, taking North China is vital to Japan. And now is the best opportunity."[27]

These views evolved into a determination to sever North China from Nationalist control and create a self-governing, economically independent region. The military were not the only ones impressed by North China's resources. In July 1937 Premier Konoe said: "I think North China is vital, particularly for our economic development."[28] This comment shows, I submit, the prevailing view of Japan's ruling elite. Deeply anxious over the loss of markets due to tariff barriers and desperate for a solution to the crisis confronting Japanese capitalism, they wanted to control North China.[29] Purely military considerations also played a part. Army leaders felt very strongly that "to create one independent government [i.e., separate from Chiang Kai-shek] in the region north of the Yellow River" was necessary in order to cut the communications lines of rebellious elements in Manchukuo and to prevent an attack from the rear by the Soviet Union.[30] As long as these economic and strategic demands infused China policy, the invasion of North China was at the top of the expansionist agenda.

A Japanese-led farmers' movement for self-government in Hopei broke out in 1935. The result was the East Hopei Autonomous Anti-Communist Council, established in November in Tungchow and headed by Yin Ju-keng, a puppet of the Japanese army. The Nationalist government also ignored popular sentiment and tried to cooperate with Japan by creating the Hopei-Chahar Political Council, headed by Sung Che-yuan. Despite this concession, political warfare against Chiang continued. To vitiate the Nationalist currency reforms, which began in November 1935 with British assistance, the military planned to block the shipment of North China cash to the south. From about 1936, Takeshita Yoshiharu, chief, Shankaikwan Special Service Unit, ran an operation to get funds for the East Hopei administration. A vast smuggling racket was carried out under army protection, and China's customs collections fell sharply. Kwantung Army aircraft flew all over North China, even as far as distant Paoting, Hsuchow, and Chingtao. China's sovereignty was treated as a scrap of paper; all protests were summarily rejected.[31]

It is hardly surprising that these simmering conflicts burst into full-scale war in July 1937. The immediate cause, the clash between Japanese and Chinese forces at the Marco Polo Bridge, differed from the Manchurian Incident in that it was not a planned provocation. Yet the abundant predictions and rumors that "something will happen" attest to the volatility of the situation.[32]

The Konoe cabinet was in office. With the demise of party cabinets after the May 15 Incident, the earlier pattern of bureaucratic leadership had reappeared. The Saitō Makoto and Okada Keisuke administrations, which had been in power until the February 26 uprising in 1936, were "national unity cabinets" responsive to the emperor, Genrō Saionji Kimmochi, and the senior advisers who had attempted to check the military. The Konoe cabinet took a different tack. Konoe favored a strong foreign policy and intervention in China, views that made him popular among the "reform" faction of army officers. Even if it was not Konoe's personal intention to launch an all-out war with China, his cabinet's actions expanded a clash that might have been limited to the area where the clash took place. The government sent three divisions to North China. This severe provocation made the situation worse. The second Shanghai Incident occurred in August, more troops were sent there, and intense fighting continued. The battles spread across China without either side declaring war. Tokyo labeled the fighting the "China Incident." The six years of intermittent military action and political intrigue after the Manchurian Incident suggest that 1937 marked a new phase of a war already well underway. It is impossible to delineate the major "incidents" as separate crises; in fact, it is probably more accurate to treat events from 1931 on as a single conflict.

The China campaign caused a serious rift in the army between proponents of ever-wider military operations and those who argued for a limited commitment of forces and a quick negotiated settlement. Expansionists and anti-expansionists disputed at the center in Tokyo and within the forces in the field. The army general staff was a stronghold of the anti-expansionists. After the war they tried to pin the blame for defeat on the officers who widened the war in China. An objective assessment suggests that the differences were a good family squabble over means, certainly not a dispute about ultimate objectives. Horiba Kazuo, a leading anti-expansionist in the war guidance section of the army general staff, has written a memoir, *Shina jihen sensō shidō-shi* (Operational History of the China Incident), critical of how the war was prosecuted. According to Horiba, on July 10, 1937, his section took the position that if additional troops were sent, it would be the start of an unlimited commitment to fight in the vast heartland of China. They doubted that the nation had sufficient power to win such a war. Japan's first priority should be to develop Manchukuo and to strengthen its defenses against the Soviet Union. Not one more soldier should be sent to China. If national policy was to win a military victory in China, the country should go on a war footing, appropriate ¥5,500 million for war expenditures (the entire 1937 budget was ¥3,000 million), and be prepared to mobilize fifteen divisions. These views did not prevail. A compromise was adopted —more troops but not full mobilization. As Horiba had predicted, the war got out of hand. It could neither be won nor stopped.

Horiba's section was part of the operations division, whose chief was Ishiwara Kanji. Ishiwara had been a leading spirit in the seizure of Manchuria, but he switched to the anti-expansionist camp on the China Incident. In 1939, two years after the shooting started at the Marco Polo Bridge, Ishiwara told Prince Takeda that Japan had two choices. The first was "to give up its special political rights and form an East Asia League with China in exchange for Chiang Kai-shek's recognition of Manchukuo." The second choice was to attack Peking and Nanking, force Chiang to surrender, obtain recognition of Manchukuo, and then withdraw all troops from China proper and form an East Asia League." But "Japan can do neither and drifts along without a coherent policy or plans."[33] Both Horiba and Ishiwara advocated clear-cut alternatives: either abandon a military solution or mobilize for a massive, protracted war.

The anti-expansionists were not doves. They did not renounce war against China. They were hawks with a different war on their minds, the next war against the Soviet Union, and they were obsessed with the need to develop Manchukuo as a forward base against the USSR.[34] Under their terms for the restoration of peaceful relations with China, Japan would keep Manchukuo. Their "anti-expansionist" position required China to accept earlier Japanese expansion.

To keep Manchukuo and to prevent China from becoming communist were the absolute minimum objectives of the military and Japan's civilian leaders. With the exception of a very few dissenters, there was a broad consensus about these goals. Japan rejected the peace negotiations carried on through Oscar Trautmann, German ambassador to Nanking. The anti-expansionists on the general staff recommended that army forces stop short of Nanking and not attack the capital and that a special envoy be sent to negotiate directly with Chiang Kai-shek. The strategy of keeping the troops in place and negotiating was overruled.[35] In November 1937 the Imperial General Headquarters, a supreme war council to improve coordination between army and navy general staffs, was set up to press an expanded war. In North China all opposition was driven out of Peking and the Tientsin area by late July, and Japanese forces crossed the Yellow River and advanced south. In central China, Japanese forces had broken out of Shanghai after very hard fighting and drove forward to occupy Nanking on December 13. The Nationalist government moved to Chungking and continued to resist. In October 1938 army units were landed in South China and occupied Canton. Other troops in central China attacked and seized the three Wuhan cities along the Yangtze River. The fighting had spread all across China.

The army left a string of puppet governments in its path. In December 1937 a Provisional Government of the Republic of China was established in Peking (incorporating the Hopei-

Chahar Political Council); the Reform Government of the Republic of China was set up in Nanking in March 1938. Two months earlier, the Konoe cabinet had announced that it would no longer deal with the Nationalist government, the famous *aite ni sezu* statement. Tokyo began negotiations with Wang Ching-wei, a prominent Kuomintang member who defected from Chungking in December 1938 and advocated peace with Japan. The discussions led to the formation of a government headed by Wang in Nanking in March 1940. To summarize events from the summer of 1937: Japan used military force all across China, refused to deal with the Chiang government, and established and manipulated various puppet regimes—all in an attempt to enslave China.

But Imperial Army control extended only to the major cities and railroad lines, just "points and dots" on the map of China. Even that limited degree of control did not reach the interior. A glance at the map shows that the military could not hope to occupy the whole country. Realizing this fact of life, the army tried several times to reach a negotiated settlement with the Chiang government (Chiang Kai-shek's reasons for wanting peace are discussed in the next chapter). The negotiations always foundered on the twin demands for recognition of Manchukuo and for Japanese troops to be stationed in China as a defense against communism.

The war guidance section of the general staff prepared a set of "liberal" peace terms in August 1937. The terms included relinquishing all special rights in North China, such as the East Hopei and Hopei-Chahar administrations, the East Hopei smuggling, and the concessions gained from the Umezu-Ho and Doihara-Ch'in agreements. A major demand of these "radical" terms was joint Japanese-Chinese cooperation in "defending Japan, Manchukuo and China against communism."[36] An Imperial Liaison Conference on January 12, 1938, decided on terms for peace negotiations with China. They included the following: "China will formally recognize Manchukuo"; "Regarding North China, a suitable administration will be established under Chinese sovereignty to accomplish the mutual prosperity of Japan, Manchukuo, and China. It will be given wide authority, and it will place special emphasis on economic cooperation by the three states"; "An independent, anti-Communist government will be established in Inner Mongolia"; "To ensure attainment of these objectives, Japanese troops will be stationed when necessary in certain areas of North China, Inner Mongolia, and Central China."[37] China was to be kept under firm military control.

The demands were pressed against collaborators and Nationalists alike. Army representatives Kagesa Sadaaki and Imai Takeo signed an agreement with Kao Tsung-wu and Mei Ssu-p'ing, who were representing Wang Ching-wei before he fled Chungking, which provided for recognition of Manchukuo and the stationing of troops to defend against communism.[38] Imai later held secret peace talks in Hong Kong in March 1940 (dubbed Operation Kirin by the army) with Nationalist emissary Chang Yu-san. Chang's position on Manchukuo was that recognition should be deferred. On the second point, the Nationalists had no objection in principle to Japan-China cooperation against communism, but wanted the military aspects left to them. To agree to keeping Japanese troops in China was impossible, Chang insisted. Neither side would compromise, and the talks failed.

The Supreme Headquarters, China Expeditionary Army, insisted upon recognition of Manchukuo, and the operations division of the army general staff wanted to station troops in China. Imai had a broader perspective and was convinced that Japan had to end the China war. He recommended to Itagaki Seishirō, now chief of staff, China Expeditionary Army, that the peace terms be softened. But Itagaki, one of the chief plotters in the creation of Manchukuo, took an even harder line and said recognition of the new state was an "absolute demand."[39] That slammed the door on a negotiated settlement. Rigidly insisting on these demands, Japan poured more energy, treasure, and blood into farflung battle lines on the continent.

5

The War in China: A Clash of Political Values

The Anti-Communist Crusade

Japan's war objectives were diverse, although economic domination of China was undeniably a major desideratum. But in the various abortive peace negotiations, war goals were reduced to two: the retention of Manchukuo and the stationing of troops in China for joint defense against communism. In view of the fact that Manchukuo was valued partly as a forward military base against the USSR, the war seems very much like a preemptive strike against communism.

Japanese leaders often described national objectives in terms of anticommunism. In May 1931, Itagaki Seishirō said that if Manchuria was occupied, Japan would have a decisive military advantage over the Soviet Union and that "our power will naturally have to extend to the Maritime Province as well."[1] At a meeting attended by Kido Kōichi, Konoe Fumimaro, Harada Kumao, and others in April 1933, Suzuki Teiichi, later a member of the cabinet, asserted, "There are absolute enemies and relative enemies. A country like the USSR, which will attempt to destroy our national polity, is an absolute enemy."[2] In January 1934 Katakura Tadashi and other young officers submitted a memorandum to their superiors advocating that while a nonaggression treaty should be concluded with the Soviet Union, "we should carry out covert operations aimed at its collapse from within."[3] In December

1935, Kwantung Army headquarters criticized the Nationalists: "The Nanking government's list of outrageous acts includes the resumption of a pro-Communist policy, a friendly attitude toward the Soviet Union, and allowing the Chinese Communists freedom of movement toward the western part of Shensi province."[4] The Privy Council's review committee met on November 20, 1940, to consider the "basic treaty" to be concluded with the Wang Ching-wei government. Premier Konoe testified: "That the present conflict is a holy war should be most evident in the defense against communism. Regardless of our relations with the Soviet Union, we are absolutely determined to pursue a strong anti-Communist policy."[5] That message was taken to occupied China with huge wall posters proclaiming a common Japanese-Chinese heritage and objectives: "Same script, same race. Defeat communism, restore peace."[6]

Tokyo and Chiang's Nationalist government certainly talked the same language about anticommunism. The Nationalist revolution succeeded on the basis of mass support, including that of the Communists. Once the warlords were defeated, Chiang turned on the Communists and tried to destroy them, bringing on the civil war. After he was placed under house arrest by Chang Hsueh-liang in Sian in December 1936, Chiang reversed himself. He promised to resist Japan and switched to sweet reasonableness toward the Communists. In August 1937, Chiang appointed Chu Teh, who was leading Communist forces, as commander of the Eighth Route Army, and the next month he issued a formal manifesto announcing Kuomintang-Communist reconciliation. After the major Communist forces and leaders had made the Long March to Yenan, Chiang brought the forces remaining in South China under Nationalist authority as the New Fourth Army. In order to concentrate on fighting Japan, Chiang had formed a united front with his erstwhile enemies. It was a remarkable turnabout.

But it was only a tactical and expedient shift; Chiang's anti-Communist convictions were not modified. Nationalist-

Communist friction soon broke out again. The clashes included fighting between Nationalist and Communist forces in November 1938 in Hopei province right in front of the Japanese army. The Kuomintang's fifth national conference in January 1939 adopted an anti-Communist policy. The Law to Restrict the Activities of Other Political Parties was secretly enacted. The Nationalists directly attacked the New Fourth Army at Pêwan in 1941. Chiang's first priority was suppression of the Communists; his resistance to Japan was little more than acquiescence to the surging nationalism of the Chinese masses. Chiang was unwilling to commit his major forces and energies to fighting Japan; he wanted to make peace with Tokyo and get back to eradicating the Reds. He therefore regarded concessions to Japan as unavoidable.[7] Chiang reportedly told a close associate, "If Japan will be satisfied with just Manchuria, well, we aren't happy about it but we can pretend they aren't there."[8] It does not seem like an apochryphal tale.

This outlook explains why Chiang repeatedly sought peace negotiations even after general war was being waged across China, including Operation Kiri. In the Operation Kiri talks, Nationalist delegate Soong Tzu-liang (T. L. Soong) told Imai Takeo, "If peace is achieved, we are fully prepared, as fast as you can say 'truce,' to launch a military operation against the communist bandits."[9] What a candid confession that the Nationalists' real enemy was not the Imperial Army but the CCP. When Japan was facing certain defeat by the Allies, the Nationalists wanted Tokyo "to end the war quickly before Japan is destroyed" so it would have enough military power left to join the fight against the Communists in China.[10] Chiang was itching to drop out of the war with Japan. He stayed in only because resistance was demanded by the Chinese masses, sparked by the Communists. If Japan's leaders had been magnanimous enough to make some face-saving concessions to Chiang and wise enough not to force him into continuing to resist—by suspending military operations in the countryside, for example—peace terms could have been worked out. General Joseph Stilwell, sent to strengthen Chinese forces so they could fight against Japan in Southeast Asia, was a perceptive critic of Chiang Kai-shek. Stilwell saw that the regime was a corrupt, morally bankrupt dictatorship that barely stayed in power through a "Gestapo and party intelligence organ." Stilwell called Chiang a "peanut" and nicknamed the generalissimo's mountain villa at Huangshan "Berchtesgaden" after Hitler's famous retreat. To Stilwell, Chiang was a minor league version of the Nazi leader.[11] If we accept the American general's opinion, Chiang's regime rightly belonged with Japan and Germany in an anti-Communist front rather than in the Allied camp.

By the same token, it was by no means inevitable that America and England would go to war against Japan. The Manchurian Incident broke the status quo by force and contributed to the upsurge of fascism in Europe. A Nazi dictatorship was established in 1933, and two years later Germany renounced the Versailles Treaty and proclaimed rearmament plans. Under the dictatorship set up by Mussolini several years earlier, Italy invaded Ethiopia in 1935, occupied Addis Ababa several months later, and turned the country into a colony by May 1936. Germany occupied the Rhineland and annexed Austria in 1938. Hitler next seized the Sudeten areas in 1938 and dismembered Czechoslovakia the following year.

Despite Japan's attack on China and the string of aggressive acts in Europe, England and the other Western countries made only formal protests and avoided imposing effective sanctions. The most famous instance was the Munich Conference on September 29–30, 1938, the prelude to the seizure of the Sudeten areas. England's Neville Chamberlain and France's Edouard Daladier met with Hitler and Mussolini and assented to German aggression, thereby avoiding a showdown with the Fascist powers and making Munich a synonym for appeasement.

Spain was another case of dalliance by the democracies. A Popular Front government was established in 1936, but General Francisco Franco led a rightist uprising and triggered the civil war. Nazi Germany and Fascist Italy sent large forces to help Franco; England and France, using "nonintervention" as an excuse, refused to take firm measures to prevent the defeat of the Republicans.[12] America's willingness to provide Franco with vast amounts of oil was one of the actions that indirectly contributed to the defeat of the Popular Front government.[13]

England and America responded to Japan's aggression in the Far East with the same policy of appeasement they tried in Europe and Africa. Of course, just as the expansion of Nazi power in Europe was a threat that could not be ignored indefinitely, Japan's attack on China posed a danger to their imperialist interests on the Asian continent. They therefore repeatedly protested against and criticized Japanese actions, provided aid to the Nationalist government, refused to recognize Manchukuo, and otherwise showed their displeasure. Japan responded by condemning the foreign assistance to Chiang. Despite this level of antagonism, neither London nor Washington was inclined to act resolutely against Tokyo's aggression. In July 1940, England agreed to a Japanese request and closed, albeit only temporarily, the Burma Road, the route for aid supplies to Chungking. Admittedly, this policy was dictated by complex international and domestic factors and British military weakness. Yet it was the latent common interest in Japan's anti-Communist crusade that made America and England willing to tolerate even a considerable erosion of their position in China. Many members of the ruling elite in both Western countries considered Japan a bulwark against communism in the Far East and felt a certain fraternal bond with Japan. At a 1936 meeting of Japanese and American businessmen, for example, an American speaker acknowledged the reality of Manchukuo and said: "In my view, it is a pity that Japan alone is carrying the fight against communism in Manchuria, and I will go so far as to say that other countries should bear a portion of the costs."[14]

These international relationships in the 1930s were one factor that helps to explain Japan's rapid seizure of Manchuria. When full-scale war broke out in 1937, the Chinese masses fought back with unexpected fury. The Imperial Army found itself bogged down in the vastness of China. Yet Tokyo was able to continue the onslaught for more than four years without substantial interference by the European countries or America because of that same underlying pattern of shared imperialist interests.

But Japan's ultimate objective was not just to dominate China. There was also the decisive struggle against international communism, which entailed much more than just avoiding a clash with the Powers over China. In November 1936 Japan concluded the Anti-Comintern Pact with Germany, ostensibly to counter the Comintern's efforts to spread communism. Italy was brought into the pact in 1937, the same year that Japan recognized the Franco government the instant it scored a major military victory. Spain joined in 1939. In September 1939 Germany invaded Poland; England and France abandoned appeasement and went to war. World War II had begun. German forces defeated the Allies in the Low Countries and France in 1940; the British Expeditionary Force made an ignominious retreat from Dunkirk. Paris fell, and France surrendered.

Bewitched by these blitzkrieg victories, the Japanese army insisted upon making a tripartite military alliance with Germany and Italy, which had joined the war just before the surrender of Paris. The Yonai cabinet opposed the scheme and was forced to resign. The Tripartite Treaty of Alliance was concluded in September 1940 by the second Konoe cabinet. The Japanese army was now linked to Hitler's Germany and Mussolini's Italy in a Fascist front with global ambitions. The Tripartite Treaty of Alliance changed the balance of world politics: Tokyo was no longer simply on the march in China, challenging European imperialistic interests in the Far East. Joining the Fascist camp moved Japan several steps closer to a military showdown with the anti-Fascist, capitalist democracies and with international communism.

As these events unfolded, disagreement arose among the hawks in Tokyo over strategic priorities. Some advocated the "traditional" policy: attack the Soviet Union if the opportunity presented itself, thus striking hard at the only Communist state and the wellspring of international communism. Others championed action in the opposite direction, to the south: take advantage of the Allied defeats in Europe by invading their colonies and possessions in Southeast Asia and the Pacific.

The army had long wanted to attack the Soviet Union.[15] Japanese forces had advanced after the Mukden Incident through northern Manchuria to the Russian border. The disputed boundary was a source of friction and many minor disagreements. But it was no garden-variety border clash in June 1937, when Japan intentionally attacked the Soviet garrison. According to Nishimura Toshio, the clash "occurred a month before the China Incident and was a good reconnaissance in force."[16] The probe reportedly verified that the USSR did not intend to attack; the army was able to strike at China without fear of an attack from the rear. The fighting at Changkufeng on the northeastern border between the USSR and Korea in July 1938 was another provocation, a "reconnaissance in force," to test Russian intentions before launching the Wuhan offensive to the south. Moreover, Odaka Kamezō, commander, 19th Division, attacked in violation of a direct imperial order. Odaka covered up his action by falsely reporting to Tokyo that he had counterattacked after a first strike by Soviet forces.[17]

The Changkufeng attack, like the Manchurian Incident, was a war crime because it was a violation of international law; it was also a violation of Japanese law. The army's criminal code, Article 37, regarding exceeding authority, and Article 57, on insubordination, were both applicable. The latter stated: "Resisting or failing to obey the order of a superior, if the infraction occurs in the face of the enemy, shall be punished as follows: by death, indefinite imprisonment, or imprisonment for more than ten years." (Of course, in this instance as well, there was no criminal prosecution.)

The Soviet Army, crippled by Stalin's purge, especially the execution of Marshal Tukhachevsky in June 1937 on false charges, had to fall back before these early provocations. Loss of leadership also prevented the USSR from effectively countering Nazi Germany's intervention in the Spanish civil war; the Soviet Union was equally remiss, with England and France, in not preventing Franco's victory. The Japanese army, arrogant over its victories, launched a similar attack in 1939 at Nomonhan on the border between Outer Mongolia and the USSR. To the army's astonishment, this time Soviet forces led by a mechanized infantry division counterattacked vigorously. Imperial Army units were completely encircled in late August and suffered enormous losses, including more than 18,000 killed (the Japanese government kept these statistics on battle deaths classified until 1966). The Kwantung Army violated orders from Tokyo during the fighting and made an air attack on Tamusku on June 27, another case of insubordination.[18]

Nomonhan was a stunning defeat. It revealed that that the army's equipment was ridiculously outdated. Japanese troops had only primitive weapons; they tried to stop Russian tanks with hand-thrown fire bombs made by filling bottles with gasoline. The wholly provocative and illegitimate nature of this attack was no less apparent. While Japan was reeling from this disaster, Anti-Comintern Pact ally Germany suddenly concluded the German-Soviet Non-Aggression Pact on the night of August 23–24, 1939. Tokyo now suffered a devastating diplomatic setback on the heels of the military defeat and had no alternative but to conclude a truce that accepted Soviet border claims. The Moscow Pact with Germany was a desperate bid by the USSR to protect itself at a time when England and France were appeasing Hitler. A brilliant Machiavellian maneuver, it left Japan's wholeheartedly pro-German leaders stupefied. The Hiranuma cabinet, adrift in the "complex mysteries" of shifting international alignments, resigned, and a cabinet headed by General Abe Nobuyuki was organized in late August.

Temporarily secure in the east, Hitler invaded Poland and touched off World War II. Japanese leaders, impressed by the initial German victories, signed the Tripartite Treaty of Alliance. A temporary peace agreement with the Soviet Union was the next move in order to secure Japan's northern flank prior to moving southward. Discussions began in 1940, and after extensive negotiations, Foreign Minister Matsuoka Yōsuke signed the Japan-Soviet Neutrality Pact in Moscow in April 1941.[19] Two months later, Germany broke its treaty with the USSR and invaded Russia on June 22. Seeing Soviet defenses crumble and the Red Army desperate, Matsuoka reversed himself and began to advocate war with the Soviet Union. At the Imperial Conference on July 2, 1941, Hara Yoshimichi, president of the Privy Council, also argued for an attack on the Soviet Union:

> The Soviet Union is spreading communism throughout the world, so it must be attacked sooner or later. . . . The public is all in favor of an attack on the USSR. . . . Some people say that because of the Japanese-Soviet Neutrality Pact, to attack the Soviet Union would be an act of treachery, but the USSR is habitually treacherous. No one will accuse us of bad faith for attacking the Russians. . . . The Soviet Union should be destroyed. Thus I hope that preparations will be made to hasten the commencement of hostilities.[20]

Advocates of an immediate attack lost out to a wait-and-see decision: "If the German-Soviet war develops to the advantage of our Empire, we will use military force to settle the Northern Question and assure the security of the northern area."[21] But although an immediate attack was rejected, this was in fact a conditional decision to attack the Soviet Union.[22] With the emperor's approval, on July 7 the generals began "the largest [mobilization] in the history of the army," and the Kwantung Army was quickly increased to 700,000 men. The army general staff prepared plans for the status of Manchukuo in a war with the Soviet Union and began research on the administration of areas to be occupied by military action. To maintain secrecy, the preparations were called "Kwantung

Army special maneuvers." They were not "maneuvers," of course, but preparations for the army's cherished destruction of the USSR.[23]

Subsequent events, however, precluded the coup de grâce. The German advance into Russia stalled, contrary to expectations in Tokyo. And Japan moved southward, hitting at the United States and England, instead of north against the USSR. Nevertheless, these military steps in 1941 constitute for all practical purposes the unilateral abrogation of the Japanese-Soviet Neutrality Pact. Certainly they betrayed the pledge in Article 1 of the agreement that both countries would "maintain peace and friendly relations." The military buildup was preparatory to aggressive war. They contravened the territorial inviolability promised in Article 2 of the pact. According to the International Court of Justice regulations (Article 38, Section 1, Part 2), "The general principles of law recognized by civilized nations" became the basis for the court's judgments in international law. Regarding serious crimes there is a general legal principle that a conspiracy, acts in preparation for a crime, or an attempt to commit the criminal act are all punishable. By this criterion, Japan's actions toward the Soviet Union in 1941 were a violation of international law.

Strategic necessity required peaceful relations with the Soviet Union. All Japan's military power was concentrated in China and then against the United States and England. Nevertheless, the ultimate objective of the war, including the fighting in China, remained the destruction of communism. In military and diplomatic moves, in the implicit assumptions behind policies, always the overriding goal was to eradicate communism. If one fundamental distinction between bourgeois democracy and fascism was the latter's attempt to destroy communism not by ideological but by military means, Japan's protracted aggression was assuredly a Fascist war. It was a projection into international politics of the domestic suppression of communism by force. The fifteen-year war may be seen as an attempt to impose the Peace Preservation Law on other nations.

Resistance: The New China

The war in China began in earnest in the summer of 1937. Japanese forces occupied the major cities, including the capital of Nanking, but the Nationalist government dug in at Chungking and continued to resist. The frequent peace feelers and discussions between Tokyo and Chiang Kai-shek came to nothing; a compromise was never reached. The Japanese army seemed able to hold a vast amount of territory, yet could not compel China to surrender: The anticipated quick victory proved forever elusive. How did Japan make this colossal blunder? The answer lies in the fact that Japanese leaders were so disdainful of China they could not see that the sleeping dragon had stirred and would never be the same again. Policy was based on fundamental misconceptions. Ikezaki Tadakata's underestimation of China, the belief that China could be conquered with three or four divisions and a few gun boats, was previously cited. Civilian amateurs were not the only ones who thought this way; military specialists had the same contempt for China.

The army had prepared carefully for war against the Soviet Union,[24] but it had done no planning worthy of the name for a general war with China. Army leaders could not conceive of the Chinese putting up a good fight against the Imperial Army. Army Minister Sugiyama's remark to Lord Keeper of the Privy Seal Yuasa Kurahei immediately after the Marco Polo Bridge clash shows how the army totally underestimated the Chinese. Sugiyama said, "We'll send large forces, smash them in a hurry and get the whole thing over with quickly."[25] In the words of one general, "Everybody thought we would send about three divisions at first and even if the fighting spread, two more divisions would be enough."[26]

The army general staff was equally optimistic: "We thought China would soon throw up its hands and quit."[27] Civilians advised Major General Kawabe Torashirō that great changes were taking place in China which Japan could not ignore. Kawabe passed this analysis on to Itagaki Seishirō, vice-chief of staff, China Expeditionary Force. Itagaki ignored the advice: "China is still China. Some young Japanese say the kind of things you have heard. But that is not the full picture. The situation is not as serious for us as you have been told."[28] The military had no monopoly on stupidity about China. Yet the ingrained contempt for the Chinese, the image of them as ineffectual "Chinks," was especially flagrant among the army and navy, with their exaggerated notions of the effectiveness of military power.

Did everyone in the 1930s think China could be so easily conquered? Some of the policymakers would have us believe that Japan was following a reasonable course of action under the circumstances, and that postwar criticism is Monday morning quarterbacking. In a roundtable discussion in 1965, Hoshino Naoki, a former high official in Manchukuo, took this line. Morishima Morito, the diplomat at Mukden during the Manchurian Incident, said that even if Japan had stopped with the seizure of Manchuria, there would still have been a war with China. He reasoned that China would never have acquiesced to the loss of Manchuria and eventually would have tried to recover her territory. Hoshino disputed this interpretation "as something that could only be said after the fact," nothing but second guessing.[29] Yet Hoshino's implication that no one had foreseen China's resurgence or predicted disaster is quite inaccurate. A few individuals did understand that China was changing profoundly.

Diplomat Nishi Haruhiko happened to meet an old middle school chum by the name of Onohara in Hankow in 1936. According to Nishi's account of their conversation, Onohara had a better grasp of Chinese determination than the general staff: "If war breaks out between Japan and China, the Nationalist Government has made secret plans to resist to the bitter end. If their Shanghai-Nanking defense line is broken, they will withdraw to a Nanchang-Kiukiang line. If that line cannot be defended, they will retreat to Hankow. If the Wuhan defense collapses, they will shift to Chungking."[30]

Yanaihara Tadao, a specialist on colonial policy, said in a lecture in November 1936: "Assertions that the Chinese have no sense of nationhood and so forth are outdated. The Chinese of today are not the Chinese of old. I have heard that there are Chinese who say, 'If China goes to war with Japan, we will probably lose at first. But there are 400 million of us, so we can afford to lose 300 million and still have 100 million left. With three Chinese soldiers to every one Japanese, we must resist and defend our nation's sovereignty.' "[31] In an essay in the February 1937 *Chūō Kōron,* Yanaihara declared:

> The key to our relations with China lies in understanding that China is a national state on its way to unification and reconstruction. Only a policy based on a perception of China which affirms and assists that national unity will help China, help Japan, and contribute to the peace of Asia. Implementation by force of arbitrary policies contrary to this rational view will bring a disaster that will haunt us for generations, will inflict suffering on China, and will destroy the peace of Asia.[32]

Kiryū Yūyū was another voice of reason and restraint. In the February 1937 issue of his privately circulated personal magazine *Tazan no Ishi* (Stones from Other Mountains), Kiryū called attention to the new consciousness of the Chinese people and added "a demand that Japan awake from its dream of military victory and show a great resolution."[33] Those last words were understood by his readers as a call to end the war. In the January 1940 issue he bravely quoted from the writings of "the leader of the Chinese Red Army, Mao Tse-tung": "Since China is a vast country, even if Japan has occupied enormous stretches of territory where 120 million people live, we are still not defeated." Mao said that China had not lost the war and would inevitably triumph. Kiryū added, "The Japanese must think very carefully about what Mao has said."[34]

Nakae Ushikichi was another of those perceptive few who saw the strength of Chinese nationalism. He wrote to Suzue Gen'ichi in February 1941 that "the currents that began flowing ten years ago have meandered back and forth but now form a raging stream. Though still hidden, the torrent is fast approaching the ocean. That stream has started an undercurrent, as yet not in view, but unmistakably wavelike in its surge. Darkness obscures the scene but the wave's roar confirms its course." Metaphorical though his language was, Nakae's prediction of how the invasion of China would end was prophetic.[35] Ozaki Hotsumi also had to be careful in his choice of words in his *Gendai Shina-ron* (On Modern China) published in May 1939. Using a different vocabulary to disguise his meaning, he pointed out that the anti-Japan national front movement was "demanding a fundamental resolution of China's semi-colonial and semi-feudal position and an end to its long historical stagnation."

Unfortunately, freedom of speech and expression were drastically curtailed in Japan; minority views were labeled subversive and crushed; and irrational policies were forced on the country. A small number of far-sighted men had offered sound advice, but it was not enough to deflect Japan from its rendezvous with disaster.

While the Japanese clung to the "Chink" image, the real Chinese were undergoing a transformation of values. Far from being crushed by the Japanese onslaught, the nationalistic consciousness only grew more intense and determined. In 1934 Sun Yat-sen's widow, Soong Ch'ing-ling, and others organized a program for resisting Japan. Several hundred thousand persons signed the statement, including members of the Kuomintang's right wing. The next wave of nationalism hit in December 1935. Nanking had reached a compromise. The Japanese army was demanding that North China be made completely independent of Nationalist control. A separatist government, the Hopei-Chahar Political Council headed by General Sung Che-yuan, was about to be established. On December 9 students in Peking staged demonstrations and distributed leaflets with such slogans as Oppose the Anti-Communist Self-government Movement, Immediate War against Japan, and Down with Japanese Imperialism. The student demonstrations, later known as the December 9 Movement, were so disciplined and dramatic that formation of the council was delayed.[36]

Nationalism affected the older generation too. The Japanese occupation of Jehol brought the former warlord Feng Yu-hsiang out of retirement in 1933. He joined with Communist forces to form a People's Federated Anti-Japanese Army which fought well in Chahar. In 1936 an Inner Mongolian puppet army set up by Kwantung Army Staff Officer Tanaka Ryūkichi invaded Suiyuan. Fu Tso-yi's Chinese forces fought them off. On December 2 the Mongolian troops, equipped with Japanese weapons and provided with Japanese air support, attempted to recapture Pailingmiao, but were driven off. The Kwantung Army's strategy failed miserably.[37] The victory news was transmitted across China and sparked further resistance. Imai Takeo, military attaché in Peking, watched a newsreel of the victory in a local theater. He described the audience "as wildly excited, clapping their hands and stomping their feet." Whenever a closeup of Chiang Kai-shek and Fu Tso-yi flashed on the screen, the audience stood up with "a storm of applause." Imai was shaken by the "fervent patriotism and excitement."[38] Anti-Japanese emotion swept China. The writer Lu Hsun, previously criticized by the radical Left for placing literature above politics and resistance, showed his mettle about this time as a champion of the anti-Japan movement. The Kuomintang preferred to "suppress the Communist bandits" rather than fight Japan. The depth of the anti-Japanese sentiment forced them to resist.

My earlier statement that the invasion of Manchuria was rapid and a total success was meant in a relative sense, as compared to the military operations to the south. To be more precise, the new "state" of Manchukuo managed to impose a temporary, superficial control over all Manchuria. But anti-Japan guerrilla fighting led mainly by Communists broke out soon after the takeover and was never fully suppressed. The Japanese government labeled the resistance "bandits," and the public pictured them as armed bands of brutal, raping desperadoes. To the Chinese, however, they were guerrilla units fighting to recover the fatherland. The Japanese army in Manchuria carried out many "bandit-suppression expeditions" with the puppet Manchukuo Army in an effort to exterminate all opposition. With so many peasants desperately poor, much of the farm population was sympathetic to the Communists and their call for land reform. The local people provided clothing and food to the resistance. When Japanese forces attacked the guerrilla base areas, the peasants hid in the mountains. If the farm children were asked the bandits' hiding place, they all replied, "There are no bandits here." Even the Japanese authorities were forced to admit the deep solidarity between the guerrillas and the people. And no wonder. Large numbers of settlers from Japan were sent to colonize Manchuria; the land they received had been taken from the local populace. No matter how many bandit-suppression operations the army launched, there was no way they could cut the close ties between the guerrillas and the people.

Japanese records show the magnitude of the resistance movement. Under the loose authority of the Northeast People's Anti-Japan Allied Headquarters in 1936 were the People's Revolutionary First Army, the Anti-Japan Allied Forces First Army, and sixteen other subordinate military units.[39] Even Manchukuo, which seemed to be under control, was rife with guerrillas and anti-Japanese sentiment. Japanese authority was even less secure in North China and to the south, where the China Expeditionary Army was hard pressed to hold "points and lines" on the map. Japanese troops in the cities and on the railroad lines were surrounded by a hostile sea of Chinese.

On August 1, 1935, the CCP issued a "Letter to the Whole Nation for Resistance against Japan and National Salvation." The August First Declaration was an appeal for national unity against Japan. In a policy switch, the Communists stopped revolutionary activity and began to cooperate with the Kuomintang. As noted earlier, Chang Hsueh-liang's arrest of Chiang Kai-shek in Sian in December 1936 forced the generalissimo to suspend the sixth bandit-suppression campaign and revive the Nationalist-Communist partnership he had abandoned in 1927. Communist forces were placed under Nationalist authority and organized into the Eighth Route Army and the New Fourth Army. The Japanese army now had to contend with the much stronger Chinese forces. As the records of Japanese army campaigns in 1939 attest, the Kuomintang troops directly controlled by Chiang Kai-shek were a far cry from the ragged warlord armies. The following notations appear in unit documents: "The enemy 74th unit shows high morale and battlefield aggressiveness, especially the officers. In all areas they have been in front of their troops leading the attack with great bravery." And: "Twenty-three enemy prisoners of war were interrogated. Despite every kind of duress, they all refused to reveal military information. One very tough soldier, apparently a squad leader, said: 'You are a soldier. I am too. To discuss military information is wrong. Kill me quickly!' "[40] The quality of Chinese troops steadily improved, although the combat efficiency of Kuomintang units was impaired by the Nationalist government's ambiguous attitude toward Japan and by its ineffectual and corrupt leadership.

Japanese forces held their own against the Nationalist units, but the Communist Eighth Route Army was a different story. Never in the earlier wars against the Manchus, tsarist Russia, Imperial Germany, Chinese warlords, or Chiang Kai-shek had the Imperial Army come up against troops like those of the Eighth Route Army: they defied conventional military modes of analysis and bloodied the Japanese army. The unique qualities of the Eighth Route Army are documented in the detailed accounts of American journalists like Edgar Snow and Agnes Smedley and the German Gunther Stein and in General Stilwell's reports.[41] The Communist forces' greatest asset was their close ties with the peasantry. That relationship dated from the civil war years; it became much stronger during the resistance to Japan. Agnes Smedley wrote: "The strength of the Eighth Route Army and the Communist party that leads it is not in military power but because they are organically linked to the people." Local peasants told the Japanese nothing about the Eighth Route Army's movements. These same farmers provided the Communists with intelligence about the Japanese, showed them the local terrain, and guided them to better tactical positions. The peasants did more than serve as the eyes and ears of the Eighth Route Army. Everywhere the army moved local residents became guerrillas, cut Japanese telephone and telegraph lines, destroyed roads and bridges, and attacked Japanese units. A Japanese brigade commander's captured diary contained the following entry: "In this area even Chinese women are in the fighting. They throw hand grenades at our men."

The guerrillas lacked weapons to engage elite Japanese troops in direct combat. They used surprise attacks against small units and stragglers to get arms; the Imperial Army gradually became the guerrillas' main supplier of weapons. Nearly everything the Eighth Route Army needed—pistols, rifles, machine guns, trucks, tanks, provisions and fodder, uniforms—was captured from Japanese forces. Chiang Kai-shek hesitated to engage Japanese units partly because of their superior equipment and firepower. The Eighth Route Army, confident that the excellent equipment would fall into their hands, saw this disparity as an opportunity. Of course, they made no stupid frontal attacks on superior Japanese forces. They continually harassed the China Expeditionary Army with flexible tactics: "If the enemy advances, we retreat. If the enemy defends, we harass. If the enemy is exhausted, we attack. If the enemy retreats, we advance."[42] Japanese forces were encircled by invisible enemies who might—and did—attack at any time.

How was the Eighth Route Army able to forge such solid ties with the people? The Communists reduced the land rent and abolished usury, thus liberating the peasants from the twin scourges of the countryside. They also fostered new industries to improve the standard of living and established schools and educational programs to end illiteracy. The control of landlords and petty bosses was ended, and a miracle occurred in the lives of China's tenant farmers: they could protest to landlords about tenancy terms! With economic reforms went political changes. Men and women above eighteen years of age were given the vote, self-governing bodies were established in the villages, and in some places the peasants served on juries. Several reforms were directed at women, including recognition of marriages without parental consent and an end to concubinage. In short, by liberating a populace that was financially exploited, politically oppressed, and beaten down spiritually, the Communists created a spontaneous following in the countryside. The Communist party also sought cooperation with other political groups, including the Kuomintang, in order to fight Japan. To that end the party advocated a New Democracy,[43] shelved its radical revolutionary policies, stopped the confiscation of land, and restricted Communist members to one-third of elected self-government bodies. Although the Communists refrained from unilaterally imposing their policies, these epochal improvements were steadily achieved during the resistance to Japan. Compared with life in the Kuomintang areas, where dictatorship and exploitation continued unabated or, of course, in the areas controlled by the Japanese army, with its hideous atrocities, life under the Communists was worth living. The peasants' acceptance of the Communist forces was perfectly natural.

It is worth noting that the Eighth Route Army, which gave the peasants their first taste of democracy and control over their own lives, was itself one of the most democratic armies in the history of military organizations. All during the civil war this was the great difference between the Communists and all other Chinese military forces. In the Communist army "everyone from the commanders to the privates ate the same food and wore the same uniforms."[44] Symbols of rank were not used, everyone was a "comrade," and military discipline was maintained by "persuasion" and not by "orders." Before going into battle, "there was always a conference to discuss their own and enemy positions, relative strengths and weaknesses, the possible consequences of defeat, and so on." When the battle was over, "There was always a meeting where the battle was analyzed, mistakes acknowledged, and outstanding performances praised." Democratic methods were used right on the battlefield. Democracy within the army enabled the soldiers to be fair and considerate with the civilian populace. Military discipline was a Communist army hallmark. The troops had strict orders and followed them to the letter: "Don't take one needle or piece of thread from the peasants"; "When you leave a household that has given you shelter for the night, put all the shutters and the straw mats you used for beds back the way they were"; "Pay for everything you break"; "Never fool around with the women in a household"; and "Don't mistreat prisoners."

This is not a fictionalized description of the Communist army by pro-Communist Western writers. It is substantiated by considerable testimony, although in fragmentary form, from Japanese military men and civilians. For example, Kitahara Tatsuo had five years experience, starting in 1938, as a specialist on communism for the North China Army. According to army directives distributed in North China, the key to discovering a Communist party member was to watch the prisoners at mealtime: "If someone willingly gives the good food to others and quietly takes the worst, generally he will be a Communist."[45] After the war, Japanese residents in Manchuria were badly treated by Russian forces and the local populace. Only the Chinese Communist units that entered Manchuria behaved scrupulously. They always returned borrowed cooking utensils. Even when the Communist soldiers had to eat inferior food and saw the Japanese furtively cooking white rice, they did not get angry. They said, "White rice is daily fare for you Japanese, so go ahead and eat it."[46] Large numbers of returnees from Manchuria have testified to this generous treatment.[47]

Prince Mikasa Takahito, who was a staff officer with the China Expeditionary Army, has written that the Eighth Route Army's "discipline toward the people, especially toward women, was incredibly strict. One North China Army staff officer even said, 'I wonder if the Eighth Route Army soldiers don't have different sexual needs than our men!' "[48] In Matsumoto Sōkichi's report of his trip to China, published in 1942, we find the following: "The strangest impression I had was that the links between the enemy forces and the ordinary people were very strong; there is a deep and affectionate relationship. Although the people in the lower Yangtze River delta were severely exploited by enemy forces, especially the New Fourth Army, they did not try to throw off the Communist yoke."[49] In the Japanese-occupied area, the military looted, burned, raped, and routinely slaughtered innocent civilians, all the while proclaiming "anticommunism and peace." The Communists improved the people's lives and gave them their first democratic rights. Popular support was not "strange" under these circumstances but axiomatic. Not appreciating this was Japan's tragedy.

Communist forces suffered fluctuations in the fortunes of war. At one point they were in grave danger of defeat by the better-equipped Japanese army. The situation seemed most serious in 1942.[50] But their vastly superior strategy and tactics saved the day; the Communists withstood the threat and steadily improved their combat capability. In early 1945 the Communists controlled eighteen "liberated zones" comprising 311,000 square miles and an estimated population of 94 million. One "liberated zone" had even been carved out in southern Manchukuo. Eighty-four percent of the 220,000 Japanese troops in North China were assigned to fight against the Eighth Route Army.[51] The Japanese public was not only completely uninformed during the war about this tough resistance by the Communist forces, but remained unaware even after 1945. Veterans of the China campaign wrote only about the fighting against the Nationalists.[52] The Japanese people do not seem to have a correct understanding of the role of the Communist military forces during the decade and a half of warfare. The invasion of China and the subsequent military operations there were the core of the Pacific War, in my view. China remained the main war theater even after hostilities with America and England began. The principal opponent in China was not the Nationalist government's armies but the Communist units. Because of the Communists' tenacious resistance, Japanese forces became bogged down in China. In desperation Japan attacked the United States, and started a hopeless war that ended in national ruin. These basic facts must not be forgotten. Furthermore, Japan's inability to destroy the Communists despite a superiority in weapons was due to the democratic power of the Red armies.

The Chinese Communist army proved that in a national crisis only democracy can inspire patriotism, raise national consciousness, and galvanize it into fighting power against aggression. In other words, true nationalism grows only in democratic soil. America's material superiority may have struck the decisive blow, but Japan had already been defeated by Chinese democracy.[53] This is crucial to an understanding of the essence of the war from 1931 to 1945. In support of this assertion, in the next chapter I shall show that while democracy was growing in China, it withered and died in Japan and in occupied areas. It is unscientific and unscholarly to analyze the war only through some dramatic battles in the Pacific. The conflict was more than a clash of armies and navies. It was a struggle of political values: the democracy of China versus the militaristic absolutism of Japan.

6

The War at Home: Democracy Destroyed

Military expansion abroad required repression at home. To the government, of course, the growth of a political movement based on free choice and popular aspirations, a political force capable of presenting alternatives to the leadership's domestic and foreign policies, was anathema. Antisubversion laws and public education were designed to discourage liberal tendencies. After Japan was at war, controls on intellectual and political activity were tightened again and again until civil rights virtually ceased to exist. National leaders naturally would not tell the people the truth or permit criticism of their attempt to wage an immoral, premeditated aggressive war. There was no way to stop the escalation in the 1930s; there was no freedom to demand an end to the war in the 1940s even when it was obviously lost. The meaningless slaughter continued until Japan's cities were smoldering ashes and atomic bombs brought the Japanese people to the brink of genetic holocaust. If the popular will had influenced national policies, the conflict might have been avoided or at least shortened. It was a vicious cycle: the weakness of democracy was one cause of the war, and the war further eroded freedom.

The End of Civil Rights

In January 1934 Army Minister Araki Sadao presented a study to Premier Saitō which shows the hawks' attitude toward civil liberties. Among Araki's recommendations and proposals were the following about "controls on journalism and publication": "Direct publishing activities so that they contribute to state prosperity, social order, the smooth functioning of national life and to wholesome public entertainment"; "Ban views which would impair fundamental national policies"; "Tighten controls over rumors, gossip, speech, and publications that would harm the state." On the "Purification of thoughts," Araki recommended: "Tighten controls over subversive organizations. The most severe methods should be employed against Communist or treasonous activities carried out by legal groups which disseminate antiwar and anti-imperialist ideas. The populace should understand the danger, oppose these subversive movements, and support their dissolution"; "Strengthen public unity for national mobilization by making participation in the Reservists' Association and youth training mandatory and by encouraging organizations such as the Youth Association, Boy Scouts, Patriotic Women's Association, National Defense Women's Association, Red Cross Society, Harmonization Society, Medical Relief Society, Soldiers' Support Association and religious, social welfare and spiritual associations."[1]

Araki sought to eliminate all journalism, publishing meetings, and groups with negative views on "national policy" (i.e., the hawks' political objectives). And he wanted to go a step further and encourage progovernment groups and organizations to mobilize the nation in support of war efforts. The controls subsequently imposed in Japan closely followed Araki's proposals.

The government's first step was to restrict freedom of thought and speech by tightening the existing antisubversion laws. Their scope was broadened by amendments. The Peace Preservation Law, which had been amended by an extraordinary imperial ordinance in 1928, was further amended in 1941 to allow preventive detention of political activists and indefinite detention of political prisoners. The latter could be kept in prison after serving their terms, detained forever in fact, unless they recanted their beliefs. These provisions destroyed freedom of conscience. The government's next move was to enact new restrictive legislation. It included the National Defense Security Law of 1941, which stipulated that important government business, such as the discussions in the Liaison Conference and cabinet meetings, were "state secrets," and established severe penalties for obtaining or revealing such classified information. One clause provided for punishment of "anyone who transmits information damaging to public order for the purpose of aiding a foreign country." Freedom of expression was sharply abridged. In addition, the Provisional Law for Control of Speech, Publications, Assembly, and Association instituted a prior approval system for the activities of political groups, political meetings, and publication of newspapers and magazines. The law contained harsh sanctions for spreading of "false reports or rumors" and "information that confuses public sentiment." In 1943 the Special Law on Wartime Crimes, enacted only a year before, was revised to include interfering with government administration: "To disseminate information during wartime which will harm public order for the purpose of interfering with national administration or public order" became a crime. The revised laws also simplified criminal procedures to the detriment of defendants' rights, making arbitrary action by law enforcement authorities much easier.[2]

These oppressive laws were strictly enforced, of course, but constraints on freedom of expression were less a matter of legislative authority than of the gradual tightening of controls through the arbitrary decisions of law enforcement officials. As the war situation grew more serious, the authorities became more lawless. The Cabinet Information Committee established in July 1936 marked a new stage in handling the news and the media. The June 19 cabinet resolution stated: "It is no longer adequate to just maintain public order by the Ministry of Home Affairs and the Ministry of Communications' police powers over the dissemination of information.

We must take the initiative regarding news, actively manage it, and thereby contribute to the national interest." By December 1940 the committee had grown into the Cabinet Information Bureau, a powerful agency staffed by military men on active duty. State control had evolved from censorship and restrictions to overt propaganda and manipulation. The mass media became a conveyor belt for government handouts. Opposing views were stifled while the public was inundated with official "news." Already able to ban publications and employ criminal sanctions, the state gained another weapon through the allotment of newsprint and paper as supplies grew short. The press was at the mercy of the government.[3]

Truth was the first casualty of the China fighting. The immediate impetus for tighter controls was the government's desire to prevent any criticism of its actions there. When full-scale war began in the summer of 1937, newspapers and magazines were instructed about how to handle the news. The Cabinet Information Committee's notice entitled "The Treatment of News about the Present Situation" informed the media that: "It is expected that you will exercise self-restraint and not print statements that in any way damage our national interests or impair international trust." Examples were: "Antiwar or antimilitary opinions or news items that reduce civilian support for the military"; "articles that might give the impression that our foreign policy is aggressive"; "in reporting the views of foreign newspapers, especially the Chinese press, articles which slander Japan, articles contrary to our national interests, or opinions which approve or affirm such negative statements, and items which may confuse the general public's understanding of issues."[4] The day after the declaration of war on America and England, newspaper, magazine, and publishing officials were summoned to the Cabinet Information Bureau and informed of "articles that cannot be printed." Included were "views that intentionally distort our true war aims or slander the imperial government's legitimate policies," "allegations of conflicting views between the military and civilian leaders," "comments that show popular unwillingness to follow government directions or indicate a lack of national unity," "comments that would increase antiwar sentiment or war weariness among the populace," and "opinions that would stimulate peace sentiment or harm national morale."[5]

Controls were first applied to factual reporting and editorial comment about the progress of the war. News was gradually limited to announcements from Imperial Army Headquarters, and only brilliant victories were splashed across the front pages. Banner headlines told of the Pearl Harbor attack and the sinking of the *Repulse* and *Prince of Wales*. There was always room on the front page for the brave exploits of Japanese soldiers and sailors, for the glorious, dramatic face of war. News of the defeat at Midway, the disastrous Imphal campaign, and other setbacks was suppressed. Defeats were covered up by euphemisms: the retreat from Guadalcanal became a "transfer of forces"; the atomic bomb was minimized as just a "new type bomb." The authorities wracked their brains devising ways to cover up the truth. The public had no way of knowing about the criminal acts committed by Japanese forces in China and other occupied areas. The March 1938 issue of *Chūō Kōron* carried a story by Ishikawa Tatsuzō based on firsthand observation of atrocities committed by Japanese troops fighting near Nanking. Ishikawa's original manuscript had phrases like "stabbing the woman's breast with a bayonet," "jabbing it into her three times," "slashing the head and breasts with a sword," and "the smell of fresh blood." These were all deleted from the published version,[6] but the issue was still banned. Ishikawa was prosecuted and convicted to deter other journalistic exposés.

Three Japanese translations of Lin Yu-tang's 1939 book *Moment in Peking* were published the next year. However, they bore little resemblance to Lin's vivid, angry description of opium smuggling under the East Hopei puppet government, the destructive effects of opium on the Chinese, and the haughty, abusive Japanese behavior in occupied China. Critical sections were either deleted or altered to obscure the events.[7] It was impossible to publish the truth about what was happening in China. In 1966, more than two decades after the war ended, the *Mainichi Gurafu* published a two-volume special edition called "Japan's War Record" which included some of the never-before-published news photographs taken in China. Among these sensitive materials were snapshots of Chinese prisoners of war. Even these innocuous pictures had been censored. It is no wonder that the Japanese public could not appreciate the terrible acts committed in China.[8]

Lest censorship make the war seem vague and far off, the government churned out fabricated stories to drum up enthusiasm. The famous Three Human Bombs of the Shanghai fighting was a notorious example. Three engineer soldiers were accidentally killed by a short fuse on a charge they set. Intelligence operative Tanaka Ryūkichi concocted the story that the men had wrapped explosives around themselves and died heroic deaths in a valiant assault on the enemy.[9] Another fabrication was the myth that every fighting man died with the emperor's name on his lips. The last cry of most Japanese soldiers as they went to their deaths was for their wives or mothers. *Okachan* or *okasan* (Mother) were the last mortal words of innumerable Imperial Army soldiers. Many who served at or near the front lines (soldiers, nurses, journalists) have attested to this fact.[10] But it was never reported during the war. The official line was that all Japanese troops died shouting "Long live the emperor!" (Some did, of course.)

At the start of the China war the press maintained by inertia some critical objectivity. The *Tokyo Nichinichi Shimbun* (February 3, 1932, evening edition) headlined the news from China: "General Offensive Intensifies in Shanghai. Cannon Fire Rocks City." In a corner of the same page there was a fairly long column entitled "Avoid an International Catastrophe. Levelheaded View Necessary." The article quoted an unidentified "member of the House of Peers" as saying: "I

hope that this temporary and limited disturbance can be re-
solved without further damage to our international position.
Continued reckless acts at this time can only lead to national
disaster." The author was identified only as a member of the
House of Peers (by 1932 even this degree of dissent could only
be written anonymously). The jingoistic effects of the war in
China can be seen in the same newspaper a few years later. On
July 21, 1937, the headlines read: "Three Battles with Demor-
alized Chinese Troops, Japanese Forces Advance against
Heavy Enemy Fire and Annihilate Foe." On July 30 extra
large letters proclaimed: "Disorder Ends in North China,
Japanese Forces Bring Justice and Decency," and "Fighting
Ends. Peking-Tientsin Region Completely Occupied in Two
Days." After Pearl Harbor, journalism's role was to whip up
hatred of the enemy. In the most emotional and vulgar lan-
guage, the daily press shrilled a message of destruction to the
white imperialists. A few choice phrases will give the flavor:
"Fiendish American Forces on Bataan Wiped Out" (*Yomiuri
Shimbun,* April 14, 1942) and "Attack! Those Savages: The
Americans Yell, 'Kill the Japs'" (*Asahi Gurafu,* March 1,
1944). Journalism did a complete about-face from balanced
dissent to inflammatory cheerleading.

The authorities broadened the oppression and "guidance"
to bring every aspect of culture under their control. All books
related to Marxism were banned, from the classics of Marx,
Engels, and Lenin to modern Japanese writers. The purge
soon swept far beyond Marxism to writing totally unrelated
to progressive politics. Men who had long been the academic
and bureaucratic Establishment and whose authoritative
scholarly works had been published in several editions over
many years were also added to the list of proscribed authors.
Two of the most famous works were *Keihō tokuhon* (A
Reader on Criminal Law) by Takigawa Yukitoki, professor at
Kyoto Imperial University, and *Kenpō satsuyō* (Essentials of
the Constitution) by Minobe Tatsukichi, former professor at
Tokyo Imperial University, a member of the Imperial

Academy, and an imperial appointee to the House of Peers. Other banned works included Waseda University professor Tsuda Sōkichi's *Jindai-shi no kenkyū* (A Study of the Age of the Gods) and *Kojiki oyobi Nihon Shoki no kenkyū* (Research on the *Kojiki* and *Nihon Shoki*). The propagation of liberal legal or academic theories was also prohibited. Takigawa was forced out of Kyoto Imperial University in 1933. Later, Yanaihara Tadao, Kawai Eijirō, Ouchi Hyōe, and others lost their posts at Tokyo Imperial University. Neither university autonomy nor academic freedom withstood the chill blasts of government interference.[11]

The lively world of political and social criticism fared no better. In 1937 the authorities ordered that publication of manuscripts by seven writers be "deferred": Oka Kunio, Tosaka Jun, Hayashi Kaname, Miyamoto Yuriko, Nakano Shigeharu, Suzuki Yasuzō, and Hori Makoto. Gradually other names were added to the list, including Mizuno Hironori, Baba Tsunego, Yanaihara Tadao, Yokota Kisaburō, Kiyosawa Kiyoshi, and Tanaka Kōtarō.[12] Even Kawai Eijirō, who had formerly worked zealously for the Ministry of Education on a committee to counter Marxism and provide "proper guidance of public thought," found himself indicted and convicted because of his *Fashizumu hihan* (Criticism of Fascism) and other works.[13] The monthly intellectual journals remained critical longer than the other media, but after Pearl Harbor they too were reduced to current affairs magazines full of innocuous or progovernment articles. *Kaizō* and *Chūō Kōron,* two of the oldest and most influential monthlies, were finally forced to suspend publication in July 1944.[14]

Literature also felt the censor's lethal grip. The proletarian writers had long been harassed and restricted; now the authorities turned to novels devoid of any ideological taint. Included among the new targets were Niwa Fumio's *Chūnen* (Middle Age) and *Aisomete* (Indigo Blue), Tokuda Shūsei's *Shukuzu* (Miniature), and Tanizaki Jun'ichirō's *Sasameyuki* (The

Makioka Sisters). They were banned for being mere love stories irrelevant to the current emergency.[15] Once warmed up, the censors went after semi-classics like Tokutomi Roka's *Shizen to jinsei* (Nature and Life) and Tayama Katai's *Ippeisotsu* (A Soldier), and finally to the classics of the feudal period and antiquity. The literary works of Nichiren, Nō chants, and the essays of Ueda Akinari all suffered deletions or revisions of "inappropriate sections." Altogether an impressive display of industrious official idiocy.[16]

Conformity was similarly imposed on the other arts. First proletarian art was banned. Later the Nikakai, a private association of Western-style painters, was disbanded and the Free Artists Association was forced to delete the word "free" from its name.[17] In 1943 the Cabinet Information Bureau banned 1,000 musical compositions; American and British works could no longer be performed. In April 1944 steel guitars, banjos, and ukeleles were outlawed, another stroke against baneful foreign influences. The Takarazuka Girls Chorus was also ordered to disband, although less for ideological reasons than because its frivolous entertainment was inconsistent with the war effort.[18] The new Western-style drama groups in the legitimate theater were most affected. Two drama groups, the Shinkyō Gekidan and Shin Tsukiji Gekidan, were both forced to disband in 1940. Some theaters were required to change their names: the Tsukiji Little Theater became the National Little Theater; the Moulin Rouge became the Sakubunkan. Finally, the Nippon Idō Gekijō (Japan Touring Theater) was formed under Cabinet Information Bureau aegis and all theatrical groups were coerced into participating.[19]

Public education, being under government purview, was much easier to adapt to state purposes than private cultural activities. Even in the public school system some teachers resisted the Ministry of Education and refused to be rote purveyors of the official curriculum. They tried to develop the students' individuality and social perspective. There was no textbook for composition, so intrepid teachers had some lee-way for real instruction. They used composition themes and other methods to provide a liberal, dynamic element in the curriculum. These teachers were charged with imparting a proletarian education, arrested, and removed from the class-rooms.[20]

The educational system was changed to better serve the new priorities. Elementary schools were renamed national schools (*kokumin gakkō*) in 1941.[21] The nationalistic nomenclature better fit their dedication to "following the Imperial Way" and "providing fundamental spiritual training for the people." In 1943 the middle schools were required to use government textbooks, thereby losing the right to select from among ap-proved texts. These changes were all important in molding mass conformity. However, only one aspect of expanded offi-cial controls will be discussed here: changes in educational content. The fourth edition of government textbooks was used in elementary schools for the first time in 1933. The *Japanese Reader* in this set was quite advanced technically. It was the first to have color illustrations and other innovations. Unfor-tunately, when first-grade students opened the reader to the first double-page spread, there was a picture of three toy sol-diers with the caption "Advance! Advance! Soldiers move forward!" The introduction of such militaristic themes to first-grade children suggests how deeply the aggression in Man-churia affected educational content. This trend was more pronounced in the fifth edition of national textbooks adopted from 1941. The most egregious examples, however, were in the national history text in the sixth edition published in 1944 (only the Japanese history text was revised for this edition). It resembled a collection of fairy tales with its simplistic, exaggerated prose style and numerous pictures, an imagina-tive combination to pique the children's interest. The first chapter, "Land of the Gods," was a lengthy account of the legendary deities who created Japan. The chapter had an illus-tration of the descent of Ninigi-no-mikoto, grandson of the sun goddess, Amaterasu, from the Plain of Heaven to earth. Although the detailed stories about the age of the gods that appeared in textbooks from the third edition on were a distinct setback for a scientific historiography, at least they had not been illustrated. Now a national history textbook carried a picture of the descent of the august imperial grandchild from the plains of heaven. (The use of an illustration in a Japanese language textbook in order to teach the ancient myths as literature would not have been so bad.) In the classwork on this section the teachers used a scroll which depicted the imperial descent: the deities Izanami and Izanagi created the Japanese islands by catching up pieces of land as though fishing. Any youthful doubts were promptly squelched. A child in the Kawawada elementary school, Ibaraki Prefecture, responded to the scroll of Ninigi-no-mikoto's descent with "Teacher, isn't that just a made-up story!" The teacher yelled, "You're as disrespectful as Ashikaga Takauji, you impertinent little bastard" and walloped the little subversive on the head with a wooden *kendō* (Japanese fencing) stick.[22]

Every facet of the curriculum was permeated with emperor worship and militarism. The manipulation and distortion of rational and scientific data was too ubiquitous to discuss in detail here. Young children were indoctrinated to believe that the Greater East Asian War was a holy war. At a school in Yamagata Prefecture, the students were dissecting frogs. One child burst out crying, "Oh, this is disgusting. The poor frog. What a shame." The teacher rapped him hard on the head twice with his knuckles and said, "Why are you crying about one lousy frog? When you grow up you'll have to kill a hundred, two hundred Chinks."[23] Subtler forms of inculcation were not overlooked. The final examination at the Maebashi middle school, Gumma Prefecture, in March 1941 included the following questions on ethics: "1. Why are loyalty and filial piety united in our country? 2. Discuss the necessity for overseas expansion. 3. Why is Japan's Constitution superior to those of other nations? 4. What kind of spirit is required to overcome the present difficulties facing the nation?"[24]

Bessho Makiko recalled with embarrassment many years later that as an elementary school student she had participated in a contest for a slogan to encourage young volunteer servicemen. Her entry was "Our brave warriors die with honor. Carry on the fight, youth volunteers!" She had also inserted notes in the little care packages her family sent to soldiers at the front.[25] A typical message said, "Please fight well and die a glorious death." Schoolgirl Nakane Mihoko prayed devotedly for victory as she endured the hardships of evacuation to the countryside during the Allied bombing. She was certain Japan would eventually triumph. Her diary was full of a sense of duty, a determination to do her best.[26] Twenty years after the war she wrote: "I think we were really well trained. The teachers were excellent instructors, so I cannot criticize them, but they never made us think about anything. We just earnestly memorized everything. That approach was probably very effective in destroying human feelings. Because in wartime human beings become inhuman."[27] Japanese schoolchildren were so "really well trained" that they could not have the slightest doubts about the righteousness of the war.

The high schools, universities, and colleges had been regarded as hotbeds of liberalism and communism. They now followed the same nationalistic trends, although not to quite the same extent. I entered higher school in April 1931 and was astounded at my classmates' knowledge of Marxist dialectics. About 1943, when I had been teaching in a higher school for two years, the students asked me to stop using the Christian era for dates. In a little more than a decade there was incredible change in student politics and interests. The same transformation occurred in the universities. By the time I began college, in 1934, the student movement and political activities had completely disappeared. University autonomy and academic freedom had gone with them. Kyushu Imperial University even curried favor with the authorities to the point of naming an admiral president of the school.[28] Many students went off to military service without ever having a chance to read the Marxist classics or the great works of liberalism. No wonder that later a large number of them thought: "It was only when I joined a naval air (suicide attack) unit that I realized the path of eternal duty. The petty individual or the family are insignificant compared to the three-thousand-year history of the Empire." A youthful patriotic zeal untempered by a critical capacity and liberal influences led students into the suicide attack units.[29] It is not surprising. They were educated for it from nursery school.

Religion was also enlisted for the war effort. Students were taken regularly to Shintō shrines as an act of patriotic worship. Passengers on streetcars were required to stand and bow reverently when passing the Imperial Palace or Yasukuni Shrine. The conductor used to say, "We are now passing the Imperial Palace. Please bow." To refuse was almost unthinkable. State Shintō was drilled into the populace as a nationalistic creed. The other side of the coin was the persecution of Christianity as foreign and subversive. Officials of the Salvation Army, the Holiness Church, the Plymouth Brethren, and other sects were arrested. Japanese were forced to choose the Christian God or Amaterasu Omikami and the emperor.[30] The pressure for apostasy was no less intense than it had been for the seventeenth-century martyrs who were given the choice of trampling on a likeness of Christ or suffering the consequences. Asami Sensaku, a member of the Christian Non-Church movement, was imprisoned for advocating pacifism.[31] Mission–affiliated schools were subjected to steady overt and covert harassment.[32]

Surveillance and disruption of political meetings and associations that might lead to direct physical resistance increased. The Communist movement was destroyed by strict enforcement of the revised Peace Preservation Law. Labor unions that followed completely legal methods and even some that eschewed militancy and advocated labor-management cooperation were driven out of existence. In December 1937 the leftist Nihon Rōdō Kumiai Zenkoku Hyōgikai (National Council of Japanese Labor Unions) was ordered to disband. The only remaining national labor organization, the "moderate" Nihon Rōdō Sōdōmei (Japan General Federation of Labor) lasted until July 1940, when it was forced to dissolve. In November 1940 the Dai Nippon Sangyō Hōkokukai (Greater Japan Association for Service to the State through Industry) was organized. Labor representatives served with capitalists in a cooperative effort for the sake of "industrial patriotism." As a result of these government actions, there was no longer any independent labor organization. Organizers attempted to form peasant unions. However, the Japan Peasants Union was prohibited in March 1942. An attempt to form a Federation to Reform the Agricultural Land System (Nōchi Seido Kaikaku Dōmei) in order to maintain a limited peasants' organization failed. Organizers hoped to take advantage of the government's policy of increasing food production to safeguard tenant-cultivator interests. The organization was prohibited in March 1942. All organizations representing the class interests of the working masses in the factories or the fields were destroyed.[33]

After the Manchurian Incident, the legal proletarian political parties quickly began to support aggression in China. Political organizations representing proletarian interests were so grievously weakened as to present no threat to the government. Nevertheless, the authorities saw the war and the Fascist mood of the 1930s as a chance to deliver the coup de grâce to the Left. Yamakawa Hitoshi and others were arrested in December 1937 for allegedly planning to organize a popular front. In a followup move, the government banned the two organizations allegedly behind the popular front, the Japan Proletarian party (Nihon Musantō) and the National Council of Japanese Labor Unions. In 1940 Abe Isoo and others left the Social Mass party (Shakai Taishūtō) in protest against the party's stand on the expulsion of Saitō Takao from the Diet in February 1940. Saitō came under fire because of an extraordinary speech criticizing the war in China. With a few individual exceptions, the political parties left him twisting in the wind. Abe and his followers organized a preparatory meeting to form a new party tentatively named the Rōdō Kokumintō (National Labor party). The government immediately prohibited the group. The official reason was that "Police controls should always adapt to changes in society. During wartime, activities to preserve public order should, of course, be much stricter than during peacetime. Furthermore, positive efforts to remove obstacles to social harmony and ensure the smooth functioning of state activities, obviate conflicts and friction, and strengthen the wartime system all stem from a desire to achieve flawless public order at the present time." At least the inevitable incompatibility of war and democracy was candidly admitted. Time ran out on the Social Mass party in July 1940. It was disbanded, and the proletarian parties were no more.[34]

Bourgeois political parties were the next to succumb. Some military men and civilian rightists had long advocated the overthrow of the *zaibatsu* (conglomerates) and the major parties. If the rightists had carried out a basic reform of Japanese capitalism and the landlord system which sustained it, they would have destroyed the foundation of the emperor system they were trying to protect. The right wing's "reform" obviously could not entail a fundamental change in the social structure. Their real objective was to get rid of bourgeois democracy and establish a dictatorial system headed by the military. In the sense that the Right as a political movement resembled Nazism and Italian fascism, the term fascism has a certain validity for Japan also. The rise of fascism inevitably brought an end to the orderly parliamentary politics that had taken hold fairly firmly during the 1920s. The political parties' very existence was soon imperiled. They dug their own graves by timid capitulation at several crucial junctures. In 1935 Minobe Tatsukichi was attacked because of his legal theory that the emperor was an organ of state. Instead of defending the scholar, the Diet passed a resolution enjoining the government to initiate a "clarification of national polity," an endorsement of reaction and an invitation to totalitarianism. The Diet's bowing to army pressure and expelling Saitō Takao in

February 1940 was another case of weakness under fire.[35] The Seiyūkai disbanded in July 1940; the next month it was the Minseitō's turn. The bourgeois parties, with a history dating back to the Jiyūtō in 1881, were finished. In August 1940 the Fujin Senkyoken Katutoku Dōmei (Federation to Acquire the Vote for Women) was disbanded and the suffragette movement ended. Its demise symbolized the fate of bourgeois democracy on the eve of the Pacific War.

But Japanese fascism differed from its German and Italian counterparts. They were broad movements from below. Charismatic leaders established dictatorial systems based on mass organizations, the Nazi party and the Fascist party. In Japan fascism was imposed from above by the military and the bureaucrats, aided by their junior partners, the civilian rightists (whose money came from secret army funds and similar covert sources). A "new political structure movement" was planned and the Imperial Rule Assistance Association (IRAA) was established in October 1940.[36] It was not comparable to the mass parties of Germany or Italy and was not very effective in organizing or mobilizing the populace. The government supported certain candidates in the April 1942 election (the "IRAA election")[37] and managed to elect many of them. The IRAA used local organizations such as the hamlet and village associations, neighborhood associations, civil defense associations, and the reservist associations to constantly interfere in the people's lives through ration distribution, air raid drills, official sendoffs for draftees, and memorial services for war dead.[38] These organizations got into the act by forcing women to stop wearing long-sleeved kimonos and getting permanent waves, and insisting that citizens put on the prescribed air raid "uniforms" of puttees and khaki caps for men and *monpe* (women's work pants gathered at the ankle) for women. The IRAA did succeed in imposing scores of petty regulations.[39] However, it failed to become a powerful mass organization capable of mobilizing spontaneous enthusiastic cooperation with the war effort.

The Nazis destroyed the Weimar Republic and established a dictatorship. No such clear break with the past occurred in Japan. The Meiji Constitution was never revised or suspended. The Diet was rendered impotent but it continued to exist. About the only major legal shift was the 1938 enactment of the National Mobilization Law. Although probably unconstitutional, its sweeping provisions broadened the state's administrative authority, imposed new duties on the citizenry, and curtailed civil rights.

Despite the differences, Japanese fascism was no less effective in destroying political freedom. Threats and the use of physical force by the police and Kempeitai were the ultimate weapons. Marxists, Christian pacifists, anyone considered even slightly opposed to the war was arrested and incarcerated under regulations that in effect voided the Criminal Prosecution Law. Some prisoners were tortured and physically mistreated; others were held indefinitely, placed in a psychological limbo. Political prisoners were pressured to make false confessions and to recant their political beliefs.[40] Among the famous cases of brutality against prisoners was the 1933 killing of proletarian novelist Kobayashi Takiji. He was beaten to death by detectives at the Tsukiji Police Station in Tokyo.[41] Another was the 1944 case fabricated by the Kanagawa Prefecture Special Higher Police against the editorial staffs of *Kaizō* and *Chūō Kōron* magazines. Hosokawa Karoku and others were accused of planning to revive the Communist movement, arrested, and tortured. One woman prisoner was sexually assaulted as a form of "erotic terror" to force a confession.[42] The assistant police inspector in charge of the case, a man named Takeshima, tried to intimidate Kuroda Hidetoshi, the chief editor of *Chūō Kōron*. Takeshima reportedly said, "We know very well that you are not a Communist. But if you intend to be stubborn about this, we know how to handle you. We'll just set you up as a Communist. We'll do a good job on you. We can easily frame one or two people as Commies. It doesn't matter what happens to a Communist.

We can kill Communists. Our superiors will not mind. It'll be quite all right." It was no idle threat. There were people who died from the effects of long years in prison, the indirect victims of police mistreatment. Tosaka Jun, the philosopher of Marxism, who died just before the war ended, was one. Another was the philosopher Miki Kiyoshi, who died shortly after Japan surrendered.[43]

Police spies and informants were everywhere. The authorities' willingness to fabricate evidence and charges meant that not even the most innocent person was safe. A person had to be extremely careful of everything he said and did.[44] It was dangerous to confide one's real feelings in a diary.[45] The police did not respect individual privacy. Detectives always rode the trains in Korea and on the Sanyō Line from Shimonoseki to Osaka because of the many Korean passengers and other travelers returning from the continent. The police made a practice of going through the passengers' baggage. Haruno Yoshie was confronted by a policeman who had read her diary and accused her, "You're a Red!" She was taken off the train and detained.[46] Matsumoto Chizuko recalled that she and a college student friend from the same labor service unit were listening to a record of "La Cumparsita" when two Kempeitai burst into the room. "You traitors! The nation is in a grave emergency but you listen to enemy music!" They shouted and stomped around the room with their boots on and broke many records before leaving.[47] Innumerable such incidents occurred in Japan during the war years. Concentration camps, the extermination of millions of Jews, and the public execution of many opponents were grim features of Nazism.[48] There were no concentration camps or mass killings in Japan. Except for Ozaki Hotsumi, implicated in the Sorge spy ring, no one apparently was executed for treason (not counting battlefield executions).

Strangely enough, this may only mean that oppression was actually greater in Japan. Every aspect of life was so regimented and controlled that no one could plan a treacherous act worthy of the death penalty! The public prosecutor winked at police and Kempeitai lawlessness. The supposedly independent courts should have seen that the police and prosecutors were exceeding their authority and protected the rights of criminal defendants. But sometimes intentionally and sometimes inadvertently, the courts cooperated with the police.[49] All government authorities, including the judges, did their best to eradicate freedom.

The populace remained silent, unable to learn the facts or discuss politics or the war. Government officials were prisoners of their own restrictions and censorship. National policies had to be decided on the basis of information from which unpleasant facts had been filtered out. Divorced from reality, the government inevitably made even more disastrous mistakes. A few military men and bureaucrats realized that all the victories were not glorious. Horiba Kazuo found no pleasure in the capture of Hankow. As a general staff opponent of expanded military operations in China, Horiba realized that each "victory" increased the certainty of ultimate defeat. The *banzai* victory cries as Japanese forces marched into the city left Horiba with "a plaintive feeling."[50] He understood that the shouts were a last hurrah for a hollow victory. Ogata Taketora, the chief censor, as director of the Cabinet Information Bureau, bemoaned his lack of reliable information. He no longer had access to the valuable news sources of his journalist days and felt "utterly out of everything, shunted off to the peanut gallery."[51] The government silenced the public at the cost of isolating itself. The decision makers had to lie in the same bed. Robbed of information and freedom in the first instance, the Japanese people paid again for official ignorance and errors with vast meaningless sacrifices and loss of life.

The weak appreciation of civil rights was one cause of the Pacific War. The populace did not defend its prerogatives. More important, the authorities stressed only obligations and ran roughshod over the citizenry. The abrogation of human rights kept pace with the intensified war; Japan was on a one-way road to disaster. This is the greatest issue of the war as far as domestic history is concerned. The failure within

Japanese society was exported with the military to occupied areas. The mistreatment of local residents by our military during the Pacific War eternally blemished Japan's record as a civilized nation.

A prewar dictionary defined "human rights" (*jinken*) first of all as an obligatory right (*saiken*).[52] An obligatory right was a property right whereby a lender was entitled to recover money or collateral from a borrower. The contemporary sense of basic human rights appeared only in the compound "infringement of human rights" (*jinken jūrin*). This suggests that prewar Japanese enjoyed human rights only in an "infringed" form. The army minced no words about human rights: "The loci of sovereignty [the emperor] and fostering of national morality underlie the attainment of national defense. The protection of individual life and property are not inviolable goals. On the contrary, they will often have to be sacrificed for national defense."[53] When the military gained power in the Greater Japanese Empire, human rights were crushed under army boots. The basic rights that should have been a raison d'être for protecting the nation were sacrificed in the name of national security, just as the people themselves were sacrificed.

Cooperation and Cooption: Intellectuals, Artists, and Popular Support for the War

Civilian politicians were still in power when the army struck in Manchuria in September 1931. A Minseitō cabinet had overridden military objections and pushed through the London Disarmament treaty the year before. It was still possible to advocate international cooperation. Men like Yokota Kisaburō, who lectured on international law at Tokyo Imperial University, could still be quite outspoken. Yokota published an article in the university newspaper disputing the Kwantung Army's right of self-defense in the occupation of Mukden and Kirin. He also strongly supported the League of Nations resolution calling for the removal of Japanese forces from Manchuria.[54] Despite relentless government pressure, the Communist party's underground activities continued.

Marxist slogans against the imperialist war were ingeniously publicized. The *Rōdō Shimbun* (Labor News) published by an auxiliary organization of the JCP, in an extra edition on September 23, 1931, exhorted, "Block the shipment of ammunition, weapons and troops! Stage a general strike and mass rallies to oppose the war." A special issue a few days later called the railroad bombing near Mukden a pretext for military action and labeled the fighting "a war of plunder" to shift the burden of economic depression to the working masses. On September 25, the *Rōdō Shimbun* boldly asserted, "A war of plunder will not cure the economic depression. The only answer is to change the war into an insurrection to overthrow imperialistic governments."[55] The policy line of "transforming imperialistic war into civil war" had been adopted at the Sixth Comintern Congress in August 1928.[56] The Communists followed this thesis in building a movement to oppose the aggression in China.[57] The Zenkoku Rōnō Taishūtō (National Labor-Farmer Mass party), a legal proletarian party, also opposed military expansion. Immediately after the Mukden clash, the party's central executive committee approved a protest statement and formed a committee to oppose the war headed by Oyama Ikuo. The committee prepared a report which called for "absolute opposition" to the China policy of Japanese finance capital, which was "trying to stop the growth of Chinese mass movements." The report prophetically stated that "The fighting in Manchuria and Mongolia will soon inevitably bring a second world war."[58] Anarchist Ishikawa Sanshirō ridiculed expansionism in the August 1931 issue of his private magazine *Dinamikku* (Dynamic). Under the caption "Dancing in Manchuria and Korea to increase national prestige," he printed a cartoon of a skeleton wearing a military cap and carrying a Rising Sun flag dancing over Manchuria and Korea. Ishikawa's editorial on the Manchurian Incident in the December 1, 1931, issue said: "Despite the 'success' of our foreign policy based on military force, future generations of

Japanese will bear the agony and shame of this 'success.' " A month later Ishikawa wrote "What Is Love for the Fatherland?" and concluded that "If we desire a more glorious destiny for our beloved Japan, we must stand in the front ranks of the world's peoples as a nation of peace and justice."[59] Many publications were banned from October 1931 to December 1935 because of their antiwar content. These ideas were expressed and circulated for several years after the push into Manchuria, but only a relatively few persons were involved.

The Communist analysis of continental expansion deserves the highest marks for understanding it as an imperialist war. However, some of their public appeals precluded mass support. For example, the *Daini Musansha Shimbun* (The Second Proletarian News) on October 24, 1931, explained that "Opposition to the war was not from pacifist scruples but as part of a struggle to topple the present government and establish a new government of workers and peasants."[60] The Communists' slogan of From War to Rebellion was linked with Overthrow the Monarchy and Protect the Soviet Union, propositions with decidedly limited appeal.[61] Rigidly sticking to the Comintern's anti-imperialism thesis ruled out cooperation with many who shared the Communists' antiwar views —bourgeois democrats, Socialists, democrats, anarchists, and liberals. To the Communists, anyone who did not give complete support to their program was the enemy. Official repression alone did not cripple the antiwar movement; ideological deficiencies and tactical errors inherent in the Communist analysis were a congenital defect. The antiwar struggle disappeared with the collapse of the Left social movement of labor unions and proletarian parties.[62]

Young intellectuals from Kyoto Imperial University made a valuable effort to provide a theoretical basis for a broad-based, unified antiwar movement. Nakai Shoichi, Shinmura Takeshi, Mashita Shin'ichi, Kuno Osamu, and others were inspired by the anti-Fascist movement in France, Italy, and Spain. In February 1935 they started the magazine *Sekai Bunka* (World Culture), which carried articles on antiwar and anti-Fascist intellectual currents in Europe. Although *Sekai Bunka* was certainly a highbrow journal removed from the masses, the Kyoto intellectuals were advocating consensus politics. In November 1937 they were all arrested, and the journal stopped.[63]

Police allegations that the *Sekai Bunka* intellectuals were part of a Communist movement were a total fabrication. The decision to start the journal was in no way related to the Communist party or the Comintern. By coincidence, however, the seventh meeting of the Comintern, held in the summer of 1935, had adopted a popular front strategy on the basis of the Dimitrov report.[64] The Comintern and the JCP had engaged in self-criticism about the "sectarian mistake" of concentrating on the "abstract propagation of revolutionary slogans." The new emphasis was on "the people's basic democratic rights," an attempt to bring politics into the reality of everyday life. To protect these rights, the Comintern called for the widest possible united front in "opposition to fascism and war."[65] By this time, however, the objective conditions for a broad, unified antiwar movement no longer existed. The Communist movement itself was virtually dead. It was too late for a change of tactics.[66]

Sporadic antiwar actions continued, however. To cite only a few colorful examples, in January 1938 someone scribbled in a toilet at a Nagasaki department store: "Oppose the imperialistic war! We don't want the miserable fate of the Italian and German peoples!" Leaflets printed on unit paper were scattered at the 24th Infantry Regiment, Miyakonojō, Kyushu: "Stop this imperialistic war and end conscription! There is a shortage of labor on the home front. Soldiers know that if the war continues, their families will be ruined. Destroy imperialism, its contradiction and oppression!" Gestures of opposition, including within the military, were too numerous to recount.[67] Despite these sentiments, there was no political force capable of organizing a mass movement.[68]

Bourgeois democratic intellectuals also criticized the war. Ishibashi Tanzan of the *Tōyō Keizai Shimpō* (Oriental Economic News) was a far-sighted advocate of an enlightened foreign policy. As early as the 1921 Washington Conference, he had suggested that Japan should get rid of Korea, Taiwan, and Manchuria and pull out of China. Ishibashi believed that if Japan went to the conference table with this resolve, its international position would vastly improve. On February 13, 1932, his journal editorialized against military adventurism: "Some of the younger army officers making names for themselves in Manchuria reportedly believe they can create an ideal state in Manchuria and Mongolia. But can ideals unattainable even in Japan be realized on Chinese territory? To recognize that Manchuria, Mongolia, and China are inhabited by Chinese is to realize that such an incredible fantasy does not warrant a second thought." On May 21, 1932, less than a week after the May 15 Incident, a *Tōyō Keizai Shimpō* editorial said, "It is not possible to speak freely in this country about foreign relations, the military, or anything of real importance." "Misinformation and narrow-minded myopia" were causing incalculable damage to Japanese society. Despite later restrictions on the press, Ishibashi remained a proponent of a moderate foreign policy and freedom of speech.[69]

Other liberal intellectuals wrote against the impending militaristic deluge. Yanaihara Tadao published *Minzoku to heiwa* (The Nation and Peace) in 1936 and started a privately circulated magazine called *Tsūshin* (Communication) to advocate Christian pacifism (the name was later changed to *Kashin* [Auspicious News]). The critiques of fascism in private magazines, each with a unique perspective, included the journalist Kiryū Yūyū's *Tazan no Ishi* (Stones from Other Mountains), Ubukata Toshirō's *Kojin, Konjin* (Ancients and Contemporaries), and Masaki Hiroshi's *Chikaki Yori* (From Nearby).[70]

Yanaihara Tadao, in a commemorative public lecture for his liberal friend Fujii Takeshi on October 1, 1937, lashed out passionately: "I have something to say to the Japanese people. Stop this war quickly! . . . Today we witness the burial of the 'ideal' of our beloved Japan . . . Please, everyone, if you have understood my remarks, let us bury this country in order to revive the ideal Japan." These remarks cost Yanaihara his position at Tokyo Imperial University; he had to resign two months later. Government officials forced Kiryū to stop publication of *Tazan no Ishi*. Fatally ill, he announced suspension of the journal with a prophetic tirade against the military: "Contrary to what one might expect, I am joyful at the prospect of disappearing from the face of the globe, which is rapidly degenerating toward ultrabestiality. My sole regret is that I will not be here to see the fulfillment of the dream I have cherished for so long, the demilitarization which will inevitably occur after the war." Yanaihara and Masaki continued publishing their defiant little magazines throughout the war, but these sterling efforts were unable to stem the tide.

Generally speaking, the intellectual community not only caved in under pressure but accommodated with alacrity to the new order. Many intellectuals veered hard right to support militarism. In November 1931 the central committee of the Shakai Minshūtō, the strongest of the legal proletarian parties, came out in favor of protecting Japan's interests in Manchuria and Mongolia.[71] A month later Home Minister Adachi Kenzō, a Minseitō man, advocated a national unity system, by which he meant a multiparty cabinet committed to working closely with the military. This betrayal from within broke up the Wakatsuki cabinet. In April 1932 Akamatsu Katsumarō and others left the Social Democratic party and formed the Nihon Kokka Shakaitō (Japan National Socialist party) in a left to right flipflop. Fourteen months later, the imprisoned Communist leaders Sano Manabu and Nabeyama Sadachika published their apostasy declaration, "A Letter to Our Comrades in Prison," left the party, and embraced ultra-nationalism. These are only a few examples of a political accommodation that transcended party lines. From bourgeois ranks, from the Socialists and from the Communists, many flexible politicians saw which way the wind was blowing and adjusted their views.

The police and prosecutors worked especially hard to break the imprisoned Communists. They skillfully exploited the emotions of loved ones, pointing out the heartbreak a prisoner's mother was suffering because of his misguided stubbornness. In other cases the authorities used physical and psychological pressures to break the prisoner's will. Most of the Communists, either under duress or voluntarily, disavowed the party.[72] Some tried to maintain as much personal integrity as possible despite the apostasy. But an evaluation of prewar Japanese Marxism must note the fact that many Communists switched from the vanguard left to the far right of nationalism and aggression. Among the reasons were their formalistic radicalism and blind adherence to Comintern and party dictates and, despite their advocacy of "democracy," a lack of real experience or understanding of human rights. Although prewar Marxism was a sharp thrust to the left and away from tradition, its psychological structure had much in common with the ideology of the emperor system, a rote submission to authority. In one sense, Marxism was simply the reverse coin of a *banzai*-shouting, emperor-worshipping statism. That partially explains why these committed Communists reversed themselves so much more quickly and totally than moderate dissidents. Two major failures stand out in retrospect. These people lacked a moral and psychological resistance against "conversion" to a state-approved ideology. Second, there was a fatal inability to develop an effective antiwar movement involving mass participation and a coalition of individuals and groups of different ideologies.[73] Both Marxist and non-Marxist intellectuals share a responsibility for the war. Not the criminal culpability of the conservative decision makers who led Japan, but a responsibility for failing to stop the war.

Academia had its share of turncoats too. Kōsaka Masaaki, Kōyama Iwao, and others of the Kyoto school of thought staunchly supported the war and churned out flimsy rationalizations for aggression. Watsuji Tetsurō's July 1944 book *Japanese Loyalty and the American National Character* is another testimony to the "Kyoto philosophers'" intellectual shallowness. It is not surprising that the citadel of a positivist "value free" historiography devoid of ideological rigor should spew forth a large number of opportunistic scholars. They were as free of values as their scholarship. It is surprising, or at least amusing, to find in the introduction to a book on *ukiyoe* prints, a subject about as far from the grim horrors of war as one might imagine, the insertion: "On that glorious day when we have triumphed in the Greater East Asian War, when America and England have been conquered, and the radiant splendor of Japanese culture shines throughout the world, Japanese arts will illuminate the universe."[74] Kawakami Hajime's *tanka* (poems), written in December 1942, poignantly caught the disgrace of the academy: "How pitiful are those academics who sell out to the government like courtesans changing patrons."[75] The same words applied to organized religion. Buddhism had always lacked the capacity to challenge the state, and Japanese Buddhism rallied behind the war. A very few Christians withheld support—the Non-Church Christians like Yanaihara and a very few others to be discussed in Chapter 10. Nearly all the other Christian groups enlisted in the "holy war."[76]

When the Dai-Nippon Bungaku Hōkokukai (Japanese Literature Patriotic Association) and the Dai-Nippon Genron Hōkokukai (Japanese Journalism Patriotic Association) were formed, many writers and journalists joined up and cooperated with the war effort.[77] Artists also did their share. From about 1937, there were "war" art exhibitions, "holy war" art exhibitions, and "Greater East Asian War" art exhibitions. Many well-known artists painted pictures of battlefield glory and the empire's victories.[78]

The cooperation of many individuals in the wartime organizations was neither voluntary nor expedient opportunism. Former Marxists were constantly hounded by the Special Higher Police and never knew when they might be thrown back into prison. Understandably, they often had to pretend to be more enthusiastic about the war than persons without such political pasts.[79] In other cases, writers and artists were dispatched to the combat zone. They *had* to write or draw something. There were also individuals who tried to work from within, to moderate policies and avoid national disaster. They ended up being manipulated like the rest.[80] Frequently the difference between collaboration and resistance was paper-thin. A hasty judgment based on appearances—an affiliation, an article, a painting—is often incorrect. A careful reading of an individual and his work is especially necessary for those persons who tricked the authorities with "faked conversions."[81]

These caveats notwithstanding, many individuals flocked to the government, trumpeted the inane braggadocio about the empire and sacred mission, and became self-righteous patriots and exemplars. Some even became informers for the police and Kempeitai.[82] Kiyosawa Kiyoshi's diary shows the anguish of a sensitive intellect forced into silence: "Fools and opportunists are the most influential people in Japan today" (June 19, 1943); "The greatest frustration now is that there is no criticism of the vulgar ideas passing for wisdom. They are lowering the public understanding to the imbecile level" (September 12, 1943).[83] The flood of crude, officially sanctioned "information" during the war years turned Japan into an intellectual insane asylum run by the demented. The whole population suffered brain damage from the incessant propaganda shock treatment. Sensitive people who remember the war period will regard even this assessment as an understatement.

The media beat the drums for the "holy war," "all the universe under one Japanese roof," and "the construction of a Greater East Asia." The newspapers reported only the "great military achievements" of the "invincible imperial forces." Denied the facts and honest analysis, the public enthusiastically supported the war. The militarist influence on education had produced a nationalistic people full of naive ardor for the war effort. The state had gotten exactly what it wanted from the school system. Certain strata of the population also found the war presented opportunities to increase status and authority. Former peasants who became noncommissioned officers and regular army men were able to vent all their pent-up anger and frustration, the rage accumulated from the social and economic deprivation they had suffered in the countryside. In their positions of minor authority they made life miserable for the recruits. Their civilian counterparts were the heads of neighborhood associations, civil defense organizations, and local chapters of the reservists' association. Bossing others around and claiming special privileges because of their "superior" commitment, they were an obnoxious breed of local self-seekers.[84]

Their opportunism was of a somewhat different quality from that of the intellectuals and the "men of culture." The authoritarian hierarchical structure of the military was a microcosm of Japanese society. During wartime, the whole nation became a huge barracks, and civilian society took on aspects of military society. The drill field discipline of the army flowed back to the civilians and produced hordes of petty authoritarian "patriots." They came from the strata of small business proprietors, local factory owners, small independent farmers, and local government officials. They were in positions of paternalistic authority in the social system of small, vertically integrated units with the emperor at the apex. While they had an inferiority complex toward government authorities and the upper classes, these objective conditions made them flag-waving enthusiasts for militarism.[85]

Ordinary citizens were harassed and bossed around by the "patriots." The average Mr. Watanabe often resented their excesses but, like soldiers in the army, still had to obey orders. Eventually most able-bodied men were drafted and became obedient, courageous soldiers. Lest this petty coercion be overstated, there was popular support for the war and it predated the destruction of the Left. About December 1931, an *Asahi Gurafu* reporter asked a father carrying a child on his back about the Manchurian issue. He replied, "We have to move faster and faster. We're protecting Japanese interests. We shouldn't hesitate." Mori Isao, whose father was a lacquerer, wrote in his diary on February 16, 1942: "I believe totally in cooperating with the war effort."[86] Mori's commitment was beyond question. His autobiography, *Shōwa ni ikiru* (A Life in Shōwa), published after the war, has the following line: "I still believe that my efforts for the war were utterly sincere." Kurita Sadako remembered a conversation with the head of the local youth group in early 1942 when Japan was scoring one victory after another: "Look how we're doing. Our Japanese spirit is wiping them out. We've got our hands on wool and gasoline. He talked big."[87] Yoshioka Yukio's father died from the atomic bombing of Hiroshima. He recalled that his father "was head of the neighborhood association, bought all the national war bonds he could, and always said, 'Japan will never lose.' He stubbornly refused to build an air raid shelter." Even after the atomic attack, "He talked about the Japanese military winning until he heard the imperial proclamation ending the war."[88] Many people selflessly sacrificed themselves and their families, convinced of Japan's victory until the very end.

Yet the millions of bereaved wives and parents who sent their husbands and sons off to the battlefields never to return had reason to hate the war. And the many more millions whose lives were disrupted by shortages and wartime regulations also had ample doubts about how it would all end. Grief and war weariness were hidden for the most part. A draft notice brought "congratulations" from the neighbors. At the flag-waving, *banzai*-shouting sendoff, the draftee bravely pledged "I'll come back victorious." But on the edge of the crowd there was often a wife "holding a child, shaking and crying."[89] Kajikawa Hiroshi, whose father was killed in the war, was a fourth-grader in 1941 when he wrote in a composition, "My mother sometimes kneels in front of my father's photograph and weeps."[90] Even in the farm villages, the greatest source of dedicated soldiers, there was mumbling by fathers whose sons were drafted:

> If only Osamu had not been drafted I could have gotten by without help from others. But look at the fix I'm in. They didn't give any advance notice. Suddenly there was

a draft notice and he was gone. Just like a cat dragged off by the scruff of its neck. Now I'm stuck since he left. No matter how many other countries we occupy or how many victories we win, it doesn't add one inch to my paddy fields. Talk about something that doesn't pay. There's nothing as stupid as war.

No patriotic rhetoric could console a mother's bitterness at the loss of a son. The official messenger recited the words of condolence, "Please accept this notice comforted by the knowledge that your son died for his Imperial Majesty, the Emperor." One mother said, "Uh, did you say the Emperor? I don't want to hear any more of that crap." Flushed with rage, she added that the Emperor ought to go into the front lines himself. "Then he would understand what it is for sons to be killed off."[91]

"Songs from the Homefront during the China Incident" contained many songs like Kamimura Teruko's glorification of the war: "What joy! My child has been called to be a warrior for the Emperor." However, many other lyrics evoked the agony of those who waited in vain. There was Karigane Hachirō's "Suddenly one day I realized that I have gotten used to reading articles about the terrible battles." And by Kiyama Shinako: "Whose mother is she? That old woman waving the Rising Sun flag and wiping away her tears." Or Kojima Yoshiko's "Standing close to the train window and facing my husband. My heart tells me to cling to him." As the war turned against Japan and conditions grew intolerable at home, disaffection spread to the pure of heart. Ezaki Tsuneko, then eighteen years old, confided her innermost feelings to her diary in 1945: "I wish I had been killed in that bombing. If there wasn't any war, we wouldn't have to go through this hell" (July 21); "This war. What will happen to Japan? I think most people are sick of the war now" (July 24); "Everything is hateful. I'm tired of living" (August 9).[92]

Whether for or against the war, people asked themselves, "When will my number be up?" As Japan was losing the war and falling under the Allied torch, many felt an intensity about life, a determination to use the little time left to them to the fullest. Some found an answer in an exultant last fling, a libertine "Live now, for tomorrow we die." Others were overwhelmed by despair and lassitude, and lost interest in everything.[93] Only those who experienced the war, the constant imminence of death, can appreciate these feelings.

7

Japan Extends the War to the Pacific

The Imperial Army march into Manchuria was presented as an act of self-defense to guard "Japan's lifeline," which had been acquired at great cost in blood and treasure in the Sino-Japanese and Russo-Japanese wars. Next, North China and Inner Mongolia had to be controlled to guard Manchuria. Protecting these areas required further advances into the heartland of China. This pattern of ever-expanding military operations confirmed a truism about international conflict: once started, a war escalates uncontrollably in the quest for elusive victory.

How could China be brought to its knees? That was the intractable problem. Unable to get a negotiated settlement on favorable terms or to win a final military triumph, Japanese leaders sought victory by expanding the conflict. Some thought Japan had to bring more military power to bear on China by attacking the Soviet Union and eliminating the threat from the north. Others argued that Japan had to control the natural resources of Southeast Asia and the Southwest Pacific in order to fight a protracted war and wear the Chinese down. A move in the latter direction entailed a clash with America, England, and Holland.

The dilemma began with the successful conspiracy at Mukden. From that modest start Japan soon found itself, with Germany and Italy, at war with most of the world. In his classic *On War*, Carl von Clausewitz states that the essence of war is its "unrestricted nature." He adds, however, that political constraints do impose limitations. (The Japanese army recognized the first point. A 1933 Army Ministry handbook says, "Operational needs are absolutely limitless.") But in the case of Japan after the seizure of Manchuria, there were no domestic constraints to perform a limiting function. Political brakes stripped, the war machine could roll on and on.

The military services alternated in slicing up China. The advance into North China was at army initiative; the moves from central China southward were pushed by the navy.[1] The navy general staff reacted firmly to the Gulf of Pohai incident of September 1936. No more Chinese "insincerity" would be tolerated: "If the anti-Japan movement increases, we will, depending upon the situation, occupy Hainan Island or Tsingtao."[2] The navy was more hawkish than the army during the Shanghai fighting in 1937. In February 1939, the navy occupied the long-coveted Hainan Island.

In May 1940 Allied forces were routed in France, and Holland and Belgium fell to the Germans. A month later France surrendered. Every German success whetted navy appetites. The advocates of southward expansion felt the time had come to strike. In a broadcast on June 29, 1940, Foreign Minister Arita Hachirō advocated the inclusion of certain "South Seas areas" in the "New Order in East Asia" as a "stabilizing force" for Japan. It was the first public expression of the policy of expanding to the south.[3] The policy was implemented by a "request" that the Vichy government of France permit the stationing of Japanese troops in northern Indochina. French authorities bowed to the demand in September 1940. Japan's objectives were threefold: to prevent the supply of munitions and arms to China, to place military forces in more advantageous positions, and to obtain certain vital materials. In effect, the China war zone of operations was expanded by a flanking operation.

Although the French authorities had agreed beforehand, Japanese military units on the scene ignored orders from Tokyo that the occupation be carried out peacefully and provoked fighting with French forces. It was another clear case of insubordination. Satō Kenryō, vice-chief of staff, South China Army, believed that such a "last-minute order to cancel a troop landing would impair command authority." Satō unilaterally blocked the order. Corps commander Nishimura Takuma hid in the ship's hold, his chief of staff Chō Isamu hid in the deck lifeboat to avoid accepting the cancellation. Senior Imperial Army officers acted like boys on a cruise instead of facing their legal responsibility to comply with higher authority.[4] Central headquarters went through the motions of disciplining the culprits, but they later turned up again in important positions. The failure to punish insubordinate officers was similar to the cases discussed earlier.

The Indochina operation was completed several months later when an Imperial Headquarters–Cabinet Liaison Conference decided in January 1941 to use force against French Indochina if necessary to improve Japan's military position there and in Thailand.[5] The French again acquiesced; southern Indochina was occupied without incident on July 27–28, 1941.

Another phase of the move southward had been approved several months earlier. The government decided in October 1940 that in order to develop and utilize the rich resources of the Netherlands East Indies, the islands "should be obtained as a link in the Greater East Asia economic sphere formed around Imperial Japan."[6] In January and May 1941, Japan demanded that Dutch officials supply oil and other essential resources. The Dutch responded in July by restricting oil exports to Japan.[7] Japan had to have the oil and other resources of the Dutch East Indies if it was to continue combat operations in China.

As long as Japan kept troops in China and had a military alliance with Germany and Italy, England, Holland, and the United States, which was stretching its nonbelligerent status to the limit to prevent England's defeat, could not stand idly by and allow Japan to move southward. The Americans, the British, and the Dutch, plus the Chinese, formed the ABCD group to block Japan. When northern Indochina was occupied, America immediately prohibited the export of scrap metal to Japan. On July 26–27, 1941, just as Japan was moving into southern Indochina, the United States, England, and Holland froze Japanese assets. A few days later, on August 1, America imposed an embargo on oil exports to Japan. The ABCD encirclement had thrown an economic noose around Tokyo's ambitions.

The United States had begun economic sanctions in 1939 by informing Japan that the 1911 Treaty of Commerce and Navigation would be terminated effective January 1940. This step was one cause of Japan's military moves toward the resources of the South Pacific. At the same time, Japanese actions in French Indochina and Thailand also threatened America, England, and Holland. A cycle of mutual provocation had begun. England had supported the American bid to deter Japan by also freezing Japanese assets, abrogating the mutual trade treaty, and joining in the economic blockade. The occupation of southern Indochina placed the great British base of Singapore within range of Japanese bombers, a grave threat to English interests in Asia. By mid-1941, relations between Japan and the ABCD countries had reached the point of no return.[8]

If the economic offensive continued, Japan would soon run out of raw materials, especially oil, and be unable to sustain the war in China. A choice had to be made: stop the fighting in China or expand it to the United States, England, and Holland to get oil. The former entailed withdrawal from China, an impossible course of action at that late date. Attacking the other countries was only a means to an end: to obtain oil for victory in China. Director of the Planning Board Suzuki Teiichi, a member of the cabinet that decided for war, has said that "although some people have charged that Japan went to war despite a lack of resources," the decision was actually made for the opposite reason: Japan went to war *because* its resources were insufficient.[9] Okazaki Ayakoto was in a position to know military attitudes at the time. As chief, second section, Ordinance Bureau, Navy Ministry, Okazaki was responsible for resources mobilization. He later wrote: "The problem was oil. If our reserves were dribbled away, Japan would grow weaker and weaker like a TB patient gasping along till he dropped dead on the road. A grim and humiliating end. However, if we could strike boldly and get the oil in the south. . . ." According to Okazaki, this kind of "[desperate] attitude was the basis for going to war."[10]

America opposed Japan's aggression against China but had no intention of intervening militarily. The attitude toward Europe was different. While mollifying the isolationists as best it could, the Roosevelt administration gradually became more deeply involved in the European war in a bid to save England and prevent a Nazi victory. Another change over the course of the New Deal years was a more liberal attitude toward communism.[11] Roosevelt had recognized the Soviet Union early in his first term. The stubborn Russian resistance to Germany won the U.S. president's respect, and he sought to improve relations with the USSR. America's attitude toward Japan gradually stiffened. When Tokyo posed a threat to the Southwest Pacific by its moves in that direction, the U.S. became determined to stop Japan even if it meant war.[12]

The United States and Japan were inexorably moving toward a bloody collision in the Pacific. Several individuals and groups tried to stop the drift toward war and stimulate productive Japan-U.S. talks. Through the efforts of Bishop James E. Walsh, a Catholic Maryknoll priest, and others who had close contacts with Japanese leaders anxious to avert war, negotiations began in Washington between Ambassador Nomura Kichisaburō and Secretary of State Cordell Hull. By this time in 1941, however, Japan had only two grim alternatives: reach a compromise with the U.S. or take the great gamble of going to war.[13] Given the vast differences between the two positions, prospects for a satisfactory resolution were dim. The American government was in no mood to compromise and insisted that Japanese troops be withdrawn from China. Tōjō Hideki, army minister in the third Konoe cabinet, spoke for the military: "The army's position is that there can be no compromise on the stationing of troops in China. It affects military morale. . . . Troop withdrawals are the heart of the matter. If we just acquiesce to the American demand, everything we have achieved in China will be lost. Manchukuo will be endangered and our control of Korea will also be jeopardized."[14] Tōjō found these compelling reasons not to budge on China. Premier Konoe, however, "thought it manifestly unwise for Japan to plunge into an unpredictable war at a time when the China incident is still unresolved." He resigned on October 16, 1941.[15]

Tōjō succeeded Konoe as premier, and the die was cast. Foreign Minister Tōgō Shigenori kept trying for a compromise on troop withdrawal that would permit an agreement with the United States. There was as little conciliatory spirit in Tokyo as in Washington. He got no support from Navy Minister Shimada Shigetarō, who at one point said: "On the basis of what I learned as commander of the China squadron, if our forces are removed our businessmen will have great difficulty in continuing their operations. Their personal safety might be endangered. Furthermore, no matter what happens on the mainland, I will oppose the removal of our forces from Hainan Island." Even previously moderate Finance Minister Kaya Okinori insisted that "My experience as president of the North China Development Company indicates that a troop presence is vital for our business enterprises in China." Tōgō felt "totally isolated, a voice crying in the dark."[16]

A war with the United States would be fought mainly at sea. No decision for war should have been made unless the navy was sure of a good chance of victory. The admirals never made such sanguine claims. Fukudome Shigeru, chief of the first division, navy general staff, bluntly told his colleagues at a meeting of army and navy division and bureau chiefs on October 6, 1941, that he "had no confidence that Japan could win the war."[17] Such candor was excruciatingly embarrassing to senior political figures. Chief of the Cabinet Secretariat Tomita Kenji appealed to Navy Chief of Staff Nagano Osami and other admirals for a candid assessment of Japan's chances for victory. According to Konoe, "The navy would not officially say it did not want the war. The admirals would only say with great force that they 'leave all decisions to the prime minister.' "[18] What an incredible paradox: the admirals agreed to a war they had no confidence of winning. Fear of an army revolt if Japan backed down carried some weight with the navy leadership.[19] Admiral Koga Mineichi found this concern misguided: "History shows that no country has been destroyed by an internal revolt. The responsible officers should have ignored the possibility of a coup d'état and courageously prevented the war."[20] Firm words, but the war had already started when Koga uttered them. It was a bit late for a storm warning; the typhoon had begun.

The decision to take military action in early December if the United States still refused to compromise was made at the Imperial Conference on November 5. Diplomacy was given a last chance; Kurusu Saburō was sent to Washington to help Ambassador Nomura in a final effort to reach an agreement. On November 26, Hull's tough memorandum containing demands for unconditional troop withdrawal from China and French Indochina, abandonment of the Wang Ching-wei regime, and other unacceptable points was presented to the Japanese representatives.[21] Now even Foreign Minister Tōgō concluded that the American response left Japan with no recourse but war. The Imperial Conference on December 1 made the final decision to fight. Japan chose war because it could not accede to U.S. demands which "ignored our national sacrifices during more than four years of the China incident."[22] As stated, the clash with America stemmed from the invasion of China and ultimately from the officer's plot at Mukden. It can hardly be overstressed that aggression against China was at the heart of the fifteen-year war.

While the negotiations in Washington edged toward their futile climax, the Pearl Harbor Strike Force left Hitokappu Bay in the Kuriles under the strictest secrecy and headed for

Hawaii. At 7:49 A.M., Sunday, December 7, carrier-based planes began their assault. They found most of the U.S. fleet at anchor and destroyed it. Invasion of the Malay Peninsula began simultaneously with the Hawaii attack. The blitzkrieg against America and England was underway.

The Japanese government had intended to inform the U.S. Department of State immediately before the attack on Pearl Harbor that diplomatic relations were broken. There were delays in Washington, however, because the embassy staff had difficulty with the last long message from Tokyo. When Nomura and Kurusu met Hull to present the final notification, the secretary of state already knew of the attack on Pearl Harbor.[23] The charge that Japan planned a perfidious attack without any prior warning is incorrect. The Nomura-Kurusu note, however, simply declared that relations were severed; it was not an explicit declaration of war. Furthermore, British forces were attacked without any advance notice. The Imperial Rescript declaring war was not issued until 11 A.M., December 8 (Tokyo time), several hours after the raid on Hawaii. This clearly violated the provisions of the Hague Convention of 1907 on the commencement of hostilities, which Japan had ratified in 1911. The first article of the convention states: "The contracting parties accept that hostilities should not be opened unless there has been an explicit prior announcement in the form of a reasoned declaration of war or a final ultimatum which includes conditions."

Japan ignored this international agreement. Domestic precedent as well was shattered by the December 8 Imperial Rescript. The rescript at the start of the Sino-Japanese War stated: "We command that our subjects make every effort in the performance of their official duties to ensure that international law is not transgressed." The Imperial Rescript for the Russo-Japanese War included a similar injunction. And the rescript declaring war on Germany in World War I said, "We also command all our competent authorities to make every effort in pursuance of their respective duties to attain the national objectives within the bounds of international law."

However, the rescript declaring war on America and Britain stated: "The entire nation with a united will shall mobilize its total strength so that nothing will miscarry in the attainment of our war aims." A phrase calling for the strict compliance with international law was intentionally omitted; international agreements and codes were openly flaunted throughout the conflict.

American intelligence knew that Japan was preparing to attack, but the Philippines were regarded as the probable target. Caught by surprise, the United States suffered its worst military disaster. The Japanese public, tired of the endless, inconclusive fighting in China, got a temporary emotional lift from the great victory. Yet the American government gained an even greater psychological advantage. By allowing Japan to strike the first blow, even the isolationists were swept up in the patriotic clamor for war and victory. Popular outrage at Japan's "sneak attack" was expressed in the slogan "Remember Pearl Harbor." American determination to avenge the humiliation at Hawaii never faltered.[24] England was also a beneficiary of the Pearl Harbor attack. Now America's enormous military potential and industrial power were brought into the conflict on Great Britain's side. From the brink of defeat, England could now anticipate the defeat of Germany and Italy and the isolation and eventual defeat of Japan.[25]

From Jubilation to Disaster

The hawks' first miscalculation was the inability to defeat China. Their second was in attacking the United States and England. A famous student of war, Mao Tse-tung, found wisdom in Sun-tzu's *Art of War:* "Know your enemy and know yourself, and you can fight a hundred battles without disaster." Mao wrote that war, the highest form of struggle, is the most difficult social phenomenon to understand correctly. Yet man inevitably goes to war and when he does, his mistakes arise from ignorance of the enemy and himself.[26]

Japan's defeat stemmed from just that "ignorance of them and us," what Ishiwara Kanji, Shigemitsu Mamoru, and other leaders later called the result of mistaken "comprehensive assessments" and "in-depth analyses." Why was Japan so tragically wrong? The reasons were twofold: (1) an educational system and internal security laws that prevented Japanese from developing the ability to perceive the historical and social realities of the world and their own country; and (2) the emasculation of academic freedom, without which objective and scientific knowledge could not be acquired and diffused. Surrounded by inaccurate information and opinions tailored to their prejudices, Japanese leaders tied the blinders over their own eyes and rushed lemming-like toward the precipice. Destruction on the rocks below was the only possible outcome.

Ikezaki Tadakata, who brandished both pen and sword as a literary critic and military commentator, wrote *Why Fear the United States?* in 1929. He said that "America has a surfeit of money and material things," but it was stupid to fear America for "just that reason." Ikezaki insisted that a comparison of Japanese and American battleships and the quality of their respective armies left no doubt about Japan's superiority. He concluded that "If at the outset Japan just seizes Guam and the Philippines, we can fight on with our bare fists if necessary." By 1932, when Ikezaki's *Taiheiyō senryaku-ron* (Strategy for the Pacific) was published, Japan's military position had slipped. The increased importance of the airplane had changed tactics, and the new fleet ratios left the Imperial Navy in a still less favorable position. Nonetheless, Ikezaki reprinted his earlier essays in the new book without change and reiterated the same line: Japan's invincibility.

Ikezaki was so committed to a strong military position that he entered politics, got elected to the Diet, and helped to carry out the military buildup of the 1930s. For all his promilitary views, Ikezaki was still a civilian. That the professional military and the senior civilians, who should have had access to all the classified information about Japan's capabilities, could share Ikezaki's simplistic notion of America as a paper tiger would seem very strange indeed. Yet the official assessment of the United States actually varied little from Ikezaki's.[27] An Imperial Conference was held on September 6, 1941, to report crucial decisions for war reached three days earlier. The background materials and supporting documents for the draft policy proposals merit lengthy citation. They were prepared by the chief, cabinet secretariat, and the chiefs, military affairs bureaus, Army and Navy Ministries.

> Although America's total defeat is judged utterly impossible, it is not inconceivable that a shift in American public opinion due to our victories in Southeast Asia or to England's surrender might bring the war to an end. At any rate, our occupation of vital areas to the South will ensure a superior strategic position. Our development of the rich resources of the region and our use of the economic strength of the Asian continent will provide the economic base for long-term self-sufficiency. By cooperating with Germany and Italy, we will shatter Anglo-American unity, link Asia and Europe, and we should be able to create an invincible military alignment.

At a meeting of the Imperial Headquarters—Cabinet Liaison Conference on November 1, 1941, Vice-chief of Staff Tsukada Isao said: "There is a strong probability that our advance to the South will enable Germany and Italy to defeat England. It will also greatly increase the probability that we can force China to surrender and then even the Soviet Union. By seizing the South, we can also strike a heavy blow at America's source of strategic materials. We should be able to ring off Asia, conquer those countries hostile to us one by one, and defeat America and England. If England falls, America should reconsider." Tsukada immediately added a significant reservation: "There is, of course, no way of knowing what the strategic, political, or diplomatic situation will be five years from now."[28] At the same meeting Nagano Osami, chief, navy general staff, said, "We can fight effectively for about two years, but no prediction can be made for after that."[29] This statement shows that neither the army nor the navy was certain of success. Premier Tōjō said at the same meeting: "In war a reasonable prospect of victory is enough. Even if there is apprehension that we may be defeated, the nation should trust the military and move ahead."[30] The truth was that the military were in a dilemma over whether to continue the war in China or withdraw all Japanese forces with the attendant loss of special economic rights. They plunged the country into war with America and England in the hope of cutting the Gordian knot in China.

The prowar faction could not have advocated an attack on the U.S. and England without optimistic assessments that, as a result, Japan could continue the war or at least prosecute it for a longer period and more effectively. Indeed, they could not possibly have recognized the prospect of certain defeat and still insisted on going to war. The ability to sustain hostilities against the United States depended completely on whether Japan could transport sufficient petroleum from the Dutch East Indies to the home islands and to operational areas. An adequate supply of oil depended on the nation's capacity to maintain enough tankers in service, taking into consideration losses from enemy attacks. The military officers responsible for calculating shipping losses, replacements, and supply feasibility came up with extremely optimistic conclusions.[31] Civilians showed the same tendency to view the world through rose-colored glasses. At the Imperial Headquarters–Liaison Conference noted above, Finance Minister Kaya Okinori and President of the Planning Board Suzuki Teiichi stated that "food supply is not much of a problem."[32] These judgments show beyond any doubt that the decision makers overestimated Japan's strength and underestimated the enemy's ability to counterattack.

The possibility of air raids on Japan was also treated cavalierly. For example, the *Asahi Gurafu* on September 29, 1937, carried a picture of people passing water buckets by hand. One was saying, "They dropped incendiary bombs." The caption said, "Wartime air raid drill." The same journal on December 7, 1938, carried a similar photograph with the caption: "This is how we can defend our cities of wooden houses and buildings." The pictures and instructions became a bit more specific though no more realistic under the threat of imminent Allied air raids. The *Asahi Gurafu* of April 14, 1943, showed a picture of incendiary bombs with the caption, "Don't be afraid of this bomb. Characteristics of and defense against large incendiary bombs." As the pictures and text showed, Japan's leaders planned to defend cities against air attack by the use of bucket brigades manned by neighborhood associations. Defense against modern aerial warfare was to be handled by volunteer firemen. On the basis of such casual assumptions the hawks pushed for war.

Shoddy analysis of America's war potential was but one case of the extreme lack of objectivity in planning. Among the major elements that contributed to the optimistic predictions about the war were the high evaluation of Germany and the denigration of British and Russian military capacity. The army was particularly prone to the former error because of the influence of officers who had studied in Germany; until late 1943, officers firmly convinced of German victory were the mainstream of the army.[33] In the navy as well there were intelligence specialists who predicted that German air power and submarines would defeat England.[34] The military comprehension of world power relationships suffered from a subjective astigmatism.[35]

Some perceptive Japanese, of course, knew that attacking America and England was the height of folly. In the midst of the excitement about sinking the U.S. fleet at Pearl Harbor, Onozuka Kiheiji, former president of Tokyo Imperial University, whispered to a colleague in the dining hall, "This means that Japan is sunk too."[36] A considerable number of ordinary citizens also sensed that "We had started something really stupid" that would end in tragedy.[37] However, these perceptions had already been blocked out from the national decision-making process. This was true for even those members of the political elite who belonged to the cautious school of thought.[38] Their point of view is seen in comments made at the Senior Statesmen's Conference by Wakatsuki Reijirō: "Do we have adequate resources for a long war or not? The government has presented its estimates, but I am still concerned about this problem." Yonai Mitsumasa said, "In attempting to prevent Japan from being gradually weakened and reduced to a minor power by embargoes, pressure to withdraw from China, and so on, the government should be very careful that the result is not instead our rapid defeat and destruction." Premier Tōjō no longer paid any attention to these doubts. His standard reply was, "Please have trust in the government."[39]

Good luck seemed to be on Tokyo's side. The Pearl Harbor strike force reached its target undetected and caught the U.S. Navy napping.[40] The landing on the Malay Peninsula was also a success, and on December 10 Japanese bombers sank the new British battleship *Prince of Wales* and the heavy cruiser *Repulse,* virtually destroying England's Far Eastern squadron. Saitō Mokichi's song[41] caught the public mood. "More victory news on the radio! I can't sit still, the excitement, the joy. Aren't our men superb, divine heroes in action." A jubilant public cheered this string of triumphs.[42] The victories assuaged a latent Japanese inferiority complex toward two of the great world powers, America and England. Military successes also temporarily dispelled the foreboding over the stalemate in China and the guilty second thoughts over aggression on the continent. However, in view of the fact that the expanded war grew out of the deadlock in China, it was in no sense an Oriental counterattack against Western imperialism, as some revisionists assert. Even those leaders who believed that the new war would definitely improve the overall military situation had mixed emotions. Crippling the British and American fleets temporarily was one thing; conquering China was another. No wonder that some Japanese were overwhelmed with despair at the thought that the nation had started down the road to ruin.

Germany and Italy declared war on the United States the

day after the sinking of the *Prince of Wales* and the *Repulse,* December 11, 1941. The separate and localized fighting in the Far East and Europe now merged into a truly global struggle, World War II. The German offensive against Moscow was stalling, and the Soviet Union was about to launch a counterattack. Germany was on the brink of retreat when Japan joined the fray, just in time to share a roller coaster ride to disaster.

But defeat was unthinkable in the early months: the carefully planned "Oriental blitzkrieg" advanced with clockwork precision. Hong Kong was occupied on December 25 and the expeditionary force in the Philippines seized Manila on January 2, 1942. Units in the South Pacific occupied Rabaul on January 23, and on February 15 paratroop units seized Sumatra's Palembang oil fields. Singapore surrendered the same day. The victories continued: Batavia on the island of Java was occupied on March 5; Rangoon, three days later; on May 27 stubborn American and Filipino resistance ended and Corregidor surrendered; and by the end of the month nearly all of Burma was under Imperial Army control. The six-month offensive had taken the Japanese military into a vast region bordered on the east by the Indonesian archipelago and on the west by Burma. Throughout Japan small Rising Sun flags were stuck into maps of Asia to mark the swath cut by the Imperial Army.

Disaster was equally swift and overwhelming. The attack on Midway Island, planned by Commander in Chief of the Combined Fleet Yamamoto Isoroku, an instant military genius after his Pearl Harbor feat, was carried out despite strong staff objections. An American carrier squadron surprised the Japanese fleet and sank four irreplaceable carriers on one day, June 5, 1942, a catastrophic loss.[43] Japan's offensive capability was blunted, although the defeat was concealed from the public. The Allied counteroffensive was underway far faster than anticipated. U.S. forces landed on Guadalcanal on August 7. The Japanese garrison, its air supremacy gone and its food supplies cut off, was reduced to starvation. After suffering enormous casualties, Japanese forces abandoned the island on December 31, 1942. The retreat was disguised as a "strategic withdrawal," but the public got its first faint whiff of defeat. The ghastly battle for Guadalcanal was described in *Gadarukanaru-sen shishū* (Poems from the Battle of Guadalcanal) by Yoshida Kashichi, a noncommissioned officer who survived the ordeal.

> No matter how far we walk
> We don't know where we're going
> Trudging along under dark jungle growth
>
> When will this march end?
> Hide during the day
> Move at night
> Deep in the lush Guadalcanal jungle
>
> Our rice is gone
> Eating roots and grass
> Along the ridges and cliffs
> Leaves hide the trail, we lose our way
> Stumble and get up, fall and get up
>
> Covered with mud from our falls
> Blood oozes from our wounds
> No cloth to bind our cuts
> Flies swarm to the scabs
> No strength to brush them away
> Fall down and cannot move
> How many times I've thought of suicide.[44]

By the end of the war every battlefield survivor had gone through as bad or worse than Guadalcanal.

The Allied counteroffensive advanced steadily in 1943. Combined Fleet Commander Yamamoto was killed when his plane was ambushed and shot down on April 18. Attu Island in the Aleutian chain, which had been occupied in June 1942, was recaptured by American forces on May 29 with the loss of all Japanese defenders. Cut off and without reinforcements, the garrison was left to be wiped out. The government called this miserable fate "an honorable death." U.S. forces continued their island-hopping campaign, and one Japanese garrison after another went to its "honorable death."

In the European theater, Soviet forces went on the offensive in late 1942 in the bitterly contested Stalingrad area and forced a German surrender in February 1943. In July 1943 Mussolini fell from power, and the Badoglio government surrendered to the Allies on September 8. One leg of the Axis triumvirate had been sheared off. The Cairo Declaration, signed by Roosevelt, Churchill, and Chiang Kai-shek on November 27, 1943, stated that Manchuria and Taiwan would be returned to China, Korea would regain its independence, and Japan would be deprived of its Pacific island possessions. The Allies agreed to fight on until Japan surrendered unconditionally. At the Teheran Conference, which began on November 28, Premier Stalin acceded to U.S. requests and secretly promised to enter the war against Japan. The Allies had major disagreements about immediate strategic priorities and postwar planning. The Soviet Union, which had been fighting almost singlehandedly against Germany, wanted England and America to open a second front in France quickly. Churchill preferred to concentrate military operations in the Mediterranean. Similar differences arose later between British (England wanted to recapture Singapore) and American-Chinese priorities. The wartime conferences never really resolved the conflicting objectives, but Allied cooperation did not break down, as the Japanese military had hoped. The alliance held together until after Japan's defeat.[45]

As the war progressed, the vast differences between Japanese and American military industrial production capacity was manifested in air power, naval tonnage replacement, battlefield equipment, front-line supply capability, and so on. Mainly due to overwhelmingly superior American air power, the Japanese navy lost control of the seas. The Pacific island front collapsed: Tarawa and Makin fell in November 1943 and Kwajalein in February 1944; the defenders were wiped out almost to the last man. A massive U.S. air attack on Truk caused enormous losses of men and equipment. At the battle of the Philippine Sea in June 1944, Task Force 58 lost its flagship, the giant carrier *Taihō,* and two other carriers. In a desperate attempt to stop a U.S. landing in the Philippines, the navy suffered a mortal defeat in the battle of Leyte Gulf. The Imperial Navy no longer existed as a fighting force. Japan's fleet had the world's largest battleships, the *Yamato* and the *Musashi,* with displacements of 64,000 tons and equipped with nine 46-centimeter cannons.[46] The rapid development of aircraft, however, made battleship cannons obsolete. The *Musashi* was sunk by air attack at Leyte Gulf. Another doomed behemoth, the 70,000-ton *Shinano,* the largest aircraft carrier in the world, was sunk by a submarine off the Kii Peninsula on its maiden voyage in November 1944.[47]

Japanese forces fared no better on land when they launched an invasion of India from Burma. The Imphal campaign of 1944 was inspired by high political considerations and mean personal ambition. On one hand, the prestige of Changar Bose's Provisional Indian Government was a consideration. On the other, General Mutaguchi Yukiya, commander, 15th Army, was motivated by personal ambition for fame and glory. A regimental commander during the Marco Polo Bridge clash, Mutaguchi used to say: "I fired the first shot at the Marco Polo Bridge and started the war. I think I'm the one to finish it up." Mutaguchi started the offensive without a food resupply plan; the troops were to eat their draft animals and forage for edible plants. Their heaviest weapons were mountain mortars and they had only a small quantity of ammunition. Inadequately prepared, the 15th Army advanced into the unexplored, forbidding mountain district between Burma and India. The British Indian Army held an area honeycombed with strong points defended by artillery and tanks, and had air support and ample ammunition and rations. When the British counterattacked, the Japanese could not possibly hold them off.

Front-line division commanders were appalled at the certain annihilation of their units from starvation and enemy action if they continued the hopeless operation without supplies. Yanagida Genzō, commander, 33rd Division, and others who were furious at the obstinate stupidity of headquarters, repeatedly requested permission to retreat. Mutaguchi flatly rejected the requests and ordered them to hold their positions. One commanding general, Satō Yukinori of the 31st Division, broke off radio communication and began to withdraw. Mutaguchi removed Satō, Yanagida, and Yamanouchi Masafumi, commander, 15th Division, who had collapsed from illness. The dismissal of three division commanders was without precedent in the history of the Imperial Army. By early July the whole force had to be withdrawn. Their food and ammunition gone, decimated by malaria, an exhausted Japanese army limped back into Burma. The wounded and sick who collapsed on the road were forced to commit suicide; no medical care or transportation was available. The army's route was marked by heaps of corpses, gruesome mile markers for a campaign of "monumental folly and death." The 15th Army started with approximately 100,000 men. About 30,000 were killed in combat and another 20,000 died from illness. Approximately half of the 50,000 survivors were sick.[48] This ridiculous offensive was a miniature version of the Pacific War. The British Indian Army pressed the attack and advanced into Burma. The Burmese Army revolted against Japanese forces, Rangoon fell in May 1945, and Burma was lost.

The U.S. offensive to retake the Philippines started with landings at Leyte in October 1944 and Luzon in January 1945. Filipino guerrillas launched attacks in cooperation with the American drive. Japanese units were cut to pieces and stragglers scattered to the hills. They were driven deeper and deeper into the jungle by relentless enemy attacks and exhausted from lack of food. The privation and suffering was worse than Guadalcanal; the total defeat was the same.[49] The Saipan garrison withstood fierce U.S. attacks and inflicted heavy casualties before being destroyed.[50] Saipan's fall was a heavy blow because the American air force was now able to launch direct bombing runs on Japan's main islands.

The military setbacks finally sent political shock waves through Tokyo. Tōjō Hideki had seemed like a dictator because he was simultaneously premier and chief of the army general staff, and dominated Navy Minister Shimada Shigetarō. Yet that preeminence was more nominal than real, and dissatisfaction with Tōjō's incompetence and vindictiveness had gradually increased. The *jūshin,* a group of former premiers, agreed that Tōjō would have to go. They forced the cabinet to resign in July 1944.[51] Koiso Kuniaki formed a new cabinet and set up the Supreme Council for the Direction of the War to improve coordination between the government and the armed services. Efforts to formulate and coordinate fundamental policies were still stymied by the independence of the supreme command. Even at this level of the government, ending the war could not be discussed.

American bombers based in the Marianas first attacked Tokyo in November 1944 with a raid by eighty B-29s. The U.S. Air Force had complete control of the skies over Japan. American ground forces landed on Iwo Jima, midway between Saipan and Tokyo. The garrison was wiped out after more than a month of bitter fighting, and the island was in American hands by about March 22, 1945.[52] Japan was now within much easier striking range for U.S. pilots. Massive air raids on Tokyo on March 10 and May 24–25 gutted major parts of the city. Nagoya, Osaka, Yokohama, and Kobe were burned out by incendiary attacks, and in June the smaller provincial cities came under the aerial torch. American forces began landing on Okinawa in April. Special Attack planes were first used during the battle for Leyte Gulf; by the time Okinawa came under attack, the military had no other weapons to "develop." The giant battleship *Yamato* had been placed in reserve for the final defense of the home islands. Most of the remaining supply of heavy oil was used to send the Second Fleet on a suicide mission against the U.S. forces attacking Okinawa. The *Yamato* got only a few miles off Kyushu when American carrier planes struck and Japan's last capital ship was lost.[53] The Okinawa garrison had been driven to the southern part of the main island when on June 22 the commander, Ushijima Mitsuru, and other officers committed suicide (civilian governor Shimada Satoshi also apparently took his own life). Approximately 110,000 Japanese troops were killed, and American forces held a corner of Japan proper.[54]

In Europe Allied forces had opened a second front in June 1944 with the invasion of northern France, and Germany was caught in a great pincer movement. In August French partisans began an armed revolt; then Paris was liberated. German forces had occupied Italy after the Badoglio government surrendered, but anti-Fascist Italians had continued the resistance. Mussolini was killed by partisans in April 1945. The Italians then attacked German units and played a role in the American offensive that liberated Italy. When the Red Army entered Berlin in April 1945, Hitler committed suicide in his bunker. In May the German Army surrendered unconditionally. The war in Europe was over, and Japan was now isolated. Other nations declared war on Tokyo, bringing the total to more than fifty. Japan was now at war with over half the world.

At the Yalta Conference in February 1945, the Soviet Union had formally promised to enter the war against Japan. As part of the secret agreement, the United States agreed to recognize the return of Sakhalin and the Kuriles to the Soviet Union after the war. When Roosevelt died in April, Harry S Truman became president. The Allied Powers began the San Francisco meetings and in June the United Nations Charter was signed. The Potsdam Conference to deal with Germany and other postwar problems began in July. The Potsdam Declaration, which specified surrender terms for Japan, was issued by the United States, England, and China (Although the USSR was a participant, it had not yet declared war on Japan and was not a signatory).

The Suzuki Kantarō cabinet had replaced the Koiso cabinet in April. The shift was a halting, indirect move toward ending the war, but Premier Suzuki blundered into an announcement that Japan would "ignore" the Potsdam Declaration. The Allies interpreted this response as a rejection of their surrender demand and concluded that Japan would fight to the bitter end.[55] America's secret work on the atomic bomb had resulted in the successful explosion of a nuclear device in July at Alamogordo, New Mexico. Some scientists objected to the use of the atomic bomb and urged delay or alternatives. Government leaders, however, in a move to break Japan's will to resist and to avoid the huge casualties expected in a landing on the home islands, went ahead with plans to use the bomb and obliterated Hiroshima on August 6 and Nagasaki three days later.[56] Acting on the secret agreement made at Yalta, the Soviet Union declared war on Japan on August 8 and launched a general offensive in Manchuria, northern Korea, and Sakhalin.[57]

The twin blows of the atomic bombings and the Soviet attack showed Japan's leaders that the war could not be continued. The flow of war materials from Southeast Asia had already been cut off by American submarines and mines dropped by airplanes along Japan's coast and in the Inland Sea.[58] By early 1945 few refineries had any oil to refine, aluminum plants had no bauxite, steel plants had neither iron ore nor coke. Production had ground to a halt. There was no gas for airplanes and no aluminum to make more planes. Without oil or steel, modern warfare was impossible. Intensified air attacks from early in 1945 on took a heavy toll of arms factories; production slowed further or ceased altogether. Japan was simply no match for the Allies with their weaponry and abundant supplies.[59] The army drafted middle-aged and physically unfit men and talked of the decisive battle for the home islands. But these recruits had no weapons. The brave talk about holding off the enemy with bamboo spears turned out not to be just rhetoric: It was to be a martial virtue born of necessity.

The awful denouement was an inevitable result of the strategic miscalculation of attacking both America and England. Japan's leaders shifted the blame to the citizenry, as if the populace had been inadequate to the task. The Japanese people were made to feel they had not tried hard enough.[60] The government used slogans like "Haven't we been lacking in dedication?" in rallies to foster greater efforts. The "approved" answer was, "We haven't tried enough. We must be more loyal." More thousands "determined to do better" were sent off to perish in a lost cause.

Until this stage in the war, Japanese troops had fought bravely despite terrible disparities in weapons and equipment. Japanese technology and industrial productivity had also accomplished some outstanding feats in weaponry: the superships *Yamato* and *Musashi*; the I-type model 400 submarine, which carried three fighter planes and could operate at sea for four months;[61] the superior Zero aircraft;[62] the No. 93 torpedo, which was twice as powerful as any turned out in America and England.[63] Yet there were fatal gaps in military technology. Japanese radar was never even adequate,[64] and during the war America completely outclassed Japan in aircraft production. While America was putting enormous scientific resources into the atomic bomb project, Japan was developing a technique of attaching bombs to balloons made of *konnyaku* (a gelatinous paste made from the Devil's Tongue plant) and launching them against the American West Coast. Washington was tapping the atom and on the verge of a new era in civilization; Tokyo was playing around with windmills in quixotic futility. In the end everything failed and the nation's fate rode on another wind, the Kamikaze units, those brave young men sent on one-way flights to death.[65]

Japan was defeated by America's enormous economic and productive power. Yet an outlook that regarded life so cheaply and devised the Kamikaze attacks was at the root of all Japan's misadventures. The spiritual qualities of the West—the freedom and dynamism behind Roosevelt's policies—were overlooked. Only American material strength was considered (and that not very well). Japan sought an "alliance" with the depraved Nazi regime, overestimated German power, and failed to perceive that a democratic spirit could generate more effective war power than a "patriotism" produced by dictatorship and oppression. This fundamental misunderstanding of the strengths of a free society was more serious than miscounting the output of southern California's airplane factories.

According to statistics released by the Ministry of Health and Welfare in the Diet in 1956, Japanese deaths from July 1937 to August 1945 from combat, combat-related injuries, and war-related fatal illnesses (military and civilians working for the military) amounted to about 2.3 million. The figure does not include tens of thousands missing and never accounted for.[66] This inglorious body count is the price the Japanese people paid for their leaders' folly.

8

The Greater East Asia Co-Prosperity Sphere: Liberation or Exploitation?

At home and abroad, a potpourri of moral imperatives was used to justify the Pacific War. The thrust into Manchuria was explained as "the right of self-defense." The puppet regime of Manchukuo was described as "the formation of a virtuous state" and "the cooperation of the five races." The former was a claim that Manchukuo would be an ideal state following "the righteous way," a Chinese utopian notion of social harmony and justice; the latter asserted racial harmony of Chinese, Manchus, Koreans, Mongolians, and Japanese. Full-scale hostilities against China were for lofty goals: "To chastise the insolent Chinese"; "the construction of a regenerated China"; "the unity of Japan, Manchukuo, and China"; and "the construction of a new East Asian order." Fresh rationales were proffered to explain the start of hostilities against America and England. Negotiations were broken off with America in order to protect "the Empire's position as the stabilizing force of Asia." War was declared because "Our Empire for its existence and self-defense has no other recourse." Candid assertions of national interest were mixed with professions of Asian solidarity.

Japan's advance into Southeast Asia allegedly had the twin objectives of "building a Greater East Asia Co-Prosperity Sphere" and liberating Asians from "American and British imperialism." As if to give substance to these claims of a new pan-Asian solidarity, in 1943 Burma and the Philippines were declared "independent" and an Indian Provisional government was established in Singapore. In November 1943 the leaders of Manchukuo, the Wang Ching-wei regime, Thailand, the Philippines, and Burma were assembled in Japan for a Greater East Asia Conference. The name Greater East Asian War was chosen to convey a sense of a new Asia throwing off the West. But were the areas of Asia that fell under Japanese control and military occupation really "liberated?" Did they enjoy "co-prosperity"? A careful examination of the realities of the Greater East Asia Co-Prosperity Sphere is crucial to an understanding of the war.

The term Greater East Asia Co-Prosperity Sphere did not mean an egalitarian solidarity encompassing the complete independence and equality of all Asian peoples. Japan's special interests were to take precedence in the region. Japan would be the political leader of the new Asia, "responsible for governance and guidance . . . of those peoples who lacked the capacity for independence." And Tokyo would "retain a preferential position in the development of those resources in the region essential for national security."[1] In March 1941 the Imperial Rule Assistance Association published "Basic Concepts of the Greater East Asia Co-Prosperity Sphere," which explicitly stated: "Although we use the expression 'Asian cooperation,' this by no means ignores the fact that Japan was created by the Gods or posits an automatic racial equality." In other words, some Asians were more equal than others. In fact, the assumption of Japanese superiority permeated relations with the rest of Asia. The Japanese Literature Patriotic Association organized a conference of writers and literary people from the Greater East Asia Co-Prosperity Sphere. Apparently taking pan-Asianism seriously, Kaneko Mitsuharu wondered if intellectuals from other countries could really accept Japan's spirit of *hakkō ichiu* (the eight corners of the world under one roof). This brought a sharp rebuke from Nakayama Shozaburō, a conference organizer: "They are not 'intellectuals from other countries.' They are members of the Co-Prosperity Sphere assembled under the august authority of the Emperor."[2]

In the highest government councils no time or sentiment was wasted on the rhetoric of solidarity. At an Imperial Conference on November 5, 1941, Finance Minister Kaya Okinori explained occupation policy for Southeast Asia: "We must ignore for the present the economic dislocation in that area and push vigorously ahead with our plans."[3] Policy for the administration of the southeast Asian occupied areas approved by a Liaison Conference on November 20, 1941, contained the following: "The local economy will be strictly controlled in order to facilitate our acquisition of essential war materials and the self-support of the occupation forces. Requests for relaxation of controls must not be allowed to interfere with these objectives." The policy directive continued: "Independence movements by the local peoples must not be encouraged for the time being."[4,5] At the Liaison Conference on March 14, 1942, Hoshino Naoki, chief cabinet secretary, said: "There are no restrictions on us. These were enemy possessions. We can take them, do anything we want to." Suzuki Teiichi, chief of the Planning Board, and Finance Minister Kaya insisted that "There should be a long period of military government. We must not promise independence to the local peoples or encourage any willful ambitions."[6] The plans for the military administration of occupied areas drawn up the same month contain the following: "Industry: The southern region for the present will be a source of raw materials and a market for our manufactured products. Measures will be taken to prevent the development of industry in this area. Wages will be kept as low as possible."[7] Even when independence was subsequently granted, as with Burma and the Philippines, it was more nominal than real. Japan insisted upon keeping complete control of the military affairs and foreign relations of both countries.[8] The southeast Asian region was used as a colonial territory just like Korea and Manchukuo.

As prologue to a detailed analysis of the vast region where these policies were implemented during the Pacific War, it is appropriate to consider the prewar Japanese colonies. Yanaihara Tadao, writing in *Kashin* in March 1941, called the colonies a litmus paper of Japan's larger pretensions. To ignore "how these non-Japanese peoples in the Empire are administered . . . and talk about unselfish and amicable policies toward Manchuria and China is pointless." The rough and exploitative rule of the colonies "contradicted the declarations of racial harmony toward Manchuria and China."[9] Yanaihara realized that the treatment of the colonial populations of Korea and Taiwan foreshadowed conditions in the Greater East Asia Co-Prosperity Sphere.

Korea

If Japan really intended to liberate the peoples of Asia from imperialism, independence for Korea should have been the first step. Anticolonialism should have begun at home. On the contrary, however, the planners of the Manchurian Incident testified that one motive for it was to ensure Japanese control over Korea.[10] A decade later independence for the people in the southern area was a sensitive subject "because there is also Korea to consider."[11] National leaders feared that the "liberation" of Western colonies might set a precedent for the Japanese empire. Yet Korea would not have been granted independence even if Japan had won the war. In June 1945 Japanese leaders unofficially sounded out American intentions as part of an effort to end the war. Even at that late date, pounded by daily air raids and facing certain defeat, the government's position was that "Taiwan and Korea are absolutely vital sources of food. Because they are essential to Japan's existence, we desire to be allowed to retain them."[12] The annexation of Korea in 1910 started Japan on the road to empire and aggression; the attempt to hang on to Korea in 1945 prolonged the final agony of defeat.

Independence for Korea was out of the question, of course, as far as Japanese leaders were concerned. Local self-rule and the franchise were permitted only to a token degree. The first moves in the 1920s were a sop to nationalist unrest. In 1933 local self-government was slightly expanded, but it was still tokenism. One-third of provincial assemblymen were designated by the governors (themselves appointed by the governor general); the remainder were indirectly elected by the metropolitan district councils and by rural district council members.[13] Important positions in the government were reserved for Japanese; salaries of Korean officials were lower than for the Japanese.[14] When Korean cooperation became essential for the war effort after 1937, including the enforcement of military conscription because of manpower shortages, certain reforms were enacted. They included the abolition of salary differences for Japanese and Korean officials and the right to elect representatives to the Diet (although in a very circumscribed way compared to Japan proper). These "reforms" were simply wartime expedients.[15]

Discrimination against Koreans was all-pervasive. The results of discriminatory education and employment policies are seen most graphically in standards of living and life expectancy. Average per capita income in 1944, for example, was ¥558 in Japan and ¥156 in Korea; Koreans earned a little less than one-third the income of Japanese.[16] The vast disparity in sanitary conditions is apparent from health statistics: of the Japanese who contracted contagious diseases in 1937, 13.1 percent died, compared to 30.5 percent of Koreans.[17] Far from being eliminated during the war to "liberate Asia," contempt for and discrimination against Koreans actually intensified. Police surveillance and harassment on trains and on the boats from Pusan to Shimonoseki became very harsh; beating and kicking of suspects were commonplace.[18] Even Korean draftees were verbally abused with racial slurs like "Don't get the idea that you are Japanese. Watch your step." Many a Korean was told, "Now you can get into the Imperial Army, so put up with a little shit along the way."[19]

Civilian life was no different as far as discrimination was concerned. Japanese employees in the Hungnam factory complex in northern Korea were provided with brick houses equipped with flush toilets, electric cooking utensils, and steam heat. Company housing for Koreans was cramped. Common toilets, common water taps, and *ondol* heating were deemed adequate. The Japanese management saw nothing improper about these disparities.[20]

While separate and unequal treatment was the rule, the government adopted and enforced a strict assimilation policy to turn Koreans into loyal if second-class citizens. The Korean language was banned from the schools.[21] Koreans were required to recite the Oath of a Loyal Citizen: "We are subjects of the Great Japanese Empire. We are loyal to His Imperial Majesty the Emperor."[22] After 1939, Koreans were "encouraged" to take Japanese surnames and stop using their Korean names.[23] All Koreans were required to attend Shintō services; Christians were singled out for special persecution through shrine attendance and in other ways.[24] Mandatory performance of Shintō rituals was especially repugnant, as shown by the fact that in an eight-day period after Japan surrendered in 1945, Koreans burned and destroyed 136 Shintō shrines and buildings where the imperial photograph was on display.[25]

As manpower shortages developed in the late 1930s, plans were made to utilize Korean labor. A large-scale forced transfer of Korean laborers to Japan was carried out after 1941.[26] Kim Dae-sik had a not untypical experience. He tried to evade the labor mobilization but was caught in 1943 and taken off in handcuffs to work in a coal mine in Kyushu. A Japanese student called up for labor service to construct an airfield on Tanegashima later recalled that although "Koreans were the hardest workers . . . they were frequently beaten with wooden clubs."[27] Manpower requirements prompted special laws to permit Koreans to serve in the military. Koreans could "volunteer" for the Japanese army after 1938 and the navy by 1943.[28] Later conscription was extended to Korea. Approximately 187,000 soldiers and more than 22,000 sailors came from the colony. If forced laborers are included, a total of 370,000 Koreans were pressed into war duty.[29] Korean women were also mobilized by the thousands and shipped off to the battlefronts as "comfort girls" for Japanese troops.

Called Chōsenpi (*pi* was soldiers' slang for "comfort girl"), they were a sexual outlet for the soldiers. The women were brought right to the front lines for fornication between combat operations, and apparently many were killed in the fighting.[30]

Within Korea, resistance was virtually impossible. Outside the country, groups led by Kim Il-song and others allied with Chinese guerrillas fought against Japanese forces in Manchuria.[31]

Taiwan

The colonial rule of Taiwan closely resembled the administration of Korea. Taiwanese were permitted fewer political rights than Koreans. Local self-government was expanded in 1935, yet half of the prefectural council members were appointed and the other half were indirectly elected by city council and town and village committee members.[32]

The Japanese language was mandatory; Chinese-language columns were prohibited in Taiwanese newspapers. It was a callous and premature policy. Taiwanese were denied Chinese-language materials before they had really learned Japanese. Functional illiteracy and cultural deprivation were the results. Efforts to switch to Roman letters and to devise a new script failed because of official antagonism.[33] Nakazawa Hiroki caught the sense of angry frustration when he asked a Taiwanese friend if Japan had acted badly on the island. The Taiwanese promptly replied, "Our language has been stolen from us."[34]

Kwantung

Discrimination and forced assimilation also characterized Japanese administration of the Kwantung Leased Territory. A few first-person accounts and anecdotal vignettes will give the flavor of Japanese rule there. A Japanese woman raised in Dairen recalled her early views of the Chinese: "It never seemed strange or unnatural to me that everyone doing manual labor—coolies, horse drivers, jinricksha pullers—and the beggars, all the lowest dirtiest jobs were done by Chinese. . . . To me as a young child, all Chinese were dirty, lazy, and tricky."[35] (A Japanese woman who had lived with her family in Taegu, Korea, until she returned to Japan to enter college grew up with a similar sense of a natural order with the Japanese on top. She described to a classmate how in Korea only Koreans hauled night soil and collected garbage and trash. She was shocked to see Japanese doing such menial work when she returned to Japan. It made her feel very uncomfortable.)[36] Discrimination was so total, so taken for granted, that no one thought about it. A Chinese student from Dairen recounted many tales of discrimination against Chinese. In Dairen rice was distributed to Japanese but not to Chinese. She came from a rich merchant family which could buy blackmarket rice and did not personally suffer. But the discrimination followed her to Japan because she had never been issued a rice allotment book and still did not have one! She also said that only when she came to Japan did she realize that not all Japanese were bad.[37] These episodes attest to how the Japanese treated the local populace.

Indoctrination reinforced Japanese superiority. Asō Fumiko, a teacher in Kwantung, described how Chinese children were taught that they were "Imperial subjects." When they asked what nationality a "Imperial subject" was, she told them a subject was precisely that, a subject, and although they were not Japanese, they must work for the emperor.[38]

Manchukuo

The Japanese army's systematic violation of domestic and international law in Manchuria has been discussed earlier. The illegitimate offspring of that sustained criminality, Manchukuo, was not the moral entity advertised in slogans like "the virtuous state." Cabinet decisions in March 1932 showed the region's real function: "Manchuria and Mongolia will be the first line of defense against the Soviet Union and China." In order to "attain and expand our national interests . . . a de facto relationship will be established" with the new state, and "we will endeavor to make [Manchukuo] a fait accompli."[39] The last point expressed the government's determination not to be swayed by criticism or other countries' refusal to recognize Manchukuo. From its inception, the new state was an instrument of Japanese military and economic power; the welfare of the inhabitants never entered into the strategic equation.

Basic policy guidelines for Manchukuo were approved by the cabinet in August 1933. The new state was to be "guided" by Japanese nationals employed by the Manchukuo government. Behind this civilian façade was the unchallengeable authority of the Kwantung Army Commander who also served as ambassador to Manchukuo. Neither political parties nor political organizations were permitted. Transportation, communication, national defense, and internal security were all placed under Japanese control.[40] The Kwantung Army commander's "Basic Concepts for Manchukuo," dated September 11, 1936, stated: "The Emperor of Manchukuo reigns by virtue of the divine will, the august will of the Emperor. He serves the Emperor and his sovereignty inheres from the splendid harmony he attains with the divine will. . . . The Kwantung Army Commander, as the Emperor's representative, is the guardian of the Emperor Pu-yi."[41] The conclusion of the Japan-Manchukuo Protocol in September 1932 confirmed the administrative agreements: Manchukuo's national defense was entrusted to Japan; defense expenditures would be borne by Manchukuo; the management and construction of railroads, port facilities, etc., required by the Japanese military would be entrusted to Japan; and Japanese recommended by the Kwantung Army commander were to be appointed counselors.[42]

This pattern of sustained manipulation and control suggests that Japan was no benign midwife who withdrew after a diffi-

cult delivery and allowed its progeny to develop as an autonomous state. The new "state" was less a creature of Tokyo,
however, than of the Kwantung Army. Pu-yi, the "Emperor
of Manchukuo," dreamed of restoring a Manchu dynasty. In
the daytime world of bayonets and power politics, his prerogatives were far from royal. The Kwantung Army regulated
every aspect of his public appearances. All his questions to
subordinates about government affairs drew a standard reply,
"The [Japanese] vice-chief handles that," or "You must also
ask the vice-chief." Pu-yi visited Japan in 1940 and received
replicas of the three sacred regalia from the emperor—a
sword, a bronze mirror, and the curved necklace. Upon his
return to Manchukuo, he was required to erect a national
Shintō shrine and to worship Amaterasu Omikami. "Emperor" Pu-yi personally had no illusions about his status.
Looking back years later, he felt he had been nothing more
than a Japanese puppet.[43]

Manchukuo's material base was as foreign dominated as the
political superstructure. Only 2 percent of capital investment
funds were by third country nationals and 1 percent was local
private capital compared to 40 percent Manchukuo state capital and 57 percent Japanese capital. Moreover, Manchukuo
state capital came from the government and the Manchurian
Heavy Industry Company, both Japanese controlled and
financed. Thus Japanese capital accounted for almost all investment. Japanese capital totally controlled transportation,
communications, new heavy industry, and the exploitation of
natural resources for that industry.[44] Manchukuo's economy
was completely subordinated to Japanese capital.

How the Japanese behaved in Manchukuo showed what the
new "state" really was: they acted as if they were in the
colonies. One long-time resident later wrote: "There were
Japanese who rode in horse cabs and then refused to pay. If
the driver demanded payment, they beat him half to death. If
the Chinaman protested to the police, the authorities always
accepted the Japanese's version even if he was in the wrong.
These things happened all the time."[45] The Japanese military

were the worst offenders. Novelist Takami Jun witnessed an incident in Harbin in November 1944 in which a first lieutenant in uniform was annoying a cabaret dancer. Unable to put up with it anymore, she finally slapped his face and ran away. The officer chased her into the dressing room and forced her to dance.[46]

The local economy was systematically looted. First, the peasants' land was seized to provide land for settlers from Japan. Many of these peasants later joined guerrilla bands and fought against Japan.[47] Second, forced labor was dragooned in the most pitiful ways. Yoshimura Mitsuo described one of these roundups: "As the war situation grew worse, the labor mobilization degenerated into abduction. Men traveling on the road near Nankuan were forcibly stopped and loaded on waiting trucks. Some were taken by the hands and feet and thrown bodily up into the vehicles. These hapless victims included persons who had just come in from the country to buy something and men returning from a visit with friends. One young man was to be married the next day and had just stepped out to make a purchase."[48] The seizure of human beings was a logical step for the Kwantung Army, which was in the habit of requisitioning horses for its annual field maneuvers. To avoid the requisition, owners blinded their animals. A Japanese visitor noted that "every single horse fit for army duty had been blinded."[49]

The slave laborers would have been better off maimed, according to an eyewitness account by Sugawara Tokio. In early 1945 a large number of Chinese were used to build fortifications at Hut'ou Shanlu on the Manchukuo-Russian border. "They were forced to work with their legs manacled. The labor was exhausting, the hours long, the treatment brutal. Many fled, some to Russia. The unlucky ones who were caught were tortured by burning and the water treatment and then strung up someplace. They were barely human after that. Other members of the escapee group received the same punishment. Chinese workers were beaten with heavy clubs in broad daylight at the work site and on the road. Because the fortifications they were building were secret, no Chinese shipped there to work were allowed to return home." They were literally worked to death and their corpses were left to rot by the roadside.[50]

The suppression of anti-Japanese "bandits" inevitably brought death and injury to ordinary peasants. The Kwantung Army acknowledged that "most casualties in the bombing raids were ordinary peasants" and that "In many cases the bandits fled and the local people were mistakenly slaughtered as bandits."[51] Patently false reporting was commonplace. An army study stated that "killed and wounded Chinese peasants were always reported as bandits." And mistreatment of the peasantry, "breaking into houses and seizing provisions," was endemic.[52] Incidents like the P'ingtingshan massacre in September 1933 were the vilest atrocities. The area was a base for the Red Spears, a secret society bandit group. Japanese troops gathered all the villagers under a cliff and mowed them down with machine guns.[53] The Kempeitai unit in Tunhwa, the area of greatest guerrilla activity, regularly brought in peasants suspected of aiding the insurgents. "The shrieks of pain and the sound of whipping continued for an hour or so" every night in the interrogation sessions.[54]

The attacks on Japanese when the war ended in August 1945 were an explosion of pent-up grievances; "the Manchurian hatred of Japanese was palpable."[55] The signs had long been there. Okura Kinmochi visited Manchuria in 1934 and found widespread antipathy to Japanese rule. A Manchukuo state minister told him: "Under the present circumstances, if a war breaks out between Japan and Russia, all Manchurians will rise in revolt against the Japanese." A "reliable Japanese" told Okura that "If our troops were withdrawn now, I am sure that all Japanese would be slaughtered."[56] These were accurate predictions of what happened at the war's end. Of course, many Japanese who neither abused nor exploited the local people were caught in the backlash. Yet the retribution was often precise. Tanaka Sutekichi was murdered for having thrown a driver who asked for his fare down a flight of stairs and crippling the man. One department store that favored Japanese customers and refused to sell rationed items to non-Japanese was set on fire, whereas another with a non-discriminatory salary policy went unscathed.[57] The Japanese reaped after August 15, 1945, what they had sown in Manchuria for several decades.

China Proper

The Imperial Army's occupation of the cities of northern and central China brought the region under Japanese economic control. Use of the puppet East Hopei Anti-Communist Autonomous Council for smuggling was an early indication of what was in store for China. The East Hopei region "began to look like a smuggling base for heroin and other items sent in from Manchuria and Kwantung." According to Yamauchi Saburō, president of the South Manchurian Pharmaceutical Company, the firm began producing a large quantity of heroin in 1933 and distributed it with "safepassage documents" provided by the Kempeitai. The major heroin dealers showed their appreciation for army protection by contributing funds to purchase military airplanes. When the war spread across China, Fujita Isamu imported heroin worth about $10 million from Persia and sold it in Shanghai. He earned almost ¥50 million for the Japanese army, which badly needed the funds.[58] The opium trade carried out under Japanese army auspices wreaked havoc on the Chinese.

New companies like the North China Development Company and the Central China Promotion Company proliferated with the spread of hostilities. Carpetbaggers rushed into the occupied areas to seize Chinese property in a frenetic bid to "develop" China. The Chinese soon found that "Japan-China friendship means a kind of economic cooperation more dangerous than being shot at by the Japanese army."[59] In his 1941 work *Senji kokusaihō kōgi* (Lectures on International Law in Wartime), Shinobu Junpei states that "enemy property" administered by the army in 1940 included a great variety of factories. There were twenty different kinds in 110 places in north China and twenty-seven categories of factories at 94 locations in central China. Shinobu defended the control of enemy property as a "temporary measure" to prevent its ruin while the owners were absent. However, the practice violated Article 46 of the Hague Convention, which required safeguards for private property.

Japanese forces openly plundered Chinese property. Troops marching into Paoting after its surrender "broke store windows, grabbed valuables, and draped the loot across their rifles."[60] In the rice-rich lower Yangtze River delta, Chinese peasants worked months in the paddy muck only to see the crop hauled away in Japanese trucks, often to already bulging army warehouses where it rotted.[61] Japanese troops shot water buffaloes for food, although the beasts were the only means old peasant women had of farming their fields and avoiding starvation.[62]

Rape was an accepted prerogative of the Imperial Army. Gomi Kōsuke, an enlisted man, saw a veteran soldier attack a Chinese woman during a short rest break. To save time, the soldier mounted the woman in full uniform with all his ammunition and gear. He pumped away while she screamed.[63] Tamura Taijirō's *Rajo no iru tairetsu* (Naked Women in the Ranks) has many provocative passages about sexual conduct. One soldier says to another, "I've been told that if our unit goes out on a combat mission, it's all right to rape the women we find. They say the raped women must always be killed." In another section, a soldier watching a regiment approaching from the distance could see "patches of white mixed in with the marching column." When the unit got closer, he saw "there were naked women" with the troops. An NCO was admonishing the men, "If you want to get your hands on these Chink broads, you better keep up with the march. Right? Keep your eyes on those Chink bitches and keep going." These descriptions were based on actual experiences.[64] A Chinese youth told of seeing Japanese soldiers force a man and woman at swordpoint to perform the sexual act. Another young rape victim, in shock from the disgrace and pain, drowned herself.[65]

Japanese forces committed atrocities against the Chinese everywhere in the combat zone.[66] A corporal back home from central China in 1942 bragged at a welcome home party about his exploits at Hsuchou: "While out foraging for supplies we got hold of a pregnant woman. We stuck our bayonets in her huge belly, skewered her like a piece of meat. . . . I wiped oil on my sword blade so the Chink's blood wouldn't stick and then I cut a coolie's head off with one stroke."[67] Kawashima Tadashi was a drafted student serving in North China when he saw soldiers "beat a Chinese with rocks until his skull split open and he fell in a pool of blood. Then they kicked him and threw more stones. Officers watched the killing and did nothing. A weeping woman, his wife I suppose, clung to the mangled body."[68]

Villagers suspected of secretly aiding the Eighth Route Army were savagely tortured for information. Interrogators tied a suspect to a ladder and forced water down his throat with a hose. Or they stripped the victim to the waist, smeared benzine on his back, and set it on fire. Other methods included forcing peasants to walk 50 meters ahead of Japanese troops where land mines were suspected. The farmers were used as human mine detectors and were blown to bits if they "found" a mine. The violence was often as random as it was brutal. Once Japanese troops patrolling in a village saw a flitting shadow. They entered a nearby house and dragged out an old woman and a young woman with bound feet holding a baby. A soldier stabbed the old woman to death. The woman with the child was shot in the back as she hobbled away. A soldier looked down at the fallen bodies and yelled, "The baby's alive. What shall I do?" The squad leader gave a two-word reply: "Kill it!"[69] These few examples of atrocities condoned by the military should suffice to indicate the pattern of troop behavior in China; there are so many atrocities recorded that one cannot even begin to list them all.

Chinese laborers were forcibly mobilized by the same methods used in Manchukuo. In March 1944 police of the Wang government closed off a section in the middle of Hankow, and "any men who seemed physically fit were seized and put on waiting trucks." At first the Japanese army carried out the actual roundup, but the Wang regime complained it was losing face as a "sovereign" government and asked to take over that part of the operation too. The Japanese army granted the request. Isoda Isamu described the human tragedy of these forced musters: "Early one morning I heard young women and children crying loudly outside. I rushed to the window and saw a long line of men with their hands tied behind their backs moving through the street. Apparently they had all been seized for labor service." Isoda ran outside: "The line stretched very far. A young woman who looked like a wife of one of the prisoners was screaming hysterically at a policeman, 'Where are you taking them? Let him go! Oh, my husband!' "[70]

Many Chinese were forced to perform labor service at the front, and a large number were shipped to Japan. A cabinet meeting on November 27, 1942, devised "delivery" measures to accelerate the supply of coolies. Chinese POWs and civilians were rounded up, packed into jammed freight cars, and moved to ports of embarkation for shipment to Japan. The Chinese laborers were assigned the worst jobs and were treated like animals. Instructions from the Kamaishi Police Station, Iwate Prefecture, in September 1944 to the Nittetsu Kamaishi Mine confirm their subhuman status. The instructions said: "The kindlier the Chinese are treated, the more demanding and impudent they become. Therefore, neither generosity nor leniency are necessary. . . . Reduce the food ration of those who do not work effectively. . . . The sleeping area need only be two or three inches higher than a person in a sitting position. . . . Bathing facilities are unnecessary because according to Chinese tradition they are offered by the defeated to the victors." Approximately 41,000 Chinese were sent to Japan as slave laborers. About 1,000 died aboard ship or shortly after arrival, and about 6,000 died at work sites in Japan. The major causes of death were malnutrition and illness due to overwork and exhaustion. A substantial number apparently were killed in escape attempts. On June 30, 1945, about 850 Chinese at the Hanaoka Copper Mine, Akita Prefecture, rioted against bad working conditions and treatment. In restoring order, the authorities killed over 400 workers.[71]

The use of POWs for forced labor was one aspect of the general violation of international law and the mistreatment of Chinese prisoners. Even Shinobu Junpei, who usually defended Japanese army conduct, expressed doubt about the lack of information on Chinese prisoners. The answer seems to be that because the army was not adhering to international law, it could not submit reports about prisoner treatment. There are many accounts of prisoners being killed to provide realistic training for Japanese recruits. Kosaka Toshikame was a new recruit when he was required to "learn the ropes" by bayoneting POWs in Ichang.[72] Recruit Ogoshi Chihaya was ordered to bayonet a Communist guerrilla captured in Inner Mongolia. The young man was tied to a wooden post and ripped to pieces.[73] Many atrocities were committed against Chinese prisoners; most were probably summarily killed and never reached the training field to serve as live target practice.[74]

Shinobu points out that Japanese authorities regarded occupied China as sovereign Japanese territory and tried to ignore the extraterritorial rights of third countries. This was a clear violation of international law. Shinobu recounted an anecdote that typified the cavalier attitude toward China. After the fighting ended in Shanghai in 1932, a certain Japanese (either a civilian official or a military man) pointed to Fudan University and asked Shinobu, "This university is crawling with anti-Japanese students. Why wasn't it burned down?" Shinobu replied that if the existence of anti-Japanese students was sufficient reason to destroy the campus, it would mean that every Chinese and foreigner who harbored views contrary to Japan's interests would have to be killed, a rather formidable undertaking.[75] International law was completely forgotten during the war in China. The Middle Kingdom had become a kind of private hunting preserve for Japanese.

The Chinese masses in the war zone suffered terribly. Army doctor Okamura Toshihiko recalled one scene on a road in the battle area: "There were more than ten corpses. One was a tiny child in her mother's arms."[76] A regimental commander on the China front told Prince Mikasa Takahito, "Our policy has been to burn every enemy house along the way as we advance. You can tell at a glance where our forward units are." If the burn and destroy policy had been prohibited, "We would not have any idea where the front lines are!"[77] The army called it an "extermination strategy"; "every village and hamlet in the operations zone was burned to the ground. Not even a single puppy was left alive."[78] Their farms ruined, millions of homeless people were left to starve. The instinct for survival led to desperate actions that were often totally misrepresented by the media in Japan. For example, the *Asahi Gurafu* on June 28, 1939, ran a picture of Chinese women who had been sold into prostitution. The caption read "sold-off women." A more accurate description might have used Ito Keiichi's phrase, "women sent out as human sacrifices to earn a little money for starving families."[79]

Attempting to create the appearance of legitimacy was a hallmark of Tokyo's military-political operations in China. The Chinese Provisional Government was set up in Peking in December 1937 and the Reformed Government of the Republic of China in Nanking in March 1938. Both were puppet regimes pure and simple. Regardless of Wang Ching-wei's intentions, the Reorganized Nationalist Government established in Nanking in 1940 was also a puppet regime. Japan endorsed the Wang administration as the legitimate government of China, concluded a treaty with it in November 1940, and observed the formalities of state to state relations. This public charade was belied by the behind-the-scenes dispute over the regime's flag.

The Wang government wanted to adopt a white sun in a

blue sky design as the national flag. Japanese authorities objected that it would be the same as the flag of Chiang Kaishek's Nationalist government and would lead to confusion, particularly in military operations. When Wang Ching-wei was adamant, Tokyo compromised with the demand that a yellow triangular pennant bearing any two of the three slogans Anticommunism, Peace, and National Construction be attached to the top of the flagpole. Wang made a counterproposal that the pennant be on a separate flagpole to stand next to the national flag. This was unacceptable to Japan. All the while the North China Army worked covertly to allow the continued use of the five-barred flag adopted by the Chinese Provisional Government in North China.[80] A regime that negotiates the color of its own flag and has to accept a foreign topknot is hardly sovereign.

Wang Shih-hui, a minister in the Chinese Provisional Government, once candidly told Tsukui Tatsuo, "Chiang Kaishek and I are both Chinese, so we have the same regard for our country."[81] Wang served as a puppet official; it was such a humiliating experience that it made him want real independence for China. To believe that Chinese who were defeated and ground down by the Imperial Army would enthusiastically cooperate with Japan was one of the stupidest assumptions underlying the Greater East Asia Co-Prosperity Sphere.

The Philippines

The Japanese occupation damaged the Philippine economy and antagonized a population supposedly being liberated. Imports ceased immediately; many sugar fields were ordered converted to cotton production, a crop more vital to the war effort. As the standard of living plummeted, Filipino antagonism rose: "The Filipinos blamed Japan for the shortages and privation. Furthermore, the presence of Japanese security forces was a serious irritant. The military arrogantly ignored local customs. An overweening victor's mentality—strutting and ordering the natives about—was a constant insult. The Filipinos watched with bitter resentment."

Granting independence to the puppet administration in 1943 did not reduce anti-Japanese feeling. Many Filipinos joined the resistance; according to American figures, there were almost 270,000 Filipino guerrillas. After mid-1944, the guerrillas received strong support from the general populace. Many Filipino men joined organized guerrilla units, but the whole populace—old and young, men and women—cooperated with the resistance. Japan had "liberated" the islands from Yankee imperialism and given the Filipinos their "independence." Nevertheless, "The whole island chain became hostile territory." When the American counterattack started, the people cooperated by providing intelligence information. The Japanese forces were desperate, cut off from supplies and surrounded by an unfriendly population.

The Japanese military struck back hard with tighter controls and terror tactics, but this only deepened Filipino hostility.[82] The Filipino prosecutor at the Far East Military Tribunal presented a long list of unspeakable atrocities allegedly committed by the Japanese army. The reaction of an *Asahi* reporter who listened to the sickening catalog was perhaps typical: "Even if the charges are somewhat exaggerated, we have to acknowledge that atrocities were committed."[83]

Many Filipinos were pro-American; they fought against Japan and welcomed MacArthur back. Not all, however. A part of the resistance, the leftist Hukbalahap (Huk) guerrillas, were not only anti-Japan but anti-U.S. as well. The U.S. Army slaughtered a large number of Huks on March 7, 1945.[84] Counterinsurgency operations continued against the Huks well after World War II ended.

Malaya

Singapore, with its large population of overseas Chinese, was a stronghold of anti-Japan sentiment. The Chinese community contributed funds to the Nationalist government and harassed Japanese supply and communications lines in Malaya. After the capture of Singapore, Japanese forces arrested more than 70,000 overseas Chinese suspected of subversive activities.[85] In a short period of time, too short for their guilt to have been established, several thousand persons were slaughtered in a vengeful massacre. According to a Japanese account, "The executions were carried out in a heinous way. A large number of Chinese were tied together, loaded on a boat, taken out to sea, and pushed overboard."[86]

Terror was a constant feature of Japanese rule. Eight Malays who broke into a military warehouse were executed by beheading, and the heads were exposed in the busiest part of Singapore. Notices in several languages were put near the heads: "They killed a Japanese sentry." Waitresses in a quayside coffee shop, bristling with anger, asked Yokota Yasuo, "Aren't there any courts in Japan? Are people so quickly condemned to death under Japanese law? Do you stick decapitated heads up on the streets of Tokyo?"[87]

The barbarous execution of resistance fighters and criminals was only part of the violent record. There were cases of rape where afterward the Japanese man took out a concealed pistol and shot the woman in the back when she tried to escape. Although it was said that "military discipline was generally satisfactory," at least compared to the China front, a veteran recalled that "Once I saw a woman's corpse with a bamboo pole stuck into her genitals."[88]

To the people of Singapore it was a strange kind of liberation. According to Yokota, "The pompous English were replaced by the rough, vulgar Japanese. Simply a change from bad to worse. The Raffles Hotel was renamed the Shōnan Ryokan, the Adelphi Hotel became the Nanto Hotel, and Singapore residents were permitted to use neither. The Japanese military took the Katon Seaview Hotel and pool for their own use. All the best theaters, the Cathay and others, were reserved for Japanese only. Forms of racial discrimination never practiced even by the British were imposed." Food became scarce and rice was rationed. Malnutrition spread as the indigenous population received only about half the ration allotted to Japanese. Schools were closed and converted to Japanese army barracks. Girls' schools became restaurants and brothels for Japanese only. Privation forced many female students and widows to work in them.[89]

Kuroda Hidetoshi was on one operation against Communist guerrillas in Ipoh in 1943. Suspected villagers were lined up to be identified by a prisoner. One young couple was picked out and loaded on a truck "as a forlorn little girl watched them taken off. Not a tear stained that young face as she turned away, still waving, and headed home." Over a dozen suspected guerrillas were brutally tortured to get the names of others. The Japanese soldiers were "covered with blood after a crazy orgy of beating and killing the prisoners." A Japanese civilian employee in the counterinsurgency unit said in disgust, "The way our army operates against these people just makes them hate us more and more."[90]

Burma

The initial response to Japanese forces in Burma, the Dutch East Indies, and French Indochina differed from that in the areas described above. At first the Japanese were perceived as liberators. It was only later that disillusionment set in, followed by hatred and resistance.

According to Kuroda, the Burmese thought that "Japan is our great friend" and "the Japanese will accept us warmly." Many Burmese, "their hearts full of anticipation . . . rushed out to greet their ally, the Imperial Army." The Japanese military responded to this warm welcome and the gift bags of rice by "slapping the Burmese about, and putting them right to work hauling logs and water." Some Burmese came limping back, "The morning's exultation gone, their faces lined with pain and despair." Disappointment followed on the heels of expectation as quickly as one Japanese soldier marched after another through Rangoon's streets.

Japanese forces originally occupied only the southern area of Tenasserim, and Burma was promised its immediate independence. Instead, the Japanese army extended the occupation to the whole country, established a military government, and used the Burmese army as an instrument of control. These actions alone were enough to trigger a Burmese reaction, but insult was added to injury. In August 1943 Burma was allowed to declare its independence. Despite that formal change of status, Premier Ba Maw was still treated like a hireling. The Japanese army even stopped the vehicles of Burmese state ministers right in front of Burmese police headquarters, a humiliating affront to a supposedly "independent" government.

Although the successful occupation of Burma was partly due to the assistance of the Burma National Army under Aung San, he was subsequently given the cold shoulder. The Burmese Army was not made an autonomous national army. When Japanese forces started to withdraw in March 1945, Aung San's Burmese troops revolted and, together with the British Indian Army, launched a sharp offensive against the retreating Japanese.[91]

India

Japanese officers organized the Indian National Army (INA) in September 1942. There were fundamental differences from the outset. Indian leaders wanted an independent and autonomous national army; Japan insisted that it participate in Imperial Army campaigns. Proposals by Captain Mohan Singh, who originated the INA, to increase the Indian forces and to issue a proclamation on Gandhi's birthday were rejected. Indian troops were sent to the Rabaul and Timor campaigns, battles and places unrelated to Indian independence. Having no desire to be a Japanese puppet, Mohan Singh left the INA.[92]

Some Indians like Subhas Chandra Bose hoped to use Japan

to gain India's independence; most Indians, however, remained loyal to England and supported the war effort. When Japan invaded China in 1937, Pandit Nehru of the Congress party formed a China Medical Committee, organized a China Day, and called for a boycott of Japanese products in support of China.[93]

Indonesia

The Dutch East Indies were by far the most important strategic jewel in the South Pacific. Japan coveted the island's oil resources; possession had been deemed worth war with the United States, England, and Holland. An Imperial Conference in May 1943 decided that "Marai, Sumatra, Java, Borneo, and the Celebes are Japanese territory and a priority effort will be made to develop them as supply areas for major natural resources."[94] Since this decision ran counter to the ostensible policy of "liberation" and co-prosperity, it was kept secret; no public announcement was made. Two years later, with defeat imminent, the policy was changed from exploitation to independence. On August 17, 1945, two days after Tokyo surrendered, Japanese navy officers assisted Sukarno, Hatta Mohammad, and others in declaring Indonesia's independence.[95] This change of heart postdated the collapse of Japan's southern front; it was not part of Tokyo's original plans to control the mineral-rich islands.

Indonesians initially welcomed Japan, but the honeymoon was short-lived. Political rights were curtailed more than under the Dutch. In March 1942, the Japanese army banned all groups and meetings and followed that in June with the prohibition of all speeches, writing, and activities related to politics. Nationalists like Sukarno and Hatta were ignored when a three-zone administration was implemented. Symbols of national unity and independence like the Merah Putih flag and the song *Indonesia Raja* (Greater Indonesia) were also prohibited. Indonesians were forced to study the Japanese language and even to stand and sing the Japanese national anthem, *Kimi ga yo,* in movie theaters.[96]

The "liberators' " behavior followed the usual insensitive pattern. It was common for "Japanese walking along the street to show their disdain for the 'natives' or to get drunk and beat up pedicab drivers ... officers would screw around with women right on the *tatami* floor of Japanese-style restaurants, and junior officers and army civilians would get drunk in bars and clubs and sing at the top of their voices, drowning out everyone else."[97]

The Japanese army undermined Dutch prestige and assiduously fanned resentment toward the former rulers. Yet Japanese control, infused with racial superiority, was discriminatory and oppressive. Antagonism and resistance by Indonesians was inevitable. An Indonesian volunteer corps was organized as an auxiliary to the Japanese administration and to help in the defense of the islands against an Allied attack. The Indonesian volunteers resented "the attitudes and training methods of Japanese officers and the better treatment given Japanese soldiers." In February 1945 this resentment exploded in a revolt by the volunteer corps unit in Blitar. There were also frequent attacks against Japanese in West Borneo by Dyak tribesmen because "the forest area they depended on for a living was ruthlessly cut down in lumbering operations."

An extremely harsh requisition of men and materials was carried out in central Java. Many farmers and workers were shipped to other areas as laborers, and nearly all died. The requisition was ostensibly a voluntary recruitment; in fact, however, "a variety of compulsory methods were used, from withholding the rations of those who did not register to randomly seizing peasants at work in paddy fields along the highway. Working conditions [of the forced laborers] were unspeakably vile." These unfortunate Indonesians, like the Korean, Chinese, and Manchurian slave laborers, learned who it was that prospered in the Greater East Asia Co-Prosperity Sphere.

Kempeitai security measures were intended to intimidate the population into submission: "The rumor was that if the Kempeitai took you away, that was the end. You would not come back alive. They wanted everyone quaking with fear." The Japanese army did its share. "Indonesian custom regards a person's head as very precious. It was taboo to even touch another person's head ... Japanese soldiers for no reason at all would hit Indonesians on the head right out on the street. . . . Indonesians were frightened of their 'liberators.' They could not even walk down the street in broad daylight." Hera Wati-dia's younger sister was raped by a Japanese and suffered a nervous breakdown from which she never recovered.[98]

War criminals were executed at Ambon after the war. "The hatred and contempt for the Japanese prisoners was written on the spectators' faces. . . . They shouted, 'Get those Japs who stole the food from our mouths! . . . They deserve to die! Kill them! Kill them!' "[99] The crowd's collective rage was the last hurrah for Japanese rule.

Sukarno, Hatta, and other prewar nationalists tried to cooperate with the Japanese military to gain independence for Indonesia. Younger Indonesians whose political consciousness was shaped during the Japanese occupation disdained such assistance in favor of winning independence with their own hands. On August 16, 1945, members of the Indonesian volunteer corps burned the Japanese flag, arrested collaborators, and created the first liberated zone in Indonesia.[100]

French Indochina

Japan also plundered French Indochina. Many rice paddies were converted to jute, and part of the rice crop was shipped to Laos and stored for contingency use. A severe food shortage occurred; nearly 200,000 Vietnamese reportedly starved to death after the war.[101]

The Vietnamese resistance to French colonialism regarded

the Japanese as a new wave of oppressors. Illegal activity began with the formation of the Vietminh Front in May 1941 to "concentrate the revolutionary power of all classes and nationalities."[102] The first Vietnam Liberation Army Propaganda Unit was organized in December 1944, and the armed struggle accelerated. A liberated zone of six counties was created in June 1945 and became the major revolutionary base. Vietnamese opposed rice requisitions and refused to pay taxes. Vietminh posters and handbills reportedly were spread even in Japanese army camps and in puppet government offices. The next stage was a general uprising ordered in August 1945. On August 14–15, the Vietminh occupied many Japanese army positions near the liberated zone. On August 16, Ho Chi Minh and other leaders decided to seize administrative control before the Allies landed, disarm the Japanese, and be ready to welcome the Allied forces. Large demonstrations were held in Hanoi on August 19 and in Saigon on August 25. Ho Chi Minh declared the independence of the Democratic Republic of Vietnam on September 2 in Hanoi. Tominaga Toyofumi recalled his astonishment at seeing a Vietminh flag whipping in the breeze over a government office in Nyattoran (phonetic) only three days after the war ended.[103]

These were the realities of the East Asian areas occupied by the Japanese military. Control was imposed by force. Tokyo attempted to legitimize that control with terms like "liberation" and "independence." But there was no "East Asian community" or "co-prosperity sphere." It was a war-wasted region where the peoples' independence and their very lives were devastated by brutal military oppression and economic exploitation.

Assertions that the independence of many Asian peoples "was largely due to the Pacific War and that therefore the conflict's positive side should be appreciated" underlie the "affirmation of the Greater East Asian War."[104] It is true that Japanese military occupation temporarily severed Western control and weakened the former rulers. But this was merely an incidental consequence: Japan did not liberate Asia. The Asian struggle for independence unfolded through the rigors of the Japanese occupation. Asians won their freedom by fighting and dying in the resistance to Japanese imperialism. To call Japan's disgraceful and bloody rampage a crusade for liberation is to stand truth and history on their heads.

9

The Horrors of War

The crumpled corpses of Nanking and Auschwitz show how easily war provokes killing above and beyond the call of any duty. The new weapons of mass destruction are incomparably more lethal. Modern warfare, in which industrial production is an extension of the battlefield and the distinction between combatants and noncombatants is imprecise or gone altogether, leads to higher and higher death tolls. In ancient times the leaders of opposing armies often met in individual combat to decide the outcome. Now huge professional military forces clash, with their societies mobilized behind them.

The Destruction of Human Values

World War II brought atrocities on an unprecedented scale, and they were an infamous hallmark of the Japanese military. A few incidents that occurred in occupied areas have already been mentioned. Here I wish to elaborate on this theme and show by concrete examples that the Greater East Asian War, which has been glorified as a moral cause, was a dirty war of sadistic cruelty.

If men hesitate or refuse to commit brutal murder, war would be impossible. But war has the power to dehumanize man, to remove his scruples about taking life. In the heat of combat where it is kill or be killed, survival often depends on being utterly ruthless to the enemy, to civilians, and even to friendly forces.[1] The nation, the military unit, and the individual act identically: each puts its own survival and victory above everything else. Thus during the Pacific War brutality was not reserved for the enemy or the inhabitants of occupied areas; it was standard fare for Japanese too. Our national leaders started the war with no assurance of victory and continued it when defeat was certain, an egregious act of cruelty against the Japanese people. A senior army officer in Osaka in June 1945 reflected the typical hawk's disdain for human life when he said, "Due to the nationwide food shortage and the imminent invasion of the home islands, it will be necessary to kill all the infirm old people, the very young, and the sick. We cannot allow Japan to perish because of them."[2] To continue a lost war was morally contemptible; under the law, it was premeditated murder. If homicidal intent was missing, surely it was criminal manslaughter.

A discussion of organized brutality should begin with the ethic of mutual triage within the imperial military forces. The wounded were an impediment to military operations because attempts to save them often resulted in more casualties or diverted manpower. A battlefield morality of "not becoming a burden to others" prevailed. The wounded were forced to kill themselves or they were shot, depending on circumstances. Hardened combat veterans used to say, "On the battlefield ruthlessness is sometimes a virtue."[3] Of course, when a battle was going badly, the sacrifice of a buddy or a friendly unit might be unavoidable to save more lives or win the day. But some commanders, indifferent to their men's suffering or because they were sadistic martinets, threw lives away with no military justification. General Mutaguchi's mistreatment of the 15th Army troops during the Imphal campaign was one example. Another was the cruelty toward subordinates of Hanaya Tadashi, commander, 55th Division, a unit of the 28th Army in Burma.[4,5]

Unable to prevent the American landing on Leyte, the military devised a desperate tactic to avoid defeat. The special attack strategy called for crashing explosive-laden airplanes into enemy warships. The originator was Admiral Onishi Takijirō, and in October 1944 a navy unit, the Navy Divine Wind (Kamikaze) Special Attack Unit, made the first strikes. Thereafter young army and navy pilots were organized into special attack units and launched in droves against the U.S. Navy in the battles for the Philippines and Okinawa.

The special attack pilots were doomed men. A "successful" mission ended when they blew themselves up against an American ship. The units were glorified as the supreme expression of the Japanese military spirit, and the impression was given that all the pilots were volunteers.[6] Takagi Toshirō's meticulous research has shown the sordid reality behind this cherry blossom myth. The units were organized from "volunteers" who had joined after intensive psychological pressure or from personnel assigned to the duty. Pilots who returned to base without carrying out their mission because of a mechanical malfunction were derided. They had to face ostracism and comments like "Why did you come back alive?" and "A coward who is afraid to die is a disgrace to the special attack unit." The condemned pilots suffered terrible mental anguish. Many were so desperate that they crashed their planes into the ground or into the ocean just to end it all.[7] Those who tried to carry out their missions did little better because of inferior planes and American air supremacy. No more than 1 to 3 percent of the suicide pilots actually hit Allied warships; most seem to have crashed short of the target. Legions of promising young men were sent off to meaningless deaths.

The suicide attacks were initially a response to the deteriorating combat situation. On January 18, 1945, the Supreme Council for the Direction of the War made the attacks official government policy. The council decided to "concentrate on converting all armament production to special attack weapons of a few major types."[8] The available weapons systems were reduced to a suicide arsenal that included special submarines of the Kōryū and Kairyū class, high-speed small boats of the

Shinyō class which exploded upon contact with enemy ships,[9] and the Kaiten human torpedo. The army's contribution was a human bomb: a soldier wrapped in explosives who hurled himself against an enemy tank, blowing it and himself to bits.[10] A military psychology insensitive to human life, to the individual's right to survive, conceived the special attack idea. The same mentality underlay the policy of requiring Japanese soldiers taken prisoner, even if they managed to return to friendly lines, to commit suicide.[11]

The military attitude toward civilians was similar. Since human rights were totally ignored within Japan, it was not likely that they would be respected on the battlefield. Prostitutes were a case in point. Prostitution is by its very nature a violation of women's rights to a decent occupation and livelihood. Prostitutes for the military, euphemistically called "comfort girls," were placed in double jeopardy. Large numbers were sent to front-line "comfort stations" to service the troops, including some who had been tricked or forced into the job. The soldiers queued up in long lines for their few minutes of "comfort"; the girls took them on one after another, probably never getting off their backs from one customer to the next. "Comfort girls" wounded in the fighting were apparently sometimes abandoned or shot to prevent capture.[12] Many of the women were Korean, but Japanese prostitutes and ordinary girls were also induced or tricked into service at the front.

The same "military necessity" that defiled women reduced noncombatants to mere pawns. In April 1945 the *Awa-maru*, which had been guaranteed safe passage by the Allies, was sunk and over 2,200 Japanese were killed. The American action was clearly illegal, but Japanese authorities had secretly loaded rubber, tin, and other prohibited war materials on the vessel. To prevent discovery of this violation of international law in case the ship was stopped, scuttling devices had been secretly installed.[13] National leaders tried to smuggle war materials even if it meant the death of innocent passengers. Their status as noncombatants was simply ignored. No one was safe, nothing was sacred.

When the battles for Saipan and Okinawa engulfed non-combatant residential areas, the military forced civilians to die with the troops. As I shall describe in the following section, on Saipan Japanese civilians were gradually forced to a cliff by advancing U.S. forces. The Japanese army then ordered them to commit mass suicide by jumping off the cliff. When one family hesitated on the edge, soldiers first shot the father and then wounded the mother. Covered with blood, she managed to escape with her two children, and surrender to an American unit. U.S. troops had watched the scene in horror.[14]

Garrison commander Akamatsu Yoshitsugu of Toka-shikijima, Kerama archipelago, Okinawa, ordered local inhabitants to turn over all food supplies to the army and commit suicide before U.S. troops landed. The obedient islanders, 329 all together, killed each other at the Onna River with razors, hatchets, and sickles. U.S. forces occupied nearby Iejima and used some of the local people to take surrender appeals to Akamatsu's unit on Tokashikijima. Akamatsu's men killed the emissaries and many members of the island's self-defense unit for allegedly violating orders. On another Okinawan island, Zamami, unit commander Umezawa ordered the island's elderly and children to commit suicide in front of the memorial to local war dead from the Sino and Russo-Japanese Wars. The remaining islanders were forbidden to pick any potatoes or vegetables. Thirty persons who violated the order were starved or shot. On the main island of Okinawa, many civilians were killed as suspected spies. Local people who fled to the main defense trenches were ordered to retreat "because of military necessity." The civilians were forced out of the trenches right into heavy American fire. As the fighting drew to an end, civilians hid with the military in the caves at the southern tip of the island. When a frightened child cried out, a soldier grabbed it from the mother's arms and strangled the child to death in front of everyone. It was a grim warning against making any noise that would reveal their location to the U.S. forces.[15]

An army so brutal against its own people would hardly refrain from atrocities against enemy forces or civilians in occupied areas. In the preceding chapter I noted the widespread brutalities committed against Chinese during the years of fighting. The worst single incident was the notorious "rape of Nanking" immediately after its capture. The documents and testimony prepared by the International Committee for the Nanking Safety Zone, organized by neutral foreigners and by other unbiased observers and survivors, tell a ghastly tale of mass slaughter. Tens of thousands of Chinese—prisoners of war, stragglers who had discarded their weapons and mingled with civilians, women and children—were massacred. Countless women were raped. Stores and homes were systematically plundered and burned.[16] According to Imai Masatake, correspondent for the *Tokyo Asahi* and an eyewitness, the units in Peking were ordered to clear the city of all stragglers before General Matsui Iwane's triumphal entry. Thousands of Chinese who looked like they might have been soldiers who had changed into civilian clothes were seized and lined up at the Hsiakuanch'ien Bridge and machine-gunned: "The area was filled with crumpled, twisted corpses piled on top of each other in bloody mounds." Coolie laborers were set to work throwing bodies into the river. Then the coolies were lined up on the river bank and machine-gunned, their bodies tumbling into the river. An officer told Imai, "There are about 20,000 dead Chinese there."[17]

Sasaki Tōichi, commander, 30th Brigade, 16th Division, wrote that before his unit entered Nanking, "Prisoners surrendered in droves, several thousand in all. Our enraged troops ignored superior orders and slaughtered one bunch after another. We had suffered heavy casualties in the bitter ten-day fighting. Many of our men had lost good friends. The unit hated the Chinese and there was a feeling of wanting to kill every one of the bastards." The slaughter continued after Japanese forces entered the city, as Sasaki relates: "Several thousand stragglers who had continued to resist on the outskirts of Nanking were steadily rounded up and executed at Hsiakuanch'ien Bridge."[18] As a professional soldier, Horiba Kazuo "deplored" the arson, robbery, and violence by the army, but he tried to shift the focus to Japanese society: "Should the military take all the blame? Most of the army are civilian draftees. The entire country should share responsibility for what happened. Actually, those men who have had only a short period of military training and the older reservists, the family men, behaved the worst.[19] But the peacetime army's values and discipline were already thoroughly brutalized. The prewar barracks and the wartime battlefield were no different as far as respect for individual rights was concerned. Granted that "superior orders" could restrain the troops, official policy often encouraged antisocial behavior. Armies from time immemorial "have had a permissive policy toward sex as a means of keeping the soldiers contented and obedient. They were allowed to indulge themselves in sexual orgies at every opportunity."[20] The Imperial Army with its "comfort stations" was no exception. The military commanders cannot evade ultimate responsibility for the atrocities (especially those related to sexual conduct) at Nanking and in other battle areas. The Rape of Nanking may have been a reaction to the fierce Chinese resistance after the Shanghai fighting, but that is in no way an excuse for its having occurred.

In addition to the looting and the killing of noncombatants, another violation of the international rules of warfare was the use of poison gas. Lieutenant General Hashimoto Mure admitted to Prince Takeda in 1939 that poison gas was used in the fighting in the mountains of Shanshi province.[21] Japan imported German equipment to manufacture Iperitto in 1933 and secretly produced poison gas on Okunoshima in Hiroshima Prefecture. Among the staff at the site, which included persons on mandatory labor service, mobilized students, and others forced to work there, about 350 died.[22]

On the battlefield men face the ultimate extremes of human existence, life or death. "Extreme" conduct, although still ethically impermissible, may be psychologically inevitable. However, atrocities carried out far from battlefield dangers and imperatives and according to a rational plan were acts of evil barbarism. The Auschwitz gas chambers of our "ally"

Germany and the atomic bombing of Hiroshima and Nagasaki by our enemy America are classic examples of rational atrocities. The Japanese military's disgusting contribution to this genre of World War II bestiality was the 731 Unit.

The 731 Unit was a bacteriological warfare research unit located in the suburbs of Harbin, Manchuria, under the cover name of Epidemic Prevention and Potable Water Supply Unit. Lieutenant General Ishii Shirō, a medical doctor, was the commanding officer. The unit was top secret; even its existence was not known to the public. After the war its activities came to light in various ways. Former unit members made anonymous detailed confessions; the USSR published captured Kwantung Army documents; and Naruchi Hideo, the Metropolitan Police Agency inspector who handled the Teikoku Bank case, investigated former unit personnel in connection with the famous bank robbery and mass murder in 1948.

The 731 Unit research included the plague, cholera, typhoid, frostbite, and gas gangrene. Their successes included a defoliation bacilli bomb that blighted an area of 50 square kilometers. A special project code-named Maruta used human beings for experiments. Several thousand persons were secretly transported from places in Manchuria and China and confined in a special unit prison. When needed for the experiments, the human guinea pigs were placed in laboratory rooms and injected with bacteria to test a germ's potency. The dead bodies were burned, both to avoid an epidemic and to destroy the evidence of the experiments. Another technique was to tie the prisoners to posts out of doors and drop a bacteriological bomb on the area to determine how many became infected. There are also indications of experiments in which bacteria were placed in bean-jam buns, on fountain pens, and in mice to spread infectious diseases among the civilian population of Manchuria. The frostbite tests also used human beings to test exposure to freezing temperatures.

According to former unit members, when the Soviet Union entered the war on August 8, 1945, the Japanese tried to destroy every trace of the 731 Unit's activities. The Maruta prisoners were given food dosed with potassium cyanide; those who did not eat the food were machine-gunned. The bodies were thrown into a pit in a huge courtyard at the unit, doused with gasoline, and set on fire. Because of the great number of corpses, they did not burn thoroughly. The charred bodies were then put into a pulverizer. Engineers dynamited the buildings, and all equipment, tools, and incriminating material were burned. Personnel of 731 Unit were given highest priority evacuation back to Japan, before the rest of the Kwantung Army or other units.

The 731 Unit truly did the devil's work. Yet the U.S. occupation was extremely lenient with Dr. Ishii. He was not arrested or charged with war crimes. American forces allegedly used Ishii's discoveries and technique in their germ warfare during the Korean War. Furthermore, according to Inspector Naruchi, only members of the 731 Unit knew how to handle the potassium compound used in the Teikoku Bank robbery. The research on "inferior peoples" had become a murder weapon turned against the citizens of Tokyo.[23]

The vivisection experiments conducted at Kyushu Imperial University on captured U.S. airmen were somewhat different from the rational cold-blooded atrocities of the 731 Unit. Anger at the devastating American air raids and a desire for revenge were partial motives. Nevertheless, the Kyushu doctors also perverted their training and ideals by committing murder. Eight captured B-29 crewmen were used in four vivisection operations conducted on May 17, 23, and 29, and June 3, 1945. The experiments were arranged by the Western Japan Military Command and Professor Ishiyama Fukujirō, director, external medicine, Kyushu Imperial University. In one experiment Ishiyama extracted a prisoner's lungs and put them in a surgical pan. He made an incision in the lung artery and allowed blood to flow into the thorax, killing the victim. In another experiment Ishiyama first removed a prisoner's stomach, then cut five ribs and held a large artery near the heart to determine how long he could stop the blood flow before the victim died. In a third, a doctor made four openings in a prisoner's skull and inserted a knife into the skull cavity. The prisoner, of course, died. Similar experiments were conducted on the other POWs.[24]

To write about these depraved acts by Japanese fills me with shame and remorse.[25] That anguish is slightly mitigated by the fact that some individuals, even in the military, refused to perform such crimes. Conscience was not completely expunged, even from the armed forces. In China, for example, Hirata Yūichi's company commander ordered him to shoot some villagers who had been tortured on suspicion of supplying information to the Eighth Route Army. Hirata conferred with his NCOs, one of whom said, "Sir, I can't kill any more Chinese." At night Hirata secretly let the villagers get away and reported to his commanding officer that they had been shot.[26] The garrison on Minamitorishima, an island north of the Marianas, was desperate from American bombing and lack of food. Captain Nakamura, a twenty-eight-year-old tank unit commander, urged regimental commander Sakata Zen'ichi to withdraw the troops to Japan so they could rest and fight again. When the suggestion was rejected with a rebuke, Nakamura shot Sakata, risking his own life to save his men from certain death.[27] There were many similar examples of humane conduct.[28] They qualify somewhat the long, brutal record of violence and death.

The atrocities committed by the Imperial Army and Navy attest to the moral degeneration of the ruling elite. The conduct of Japanese forces in World War II was far inferior to their disciplined behavior in the Sino-Japanese and Russo-Japanese Wars. Their actions as defeat loomed deserve special mention. As previously described, troops in the battle areas were provided with "comfort girls." The officers had high-class prostitutes for their exclusive use. The vainglorious Imperial Army debauched itself everywhere in the Greater East Asia Co-Prosperity Sphere. An army doctor described Batavia in 1942 as "a great place with all the women and booze you could want."[29] Troops stationed in a village on the Burmese border in 1944 recounted wild stories about the officers' whoring:

> The general staff really gets its share. Every officer has his own Japanese mistress at the Nanpūso, a fancy brothel. The girls are off-limits to the enlisted men. There are drinking parties every night and the officers get drunk and raise hell. . . . The senior adjutant sends his car all the way to Rangoon for a load of *rungi* [Burmese skirt fabric]. The girls at the Nanpūso can pick out whatever they like.[30]

The battle for Okinawa was vicious, hand to hand fighting; Japanese troops were being wiped out as the Americans advanced yard by yard. But "Colonel Udo continued his plush lifestyle in the trenches, with three women serving him hand and foot." Chief of Staff Chō Isamu "drank even in the trenches and had girls from the brothel area in Naha."[31]

Irresponsible debauchery while ordinary soldiers fought to the death had its counterpart in Manchuria when the Soviet Union attacked. Reservists were ordered to defend the area as the Kwantung Army immediately evacuated officers' dependents by train and army headquarters fled from Hsinching to Tunghwa.[32] Left in the lurch, the reservists cursed their erstwhile protectors: "Those bastards left us holding the bag. Only the Kwantung Army got away," and "Those gutless wonders. The great Kwantung Army, my ass."[33] Japanese residents in northern Korea fled southward on foot ahead of the Russians. Old people and women and children, many of them sick, trudged along the dusty roads. "The Imperial Army's front line troops and the Kempeitai, riding in trucks and ox carts, overtook the refugees and knocked and kicked them out of the way so they could escape." The army seized the railroad line and kept it for military use only. "Many civilians tried to hang on to the outside of the trains. Soldiers forced them off at sword point, yelling at the terrified men and women, "Tough shit. Get off the bastards!' "[34]

Some fleeing soldiers turned on their wounded and sick comrades and stole their rations and personal belongings.[35] The ultimate betrayal was in the Philippines, where army units had scattered to the hills. Starving bands of soldiers shot and killed stragglers from other units and ate their flesh. The Imperial Army was reduced to squads of cannibals.[36]

The arrogant Kempeitai in Tokyo panicked at the surrender announcement. Many deserted their units at the rumor that Allied forces had landed.[37] When the armed forces were disbanded, officers removed vast quantities of military supplies for their personal use, including food, fuel, horses, and draft animals.[38] It was not a sudden collapse of will and discipline. Long before their defeat in battle, the professional military were morally bankrupt.

The War Comes Home

Modern war takes a heavy toll of home front civilians as well as battlefield soldiers. Unlike the wars of 1894, 1904, and 1914, in the 1930s and 1940s millions of Japanese soldiers were sent overseas. As total mobilization occurred, every aspect of life was affected. Finally, the war came home to Japan and large numbers of noncombatants were killed. Never before in modern Japanese history had war struck the people directly. Only rarely in any country's history had a civilian population suffered such physical and emotional destitution. Personal experience taught the Japanese people the "horrors of war."

The worldwide financial crash of 1929 threw Japanese business into a severe depression. The Manchurian Incident stimulated the armaments and related industries. The new colony of Manchukuo further sparked business activity, and a good recovery seemed underway.[39] Military adventurism meant good profits to investors and the bureaucrats and high-ranking military closely allied with them. As nominal income rose and unemployment fell, expansionism seemed good for ordinary citizens too. As the war expanded and dragged on, however, prices rose sharply and the cost of living increased enormously. Workers' real wages declined, and working conditions worsened. For example, under the 1943 Factory Law Wartime Exemption, women and children were permitted to work more than eleven hours a day. The mandatory two rest days a month was suspended, and women could be assigned to night work.[40]

Millions of adult males were drafted and others were mobilized for war production. All resources and facilities were concentrated on armament production; consumer goods gradually became in short supply. Food shortages threatened much of the population with hunger and starvation. The Ministry of Health and Welfare's nutritional standard for an adult male doing "medium-hard labor" was 2,400 calories a day and 80 grams of protein. From 1942 on, the average caloric intake had fallen to below 2,000. In 1945 average daily calories were 1,793 and protein consumption was at 60–65 grams. Public health deterioration was apparent in a sharp increase in tuberculosis. The death rate from tuberculosis was over 140,000 in 1938; in 1942 it exceeded 160,000, and by 1943 it was more than 170,000 (no statistics were published after 1944).[41] A photograph in the *Asahi Gurafu* on March 24, 1943, captioned "Fighting TB in the Factory" was one indication of the link between war production and death from illness due to malnutrition.

In April 1941 the Basic Necessities Control Ordinance was promulgated on the basis of the National Mobilization Law. A rice rationing system was begun in the major cities and expanded to the entire country. Other items were added to the rationed list, including fish, vegetables, condiments, and clothing. Daily necessities were strictly controlled, but the system did not work effectively. Moreover, supplies of rationed items gradually ran out, and the populace could not get enough food through official channels to live on. A black market flourished as people tried to get necessities. Black market prices were much higher than official prices, causing a sharp increase in living expenses. Long queues for rationed goods or the few nonrationed items became a fact of life. Housewives had to go long distances looking for food. They spent far more time and energy to shop than in peacetime, with but meager results. Toward the end of the war, nearly every shop was bare.

Nagai Kafū, Kawakami Hajime, Oya Ten'ichi, and others carefully recorded these hardships in their diaries. I can add a few personal experiences. Late in 1942 I waited in line for three and a half hours in the cafeteria restaurant of the Matsuzakaya Department Store in Ueno just to get a thin gruel of rice and vegetables. We would pay anything to fill our stomachs, so inadequate was rationed food. I used to dream that I was in a store full of delicious food just like in the old days. I would think, "This is strange," but wake up before I could eat anything. What misery! I used to take vitamin B and *oblaat* (medicinal wafers that contained no medicine during the war), which were not rationed, to assuage my constant hunger. I can still taste them as if it was only yesterday.

Not everyone had hunger pangs. The privileged elite of senior army officers, high-ranking bureaucrats, and arms manufacturers had the right connections. Through special black market contacts, they got plenty of food and liquor, and they caroused nightly in the brothels of Akasaka and Shimbashi. War meant all the women and whiskey they wanted. Their houses were filled with food and goods that ordinary people could never get their hands on.[42] Kiyosawa Kiyoshi wrote in his diary for April 30, 1943, about a popular ditty with the line "Everything goes to the military, the black marketers and the big shots. Only the fools queue up." For March 16, 1944, he wrote that mobilized workers were grumbling, "Even if we work hard, the company management and the officers spend their time in the brothels."[43] Privilege for the few and privation for the many were the two faces of the Pacific War.[44]

Spiritual and moral deterioration paralleled physical deprivation. Slogans calling for "selfless patriotic service" and "a life for the country" were everywhere. Constant official exhortation notwithstanding, there never was a time of such general moral collapse. The shriller the government's demands for "selfless patriotic service," the more individuals and families looked out for themselves. Public appeals for sacrifice increased private hoarding, speculation, and cynicism. Watanabe Kiyoshi was a sixteen-year-old farm boy when he wrote in his diary for January 6, 1941, about young men facing the draft: "They'll soon go off to the front and they don't know if they will ever come back alive, so they become really desperate." There were numerous incidents of gang rape by village youths.[45] A Police Bureau publication entitled *Jūgo ikazoku o meguru jihan to kore ga bōshi jōkyō* (Crimes by Families of Military Personnel and Their Prevention) reported widespread adultery by wives of soldiers away at the front.[46]

Business activities were curtailed, and many companies closed down. The laid-off workers were directed under the mobilization ordinance into war production. Government-set wages were very low; many men could not adequately support their families. In 1943 students and young women were brought into the labor pool. Students had to give up their studies and go to work in war factories; unmarried women were organized into women's volunteer units.[47] Academic requirements for higher and technical colleges and universities were reduced to accelerate graduation. Only elementary school students were exempt from labor mobilization (some were in fact mobilized). A generation was denied its right to an education, its right to mature gradually into adulthood.

In 1943 deferments were ended for students in universities, technical colleges, and higher schools.[48] The new policy was necessary because every eligible nonstudent in the same age bracket was being drafted. Mobilization reached the lower grades informally through quotas for youth volunteers (boys fifteen to seventeen years of age) and volunteers for Manchuria-Mongolia Development Youth Patriotic Units. Made responsible for filling the quotas, teachers pressured the children directly by saying, "Any Japanese boy who doesn't get into this 'holy war' will be shamed for life." The teachers would visit a student's home and get his parents' tearful approval. Many boys in their midteens became youth pilots and youth tankers, or "volunteered" for service in Manchuria and Mongolia. These rosy-cheeked teenagers were put in special attack units and blew themselves up crashing into enemy ships. Or they were slaughtered in the Soviet invasion of Manchuria.[49]

In June 1944, in anticipation of enemy air raids, the government adopted a policy of evacuating younger children from the major urban areas. Children from Tokyo and other large cities were separated from their families and relocated to rural areas in groups under the supervision of schoolteachers. Some children were so desperately homesick that they ran away, boarded trains by themselves, and returned to the city. Despite the teachers' dedicated efforts, it was impossible to provide sufficient food. Away from their families for the first time and living in groups where personal attention was sporadic at best was an enormous strain on the young boys and girls. Everything was made worse by the constant hunger.[50] Matshushita Motoko was a young refugee: "The children got fed the same thing every meal: a bowl of gruel made of sweet potato leaves, bean husks, and what have you." They were constantly hungry and would "go outside and eat all the fruit on trees belonging to the local people. Soon the local residents began to accuse the refugee children of stealing potatoes and pilfering from the fields."[51]

"Hōboku" (Grazing) is a short story by Hayashi Fumiko based on real experiences about children relocated to a countryside inn. She recounts how homesick the children were when they saw village children munching away at large rice balls while they played. The local kids had white rice for between-meal snacks, an incredible luxury. Hayashi describes how a rumor spread that the inn kitchen was haunted because every morning the containers for leftover rice and side dishes were empty. One of the young evacuees turned out to be the culprit. When the war was finally over, many of the children returned to the cities only to discover their parents had been killed in air raids and they were homeless orphans.

Women and elderly persons were also evacuated from the large cities. Leaving behind husbands, fathers, and sons who had to work in the cities, they imposed on relatives in the countryside. The reception was not always cordial. According to Chokai Sigeko, "The country people had never experienced the bombing and they were unsympathetic and mercenary. We had been burned out and lost everything. Still they wouldn't give us a scrap of food if we didn't offer something in exchange." Ishizuka Rui's poems suggest the unhappy ambience: "We fled there, unknown to the town's people, they treated us like strangers"; and "Scorned as refugee beggars, misery in a forlorn place."[52]

As previously mentioned, military deaths in combat from the start of the war in China totaled 2.3 million.[53] The horrible suffering of wounded soldiers was another facet of that carnage. Poems caught the anguished pathos: "His chest heaving at every breath, the wounded soldier on the dirt floor chewed on a straw mat trying to endure the pain" (Ikeuchi Isamu), and "My body was squeezed in a vise, pain, pain, more pain" (Kadō Itsurō).[54] Thousands died from their wounds. Thousands more were deformed and permanently disabled. Their families suffered the mental anguish of a son or father crippled for life, the loss of a worker on the farm and support in their old age. Millions of families who waited so anxiously for their men to come home received nothing but an official death announcement and perhaps the ashes of the slain soldier. Death in battle was an "honor." Grief was inappropriate if not subversive. Widows and orphans were denied tears of grief for their loved ones.[55] Every citizen, man and woman, young and old, was directly or indirectly touched by the war.

Finally, the noncombatant populace was swept into the vortex as Japan came under attack. The slaughter of civilians began in the Pacific islands. Most Japanese residents had been evacuated from the fortified islands except for Saipan. *Time* correspondent Robert Sherwood described the grisly mass suicide of civilians when the island was attacked by U.S. forces. They were forced to retreat to Marubi Bluff at the northern tip of the island. Some families blew themselves up with hand grenades. Young women sat on the rocks, carefully combed their black hair, and then quietly jumped into the ocean. One woman was just about to give birth when she leapt into the sea. The head of the fetus protruded from her vagina as she sank under the water. Four- and five-year-old children clung to the necks of Japanese soldiers and drowned with them.[56]

The American invasion of Okinawa turned the whole island into a battlefield, with the civilians caught in the middle. In 1944 a policy of evacuating women and girls was implemented. The first evacuation ship left Naha in August loaded with children. An enemy submarine sank it on the night of August 23 with great loss of life.[57] The sinking was kept secret, but the approach of American forces was unmistakable when a massive air raid on October 10, 1944, burned out Naha. The fate of Okinawan civilians as U.S. forces struck the narrow island is best suggested by a few grim vignettes. An old woman and her grandson are fleeing from naval gunfire when the boy is hit in the leg. Blood gushes from his wound and he cannot go on. The woman gives her bag of rice and water canteen to the boy and leaves, barely escaping through the shelling. Later she cries in horrified grief that the boy probably died cursing his grandmother's heartlessness in leaving him behind. The sight of a four- or five-month-old baby abandoned in the middle of a field. A group of civilians wait for a lull in the artillery barrage. Suddenly they make their break for safety just as a shell explodes nearby, sending a burst of shrapnel in all directions. Arms, legs, and torsos scattered everywhere like ground meat. The war had reached Okinawa with a vengeance.[58]

Adult men and women were called up, formed into Patriotic Defense Units, and used in combat. High school students were also drafted. Some male students were armed and sent into combat; others were assigned to dig trenches, build field fortifications, and serve as messengers. Female students were pressed into service as nurses to care for the wounded.[59]

The military garrison and civilians were driven to the southern tip of the island into a defensive perimeter within the

Yaeju-Dake escarpment near the villages of Kiyan, Makabe, and Mabuni and the caves in the seaside cliffs. Naval guns pounded the area from the ocean side. Soldiers moved closer from the land side, their flamethrowers incinerating everything in their path. Bombers blasted the defenders from the air. Food and water ran out. The wounded and sick formed a chorus of pain. Covered with blood from the wounded and dying, the girl students stayed with their patients to the end. Many civilians wanted to surrender but were prevented by the army; they committed suicide with hand grenades or bayonets. Casualty figures show the bitter fighting. About 50,000 U.S. military personnel were killed or wounded, while Japanese forces had about 110,000 killed. Estimates of civilian casualties run to more than 160,000. The Japanese military added its own atrocities against the local residents. Foe and "friend" alike made Okinawans suffer more than any other Japanese civilians.[60]

Japan proper came under air attack about the middle of 1944. The Sino-Japanese War, the Russo-Japanese War, and World War I were fought on foreign soil. Except for the military personnel who went into battle, the Japanese people had never seen modern war up close. Now weapons vastly more destructive than those of any previous war pounded Japan night and day. The U.S. Air Force strategy was indiscriminate bombing: military and industrial targets, residential and commercial areas were all bombed with fine impartiality. Incendiary attacks burned out the large cities one after another. Civilians were blown up or burned to death in the saturation raids.[61] No more eloquent testimony to the ravages of war upon the innocent exists than the piles of corpses near Yurakuchō Station in downtown Tokyo. Or the photographs of the charred corpses of a mother holding a child, the woman's face burned into a scorched blob of flesh, eyes and nose mangled together.[62] The massive Tokyo raid on March 10, 1945, was intended to burn out the Shitamachi district by setting a ring of fires. Trapped inside a wall of flames, more than 80,000 persons were burned to death in one night.[63] The survivors found their homes and possessions were piles of ashes. Some were forced to move in with rural relatives. Others made temporary houses out of the air raid shelters in the middle of the ruins. They had no place else to go.

The *Nihon Dokusho Shimbun* on August 13, 1956, solicited manuscripts on the theme "Recollections of the War." Of the 151 manuscripts received, "A great many writers recalled that they had thought war was somewhat beautiful and heroic. After the savage air raids, their ideas about war had changed."

With little to eat and no hope for the future, under constant air attack and exhausted from overwork, urban Japanese were desperate. Getting enough food on the black market to stay alive each day was their only thought. The next day and the next person would have to take care of themselves. Chino Toshiko thought, "We have sunk to nothing but animals."[64]

Bombs dropped from 20,000 feet did not distinguish between soldier and civilian. The August 7, 1945, attack on the Toyokawa Naval Arsenal was a hideous example of total war. Labor service workers and student workers were employed at the arsenal under military supervision. Between 2,000 and 3,000 civilians were killed in the air raid. Among the dead were women's volunteer corps members, female students, and more than fifty elementary school students. An eyewitness described the carnage: "An arm lay on the ground. There was a skull split in half. A headless torso. A girl's head hung from a tree by the road, the hair caught in the branches. A young worker with no legs, face burned black, crawled around on her hands." Several hundred young women and girls were blown to bits, burned, and mutilated.[65]

For sheer horror, nothing rivals Hiroshima and Nagasaki. Residents of those two cities were human guinea pigs in the first use of atomic weapons in warfare. The *Enola Gay* took off from Tinian in the Marianas early on August 6, 1945, and released the atomic bomb over Hiroshima at about 8:15 A.M. There was a blinding flash as a force equal to twenty thousand tons of TNT exploded 1,800 feet over the city. Everything for 3,000 meters in all directions from the center was totally

destroyed. Survivors were covered with blood and nearly naked: their clothes had been blown right off by the blast. "A
woman was walking in a daze. The skin of her face was peeled
off and hung from her lower jaw." And "Under the bridge
countless corpses were floating. Only scraps of clothing were
left on them. Near the river bank a woman floated face-up,
blood gushing from a deep hole in her chest. Everywhere were
incredibly bloody and gruesome sights." Medical treatment
for the survivors was hopelessly inadequate. City government
had been wiped out in the blast. The few doctors and medical
personnel available had no idea how to treat radiation victims
or at first even that the city had been struck by an atomic
bomb. The injured suffered excruciating pain and died like
flies.[66] Three days later, on August 9, Nagasaki was turned
into an atomic furnace.[67]

Some American scientists argued in vain against using the
atomic bomb.[68] Nobel prizewinner H. M. S. Blackett has
questioned why America had to employ the bomb so hastily.
If the primary objective was to save American lives, Washington could have deferred both the bomb and an invasion of
Japan until the Soviet offensive had run its course. The Red
Army was smashing through Manchuria before the United
States could reach Japan, a situation not to the liking of the
American military. The sensational atomic attacks diverted
attention from the Russian successes. Blackett implies that
this may have been the reason why the United States rushed
to drop the bombs.[69]

I have serious disagreements with the minority opinion of
Judge Radha Binod Pal, the Indian justice at the International
Military Tribunal for the Far East. In my opinion, Judge Pal's
dissent is marred by prejudice and factual error. His intense
anti-communism led him to justify Japan's invasion of China,
and he was inaccurate about the Mukden Incident. Nevertheless, Pal was correct in stating that the decision to use atomic
bombs on Hiroshima and Nagasaki closely resembled the orders issued by German leaders brought to trial as war criminals at Nuremberg.[70] On February 27, 1963, the Tokyo

District Court ruled that the use of weapons like the atomic bomb in indiscriminate attacks on the undefended cities of Hiroshima and Nagasaki was "an illegal act under then current international law."[71] There are limits to the weaponry and tactics that may be used in wartime. Weapons like the atomic bomb, which entail mass murder and inflict unnecessary suffering on large numbers of noncombatants, violate international law. From a moral perspective, the use of such weapons is an atrocity.[72]

Research by the Specialists Committee, Japan Council Against Atom and Hydrogen Bombs, indicates that approximately 200,000 persons died in Hiroshima and 122,000 in Nagasaki.[73] According to statistics compiled in 1949 by the Keizai Antei Honbu (Economic Stabilization Board), Japanese civilian casualties in the war, not including Okinawa and foreign areas, were 299,485 persons (deaths from bombing were 297,746; deaths from naval bombardment and other causes were 1,739).[74] The *Dai Tōa sensō zenshi* (Complete History of the Pacific War) published in 1953 places the number of civilian deaths, exclusive of civilians working directly for the military in overseas areas but including Okinawa and China, at 658,595. Though not precise, these statistics show the scale of civilian casualties. The Keizai Antei Honbu also compiled figures on property damage. Approximately 62.1 million *tsubo* (1 *tsubo* is equivalent to 3.954 square yards) of buildings were directly damaged, including 1.7 million *tsubo* of private dwellings and businesses. Privately owned shipping losses were 3,207 vessels and 7.9 million gross tons. Cultural losses due to air raids included the castles of Nagoya, Okayama, Hiroshima, Wakayama, and Shuri (Okinawa), the Tokugawa family mausoleum, and the shrine of Daté Masamune in Sendai. No one could ever count the books, documents, paintings, and other treasures that went up in flames.

10

Dissent and Resistance: Change from Within

Historians must not flinch from the ignominy and suffering caused Japan and its people by the Pacific War. Grim facts must be faced and researched no matter how painful and upsetting. Presenting the people with the objective historical facts is an obligation that humanizes and dignifies scientific research. Yet fidelity to the truth requires that we also note the exceptions. During that long night from 1931 to 1945 there were a few Japanese who resolutely refused to change their political beliefs or to kowtow to the authorities. They remained critical of the war and aggression.

The existence of these intrepid individuals enables us to find even in this disgraceful period accomplishments worthy of Japan's best traditions. These persons kept the flame of conscience burning during the mad storm of tyranny and aggression. They added a distinguished chapter to Japan's long history; they have bequeathed a valuable legacy to later generations. The dissidents also constitute eloquent testimony in the vigorous debate over the Pacific War. It is said that Japan's actions were unavoidable under the international conditions then prevalent. Or it is argued that once the war started, citizens naturally had to work for victory. The dissenters undermine that argument. They also suggest that an individual or a society's choices are not predetermined.

Official repression forced the open resistance of the early period previously discussed and the dissidents who survived the destruction of the organized antiwar movement to adopt various distinct modes of action. A general classification would include (1) passive resistance and (2) active resistance. Under the former may be subsumed (a) "perfect silence," a refusal to endorse the war in any way, and (b) ignoring the war and continuing one's nonwar professional work. The second general category may be further subdivided into (a) legal resistance and (b) illegal resistance, with the latter including refusing induction into military service, secret dissident activities within Japan, resistance in prison, and overt antiwar activities abroad. The extremes in each category were perfect silence and illegal resistance; people in these polar modes were able to oppose the war clearly and unequivocally. The other categories include numerous gray areas. Many individuals for different lengths of time and to varying degrees had to pretend tacit approval of the war in order to avoid repression. The distinction between these modes of resistance and opportunistic cooperation with the government was very fine. The dissidents were frequently placed in ambiguous situations in which an outsider cannot judge their real motives.

Passive Resistance

When what a person said and did had to appear to support the war, or inevitably became a kind of approval of the conflict, one method of preserving personal integrity was by perfect silence. Arahata Kanson chose this method and "held [his] breath for several years during the war."[1] Some writers saw they would have to toe the line in journalism and switched jobs completely. Ishikawa Sanshirō went into farming and Hattori Shisō worked for a soap company.[2] Changing jobs to avoid both cooption and compromise of one's principles may seem like avoidance of responsibility rather than a form of resistance. But there was the danger that, as Ooka Shōhei put it, "anyone who opposed the army would be killed." When it meant that the military could "deal with the dissident anyway they wanted,"[3] silence should not be denigrated.[4]

There were also a few cases, long locked in mystery, of "domestic exile." Some individuals hid successfully within

Japan. This self-effacement was perhaps the supreme form of "perfect silence." The poet Shōbara Teruko reportedly dropped out of sight to escape the police and is still living incognito.[5]

The attempt to continue cultural life while avoiding as much as possible the official rhetoric of "Japan's divine mission" was also a legitimate response to the war. For example, the political step backward of ideological conversion turned out to be an artistic step forward for some proletarian writers. No longer didactic, their values internalized, they were more skilled craftsmen. Many outstanding literary works were turned out in the period after 1935.[6] They included: in 1935, *Oguma Hideo shishū* (Collected Poems of Oguma Hideo) and *Yoake mae* (Before the Dawn) by Shimazaki Tōson; in 1936, *Fuyu no yado* (Winter Lodging) by Abe Tomoji, and *Fugen* (The Merciful Bodhisattva) by Ishikawa Jun; in 1937, *Robō no ishi* (Stones by the Roadside) by Yamamoto Yūzō, the completion of *Anya koro* (A Dark Night's Passing) by Shiga Naoya, *Hokutō no kaze* (A Cold Wind) by Hisaita Eijirō, *Yukiguni* (Snow Country) by Kawabata Yasunari, *Kisha no kamataki* (The Stoker) by Nakano Shigeharu, *Bokutō kidan* (A Strange Tale from East of the River) by Nagai Kafū, the poem *Same* (Shark) by Kaneko Mitsuharu, and volume 1 of *Kazan baichi* (Soil of Volcanic Ash) by Kubo Sakae; in 1938, *Marusu no uta* (The Song of Mars) by Ishikawa Jun, *Kaze tachinu* (The Wind Rises) by Hori Tatsuo, *Sorori banashi* (Shinzaemon's Tales) by Ishikawa Jun, volume 2 of *Kazan baichi,* and *Ishikarigawa* (The Ishikari River) by Honjō Mutsuo; in 1939, *Uta no wakare* (Taking Leave of Poetry) by Nakano Shigeharu and *Fūsetsu* (Wind and Snow) by Abe Tomoji. Works like those of Kaneko and Ishikawa were positive statements of resistance skillfully camouflaged in complex styles.

As one might expect, after 1941 most published writing was a far cry from real literature. Yet a few masterpieces appeared, including *Naoko,* by Hori Tatsuo, *Shukuzu,* by Tokuda Shūsei, and *Hikari to kaze to yume* (Light, Wind, and Dream), by Nakajima Atsushi, in 1941; and in 1943, *The Makioka Sisters* by Tanizaki Jun'ichirō and *Ri Ryō* (Li Ling) by Nakajima Atsushi. When the authorities prohibited serialization of *The Makioka Sisters,* Tanizaki continued writing the novel in anticipation of later publication. Nagai Kafū did the same.[7] Funabashi Seiichi's *Shikkaiya Yasukichi* (Yasukichi the Kimono Dealer) was published during the heavy air raids in May 1945. After the war, Funabashi described his mood at the time: "They said you can't do this and you can't do that. I decided I was going to do something. I thought I would get killed in the air raids anyway. If I was going to die, I wanted to produce at least one solid work. I wrote in a frenzy of exultant desperation."[8] Funabashi's life style was a kind of freakish resistance to the deluge; he "slept with all the women he could and forgot the war,"[9] and singlemindedly described eros and love.

These few selections show that even though the propaganda mill flooded the nation with hack pieces, there was also some writing worthy of the best in Japan's literary tradition. Literary criticism also continued. A partial list would include: in 1937, *Shinzō no mondai* (The Problem of the Heart) and *Rekishi o gyakuten saseru mono* (Reversing History) by Hirotsu Kazuo; in 1939, *Fuan no katachi* (The Shape of Anxiety) by Ayukawa Nobuo; in 1940, *Bungaku no setsuri* (The Providence of Literature), also by Ayukawa; in 1941, *Sakkaron* (On Writers) by Masamune Hakuchō and *Mori Ogai* by Ishikawa Jun; in 1942, *Saitō Mokichi nōto* (A Note on Saitō Mokichi) by Nakano Shigeharu;[10] in 1944, *Ro Jin* (Lu Hsun) by Takeuchi Yoshimi.

A survey of all the diverse fields of academic research, even a broad overview such as I attempted for literature, is not feasible. I shall offer a few examples that I happen to know about: in 1936, "Iinkai no ronri" (Dialogue and Truth) by Nakai Masakazu,[11] "Fuorierubatha ni tsuite, daiichi tēze no kaishaku" (On Feuerbach, An Interpretation of the First Thesis) by Katō Tadashi,[12] and *Nihon ideorogi-ron* (On Japanese Ideology) by Tosaka Jun; in 1937, *Senkyo bassoku no kenkyū* (Research on Criminal Penalties in Election Laws) by Minobe

Tatsukichi, and *Nihon shakai seisaku-shi* (A History of Japanese Social Policy) by Kazahaya Yasoji; in 1939, *Mikeruanjero* (Michelangelo) by Hani Gorō, and *Gendai Shina-ron* (On Modern China) by Ozaki Hotsumi; in 1940, "Meiji Ishin kenkyū" (Research on the Meiji Restoration) by Hani Gorō,[13] "Kinsei jukyō no hatten ni okeru Soraigaku no tokushitsu narabi ni sono kokugaku to no kanren" (The Unique Characteristics of the Sorai School in the Development of Tokugawa Confucianism and Its Relationship to National Learning) by Maruyama Masao,[14] and "Iwayuru nōdo kaihō ni tsuite" (On the Emancipation of Serfs) by Takahashi Kōhachirō; in 1941, "Kinsei Nihon seiji shisō ni okeru 'shizen' to 'sakui' " (Nature and Invention in Tokugawa Political Thought) by Maruyama Masao;[15] in 1942, *Doitsu chūsei-shi no kenkyū* (Research on Medieval Germany) by Uehara Senroku, *Kokka to shūkyō* (State and Religion) by Nambara Shigeru; in 1943, *Chūka minkoku sanjūnen-shi* (A Thirty-Year History of the Chinese Republic) by Matsumoto Shin'ichi (published under the name of Tachibana Araki), "Utsubo monogatari ni tsuite no oboegaki" (A Study of the Utsubo Monogatari) by Ishimoda Sho; in 1944, "Shihonshugi to shimin shakai" (Capitalism and a Civil Society) by Otsuka Hisao[16] and *Keizai keihō no kisō riron* (Basic Theory of Economic Criminal Law) by Minobe Tatsukichi.

The authors of these works implicitly opposed the nation's aggressive policies or they put their energies into subjects totally unrelated to the war. Their scholarly output was remarkable considering the adverse conditions. For many years, Minobe had published annually the *Kōhō hanrei hyōshaku* (Commentary on Public Law Cases). The journal, like Minobe's other wartime writings, registered his opposition as a legal scholar to the current abuses of state authority. Minobe sent off the last volume, the issue covering calendar year 1942, during the intensified air raids in March 1945.[17] The Marxist historians Watanabe Yoshimichi, Ishimoda Shō, Matsumoto Shinpachirō, and Tōma Seita continued their collaborative research in secret, confident that "our spirit will be taken up by the next generation and that a better day is coming."[18] Ishimoda wrote *Chūseiteki sekai no keisei* (The Formation of the Medieval World) during the war, finishing the preface in October 1944 (it was published in June 1946). The solid research of a small number of scholars during the war was a crucial contribution to the vigorous postwar revival of the social sciences.

Literature and academic research permit a certain amount of political dissembling. If an individual could hide behind the technical craft of his special field, it was possible to do honest work. In social criticism, however, there was no place to hide; candor was virtually impossible. If a person had been really critical of the government, the only outlets were diaries and private correspondence. This required great courage because of the possibility of discovery. The diaries and private letters of Nakae Ushikichi,[19] Nagai Kafū,[20] Mizuno Hironori,[21] Kiyosawa Kiyoshi,[22] and Morishita Jirō[23] contain sharp criticism of the authorities and accurate prophecies about how the war would end.[24] Even in this period, when all Japanese seemed to have lost their critical faculties and lapsed into a psychotic frenzy, there were some perceptive persons with a firm grasp on reality.

Active Resistance

To the extent that it can be distinguished from sycophancy and opportunism, passive resistance was certainly a form of defiance. Yet passive resistance had no societal effect in directly impeding the war. Its significance lay solely in preserving individual conscience in preparation for postwar reconstruction. Active resistance was carried out by individuals not content to watch and wait. Any really determined action to stop the war and prevent a national disaster inevitably entailed illegal resistance. As shall be described in detail below, there was almost no organized illegal resistance in Japan. Most dissenters believed that to have even a little influence on society, it was more effective to operate within the law, doing so as courageously and militantly as possible.

Communism and other revolutionary movements were destroyed, but elements of the labor and farmer movements were still around. For example, in 1943 there was reportedly a well-organized group of printing workers. They cooperated with the authorities but protected their own interests by continuing their union activities as a workers' club. Statistics on labor disputes indicate some unrest: 417 incidents involving 14,791 workers in 1943; 296 incidents involving 10,026 persons in 1944; and 13 incidents and 382 workers to August 15 in 1945. Tenant farmer disputes also continued through the war: 17,738 tenants were involved in 2,424 disputes in 1943, and 8,213 tenants in 2,160 disputes in 1944 (figures for 1945 are not available). Though reduced in scope, tenant disputes continued until the end of the war.[25]

As professional journalism gradually succumbed to government pressure, private magazines appeared as forums for critical comment. Those mentioned earlier were typical. After Kiryū's *Tazan no ishi* was banned and Ubukata's "self-control" ended his open opposition, Masaki's *Chikaki yori* and Yanaihara's *Kashin* were the most open forms of legal intellectual opposition during the war. Issues of both journals were frequently banned, and both men were pressured to stop publication. Nevertheless, they continued to put out their magazines every month, never missing an issue and never surrendering to the official line. Even after the heavy air raids in the spring of 1945, the magazines came out in mimeographed form until the day the war ended. Masaki and Yanaihara showed equal fortitude against the Japanese police and U.S. B-29s.

I have already mentioned how Yanaihara, a specialist in colonial policy and a disciple of Uchimura Kanzō in the Non-Church movement, was driven from Tokyo Imperial University because he criticized Japan's aggression in China. Stripped of his teaching position and forbidden to write for the media, Yanaihara continued his personal critique in the pages of *Kashin*. An incident at a Christian meeting in November 1939 was the subject of the January 1940 issue. The Christians had all stood up to honor "a certain army general" (Matsui

Iwane, commander of the offensive against Nanking and the officer responsible for the Nanking atrocities). Yanaihara asked, "Would it not have been more appropriate for Christians to have demanded an expression of regret for those actions? Could anything have been less appropriate than for them to have stood up and honored him?" For all its indirectness, Yanaihara's comment was still a trenchant denunciation of army conduct in Nanking.

In the June 1940 *Kashin* Yanaihara attacked "An Announcement to the Troops" issued by Itagaki Seishirō. Itagaki had denounced England, France, and America by saying that "Europe and America had aggressively invaded China." Yanaihara noted, "There is no mention of Germany or Italy. Isn't Germany aggressive? What about Italy?" Itagaki had written that "European and American imperialism had turned China into a semi-colony. Japan's policy is to make China an independent country." Yanaihara retorted: "In view of the recent history of East Asia, one cannot say that only Europe and America have pursued a policy of making China a semi-colony. To condemn only the West's actions in China is a highly partisan interpretation supported by neither scholarship nor history."

Yanaihara's Christian faith inclined him away from a direct clash with the authorities. For example, in June 1938 he wrote, "My burning passion for Heaven rests on a complete faith in Christ's second coming. I leave retribution to God's hand." Yet in August 1941 he wrote, "The storm will not rage forever, the fire will not spread everywhere. God's judgment will be made and God's providence will be done. Righteousness always triumphs over injustice, construction always defeats destruction. God's kingdom always triumphs in this world, the glory of Christ will always be exalted." Yanaihara firmly believed that God's justice would prevail in the end. He never wavered in his determination to use the power of his pen against the storm of oppression sweeping over the earth.[26]

In contrast with Yanaihara's blend of Marxist economics

and Christian theology, Masaki's career included journalism and the law. He personified a natural militant democracy. The pages of *Chikaki yori* were alive with intriguing paradox and irony, with lively metaphors and similes. Masaki was a master of double entendre and oblique attack. But he also used fiery language and went for the jugular when incensed by a particularly stupid government policy or personality. In May 1943 he wrote: "Incompetent and unscrupulous lawyers have a bag of tricks. As they take a case they say, 'We'll win, We'll win.' Next, as they collect their fee, they say, 'Defeat would be a disaster.' Finally they say, 'If we lose it isn't my fault. I've done my best.' They don't feel responsible for an adverse verdict." Readers saw the similarity to Japan's early victories and later setbacks. In September 1943 Masaki commented on a new book, *Niūheburidesu tankenki, shokujinzoku o saguru* (Exploring in the New Hebrides: The Search for Cannibals):

That the cannibals lead such an extremely wretched life was a revelation to me. In photographs of them everyone looks wretchedly unhappy. The reason is not the natural conditions they live under or the oppression of the British and Americans. It is because of their own ignorance. Of all the living creatures in the islands, the cannibals have the most stupid and ugly existence. The animals are restrained by an instinct for preservation of the species; the islanders feel no such restraint. Neighboring tribes fight incessantly. Each village tries to wipe out the next. The "law of the jungle" literally applies: the weak are destroyed by the strong. Intravillage violence has also been institutionalized by chiefs. Their word is law and they are extremely cruel. Sometimes people are unhappy and disaffected with the chief. But the chief is surrounded with swarms of loyal opportunists who covet the special privileges of food and women the chief can bestow. The needy and powerless cannot get near the chief and must bear their miserable lot in silence. Is there such a squalid spectacle in the animal world? Hell must be like this. Reading this book made me thankful that I was born in a civilized country.

Masaki's scathing irony hit the mark more effectively than any broadside aimed directly at the authorities. He was not loath to speak directly to power. The June 1944 issue was an attack on Premier Tōjō:

> The whole country is so preoccupied with the war effort that no one has time to think of anything else. The people are quiet and obedient because of the war. There are people who take advantage of them. Suddenly drunk with power, they regard the public as stupid peasants. They exploit their countrymen's suffering for personal advantage. They are addicted to base, ugly ambitions and sully the honor of this divine land. We who believe that justice is the essence of the nation have silently endured their crude rampage. The country is now engaged in a great battle; this is not the time to punish their perfidy. Yet the righteousness of this divine land must never perish. Someday the hammer of justice will strike them. Patriotic Japanese! For that future day of retribution, we should keep a careful record of their nefarious activities.

In a combined February-March 1945 issue, Masaki spoke out against the suicide tactics, the use of human torpedoes and human bombs: "People are saying, 'There is no other way than to rely on Japanese spiritual power. Look at the young heroes of the Special Attack Units.' Well, is that really spiritual power? Isn't that Japanese spirit just like the compressed air in a torpedo? Instead of several tubes of compressed air, the spiritual power of several men is used. Spirit is used as a substitute for material. Is this any way to treat human beings?" Masaki's dissent on the suicide tactics was but one of many instances when he attacked the government head on. Perhaps the limited influence of the private magazines explains why they were allowed to continue publication. Yet it is still a mystery that *Chikaki yori* was not banned and its author not arrested.[27]

Masaki also used his legal training to fight the government. One dramatic clash with the authorities occurred when a coal mine operator asked Masaki to investigate the disappearance of one of his employees. Masaki learned that the missing man had been arrested on suspicion and then tortured to death by the police in Ibaraki Prefecture. Masaki had the corpse removed from the grave where the police had put it and had the head severed (the body had not been handed over to the family). The decapitated head was taken to the department of forensic medicine at Tokyo Imperial University, where Professor Furuhata Tanemoto performed an autopsy. His examination confirmed that the victim had died of head wounds. Masaki initiated legal action against the patrolman involved. The Mito prosecutor, the Mito district court, and other authorities had done everything they could to cover up the death and protect the police. To challenge them on their own ground put Masaki's life in danger. The police and prosecutors were not above arresting him and getting rid of him.

The struggle by lawyers and judges like Masaki to protect human rights deserves special mention.[28] In February 1942 Premier Tōjō demanded that the judiciary change its attitude. If the judges could not see their way clear to cooperating with national policy, Tōjō threatened, "Some special measures will be taken." Hosono Nagayoshi, chief judge, Hiroshima Court of Appeals, criticized Tōjō's action as an unconstitutional infringement upon judicial independence.[29] Another noteworthy case involved Chief Justice Yoshida Hisashi and his colleagues on the third civil affairs section, Supreme Court, who defied Kempeitai intimidation and ruled that the authorities had interfered in the 1942 election. In March 1945 he declared the election results invalid.[30] As these cases attest, some lawyers and judges displayed exceptional courage and dedication to justice during the war.

There were also some instances of illegal resistance: refusing military service, secret resistance at home, resistance overseas, resistance in prison. Anarchist Ishikawa Sanshirō urged Kimura Ayao, who was about to be drafted, to desert from the army. That was about 1939. A few years later Kimura got the chance and reportedly decamped in Singapore.[31] This is one of the few recorded cases of desertion for political reasons. Most evaders or deserters acted for personal reasons.

According to the statistics on defectors and deserters, in

1943, 20 men defected and 1,023 deserted. During the first seven months of 1944, there were 40 defections and 1,085 desertions. This was a very rapid increase compared to the 669 defections and desertions in 1939.[32] One army combat veteran slipped away from his unit in Sumatra, hid in the countryside, and became very friendly with the villagers, who nicknamed him "Tobin." Recounting his experiences, Tobin described the death of an Indonesian auxiliary trainee (from the puppet Indonesian army organized by Japan) wounded in an air raid. As he died, the young man screamed *Tennō Heika banzai* (long live the Emperor!). According to Tobin, the words were shouted in an affected manner which no Japanese soldier would have used. Tobin thought: "I wished I had not heard the cry. But if some bastard shouted that as he died, someone who wasn't even Japanese, an Indonesian, were not we all, every Japanese, responsible for indoctrinating him this way? I couldn't stand it any more." The Indonesians had been indoctrinated to be more Japanese than the Imperial Army. Tobin reportedly wept after he witnessed the scene.[33]

Draft-age men in wartime grasp at any straw. "If you just wait and take your chances, you might not be drafted. Even if you're drafted, you might get stationed in Japan and never leave the country. Even if the worst happens and you're assigned to a combat infantry unit, you might come back without a scratch."[34] Before the draft notice arrived, the odds against actually ending up in combat seemed fairly good. Eventually the draft notices came, however. Vast numbers of unwilling men were drafted, sent off to risk their lives and be maimed and killed at the front. A considerable number tried to improve the odds by dodging the draft under one strategem or another.[35] Draft dodging is a class privilege; few ordinary citizens can arrange it. They have to go when called. What they thought about military service was caught in an underground song popular at the time: " 'For the country' they say. How sad the draftee going off to the stupid army. A tearful parting from his lovely Sū-chan."[36]

Some individuals refused military service because of pacifist convictions. Ishiga Osamu was a member of War Resisters International, a Quaker organization. In 1939 he refused to appear at the one-day inspection callup of reservists and turned himself into the Kempeitai. While being held by the military police, Ishiga heard of another man, a member of the Buddhist Shinshū sect, who refused to take human life. Ishiga was held for a while and then released.[37]

Even after the Communist movement was destroyed, antiwar consciousness was latent in the populace and surfaced occasionally in anonymous letters to the authorities, graffiti, and private comments. The activities that came to police attention were listed in *Shakai undō no jōkyō* (The State of Social Movements), published annually until 1942. The number of dissidents who apparently were not affiliated with the Communist movement is strikingly large. A few examples will show the nature of this protest.

Elementary school teacher Tanaka Shigetoshi made the following comments at a barbershop in 1938: "We are fighting in China because the military are out of control. They keep saying it's a 'righteous war, righteous war.' But when the Japanese army invades another country, isn't it strange to call the fighting 'righteous'?" Kondō Masatarō, a sixty-three-year-old farmer, was quoted as saying at a soldier's funeral: "If the Emperor would just say the word, the war would stop and there would be no more killed and maimed. He doesn't do it, so we can understand if there is resentment against him. But why should anyone shout 'Long live the Emperor!' as he dies?" In 1939 Ono Onyū, chief priest of a Buddhist Jōdō sect temple, put up a notice on the temple bulletin board: "There never was a good war or a bad peace. A reckless war destroys in one year what man took many years to create. Franklin." (The aphorisms were by Benjamin Franklin, well known in Japan because many of his sayings were included in elementary school textbooks.) Aoto Minso, a farmer's wife in Fukushima Prefecture, said in 1940, "The state is like a selfish, unreasonable brat. We don't even have socks for our feet but they demand 'more work, more work.' And we have to do it.

There are higher taxes, higher this and that. Farmers can't take it any more. It's all because of the war. Even if we lose, I just want them to end it quickly."

An anonymous letter was sent to Home Minister Hiranuma in 1941: "Get rid of the Emperor and set up a republic. Demolish all the Imperial tombs and convert the areas to farming land. . . . End the China Incident now. If we grab China, only the military and a few businessmen with political connections will profit from it. To us ordinary folks it doesn't matter if Japan loses. We want peace now." (From internal evidence— a demand to "Abolish all prisons and deport all the criminals to Manchuria"—the author obviously was not a Communist.) A public toilet in Oita Prefecture was embellished with: "Assassinate Premier Konoe. End the war and restore peace." An anonymous letter to the home minister in 1942 said: "Citizens of Tokyo! I think you are all stupid. I'll tell you why: you're giving your lives for that fool who lives for free in the big mansion right in the middle of Tokyo. He should be gotten rid of, chased out of Tokyo. We should revolt and make a free country like America. Isn't the Emperor a human being just like the rest of us?" Only a representative selection of the innumerable statements and letters can be presented here. Granted that the logic may be a bit confused, there is no mistaking the genuine popular sentiment that grew from direct experience of the war. More important, these manifestations show a healthy commonsense skepticism toward the government exhortations and lies.

Although the Communists opposed the war on the basis of scientific analysis and made the most prescient critiques of Japan's aggression, their incredibly clumsy tactics had led to the destruction of the party and the mass apostasy of its members. They therefore played no political role in stopping the war. However, Tokuda Kyūichi, Shiga Yoshio, and other party leaders refused to renounce their beliefs and were kept under preventive detention long after their prison terms ended. Convinced that Japan would eventually be defeated, they spent long years behind bars. Tokuda, for example, was imprisoned and detained for eighteen years.[38] It was a personal resistance, for they were completely cut off from Japanese society and had no impact on events. Still, it was a remarkable record of conviction and endurance. Matsumoto Sōichirō was a singularly determined prisoner. All the inmates of Sakai prison, Osaka, had to bow every morning in the direction of the Imperial Palace in Tokyo. Matsumoto refused. The guards beat him mercilessly and knocked out all his front teeth, but he would not bow. Prison staff reports grudgingly bestowed the classical sobriquet "undaunted by authority or force" on Matsumoto.[39]

The Christian Church also had a few maverick exceptions. Akashi Junzō and other members of the Japan branch of the Watchtower Bible and Tract Society and Fujimoto Zen'emon and members of the Plymouth Brethren sect defied the government. They went to prison rather than admit the religious authority of the emperor under State Shintō, and they remained opposed to the war. When Akashi Mahito and others of the Watchtower Society were drafted, they tried to turn in the weapons on the grounds that they were instruments of murder that violated God's will. For this act they were convicted and imprisoned. Fujimoto and his colleagues were arrested in 1941, but they preached the same message in prison: "God absolutely forbids murder. Thus war is contrary to God's will. The Greater East Asian War, like other conflicts, is due to the greed of nations. It is not a 'holy war' but in fact a sin." They never deviated from their beliefs or cooperated with the war effort.[40]

But Japan was barren ground for political dissidents. The Communists who refused to apostasize were locked up, legal resistance could accomplish very little, and illegal antiwar activity was limited to sporadic and ineffective protests. Finding it impossible to function in Japan, some individuals went abroad, out of the reach of the police and the Kempeitai. Political scientist Oyama Ikuo went to America in 1932 and remained there until the war was over. Actress Okada Yoshiko slipped from Sakhalin into exile in the Soviet Union in

1938. Others sought a more positive role in the antiwar struggle by throwing in with the enemy. The best examples were the activities of some of the captured Japanese soldiers in China. One group formed the Hansen Dōmei (Antiwar League) in Nationalist-held territory. Kaji Wataru, a leftist who had fled from the Japanese settlement in Shanghai and then joined the Nationalists, was one of its leaders. The Hansen Dōmei operated at the front doing "megaphone propaganda," appeals to Japanese troops to surrender or refuse to fight.[41]

In 1939 small groups of Japanese soldiers taken prisoner by the Eighth Route Army formed the Nihon Heishi Kakusei Dōmei (League to Raise the Political Consciousness of Japanese Troops). This was the first antiwar activity by prisoners in the Communist areas. Nozaka Sanzō, a Communist leader who had fled to the USSR in 1931, secretly made his way to Yenan in 1940 and helped to establish a Yenan unit of the Hansen Dōmei. The Kuomintang soon withdrew its support from the league, but Japanese antiwar organizations grew in the areas held by the Eighth Route Army. By April 1944, 220 members were engaged in propaganda work against Japanese forces.[42] Several foreigners like the Canadian doctor Norman Bethune served with the Eighth Route Army for humanitarian reasons. Their devoted treatment of wounded and sick Communist soldiers helped to alleviate the primitive medical and hygienic conditions. A Japanese doctor, Satō Takeo, was also a member of this international medical team.[43]

Some Japanese also cooperated with the American and British military forces. Oka Naoki was in the United States when Pearl Harbor was attacked. He decided to work for the Allies because: "Once the war has started, one can only hope that Japan is defeated quickly. If the military lose, a revolution will break out. Even if the situation does not become revolutionary, once the Japanese realize their relative weakness and understand that they cannot win the war, there will be a broad-based popular movement for peace. The sooner that happens, the less death and destruction Japan will suffer."

Oka went to India in 1943 and did propaganda work for the British Indian Army aimed at eroding Japanese morale and inducing surrender.[44] Painter Yashima Tarō was also in the United States when the war started. Motivated by a belief that "Japanese soldiers should not be sent off to die in a hopeless war," he lent his talents to the Allies. Yashima created an illustrated booklet entitled *Unganashizō* (The Unlucky Soldier) whose hapless hero proved very effective. Many copies were reportedly found in the pockets of dead Japanese soldiers, grim evidence of its popularity. Yashima went to India in April 1945 to work on the *Mushozoku Heishi Butai Shimbun* (The Straggler's Unit Newspaper), a propaganda publication directed at enlisted men. It urged them to surrender and explained the procedures they should follow; it was a how-to-do-it guide for men tired of the war.[45]

Collaboration with the enemy was a unique form of resistance. These men joined the "enemy" and committed apparently treasonous acts against the "fatherland." By conventional wartime moral standards, they were "traitors." I think their behavior falls into a special category and I have coined a name for it, *tsūteki teikō* or "resistance through the enemy." Resistance movements around the world shared the common discovery that when the "fatherland" is preempted by madmen or criminals, they had to turn to the enemy camp. To obey the orders of a "fatherland" controlled by dishonorable men is hardly patriotism; to rebel against illegitimate authority is the only proper course for real patriots. A cruel paradox obtains: to save the nation one must cooperate with an enemy that is ostensibly trying to harm or destroy it. No wonder that the resisters suffered "terrible pangs of conscience and doubt." Viewed objectively, however, actions commonly regarded as treason were actually a higher form of patriotism. A tragic patriotism was appropriate when fools and criminals ruled the state.[46]

Ozaki Hotsumi's involvement in the Richard Sorge spy ring was a different mode of activity from *tsūteki teikō,* yet it falls in the same intellectual category. Ozaki's public writing showed a brilliant dissembling, an ability to mask a radical message in establishment terms. For example, Ozaki published an article called " 'The East Asian Cooperative Community,' the Concept and Objective Conditions for its Realization," in the January 1939 issue of *Chūō Kōron.* In it, Ozaki used the term Tōa Kyōdōtai (East Asian Cooperative Community), which was, of course, a euphemism for aggression in China, in its official contemporary sense. But Ozaki made the point that Chinese nationalism "was moving in a direction diametrically opposed to Japan's interests . . . because Japan makes assertions and demands that are at least objectively indistinguishable from those of the Western powers." In order to implement the concept of an East Asian Cooperative Community, Ozaki averred, an economic restructuring at home would be necessary. Ozaki was really saying that only when a socialist revolution occurred in Japan could there be a "cooperative" relationship between the two countries compatible with Chinese nationalism. It was a radical message disguised in imperialist verbiage.

Recognized as an outstanding expert on China, Ozaki was an adviser to Konoe and used his access to the premier and to classified information to gather intelligence on military and government policies. Ozaki turned the material over to Sorge, who reported to the Soviet Union. They were arrested in 1941 and subsequently executed. Ozaki said he had become a "traitor" and spied for a foreign government because he believed that to save Japan "it had to be reconstructed as a socialist state." Ozaki was convinced that "close cooperation among a China ruled by the Chinese Communist party, a Japan that has rejected capitalism, and the Soviet Union" was the only course open to Japan. According to his statement, he worked with Sorge to prevent Japan from attacking and destroying the USSR.[47] Motivated by political idealism, Ozaki's actions were a blend of socialist internationalism and home-grown nationalism. It was a seemingly contradictory patriotism whereby he "betrayed" the nation in order to save it. It was essentially the same as "resistance through the enemy" except that the category is not strictly applicable in Ozaki's case, since the USSR and Japan were not then formally enemies.

The masses' latent antiwar consciousness gradually became stronger as the consequences of the deteriorating war situation were felt at home. An August 1945 Police Bureau report entitled *Saikin ni okeru fukei, hansen/hangun, sonota fuon gendō no jōkyō*: (Recent Lèse Majesté, Antiwar/Antimilitary, and Other Subversive Activities)[48] that antiwar sentiment had increased sharply compared to 1943 and 1944. The report lists angry resentment about the authorities: "Government officials and the military just keep shouting encouragement while they allow the populace to be slaughtered. The people are being killed off by the thousands every day. Yet the nation's leaders don't seem at all troubled by the death and destruction. Do they think of us as human beings? What are we to them, just cannon fodder? I never realized till this war what a vicious, ruthless country Japan is." Demands for quick surrender proliferated. Resentment toward the emperor increased, as shown in one typical comment: "The Emperor looks very carefree in his photograph. He's killed off a million mothers' sons and he sits there looking unconcerned." The shift in popular sentiment from enthusiastic endorsement of the war to hatred of the imperial family had begun with the escalation of fighting in China in 1937. Now the trickle of disillusionment was swelling into a wave of dissatisfaction. The ruling classes' judgment that to continue the war endangered the "national polity" had ample basis in fact.[49]

Animosity toward the military even burst out in angry public confrontations. After the massive Tokyo air raid of March 9–10, 1945, a Shitamachi woman, apparently a housewife, went right up to a military work party removing corpses from the Sumida River: "You there, you soldiers! How do you feel about all these people? Can you face them?"[50] A staff officer drove up on an inspection tour of the area. A group of burned-out residents were sitting exhausted on the road. "Suddenly they all jumped up and shouted, 'This all happened because of you military men! What's the point of you coming here to look at it?' Without a word, the officer got back in his car and hurriedly drove off."[51]

Popular anger dissipated itself in these short outbursts; there were no organized uprisings. The most that happened were a few insignificant protest attempts. Major Tsunoda Tomoshige planned to assassinate Premier Tōjō in 1944, but he was arrested by the Kempeitai before taking any action.[52] Hibi Tatsusaburō, a machine manufacturer, printed a large number of antiwar leaflets and placed them under the seats of trains leaving from Tokyo Station, at public telephones, and in public toilets and similar places.[53] The absence of organized resistance in Japan contrasts starkly with the experience of other countries where Fascist dictatorships were imposed on the populace. Guerrilla movements sprang up in every country Japan occupied. Resistance in Europe was equally widespread and determined. The Spanish people rallied to the defense of the republic against Franco's forces. Spanish women fought and died alongside their men in that ghastly bloodbath. Although it proved impossible to overthrow the Nazis, many Germans of all classes—intellectuals and workers, men and women—participated in secret resistance activities. Nazi police controls and terror were more severe, yet the scope and tenacity of civilian resistance went far beyond anything in Japan.[54] This was also true of Italy, where the labor movement carried out a general strike despite great danger. In the April 1945 uprising, citizens occupied important buildings and transportation points, and the partisans, their ranks growing every day, launched attacks against German forces. Thrown back in confusion, the Germans finally surrendered. The cities of northern Italy had been liberated by the Italian resistance and citizenry by the time Allied forces reached the area.[55] These were final glorious acts of a resistance movement that had been active everywhere in Nazi-occupied Europe. From France to Yugoslavia, daring guerrillas had harassed the Germans and tied down innumerable divisions in garrison duty.[56] The citizens of Paris fought and died for the honor of liberating their own capital. They erected street barriers, disrupted communications lines, and attacked German units.[57]

Only the Japanese failed to rise up, overthrow the war leadership with their own hands, and restore peace as an act of sovereign will. The Japanese people were passive recipients of a "termination of hostilities" bestowed by the ruling elite. This remarkable docility contrasts with the spirited dynamic resistance in other countries. Why did the populace behave this way? Passivity cannot be explained as traditional behavior. Japanese history is full of violent revolts by warriors and their followers. Peasant uprisings were a common response to exploitation and misrule. But the failure of the armed revolts at Chichibu, Iida, and elsewhere in 1884 at the end of the People's Rights movement wrote finis to armed struggle in Japan. The failure to throw off fascism and fight for freedom —the lack of popular autonomy—was a crucial debilitating factor in postwar democratization.

The resistance in Japan was not strong enough to affect the course of the war. Yet human conduct cannot always be judged by immediate results: An abysmal failure may inspire another generation to do better. It may provide invaluable lessons. If one age's failure contributes to another's success, then it was not all in vain. The resistance movement in wartime Japan is a case study for future generations who may be required to resist a dictatorial government.

Toward a New Japan

Although resistance in Japan was qualitatively and quantitatively inferior to that of other peoples under fascism, the few dissenters at least kept alive the beacon of democracy and peaceful internationalism first lit in early Meiji. It burned low but was never completely extinguished during the long night from the 1930s to August 1945. The wartime repression did not break all links with earlier history. Liberal and radical alternatives to fascism, while an endangered species, survived to the post-1945 era.

Nozaka Sanzō, the Communist leader working with the

Chinese Communists at Yenan, discussed his ideas about post-war Japan with Gunther Stein in late September 1944. Nozaka said, "At the armistice, the Allies should be absolutely uncompromising in their demand for a democratic government, preferably on a republican basis." Nozaka's main points were (1) overthrow the militarists' regime, (2) a drastic curtailment of the political power of the monarchy, (3) a new, liberalized election law, giving general suffrage to men and women over eighteen years of age, (4) the guarantee of more power to parliament, (5) government control over big monopoly capitalists. Nozaka wanted guarantees of freedom of speech and the press and educational reforms because "We *must* bring about a fundamental change in the psychology of the Japanese people in order to guarantee the development of a truly democratic and peaceful Japan."[58]

Although they did not have as lucid a programmatic analysis as Nozaka, some liberals were thinking of the future. As early as 1941, Kiryū Yūyū had predicted the abolition of the military after Japan's defeat. Kiyozawa Kiyoshi's diary from 1944 to early 1945 is sprinkled with ideas about reform: "Freedom of speech must be absolutely guaranteed in the new political system. Unless government bureaucrats are accountable not to the emperor but to the people, there is no hope for administrative reform. . . . The task of education in the future is a transformation of values"; "The idea that the state is supreme and that it is a citizen's duty to support state policy must be discredited"; "There will be a period of disgust and hatred for war. A proper educational system must be implemented and decent values inculcated during those years. The status of women must be raised."[59] Kiyosawa foresaw the major reforms of the 1947 Constitution.

Novelist Morita Sōhei agonized in his diary about the shape of the new Japan. He realized that "a change in the national polity" was an urgent postwar problem: "The military are able to bluster around and dominate things because of the national polity. Unless the national polity is changed we will not be able to rectify the detestable social climate in which honesty does not pay. I have boundless love for our unique system. But when the evils have become so great, what shall we do?" (March 26, 1945). Morita also saw the curtailment of militarism: "The military will be destroyed. That's what the Japanese will get from this war" (April 12, 1945). Morita joined the Communist party after the war, a decision he had reached by the end of May 1945: "This war has shown beyond any doubt that human degradation and misery are due to the system of private property." It was a wartime conversion to communism; Morita was not jumping on the bandwagon of popular postsurrender leftism.[60]

Well-established intellectuals like Morita were not the only ones who desperately wanted postwar changes. Japanese youth were groping toward a better world, though many never lived to see the new dawn. Takushima Norimitsu was drafted from the campus of Keiō University and died in the war. In the diary left to his sweetheart Takushima had written on June 30, 1944: "I have only one ideal. That is for human freedom."[61] Matsubara Shigenobu, drafted from Dōshisha University and later killed, bared his feelings in a letter to a friend: "If I survive, there will be a time when I can talk to you about this long, long night, this unending starless black void. . . ."[62] Tokyo Imperial University student Sumiyoshi Konokichi was mobilized for labor service at an aviation research institute. On one of the rare visits he was able to make to his family, Sumiyoshi was caught in a night air raid and burned to death. His diary entry for May 6, 1945, only twenty days before his death, states: "A new Japan will be created from the ashes. I have not one scintilla of pride about the 'Imperial Throne coeval with heaven and earth.' It is because of that imperial line, because of the national polity and the oracle of Amaterasu Omikami that the military and ultraconservative patriots have become irrational, trampled on humanity and tried to block every progressive trend in society. I want to obliterate that kind of feudal indifference to human dignity. I want to be truly kind, to love my neighbors, be close to my relatives and help everyone."[63] These ill-fated young men were all forming new ideas and beliefs for a postwar Japan.

Chino Toshiko, barely out of her teens herself, taught in an elementary school in Fujimi Kōgen during the war. Her wartime notes are another record of disillusionment with jingoism and imperialism. Germany's surrender reminded her how the Germans had persecuted the Jews. She "thought an age is at hand where 'Art knows no national boundaries.' " Immediately after Japan surrendered she wrote: "I feel vindicated at last. I have long believed that it was wrong to insist that the state should take precedence over everything else. The 'human being' should be foremost. I was sure it would be fatal for Japan to turn all its energies and resources to war and ignore culture and the finer things of life. The way the war has turned out has absolutely convinced me that I was right all the time." The tone and content of all her writings show beyond doubt that these were her true sentiments at the time. They were not added after the war.[64]

Long before the war turned sour, someone had outlined a postwar program for Japan in a bit of political graffiti in a toilet at the Nakanoshima Library, Osaka:

> Tasks for reconstruction: 1. End universal conscription. 2. Reorient Japan toward democracy. 3. Create new relationships between men and women (eradicate all feudal aspects). 4. Revise the legal system. 5. Religious reform (in my opinion, individuals should find God for themselves). 6. Improve the cultural level of the people.[65]

This anonymous liberal's demand for democratic reforms and policies scribbled in June 1938 became a genuine popular aspiration during the war. It was an aspiration formed gradually, incrementally, and secretly in the minds and hearts of people sick of war and fascism. The desperate longing for peace and freedom did not, however, coalesce into an organized, powerful movement able to overthrow the war elite. That unfortunate failure greatly impeded postwar reforms.

Continuities from the war years were the historical preconditions for a new society. Just as values changed, there were changes in social relationships whether the ruling class approved or not. Rapid expansion of military industries caused a shift from light industry, which had been the mainstay of the industrial structure, to heavy industry. Although the old management-employee relationships persisted, war production stimulated the formation of a modern labor force whose major element was adult men. The dynamic labor movement after the war emerged from this industrial force.[66] To fill the labor shortage due to conscription and mobilization for armament production, women were mustered for all kinds of jobs, including many that had been held exclusively by men.[67] Although this was a temporary situation for the war effort, it probably prepared many women for the new roles they played after the war. Takami Jun noted this trend in his diary entry for September 20, 1945, in which he quoted a newspaper article: "Women who were stimulated by and enjoyed going out to work during the war tend to be dissatisfied staying at home and doing domestic chores. Almost all the 700 women at the Asahina steel works returned home when the factory closed. After a while, the women began coming back to the company dormitory in groups of twos and threes. Some returned of necessity because they had been burned out. Many of the others had places to go but preferred to continue working."

Change reached the countryside during the war. In order to meet the need for greater agricultural output, the government had to provide cultivators with incentives to raise production. The first move was passage of the Rent Control Order of December 1939, which empowered the government to reduce tenant rents. Under the Temporary Land Control Order of February 1941 (revised in March 1944), the transfer of agricultural land was controlled. After 1941 the government set up a dual price system: cultivators received a higher price than landlords. Tenant rents were substantially reduced as a result of these measures. Furthermore, the quota system of rice deliveries to the government caused a change from payment of tenant rents in rice to cash payments. These innovations shook the foundation of the landlord system—the dependency relationship between landless tenants and landowners sanctified by law and custom in favor of the latter. Wartime adjustments prepared the agricultural population for the postwar land reform.[68]

Its framers certainly had no such intention in mind at the time, but wartime social legislation proved to be a forerunner of change. Some laws passed in 1937 were designed to alleviate the hardships of the spreading war. That year saw enactment of the revised relief law, the Women and Children Protection Law, and the Military Allowance Law. Two years later, the Medical Treatment Protection Law and the Labor Pension Protection Law were passed, followed in 1943 by the National Medical Treatment Law and other legislation. These laws were far from adequate and were deceptive in intent; their purpose was to strengthen the home front as part of the total war effort. Nevertheless, they were pioneer steps toward the enactment of welfare legislation after 1945.[69]

Other more fundamental changes occurred in the economic structure. They included the rapid industrialization concentrated on heavy industry and the decline of medium and small industry, and improper collusion between government officials and capital due to wartime controls over the economy. These shifts accelerated monopoly, cemented close ties between certain elements of the ruling class bureaucracy and monopoly capital, and weakened the landlord groups. Structural changes in the economic sphere, combined with the self-destruction of the military, seriously damaged the material, institutional, and intellectual base of the emperor system. At the very time when imperial ideology was at a fever pitch, screeching hysterically about the Greater East Asia Co-Prosperity Sphere abroad and selfless devotion to the ruler at home, the whole structure was crumbling from within. The great political, social, and economic reforms centered around the "change of the national polity" carried out by the Occupation after the war were slowly taking shape deep within the imperial system.

11

Defeat

Japan's decision to end the war has attracted enormous scholarly interest. The earliest publications of primary historical material and academic research on the war were about the events leading to its end.[1] This body of material and scholarship shows that although many different actors and initiatives were involved, surrender was achieved by the senior statesmen, the *jūshin,* a group of former premiers, working behind the scenes and through the emperor. They ended the war. The mass of the populace was impotent. Nevertheless, rising popular dissatisfaction posed direct and indirect threats to the ruling class. And the apprehensive elite understood the danger. To that extent, demands from below, from the masses, influenced the authorities. But all planning and activities to end the war were done secretly in the highest councils of government, far removed from the ordinary citizen.

Ending the War in Order to "Protect the National Polity"

The senior statesmen led those who wished to end the war. It was apparent to everyone in the ruling circles that Japan's fortunes could not be reversed, that the war was lost. Everyone, that is, but the military, who insisted on a final decisive battle "to save the nation." Their strategy called for an all-out attack when the Allies invaded the home islands.[2] A massive offensive would smash enemy forces as they came ashore on the beaches. The military were asked what they would do if the Allies did not attempt a landing but "stuck to bombing and burned the whole country to the ground." They could only reply, "We'll really be in a fix then."[3] It was a defense strategy worthy of little boys playing samurai; the military were as dangerous as they were ridiculous. Refusing to surrender, they demanded a great battle to bloody the Allies on the beaches, drive off the invaders, and gain better terms. The military saw the Allied approach as the "golden opportunity," as "the divine chance" they had been waiting for. Faced with such obstinate opponents, the senior statesmen had to be extremely careful. The army might assassinate peace advocates or stage a coup d'état. Real intentions screened by secrecy, the *jūshin* maneuvered delicately toward ending the war.

Certain ideological differences aside, the senior statesmen shared a basic outlook: strongly pro-England and America, anti-Communist, and totally committed to the preservation of the emperor system.[4] They wanted to end the war, but not because they had any doubts about its morality or about the ideology and political structure that had sustained it. Konoe's motives were typical, and his views are well known from his statement at the *jūshin* conference on July 18, 1944,[5] his "Memorial to the Throne" of February 14, 1945,[6] and other documents. Konoe charged that Communist elements in the military had launched Japan into the war; he thought a revolution might occur if the conflict continued. Konoe believed that in order to "preserve the national polity," Japan had to end the war as quickly as possible. He feared revolution more than surrender and defeat.

First priority, perhaps the *jūshin*'s only moral imperative, was to preserve the national polity. Thus the moderate Yonai Mitsumasa could say on May 17, 1945: "If we can just protect the imperial family, that will be sufficient. Even if it means the empire is reduced to the four home islands, we'll have to do it."[7] The *jūshin* shared Konoe's dread that if the war was not ended, domestic unrest might sweep away the throne and everything else with it. This was their reason for ending the war. Not to save the Japanese people from more Allied air raids and naval bombardment; not even to avoid a last-ditch ground battle across the crowded home islands. Japan's leaders showed a supreme indifference to the suffering and despair of the populace to the very end. That callous determination was unshaken by two atomic bombings. The "national polity" took precedence over the people.

Negotiating an end to the war was first formally raised in an official discussion at the Imperial Conference on June 22, 1945. A plan was agreed upon to send Konoe to Moscow to request Russian good offices for peace talks. The gall of government leaders is breathtaking. Japan had planned to attack the Soviet Union if the opportunity arose. Now they asked for assistance as if Tokyo had some claim to Russian friendship![8] It was already too late: Stalin had promised to enter the war against Japan. The twin shocks of the atomic bombings and the Soviet declaration of war broke the stalemate in Tokyo. At the Imperial Conferences on August 10 and 14, Premier Suzuki Kantarō, Navy Minister Yonai, and Foreign Minister Tōgō had advocated surrender. They were opposed by the army minister and the two chiefs of staff. Tradition required unanimity, but consensus was still impossible. The emperor cut the Gordian knot by deciding to accept the Potsdam Declaration. Late on the night of August 14, the emperor recorded a surrender announcement for broadcast the next day. At noon on August 15, the imperial broadcast informed the people of Japan that "Our Empire accepts the provisions of their Joint Declaration." Most of the country realized for the first time that Japan had been defeated and the war was over.[9]

One group of army officers rejected the imperial will. They planned a coup d'état to seize power, establish a military government, and continue the war. After a few days of plotting, they broke into the Imperial Palace on the evening of

August 14 in search of the emperor's recording. They also intended to kill Premier Suzuki. Leaflets calling for continued resistance were distributed at Atsugi Air Base and other facilities.[10] The fanatics failed to stop the imperial broadcast. Most of the military knew that further resistance was impossible and quietly complied. The wretched fifteen-year war came to an end with a whimper instead of another gory bang.

That last bit of military lunacy was a fitting postscript to the conflict. Army Minister Anami initially was sympathetic to the officers' plot; he later declined to lead it but still did nothing to check it.[11] General Anami joined the criminal conspiracy or at least was guilty of neglect of duty for not suppressing the revolt. The war started with the Kwantung Army's conspiracy at Mukden and ended with an officers' conspiracy against the Imperial Palace in Tokyo.

Popular reaction to the surrender news ranged across the political and emotional spectrum. At one extreme there were comments like "Japan cannot be defeated," "It's a filthy lie," or "I'll kill my wife and children, then commit suicide." On the other side were opinions like "Now my world is bright and dazzling. Everything brims with happiness and promise for the future." Some people broke out the rationed whiskey and celebrated. There were many shadings of emotion in between.[12] The most common responses were anguished tears and misery at defeat or "deep sighs of relief that the war was over and one had survived."

Defeat had been unthinkable, surrender inconceivable. Neither rulers nor ruled were prepared for the humiliation of national failure and occupation by foreign troops. Minds recoiling from reality sought scapegoats or fantasies of revenge. Persons in authority tried to shift responsibility to the public. A speech by a schoolteacher to his students was typical: "It's your fault. Did you work as hard as you could for the nation? Didn't you forget it was a war ordered by the emperor? Yes, you forgot, didn't you."[13] Others looked impatiently ahead to a future war of victorious revenge: "Just think in terms of victory being postponed for fifty years. Endure this and let's bide our time, for the sake of the empire."[14] The government avoided the word "surrender" and used such euphemisms as "acceptance of the Potsdam Declaration" or "the end of the war." But no words were adequate to express or conceal the national trauma of defeat.

On August 14, 1945, Japanese citizens in the colonies and occupied areas were proud rulers backed by the power and authority of the Greater Japanese Empire. A day later they were a defeated people. The empire was gone, replaced by danger, privation, and death. The time of reckoning came a week earlier in Manchuria and northern Korea when the Soviet invasion struck through Manchuria and down to the 38th parallel in Korea. Japanese residents were surrounded by resentful populations that had long hated their exploiters. The whole region swiftly came under Russian control.[15]

The agricultural settlers and youth volunteer corps members in northern Manchuria were in the path of the Soviet steamroller. Of 333,000 Japanese in the area, confirmed deaths totaled approximately 80,000. The agricultural settlers were only 14 percent of the Japanese in Manchuria; they suffered 50 percent of the casualties.[16] The fate of the youth volunteers, who were mainly pressured into volunteering in the first place, was especially pitiful. They were slaughtered by the local Chinese and the Red Army. In addition, approximately 32,000 Japanese died in northern Korea. Ninety percent were refugees fleeing from the advancing Russian forces.

Many of the Japanese casualties in Manchuria were at the hands of Chinese taking revenge; the elderly, women, and children were innocent victims of the reprisals. To the settling of old scores was added the enormous violence of the Soviet invasion. Japan had violated the Japan-Soviet Neutrality Pact by the Kwantung Army Special Maneuvers, which were actually feints at Russian units in Siberia. Japan had been ready to strike at an opportune moment. Thus criticism of the USSR for formally violating the treaty and declaring war on August

8 is not to be taken too seriously. Nevertheless, the extensive plunder, rape, and acts of force by Red Army personnel were clear violations of international law and deserve severe condemnation.

Some civilians stranded when the Imperial Army decamped never had a chance to flee. Others tried to get away as best they could. The Soviet offensive swept through the area, leaving a trail of death and pillage in its wake. Half-crazed Japanese women, faces distorted with the agony of their decision, strangled or stabbed their own children to death and then committed suicide.[17] Whole families grew sick and died from weeks of exposure, starvation, and fatigue. One thirteen-year-old orphan was sold off as a slave and put to work by a local farmer on a hand mill grinding soy beans. Tied to the bar in place of a donkey, she went round and round in a circle day after day till she dropped. She went blind, probably from poor nutrition, but miraculously survived and eventually got back to Japan.[18] Other women were less fortunate. Screaming for help, girls were taken away in Russian trucks and never seen again. Refugees watched hopelessly.

Japanese military personnel and civilian adult males captured by the Soviets in Manchuria and northern Korea were sent to labor camps in Siberia and Outer Mongolia. Hunger, extreme cold, and overwork took a heavy toll.[19] Japanese prisoners were also illegally treated in China. The Nationalists used some Imperial Army units against the Communists. Many Japanese soldiers died pointlessly in other people's civil wars after the Pacific War ended[20] (this also happened in Vietnam and Indonesia).[21]

Japanese civilians in the Philippines had tasted defeat months before.[22] When American forces landed, whole families fled to the mountains and wandered from place to place until claimed by starvation and exhaustion. In one case the mother and father died, leaving a young boy and his two younger sisters, nine and six years old. The six-year-old refused to leave her mother's corpse. Later the two skeletons were found together. The boy and his nine-year-old sister went on until she said, "I can't walk anymore." Cries of "Brother, brother" ringing in his ears, the boy left her behind and staggered along until he was found more dead than alive by American soldiers.[23] Manila-born Hidaka Fusako was ten years old when the final battles took place. Her family fled to the mountains with a group of refugees. When her mother and father died, she and her nine-year-old and seven-year-old brothers trudged along with the group. Completely exhausted, the younger boy finally collapsed and made no effort to get up again. Fusako took the other boy's hand and followed after the refugees. Later during a short rest break a stranger reprimanded her: "Why did you leave your brother back there?" Two decades later that question still haunted her, its cruel implications forever seared into her conscience. She was not the only one; others made the same decision. When personal survival was at stake, many parents abandoned their children.[24] Even the end of the war was no guarantee against tragedy. On August 22, 1945, a repatriation ship from Sakhalin was sunk by an unidentified submarine. Over 1,700 people were killed, including many women and children.[25]

Japanese on the home islands were relatively well-off compared to their countrymen caught overseas at the war's end. The terror of the bombing ended with surrender; they could begin to adjust to peaceful lives again.[26] Yet the consequences of the war were not over with the emperor's broadcast or the September 2 surrender ceremony on the *Missouri*. For the widows and orphans, pain and loss persisted: their husbands and fathers never came back.[27] Maimed veterans returned to Japan minus arms and legs left on field hospital operating tables or distant battlefields. The pathetic honor for the most prolonged suffering goes to the victims of the atomic bomb attacks on Hiroshima and Nagasaki. The war never ended for them. Those residents not killed instantly were dosed with radiation. Rescue workers and outsiders who entered the city later searching for missing relatives were also exposed to toxic radiation effects. A strange sickness, the A-bomb disease, struck like an epidemic in the days and months after the attack. Thousands grew sick and died.*

Radiation victims were the living dead. Symptoms appeared without warning: An apparently healthy person would suddenly show the fatal signs, grow weak, and die. Every year for more than two decades after August 1945 many died from radiation illness.[28] Survivors were hurt professionally. Their health destroyed, many could no longer support themselves. Persons exposed to radiation were discriminated against as "contaminated."[29] Young women with faces disfigured by keloid scars could not hope to marry. Many women pregnant at the time of the atomic bombings gave birth to microcephalic children.[30]

The harsh treatment of civilians in Manchuria had its counterpart in Japan under U.S. occupation forces. Surrender avoided the mass violence and slaughter of an invasion; American forces landed and occupied Japan peacefully. The violence came later, however, in the assaults, robberies, and general mayhem committed by American troops against civilians. The Higashikuni cabinet succeeded the Suzuki cabinet on August 17 as a caretaker administration to carry out the surrender. The following day, Tanaka Naraichi, director of the police bureau, Ministry of Home Affairs, ordered all police chiefs to "establish sexual comfort facilities" for the occupation army. Brothel operators were summoned to the Metro-

---

*"Soon after the bomb fell—sometimes within hours or even minutes, often during the first twenty-four hours or the following days and weeks—survivors began to notice in themselves and others a strange form of illness. It consisted of nausea, vomiting, and loss of appetite; diarrhea with large amounts of blood in the stools; fever and weakness; purple spots on various parts of the body from bleeding into the skin (purpura); inflammation and ulceration of the mouth, throat, and gums (oropharyngeal lesions and gingivitis); bleeding from the mouth, gums, throat, rectum, and urinary tract (hemorrhagic manifestations); loss of hair from the scalp and other parts of the body (epilation); extremely low white blood cell counts when these were taken (leukopenia); and in many cases a progressive course until death." (Robert J. Lifton, *Death in Life: Survivors of Hiroshima,* New York, Random House, 1967, p. 57.)

politan Police Bureau in Tokyo and provided with ¥100 million in government funds. A special comfort association, known in English as the Recreation and Amusement Association (RAA), was established. Announcements appealed for "employees": "Women of the New Japan. Comfort stations for the occupation forces are being established as one of the national emergency measures for the postwar period. Your positive cooperation is requested." Japanese women were offered up as human sacrifices to the American GIs. The objective was to propitiate the victors with sex and save the "good women" from unwonted advances. In this way, the government of Japan "positively cooperated" with the Occupation.[31] The authorities had thought nothing of violating human rights during the war; they lost the war but not that attitude. The only difference was that now they were pimping for the occupation army. War or peace, women were victimized by the state.

Not content with official pleasure quarters, U.S. soldiers frequently accosted Japanese women on the street or sexually assaulted them. Lives ruined, many committed suicide or became common street prostitutes.[32] The truism that women suffer most in war carried over to the postwar years. Japanese women shared the same fate that befell foreign women in the areas occupied by the imperial military forces. Mixed-blood children abandoned by their Japanese mothers and GI fathers were another legacy of the war.[33] The obverse was the many mixed-blood children in the occupied areas fathered by Japanese military men. In the Philippines, where fierce hatred of Japan persisted long after the war, mixed-blood children were desperate outcasts.[34]

U.S. troops committed the other crimes that marked the Japanese army's reign, including robbery and murder.[35] Victims rarely recovered their property or received any compensation. Families of murder victims got little satisfaction from occupation authorities. Among the miscarriages of justice in the aftermath of the war was the treatment by Allied courts of the B and C class war criminals. The executed prisoners included many who had no chance to defend themselves properly and many cases of mistaken identity where the wrong man was put to death. The executions were more expedient revenge than careful justice.[36]

The San Francisco Peace Treaty ended the occupation and restored Japan's sovereignty. Not complete sovereignty, however. Okinawa and the Bonin Islands were kept under U.S. military control. The residents of the latter had been forced to leave during the war. Still forbidden to return to their homes after 1952, they eked out a meager living any way they could.[37] Okinawa had been a bloody battlefield and the prefecture had borne some of the worst fighting of the conflict. The Japanese government never bothered to consult the Okinawans when it concluded the peace treaty; the prefecture and its residents were turned over to the U.S. military government on the islands.

Once again, officials in Tokyo sacrificed the interests of Okinawans. The prefecture was donated to America as a front-line base in the aggressive strategy directed against the People's Republic of China and Vietnam. Okinawan men and women were victimized by the criminal behavior of American servicemen. Murder, robbery, and rape were commonplace. The U.S. military government itself became one of the biggest robbers as land was expropriated for bases and facilities. Denied self-government, Okinawans could not protect themselves. Their status and treatment resembled those of the oppressed peoples in the Greater East Asia Co-Prosperity Sphere.[38]

Sovereign rights and territory were lost in the north to the Soviet Union. The residents of Sakhalin and the Kurile Islands were forcefully removed to the mainland by Russian forces after Japan surrendered. The southern half of Sakhalin was acquired by the Treaty of Portsmouth in 1905; the Kuriles had long been Japanese territory and were not acquired by aggression. Ignoring this history, the United States agreed at Yalta

to give them to the Soviet Union in return for Russian entry
into the war against Japan. Under the San Francisco Peace
Treaty, Japan abandoned territorial rights to the islands. As
a result, the Soviet Union continues to occupy them as Russian territory.

In the two decades since the war, Japan has made an amaz-
ing recovery from the devastation of the war. A new prosperity glitters everywhere. Yet tucked away in the shadows,
hidden from view, are many of the war's victims. The orphans
who roamed the streets of Tokyo and other cities begging and
stealing after the war were eventually placed in institutions
and provided for.[39] Most of the war widows found the
strength to carry on, and time has eased the pain of lost loved
ones. It is the A-bomb illness victims and the maimed war
veterans who can never "recover and prosper." In late 1961
there were still 3,000 wounded veterans who had been bedridden since the war.[40] The workers injured at the Okunoshima
poison gas plant were also invalided for a long time after the
war.[41]

Koreans number among the permanent victims of the war.
Men who served with the Imperial Army or Navy and were
wounded received no assistance from the Japanese government after 1945 on the grounds that they were not Japanese.
The postwar independent Korean states regard them as traitors and provide no compensation or assistance. Crippled in
body and spirit, they lead mean and helpless lives.[42] Korean
victims of the atomic bombings are in an equally desperate
legal and medical limbo. Many happened to be in Hiroshima
or Nagasaki because they were forced to work on war labor
projects. Yet after 1945 they were denied medical treatment
because they were not Japanese citizens.[43]

Japan has a moral responsibility toward the millions of
people killed and wounded, and to their families, when the
Imperial Army and Navy triggered a fire storm of war across
Asia. Although China was a major target of aggression, Japan
has still not concluded a peace agreement; a state of war still

exists between the two countries.* That abysmal policy is compounded by an immoral military alliance with the United States, the new aggressor in Asia. The consequences of the Pacific War still plague the region.

*The state of war was formally ended in September 1972 when Japan and the People's Republic of China resumed diplomatic relations.

Conclusion

Japan surrendered after receiving a message from Secretary of State Byrnes on August 11, 1945, which stated, "The ultimate form of government of Japan shall, in accordance with the Potsdam Declaration, be established by the freely expressed will of the Japanese people."[1] That meant a "change in the national polity": abolition of imperial sovereignty and adoption of popular sovereignty.

General Douglas A. MacArthur became Supreme Commander Allied Powers (SCAP) with headquarters in Tokyo, and occupation forces, mostly American, were stationed throughout the country. SCAP began the democratization and demilitarization of Japan along lines laid out in the Potsdam Declaration. The Imperial Army and Navy were disbanded and all internal security laws were abolished except for SCAP-ordered restrictions on freedom of speech prohibiting criticism of the Occupation. A new constitution was enacted in 1947. It established a new system of government around the three great principles of popular sovereignty, guaranteed human rights, and peace. Under imperial sovereignty, the Greater Japanese Empire suppressed freedom at home and deployed enormous military power to disrupt the peace of Asia. That Imperial Japan was destroyed. In its place a new and peaceful Japan was born. To the degree that the lack of human rights and the military's authoritarianism and irrationality which flourished under imperial sovereignty were the direct causes of the Pacific War, these were epochal changes that removed the sources of aggressive expansionism.

That the Japanese people did not end the war and initiate democratic changes by revolting against the military and civilian war makers bears repeating. In a short English essay written in 1897, Uchimura Kanzō said:

> The voice of their own countrymen they have suppressed (in the name of Loyalty and Patriotism, as hypocrites and scoundrels always do, says Dr. Samuel Johnson), but the voice of the world they can never suppress. And because they oppress the poor powerless people, Nature employs, now, as of old, Nebuchadnezzars and Sennacheribs to bring these minor despots to justice. Because Freedom suffers violence in Japan, there float round that Island Empire alien fleets to guard it from the hand of the oppressors. What the Japanese people may fail to do because of their powerlessness, these foreign fleets may accomplish by their pressure upon the tyrants.[2]

Half a century later, Uchimura's prophecy came true. It was a shameful stigma on the Japanese people that liberation came from foreigners and not by their own hands. Yet perhaps historical reason—the impulse for justice in human affairs—took a circuitous route to Japan. In any case, the basic structure of the new constitution had ample Japanese support. It was not just post–Pacific War support by a few Japanese liberals. People's Rights activists of the 1870s and 1880s clearly wanted a progressive, libertarian constitution. That movement failed, however, and Japan got the authoritarian Meiji Constitution.[3] The postwar constitution realizes the ideals sought three-quarters of a century earlier in the People's Rights movement. A democratic system belatedly came into being after the people had paid a terribly high price in human and material losses for that first failure.

The new constitution has even more concrete links to the past. The Occupation's original draft adopted many parts of a draft law prepared by the Constitution Research Association, made up of outstanding Japanese academics and legal authorities. They used draft constitutions and other ideas of the People's Rights activists in the 1870s and 1880s.[4] Thus, Japanese ideals and values have also been in large measure incorporated into the new constitution. The genesis is crucial: the postwar constitution was not simply an "imposed constitution" forced on the Japanese people.

Unfortunately, the healthy growth of the democracy and pacifism articulated in the Constitution was very quickly stunted by the unwholesome postwar political environment. Defeated Japan and Germany were no longer major powers. Although victorious, England and France were greatly weakened by the conflict. The U.S. and the USSR emerged as superpowers. A new China rose from the chaotic decades of foreign invasion and civil war when the CCP gained control of the mainland and established the People's Republic of China in 1949. From semi-colonized status as the whipping dog of Asia, China emerged as a great power in the Communist camp. These rapid, momentous shifts in the international system affected the world balance of power. America responded by discarding the anti-Fascist policies of the Roosevelt era and adopting a strong anti-Communist strategy.

The consequences were immediately apparent in American policy toward Japan. New Dealers at SCAP Headquarters were weeded out and sent home. Democratization and demilitarization were early casualties. Reforms were stopped in midcourse as policy shifted 180 degrees. Now the American objective was to reorganize Japan as a link in America's anti-Communist military strategy in Asia. Rearmament began under orders from SCAP. The "reverse course" was capped by the U.S.-Japan Peace Treaty signed in 1951 and effective in 1952 and the U.S.-Japan Mutual Security Treaty, concluded at the same time. Under these agreements, America retained Okinawa indefinitely and U.S. forces were stationed on the Japanese main islands. Washington had a treaty and political structure by which it could use the Japanese archipelago as a forward outpost in the Far East.[5] Utilization actually began in 1950 during the occupation period when U.S. facilities in Japan were used against the Democratic People's Republic of Korea (DPRK) and the PRC in the Korean War. The Security Treaty enabled the U.S. to continue using Japan as a military base after the occupation formally ended in 1952.

The Police Reserve set up in 1950 by SCAP order evolved into the present Japan Self-Defense Forces (JSDF). Those units now constitute an auxiliary or puppet force for the Pentagon.[6] The JSDF are to be used if necessary under U.S. command in an anti-Communist war.[7] The significance of these arrangements may be seen in America's brutal, aggressive war in Vietnam. The Japanese government has given its complete support to American actions. Japan shares responsibility, as a partner in crime with the United States, in the illegal war against the Vietnamese people.

Let me suggest a way of looking at the postwar period. The Pacific War was the international version of Japan's peace preservation laws, which tried to crush communism by force. The Japan-U.S. military alliance revives prewar roles, albeit with different stars. America has assumed the Japanese mantle of anti-Communist crusader in Asia and helpmate Japan functions as a strategic base. This arrangement again projects internal security laws outward across Asia and employs lethal force against radical ideas. American aggression in Korea, the Taiwan Straits, and Vietnam is a replay of the Japan-China War. In its post-1945 reincarnation Japan has virtually the same relationship with the United States that Manchukuo or the Wang Ching-wei regime used to have with Tokyo. Now Washington pulls the strings and Japan dances.

One of the major principles of the Constitution, renunciation of war and nonpossession of war potential, has been emasculated by rearmament and the military alliance with the United States. There is also rapid deterioration in the field of human rights.[8] Now that the Japanese have tasted the forbidden fruit of freedom, however, it cannot be so easily denied to them. The people have responded to the attacks on the Constitution by a passionate and committed defense of pacifism and democracy. By an act of transubstantiation, the constitution enacted under the Occupation has become the flesh and blood of the Japanese polity.[9] Several broad changes in world history may help to explain this. One is the growth of a worldwide peace movement alert to the dangers posed to the human race by advanced nuclear weaponry. Another is that the independence of Third World countries has gradually made a system of world domination by a few states impossible. Whatever the reasons, the Japanese people have shown great vigor and determination in popular struggles to stop the erosion of freedom and defend peace. The mass opposition to the revision of the Security Treaty in 1960 was one sign of popular sentiment.[10] The antiwar movement in America and the cooperation of Japanese and Americans in opposition to the Vietnam war is a significant development of these trends.[11]

Only the determination not to ever repeat "the horrors of war" described in this book sustains the pacifism and democracy of the Japanese Constitution. As the postwar generation grows older and memories of the war fade, we must ensure that there is no revision of the Constitution that restricts political freedom or permits massive rearmament. We must prevent a lessening of that self-awareness so crucial to preventing a third world conflagration. A careful reconfirmation of the truth about the Pacific War and making these facts as widely known as possible are the only ways to avoid another tragedy. It is a solemn obligation incumbent upon those who survived the conflict, a debt we owe to the millions who perished in the fires of war.

Note: Changing Japanese Views of the War

The terms "Manchurian Incident," "China Incident," and "Greater East Asian War" were both official and popular usage until Japan's defeat in 1945. "Incidents" became war with the start of hostilities against the United States and England on December 7, 1941, and the government designated the expanded conflict the Greater East Asian War. The new name included the fighting in China since 1937, but did not retroactively encompass the Manchurian Incident, the Chang Tso-lin Incident, the Nomohan Incident, and the other covert operations and military clashes of the 1930s. They were thought of by the public as disparate events separate from the larger conflict.

Japan's leaders, however, regarded all the fighting after the Manchurian Incident in September 1931 as one war. Major General Kawabe Torashirō stated in 1940 that "Many reasons may be cited for the China Incident, but I think it was an extension of the Manchurian Incident which continues to the present."[1] Colonel Mutaguchi Ren'ya, a regimental commander at the clash which started the China Incident, said in 1944, "I am responsible for the Greater East Asian War. I fired the first shot at the Marco Polo Bridge and started it."[2] To these professional soldiers, from the Manchurian Incident to the Greater East Asian War was one continuous conflict. Civilian premier Konoe Fumimaro, in a February 1945 report to the emperor, echoed this view: "The Manchurian and China Incidents were provoked, the hostilities expanded, and we were finally led into the Greater East Asian War."[3]

Premier Tōjō Hideki's explanation at the Imperial Conference on December 1, 1941, when the decision to go to war against America, England, and the Netherlands was made, contains the following passage about the consequences of accepting American demands: "Japan will be forced to withdraw completely from the Asian continent. Our status in Manchukuo will be jeopardized. All our successes in China will be completely lost."[4] War with the United States and England was inevitable in order to defend Manchukuo, which was established as a result of the Manchurian Incident. The highest national leadership thereby confirms that the Greater East Asian War began with the push into Manchuria. The conflict was acclaimed as a "holy war" and enthusiastically supported in Japan. The great mass of the public sincerely believed in the cause. A small number of people, however, either because they saw it as an "imperialistic war" or for other reasons, were critical or opposed the hostilities. This dissent was completely suppressed; the attitudes and opinions openly expressed or published until August 1945 showed only total support for the war.

Japan's defeat and the Allied occupation changed the name and interpretations of the war. On December 15, 1945, the term Greater East Asian War was prohibited;[5] it was replaced by Pacific War (Taiheiyō sensō). Nakaya Ken'ichi's *Taiheiyō sensō-shi* (Historical Articles on the Pacific War), based on materials provided by the Occupation and probably the first general history of the war, was published in April 1946. As indicated by the subtitle, "From the Mukden Incident to Unconditional Surrender," the Pacific War was traced back to 1931. Allied policy was to treat all hostilities after the Manchurian Incident as related actions. The International Military Tribunal for the Far East (IMTFE) followed this policy in trying individuals for war crimes.

Although the Occupation's terminology and view of the scope of the war changed popular usage, which had superficially separated the Manchurian Incident from the later all-out conflict, they were not new to Japan's top leaders. The term Pacific War reflects the fact that to America the Pacific was the main battlefield. The wording was also used in Japan. At a Liaison Conference on December 10, 1941, the navy suggested Pacific War as the official name for the expanded conflict. But the name was considered inaccurate "if the fighting in China is included"; furthermore, it was pointed out that "no one knows when war might begin with the Soviet Union."[6] These reasons suggest that the term was not markedly at variance with Japanese thinking about the war. However, as the Liaison Conference noted, "Pacific War" was not accurate for hostilities that included years of fighting in China, and it gave excessive stress to the hostilities with the U.S. Although I have entitled this book *The Pacific War,* the name is not altogether accurate.

The Occupation's assessment of the conflict as an illegal war planned by Japanese militarists is well known; reforms of Japan were predicated on this assessment of war responsibility. The FEMT called it a war of aggression in violation of international law and a criminal act involving inhumane conduct contrary to the rules of war. Several Japanese leaders were brought to trial; those thought most responsible were designated class A war criminals, found guilty, and sentenced to death. The tribunal was criticized on both moral and legal grounds by the defense attorney Kiyose Ichirō; by Justice Radha Binod Pal in his minority opinion; and by others. The main objections were that the victors were ignoring their own responsibility for the war and unilaterally blaming only the losers, and that the penalties were based on an ex post facto law, contrary to the legal principle that both crime and punishment should be specified in the law. If the Japanese people of their own volition had determined legal responsibility for the war, these objections would not have been raised and it should have been possible to reach a clearer judgment. No such attempt was made, however, and the problem of legal responsibility for the war was limited to a moot issue: the legitimacy of the IMTFE's. The basic issue—war responsibility—was obscured in legalistic charges of "victor's justice" and never resolved.

Despite the IMTFE's imperfections, the majority of the Japanese people were certainly not opposed to the tribunal. On the contrary, legal scholars like Yokota Kisaburō and Dandō Shigemitsu have argued in favor of the proceedings,[7] and there was wide public support for the court. This was not an expedient change of opinion to curry favor with the Occupation. As I mentioned above, some Japanese opposed the war long before defeat in 1945, and their views quickly gained enormous support. A genuine shift of opinion occurred even among those who had patriotically supported the conflict because it was national policy. They had now experienced war and knew how they had been systematically deceived by the government. The public no longer thought the East Asia Co-Prosperity Sphere so glorious.

The preamble to the postwar constitution states that the Japanese people "resolved that never again shall we be visited with the horrors of war through the action of government." The renunciation of war and war-making capacity in Article IX of the Constitution bespeak a judgment about World War II. According to the *Chūkai Nihonkoku Kempō* (Annotated Constitution of Japan), written by members of the Association for the Study of Law, these provisions are based on a "soul-searching reconsideration" of the war: "We started a reckless war which inflicted vast damage on other countries and enormous loss of life and terror on ourselves. Defeat destroyed much of our country and plunged the people into the depths of terror and deprivation." When a draft of the constitution was published, although a majority of the public did not fully understand its peace provisions, there was no opposition to the proposed law. Indeed, the reaction was favorable because most Japanese had personally experienced the loss of loved ones, the bombing, or near-starvation. Their passionate hatred of war was a cry from the heart by a people who had been misled: it was not the path of glory they found, but the "horrors of war." Some of the ruling elite feigned compliance with

Occupation policies and the new constitution while sabotaging them, but the public had no reason to dissemble. Their approval was genuine.

Books about the war published at the time are full of pacifist sentiment and disdain for militarism. For example, the first edition of Takagi Sōkichi's *Taiheiyō kaisen-shi* (The Pacific Naval War, 1949) has a preface written by an unidentified editor: "Even if those who saw and felt the ravages of war as adults become critical of war and the military, the antiwar sentiment fades away when the next generation, which did not directly experience the war, comes of age. We saw this phenomenon in the rise of the Nazis in Germany after World War I. We have paid too frightful a price in human carnage to repeat this same mistake over and over again." This was a prophetic warning against the erosion of antiwar beliefs. The 1953 book *Zerosen* (Zero) by Horikoshi Jirō and Okumiya Masatake shares this view. The authors' objective was to inform a new generation of the "brilliant" feats and "great victories" of the Japanese fighter plane of that name. Yet they were fully aware of the criminal inhumanity of war: "When we think of the war in human terms, we are utterly horrified. Neighboring countries were forced into a war, the fighting and killing spread over a large area, and even though an effort was made to limit the destruction to military targets, the toll of civilians was terrible. Millions of children were orphaned and wounded, homes were destroyed, careers disrupted or ruined, and the peaceful lives of a generation shattered." From two celebrants of lethal technology this is an extraordinary statement of remorse (assuming they meant it).

We acquired academic freedom after World War II. Objective social science research proliferated, and research on Japanese history, where so much had been shrouded in taboos, accomplished the greatest breakthroughs. Marxist historians were particularly active and productive. The Rekishigaku Kenkyūkai's (Historical Association) four-volume *Taiheiyō sensō-shi* (History of the Pacific War) was published from 1953 to 1957 during this creative, dynamic period. Written when many materials were not yet available, the study has serious factual gaps. But it is unique in its candid treatment of the war as an imperialistic conflict and in the attempt at a comprehensive analysis of the essence of the war.

The Occupation's "reverse course" policy of integrating Japan into an anti-Communist bloc led by the United States subverted the pacifist spirit of the Constitution. As Japan was rearmed and became increasingly dependent militarily upon the United States, views of the war shifted again. Minister of Education Okano Seigō's remarks in the Diet in February 1953 caused a public sensation. In response to a question, he said, "I do not wish to pass judgment on the rightness or wrongness of the Greater East Asian War, but the fact that Japan took on so many opponents and fought them for four years . . . proves our superiority."[8] Thereafter favorable evaluations of the war began to recover the ground they had lost in the early years of defeat. Former Colonel Hattori Takushirō's *Dai Tōa sensō zenshi* (Complete History of the Greater East Asian War) was also published in 1953. It is a valuable historical source as a detailed record of combat operations, but the style is no different from wartime writing. For example, Hattori described the bravery of Japanese forces as "so gallant that the gods would be moved to tears." The author's objective is readily discernible from a line in the preface: "The establishment of national defense policies is manifestly important," a code phrase for rearmament.

The twelve-volume *Hiroku dai Tōa senshi* (A Secret History of the Greater East Asian War), first published in 1953 and reissued in a smaller edition the next year, contains the recollections of Japanese military men. The book's biases are transparent. The charges that the 731 Unit did germ warfare research are denounced as "utterly false accusations." The authors are contemptuous of the Chinese, who are described in the most disparaging terms: "They call themselves the Eighth Route Army, but look at the plundering mentality of the Chinese that Pearl Buck wrote of in *The Good Earth!* How long can they pass themselves off as communist soldiers? . . .

They dress up their motives as communism and they dress themselves in U.S. uniforms but inside they are still Chinese."

The authors also emphasized Japanese casualties rather than the destruction wrought by Japanese forces in China. These books revived the term "Greater East Asian War," a noteworthy semantic and political shift. The serialization of Hayashi Fusao's "Dai Tōa sensō kōtei-ron" (An Affirmation of the Greater East Asian War) in *Chūō Kōron* magazine began in 1963, and it was published in book form (two volumes) in 1964 and 1965. Hayashi gave another boost to the name "Greater East Asian War" and to more favorable interpretations of the conflict. Although the book may be dismissed as stupid and unscholarly, a ghost from the militarist 1930s and 1940s appearing in Japan's bookstores in the 1960s was significant.

It is deplorable when scholars substitute tendentious analysis for objectivity. *Taiheiyō sensō e no michi* (The Road to the Pacific War), a collaborative research project headed by Tsunoda Jun, and published in 1962–63, is an example. Not all the contributors shared Tsunoda's point of view. Nevertheless, Kamikawa Hikomatsu's plan to reassess the war because excessive emphasis on war responsibility "would produce a guilt-ridden nation," coupled with Tsunoda's ideological preferences, gives the whole study a certain thrust and tone.[9] There is an unmistakable effort to shift war responsibility away from Japan. Although the series is well-documented with new materials and facts, its basic approach is seriously flawed.

Ueyama Shumpei's *Dai Tōa sensō no imi* (The Meaning of the Greater East Asian War), published in 1964, grew out of an essay that appeared in *Chūō Kōron* in January of the same year. Ueyama argued that all major interpretations—the "Greater East Asian War" view of Japan's mission in Asia, the "Pacific War" analysis of an aggressive Japan on the warpath, the "imperialist war" approach which explained the conflict as a clash over resources by capitalist countries, and the "war of anti-Japanese resistance" interpretation which empathized the "liberation" forces—reflect value judgments based on specific national interests. Ueyama advocated instead a "universal value standard." Ueyama's essay has merit, but he is less than objective and trenchant; nostalgia replaces judgment. Ueyama used the odious name Greater East Asian War because, as he states in the preface, he was a member of a Navy suicide unit—"a human torpedo"—and the experience left him with a lingering fondness for the term. Ueyama wrote, "I cannot bear the thought that the best years of a whole generation and the lives of my comrades in arms were wasted in a meaningless war." Nostalgia also infuses Agawa Hiroyuki's essay, "Watakushi no sensō bungaku" (My Writing About the War), which appeared in the *Yomiuri Shimbun*[10] in 1964, and Ikeda Kiyoshi's review of the Hayashi and Ueyama books cited above.[11] Ikeda confessed that despite the numerous deficiencies of Hayashi's work, the author's spirit was virtually irresistible "to those of us who were totally committed" and had "burned ourselves out for the war."

Nostalgia and time are eroding the reality of the war. Those veterans who recall their "total commitment" describe the experience in Kiplingesque terms: a good, hard campaign that brought out the best in courage and dedication. (The nostalgia school were all officers; rank and privilege shape their fond remembrances. Former enlisted men, like novelists Tamura Taijirō and Gomikawa Junpei, view the war very differently.)[12] The passage of time has also dimmed perception of the real nature of the war. A new après guerre generation has grown up with no direct experience of the conflict; their innocence threatens to further weaken historical perception. The new generation's understanding of the war is largely formed by what they are taught in school and how it is presented in movies and on television. The media tend to depict only the glamour and excitement. The young are not likely to appreciate the "horrors of war" from this romanticized fare. Thus what Japanese youth are taught about the war in school is crucial.

The textbooks and other materials issued during the first

few years after 1945 clearly stated Japan's responsibility for the conflict. The Ministry of Education's *Shin kyōiku no shishin* (Guide to the New Education), issued in 1946, states: "From the Manchurian Incident, Japan followed an undemocratic political and economic course at home and acted contrary to international legal and moral tenets abroad. . . . These policies were a cause of the Pacific War. We must never repeat those mistakes." The first postwar state textbook on history, *Kuni no ayumi* (Our Nation's Path), came out the same year. It states: "The Japanese people suffered terribly from the long war. Military leaders suppressed the people, launched a stupid war, and caused this disaster." In the 1947 Ministry of Education publication *Atarashii kenpō no hanashi* (Our New Constitution), we find the following: "What did Japan gain from the war? Nothing. Was not the only result enormous grief and suffering? War destroys human life and culture. The countries that started World War II must bear a grave responsibility." *Minshushugi* (Democracy), a 1949 Ministry of Education publication, states: "Japan and Germany must accept the greatest responsibility for World War II, which caused vast suffering, distress, and dislocation to the world"; "The militarists trumpeted grandiose strategies of *kogi kokubō* (comprehensive national security), seized political power, trampled on the rights of the people, and planned a reckless war"; and "[The military] propelled Japan into the fateful cataclysm of the Pacific War." These publications were not perfect, but at least as far as the war was concerned, they were unequivocal on its "recklessness" and Japan's "responsibility."

The situation changed drastically in the 1950s. In the 1953 Ikeda-Robertson conference, the United States and Japan agreed to promote militarism among the Japanese people in a bid to increase public support for rearmament.[13] The Ministry of Education did a volte face on the official interpretation of the war. I personally experienced that change of policy. In 1963 the ministry refused to approve a high school history textbook I had written. A ministry textbook reviewer told me the book was unacceptable because "it was too gloomy on the whole." He cited the illustrations as a case in point. There were pictures of the air raid destruction, of the atomic bomb and devastated Hiroshima, and of disabled veterans begging for money.[14] I contested the decision in a lawsuit. During the trial, a government brief elaborated on the shortcomings of my manuscript. Certain phrases such as "The war was glorified as a 'holy cause,' " "atrocities by Japanese troops," and "reckless war" were objectionable because "These are excessively critical of Japan's position and actions in World War II and do not give students a proper understanding of this country's position and actions in the war."

The Ministry of Education's interpretation of the war has become the official version—what is taught to students in all history courses from the first grade through high school. This has been done by textbook approval and through administrative action, such as the questions on national scholastic examinations, and in teacher job rating reports. The results of this policy are now apparent. Whereas the great majority of students and children used to have a negative attitude toward the war, recently approval of Japan's actions has been increasing. For example, in 1962 Murakami Hyōe interviewed teenagers, the age group born at the end of or after the war. The most numerous view of the Pacific War was that "it was unavoidable." Murakami was startled when one high school student said, "The ABCD encirclement [left Japan no choice]. . . ."[15]

An enormous amount of material and scholarly research has been published and the factual understanding of details of the Pacific War has greatly increased in the two decades since 1945. There is a tendency for the factual trees to obscure the essence of the forest, the basic nature of the war. The public only wants to forget the unpleasant experience, but collective amnesia will also erase the costly lessons of the war. This book is an attempt to halt that erosion of consciousness.

Notes

CHAPTER 1. MISCONCEPTIONS ABOUT CHINA AND KOREA

1. Inoue Mitsusada, *Nihon kokka no kigen* (The Japanese State), pp. 218–20.

2. Tsuda Sōkichi, *Bungaku ni arawaretaru waga kokumin shisō no kenkyū: Heimin bungaku no jidai* (Research on Popular Values as Manifested in Literature: The Period of Commoners' Literature), Vol. 1, Part I, Chap. 2; and *ibid.*, Vol. 2, Part II, Chap. 23.

3. Ienaga Saburō, *Ueki Emori kenkyū* (Research on Ueki Emori), Part II, Chap. 3.

4. Matsunaga Shōzō, "Jiyū minkenha ni mirareru shokokushugi shisō" (Ideas about Japan as a Small Power in the People's Rights Movement), *Shichō*, No. 89.

5. Chōsen Chusatsugun Shireibu, *Chōsen bōto tōbatsushi* (The Suppression of Korean Bandits); Yamabe Kentarō, *Nikkan heigō shōshi* (A Short History of the Annexation of Korea); and Yamabe Kentarō, *Nippon no Kankoku heigō* (Japan's Annexation of Korea).

6. Naka Kansuke, *Gin no saji* (The Silver Spoon). See also below, Chapter 4.

7. Fujisawa Morihiko, *Meiji Taishō ryūkōka-shi* (A History of the Popular Songs of the Meiji and Taishō Periods).

8. Yanaihara Tadao, *Teikokushugika no Taiwan* (Taiwan Under Imperialism); Yanaihara Tadao, "Chōsen tōchi no hōshin" (A Policy for the Administration of Korea), in *Shokumin seisaku no shinkichō* (Toward a New Colonial Policy), and others.

9. See *Chōsen seisai hōki* (Punishment Laws and Regulations in Korea), and other compilations of colonial laws.

10. Hosokawa Karoku, *Gendai Nihon bunmei-shi, Vol. 10, Shokumin-shi* (A History of Modern Japanese Civilization, Vol. 10, The Colonies), and others.

11. Chang Tu-sik, *Aru Zai-nichi Chōsenjin no kiroku* (The Life of a Korean in Japan). Hosoi Hajime advocated "harmony between the homeland and Korea"; yet his lectures, published in 1925 as *Chōsen mondai no kisū* (The Korea Problem Today), showed he had no illusions about Japanese popularity on the peninsula: "The Koreans have lost all confidence in Japanese. They feel nothing toward us but resentment, malevolence, hatred and a desire to resist our rule."

12. Yamabe Kentarō, "San-ichi undō ni tsuite" (On the March First Movement), *Rekishigaku Kenkyū*, Nos. 184–85; Yamabe Kentarō, "San-ichi undō to sono gendaiteki igi" (The March First Movement and Its Contemporary Significance), *Shisō*, June and July 1955; and *GS*, Vols. 25–26, *Chosen* (Korea), Vols. 1–2, and others.

13. Kant Tok-sang, "Kantō daishinsai ni okeru Chōsenjin gyakusatsu no jittai" (Atrocities Committed against Koreans after the Great Kantō Earthquake), *Rekishigaku Kenkyū,* No. 278; Matsuo Takayoshi, "Kantō daishinsaika no Chōsenjin gyakusatsu jiken" (Atrocities against Koreans during the Great Kanto Earthquake), *Shisō,* September 1963, February 1964; "Aru zankoku monogatari e no shōgen" (Testimony about an Atrocity Story), and *GS,* Vol. 6, *Kantō daishinsai to Chōsenjin* (The Great Kantō Earthquake and Koreans).

14. *Kido Kōichi nikki* (Kido Kōichi Diary), January 20, 1931; Yamabe Kentarō, "Nihon teikokushugi to shokuminchi" (Japanese Imperialism and the Colonies), in *Iwanami kōza Nihon rekishi,* Vol. 19, and other sources.

15. "Ozaki Hotsumi no shuki" (Memorandum by Ozaki Hotsumi), *GS,* Vol. 2, *Zoruge jiken* (The Sorge Incident), Vol. 2.

16. Hirano Reiji, "Ningen kaizō" (Human Reconstruction), in *Shōwa sensō bungaku zenshū* (Complete Collection of War Literature of the Shōwa Period), Vol. 12.

17. Andō Hikotarō, *Mantetsu* (The South Manchurian Railroad).

18. Not every Japanese had this attitude toward Korea, of course. There were individuals like Yanagi Sōetsu who brought universal humanistic values to the study of Korea, even though it had become a colony of Japan and was supposedly a "stagnant," inferior culture. Yanagi had a fine appreciation of Koreans and Korean culture. *Sōetsu senshū, Chōsen to sono geijutsu* (Selected Works of Yanagi Sōetsu, Korea and Its Art), Vol. 4.

19. Shidehara Heiwa Zaidan (Shidehara Peace Foundation), *Shidehara Kijurō.*

20. Ikezaki Tadakata, *Beikoku osoruru ni tarazu* (Why Fear the United States?).

21. "Yokoyama shigenkyoku jimukan ni shimeseru Ishiwara shiken" (A Personal View by Ishiwara Kanji shown to Yokoyama, an Official in the Resources Bureau), *GS,* Vol. 7, *Manshū jihen* (The Manchurian Incident). The documents of Ishiwara's conspiratorial planning are in Tsunoda Jun, ed., *Ishiwara Kanji shiryō; Kokubō ronsakuhen* (Writings of Ishiwara Kanji: National Defense).

22. *Shidehara Kijurō.*

23. Ikezaki, *Beikoku osoruru ni tarazu.*

24. "Yokoyama shigenkyoku jimukan ni shimeseru Ishiwara shiken."

CHAPTER 2. THOUGHT CONTROL AND INDOCTRINATION

1. Naimushō Keihokyoku (Ministry of Home Affairs, Police Bureau), *Shinbunshi oyobi shuppanbutsu torishimari hōki enkakushū* (History of the Laws and Regulations Regarding the Control of Newspapers and Publications), and others.

2. Asahi Shimbunsha, ed., *Meiji Taishōshi, Vol. 1 Genronhen* (The History of Meiji and Taishō, Vol. 1, Freedom of Speech), Chap. 11, Sec. 4 and 5, passim.

3. *Meiji seishi* (History of the Meiji Period), and Itagaki Taisuke, ed., *Jiyūtō-shi* (History of the Jiyūtō), and others.

4. Ienaga Saburō, *Nihon kindai kempō shisō-shi kenkō* (History of the Ideology of Japan's Constitution); and Ienaga Saburō, Matsunaga Shozō, and Emura Eiichi, *Meiji zenki no kempō kōsō* (Draft Constitutions in Early Meiji).

5. Itō Nobumichi, "Shuppanhō to shimbunshihō ni tsuite" (The Publication Law and Newspaper Law), in *Shihō kenkyū dai jūyonshū hōkoku shosh ū yon;* Takahashi Kazuo, *Saishin keisatsu jitsumei hanreishū* (Recent Police Affairs Law Reports); Saitō Shozo, *Gendai hikka bunken dainenpyō* (Chronology of Modern Banned Publications); and Odagiri Hideo, *Hakkin sakuhinshū oyobi zokuhen* (Collection of Banned Works and Supplementary Volume).

6. Akamatsu Katsumarō, *Nihon shakai undō-shi* (History of Japanese Social Movements).

7. Matsushita Yoshio, *Meiji-Taishō hansen undo-shi* (History of the Antiwar Movement in Meiji and Taishō); and Ienaga Saburō, "Nihon ni okeru hansen shisō no rekishi" (History of Antiwar Thought in Japan), in *Nihon kindai shisō-shi kenkyū* (Research on the Modern Intellectual History of Japan).

8. "Kanshō memo" (In Appreciation), program published when the movie was reshown in 1965.

9. Osatake Takeshi, *Hanji to kenji to keisatsu* (Judges, Prosecutors, and the Police); Minobe Tatsukichi, "Keisatsu kensoku no genkai" (The Limits of Police Detention Authority), in *Gendai kensei hyōron* (A Critique of Modern Constitutionalism); and Ienaga Saburō, "Keiji soshōhō o meguru jinken hoshō no yōkyū" (The Criminal Prosecution Law and Human Rights), in *Shihōken dokuritsu no rekishiteki kōsatsu* (A Study of the Independent Judiciary).

10. Karasawa Tomitarō, *Kyōkasho no rekishi* (The History of Textbooks); and Tokyo Shoseki Kabushiki Kaisha, ed., *Kyōkasho no hensen* (Textbooks over the Years).

11. Mombushō Kyōgakukyoku (Ministry of Education, Imperial Doctrine Bureau), *Kyōiku ni kansuru chokugo kanpatsu gojūnen kinen shiryō tenkan zuroku* (Illustrated Record of Materials Displayed to Commemorate the Fiftieth Anniversary of the Imperial Rescript on Education), and others.

12. Umetani Noboru, *Meiji zenki seiji-shi no kenkyū* (Research on the Political History of Early Meiji); and Kaigo Tokiomi, *Kyōiku chokugo seiritsu-shi no kenkyū* (Research on the Proclamation of the Imperial Rescript on Education).

13. Ienaga Saburō, *Nihon kindai kenpō shishō-shi kenkyū,* Part II, Chap. 3, Sec. 1.

14. Ebihara Haruyoshi, *Gendai Nihon kyōiku seisaku-shi* (Educational Policy in Modern Japan).

15. For government textbooks, see *Nihon kyōkasho taikei, kindaihen* (Japanese Textbooks, The Modern Period).

16. *Nihon kyokasho taikei, kindaihen, shōka* (Japanese Textbooks, The Modern Period, Songs); see also *Nihon shōkashū* (Japanese Songs).

17. Kaigo Tokimi, Ed., *Rinji kyōiku kaigi no kenkyū* (Research on the Government Advisory Council on Education).

18. Kaneko Masashi, *Kyōikuhō* (Educational Laws), in *Hōritsugaku zenshū* (Complete Collection of Legal Studies), Vol. 16, Chap. 3, Sec. 3.

19. "Shōgakusei zadankai" (Roundtable Discussion of Elementary School Students, 1), *Asahi Gurafu,* January 1, 1932.

20. Miyazaki Ichimu, "Nichi-Bei miraisen" (The Future Japanese-American War), *Shōnen Kurabu,* January 1922, February 1923.

21. Kikuchi Kunisaku, "Tennōseika no guntai ni okeru itan" (Dissent in the Military under the Emperor System), *Misuzu,* November 1964.

CHAPTER 3. THE MILITARY: AUTHORITARIAN AND IRRATIONAL

1. Yamagata Aritomo, *Rikugunshō enkaku-shi* (History of the Army Ministry); and Matsushita Yoshio, *Meiji gunsei shiron* (History of the Meiji Military System).

2. For example, Inoue Mitsu, *Dai Nippon teikoku kenpō* (The Imperial Constitution of Japan), approximately 1901; Fujimura Moriyoshi, *Dai Nippon teikoku kenpō kōgi* (Lectures on the Imperial Constitution of Japan), 1902; Mizuno Hironori, "Gunbu daijin kaihōron" (A Civilian Army Minister), *Chūō Kōron,* August 1921; and *Gendai Nihon shisō taikei,* Vol. 3, *Minshūshūgi* (Modern Japanese Thought, Vol. 3, Democracy).

3. Nakano Tomio, *Tōsuiken no dokuritsu* (Independence of the Supreme Command), and others.

4. Ienaga Saburō, *Minobe Tatsukichi no shisōshiteki kenkyū* (Historical Research on the Thought of Minobe Tatsukichi).

5. *GS,* Vol. 11, *Zoku Manshū jihen* (The Manchurian Incident Continued, Vol. 11).

6. Rikugunshō gunjika (Army Ministry, Military Affairs Section), "Tōsuiken mondai ni kanshi hōseikyoku tōjisha to mondō no yōshi" (Summary of Discussions with Legal Bureau Specialist Fujita Isuguo Regarding the Independence of the Supreme Command); and "Naikaku kansei dai nana jō ni tsuite" (Concerning Article 7 of the Cabinet Regulations), in *GS,* Vol. 11, *Zoku Manshū jihen.*

7. *Hara-Takashi nikki* (Hara Takashi Diary), November 25, 27, 28, 30; December 1, 2, 3, 6, 1912; and passim.

8. *TSM, Bekkan shiryō hen* (Supplement); *GS,* Vols. 7, 11; Harada Kumao, *Saionji-kō to seikyoku* (Prince Saionji and the Political Situation), Vol. 1; *TSM,* Vol. 1.

9. Morishima Morito, *Inbō, ansatsu, guntō* (Conspiracy, Assassination, and the Saber).

10. Konoe Fumimaro, "Heiwa e no doryoku" (My Struggle for Peace), *Sekai Bunka,* February 1946.

11. *TSM, Bekkan.*
12. Tōgō Shigenori, *Jidai no ichimen* (The Cause of Japan).
13. *Ibid.*
14. Shigemitsu Mamoru, *Shōwa no dōran* (Upheavals in Shōwa Japan).
15. *Ibid.*
16. *Saionji-kō to seikyoku,* Vol. 5.
17. "Gunmuka seihen nisshi" (Military Affairs Section, Record of Changes of Government), and Hata Ikuhiko, *Gun fashizumu undō-shi* (History of Military Fascism), appendix.
18. *Ibid.,* and Otani Keijirō, *Shōwa Kenpei-shi* (The Kempeitai in Shōwa).
19. Otani, *Shōwa Kenpei-shi.*
20. Higashikuni Naruhito, *Ichi kōzoku no sensō nikki* (An Imperial Prince's Wartime Diary).
21. *TSM,* Vol. 7, and *Kido Kōichi nikki,* July 8, 16, 17, 22, 1940.
22. *Saionji-kō to seikyoku,* Vol. 2, and *Kido Kōichi nikki,* August 7, 12, 1931.
23. *Kido Kōichi nikki,* September 17, 20, 1931.
24. *Ibid.,* May 16, 17, 1932.
25. *Ibid.,* March 2, 3, 9, 1936.
26. Otani, *Shōwa Kenpei-shi.*
27. *GS,* Vol. 7; *TSM,* Vol 2; and Imamura Hitoshi, *Manshū hi o fuku koro* (Manchuria Aflame). *himerareta Shōwa-shi, Bessatsu.*
28. *Saionji-kō to seikyoku,* Vol. 7, October 13, 1938, and February 23, 1939.
29. *Saionji-kō to seikyoku, Bekkan* (supplementary volume), memorandum, May 1, 1940.
30. Kono Tsukasa, ed., *Niniroku jiken* (The February 26 Incident); Arai Isao, *Nihon o shinkan saseta yokkakan* (The Four Days That Terrorized Japan); Otani Keijirō, *Niniroku jiken no nazo* (The Riddle of the February 26 Incident); "Isobe Asaichi no gokuchū shuki" (Isobe Asaichi's Prison Memorandum), *Bungei,* March 1967; and Fujiwara Akira, "Niniroku jiken" (The February 26 Incident), *Rekishigaku Kenkyū,* Nos. 169, 171.
31. Otani, *Shōwa Kenpei-shi;* and Horiba Kazuo, *Shina jihen sensō shidō-shi* (History of the Direction of the China War).
32. *Saionji-kō to seikyoku,* Vol. 5, December 13, 1936.
33. Horiba, *Shina jihen sensō shidō-shi.*
34. Hayashi Saburō, *Taiheiyō sensō rikusen gaishi* (General History of Land Campaigns in the Pacific War).
35. Matsushita Yoshio, *Chōheirei seitei-shi* (Establishment of the Conscription System).
36. Ienaga Saburō, "Iida jiken kankei bunken" (Documents About the Iida Incident), in *Ueki Emori kenkyū,* appendix, "Jiyū minken ni kansuru shinshiryō shōkai (New Materials on the People's Rights Movement).
37. Fujiwara Akira, *Gunji-shi* (History of the Military), and Fujiwara Akira, "Nihon gunkokushugi no senryaku shisō" (The Strategic Ideology of Japanese Militarism), *Shisō,* November 1954.
38. Itō Masanori, *Kaigun gojūnen-shi* (Fifty-Year History of the Navy).
39. Fujiwara, *Gunji-shi;* and Fujiwara, "Nihon gunkokushugi no senryaku shisō."

40. Hirano Masami, "Senjinkun wa yurusu koto nashi" (The Iron Code, Army Field Regulations), in *Shūkan Asahi*, ed., *Chichi no senki* (Daddy Tells about the War).

41. "Shirami wa nanshin sezu" (The Lice Don't Move South), *Tokushū Bungei Shunjū, akagami ichimai de* (Special issue of *Bungei Shunjū*, The Draft Notice). There are many similar accounts of war experiences, such as Tsuyama Akira, *Sensō dorei* (War Slave).

42. See Chapters 2 and 6.

43. A phrase used by an army conscription officer and quoted in Takenaka Akira, "Kōryan batake de atta teki" (The Enemy in a Millet Field), in *Chichi no senki.*

44. Gomikawa Junpei, *Ningen no jōken* (The Human Condition), Part 3. One day in 1928 or 1929, while I was a middle school student, we were in the middle of military training when it began to rain. We all rushed for cover in the school. I thought the army drill officer was concerned about us getting soaked and was dumbfounded when he said he dismissed us so the rifles would not get wet.

45. Public education had prepared Japanese men to endure this brutal, inhuman treatment. That military service was a "sacred duty" had been pounded into most of the population from early childhood. They were so indoctrinated that they could not even imagine any other system. However, the idea of democratizing the military had been expressed in the 1899 book *Nihyakunengo no yume, heisotsu kaigi* (A Soldier's Meeting Two Hundred Years from Now). Presented as a dream about the future, in this book the soldiers passed a resolution demanding improved treatment. See the author's article in *Nihon Rekishi*, No. 68.

46. See, for example, the diary of Takeda Kiyoshi in Nihon Senbotsu Gakusei Shuki Henshu Iinkai, ed., *Kike, Wadatsumi no koe* (Listen, The Voices of the Sea), and the diary of Kimura Shoichirō in Takagi Toshirō, *Chiran.*

47. Statements of persons who appear in Gomikawa, *Ningen no jōken,* Part 4.

48. Statement by Lieutenant Usubuchi in Yoshida Mitsuru, *Senkan Yamato no saigo* (Last Days of the Battleship *Yamato*).

49. Itō Keiichi, *Zoku kanashiki senki* (More Bitter War Experiences), Account No. 19.

50. Noma Hiroshi, *Shinkū chitai* (Zone of Emptiness).

51. War prisoners and civilians in occupied areas were treated the same way. Satō Kenryō, *Tōjō Hideki to Taiheiyō sensō* (Tōjō Hideki and the Pacific War).

52. Army cohesiveness was abetted by the camaraderie of enlisted men sharing the rigors of war and the close personal relations with some of their immediate superiors. But the sense of collective solidarity was extremely weak compared to that of the armed guerrilla units or revolutionary armies infused by a common spirit and purpose. Competition and noncooperation seem to have been much stronger traits of the Japanese army; efficiency and performance often suffered as a result. For example, units even burned buildings and supplies to prevent other units from using them. Sakè containers were filled with urine and left for the next unit, a particularly distasteful surprise. "Okamoto Tarō no gan" (Okamoto Tarō's View), *Shūkan Asahi,* August 13, 1965; Fuji Masaharu, *Teikoku guntai ni okeru gakushū* (Training in the Imperial Army, Introduction); and Imai Yukihito, "Kohima kōryaku zengo" (Attack on Kohima), in *Hiroku dai Tōa senshi* (Secret Records of the Greater East Asian War), Vol. 3.

53. Letters of Odajima Fujimi and Tōdō Tsutomu in Iwate-ken Nōson Bunka Kondankai, ed., *Senbotsu nōmin heishi no tegami* (Letters of Farm Area Soldiers Killed in the War).

54. *Ibid.,* postscript. Wada Tsuto's "Mura no jinan" (Second Sons of the Village). *Heiya no hitobito* (The People of the Plain) has a good description of conditions. For an incisive analysis of the psychology of noncommissioned officers, see Doi Hiroyuki, "Nihon rikugun no kashikan" (Noncommissioned Officers of the Japanese Army), in *Wadatsumi no koe* (October 1964).

CHAPTER 4. THE BEGINNING: AGGRESSION IN CHINA

1. Iwamura Michio and Nohara Shirō, *Chūgoku gendai-shi* (Modern Chinese History); and Takeuchi Toshimi, Yamaguchi Ichirō, Saitō Akio, and Nohara Shirō, *Chūgoku kakumei no shisō* (The Ideology of the Chinese Revolution).

2. "Japanese journalism had such a limited perspective that they could not appreciate the changes taking place in Chinese society, particularly the essence of the Chinese revolution. The press assumed that aggressor Japan was more advanced than China, a faulty premise. As long as they believed this, the members of the press could never be able to understand or accept the new China." Itō Takeo, *Mantetsu ni ikite* (A Career on the South Manchurian Railway).

3. Morishima Morito, *Inbō, ansatsu, guntō;* and Shimada Toshihiko, *Kantōgun* (The Kwantung Army). Kawamoto carried out the bombing of Chang Tso-lin's train; Sasaki Tōichi, of the general staff, suggested the attack. See Sasaki Tōichi, *Aru gunjin no jiden* (A Military Man's Story), revised edition.

4. *Saionji-kō to seikyoku,* Vol. 1.

5. Nakano Ryōji, "Kaisō 'Manshū jihen no shinsō' bassui" (Excerpts from the Recollections, The Truth about the Manchurian Incident), *GS,* Vol. 11.

6. "Manmō mondai ni tsuite" (Concerning the Manchuria-Mongolia Problem), *TSM, Bekkan.*

7. Hanaya Tadashi, "Manshū jihen wa kōshite keikaku sareta" (How the Manchurian Incident Was Planned), *Himerareta Shōwa-shi, Bessatsu;* Ishiwara Kanji's diary, in *Ishiwara Kanji shiryō, kokubō ronsakuhen,* indicates that Ishiwara, Itagaki, Hanaya, Imada, and others met secretly from the end of May 1931 to plan the "Mukden conspiracy" and "post-occupation measures for Mukden."

8. Kanda Masatane, "Oryokkō" (The Yalu River), *GS,* Vol. 7; Hanaya Tadashi, "Manshū jihen wa kōshite keikaku sareta"; Ishii Itarō, *Gaikōkan no isshō* (The Life of a Diplomat); and *TSM,* Vol. 2.

9. Kantōgun (Kwantung Army), "Manshū jihen kimitsu seiryaku nisshi" (Secret Policy Record of the Manchurian Incident), *GS,* Vol. 7; and Sanbō Honbu (Army General Staff), "Manshū jihen-shi dai go kan an" (The Manchurian Incident, Part 5, Draft), *GS,* Vol. 11.

10. Kanda, *Oryokkō;* Toyoshima Fusatarō, "Chōsengun ekkyō shingekisu" (The Korea Army Crosses the Border), *Himerareta Shōwa-shi, Bessatsu;* and Yamamoto Shirō, "Manshū jihen no sai no Chōsengun no ekkyō ni tsuite—Mori Goroku-shi no danwa o chūshin ni" (Mori Goroku and the Korea Army's Move across the Border during the Manchurian Incident), *Misuzu,* May 1966.

11. Sanbō Honbu, "Chōsengun shireikan no dokudan to chūōbu no kore ni tsuite toreru shochi ni tsuite" (Unauthorized Action by the Commander, Korea Army, and Measures Taken by the Central Authorities), *GS,* Vol. 7.

12. *Ibid.*

13. Sanbō Honbu, "Manshū jihen-shi dai go kan an."

14. Ogata Taketora, *Ichi gunjin no shōgai* (The Life of an Admiral).

15. Sanbō Honbu, "Manshū jihen kimitsu sakusen nisshi" (Record of Secret Operations in the Manchurian Incident), *TSM, Bekkan.*

16. Sanbō Honbu, "Manshū jihen-shi dai go kan an"; and Kantōgun, "Manshū jihen kimitsu seiryaku nisshi."

17. *TSM,* Vol. 2.

18. "Manmō mondai shori hōshin yōkō" (A General Outline of a Policy for Manchuria and Mongolia), in *Nihon gaikō nenpyō narabi ni shuyō monjo,* Vol. 2.

19. *Kido Kōichi nikki,* January 21, 1932.

20. Tanaka Ryūkichi, "Shanghai jihen wa kōshite okosareta" (How the Shanghai Incident Was Carried Out), *Himerareta Shōwa-shi, Bessatsu.*

21. *TSM,* Vol. 2.

22. Gaimushō, *Ritton hōkokusho, Kokusai remmei Shina chōsa iinkai hōkokusho zenbun* (The Lytton Report, Complete Text of the Lytton Commission of the League of Nations).

23. *TSM,* Vol. 2; Oka Yoshitake, *Kokusai seiji-shi* (International Politics); Hata Ikuhiko, *Nitchū sensō-shi* (The Japan-China War); and Saitō Takashi, *Dainiji sekai taisen zenshi kenkyū* (History of the Pre–World War II).

24. "Rinji dokuritsu hikō chūtai sentō shōhō" (Combat Reports of the Provisional Independent Air Squadron), *GS,* Vol. 12.

25. Sanbō Honbu, "Manshū jihen kimitsu sakusen nisshi," *TSM, Bekkan.*

26. *Kantōgun,* "Kimitsu sakusen nisshi bassui" (Selections from the Secret Strategy Record), *GS,* Vol. 7.

27. *Saionji-kō to seikyoku,* Vol. 4, June 23, 1935.

28. Yonai Mitsumasa's diary as quoted in Ogata, *Ichi gunjin no shōgai.*

29. Tōgō, *Jidai no ichimen.*

30. "Kawabe Torashirō shōshō kaisō ōtōroku," *GS,* Vol. 12.

31. *TSM,* Vol. 3; Imai Takeo, *Nisshi jihen no kaisō* (Recollections of the China Incident); and *Saionji-kō to seikyoku,* Vol. 4.

32. Imai, *Nisshi jihen no kaisō;* "Kawabe Torashirō shōshō kaisō ōtōroku"; Teradaira Tadasuke, "Rokōkyō han no jūsei" (Gunfire at the Marco Polo

Bridge), *GS,* Vol. 9, *Nitchū senso* (Japan-China War), Vol. 2, appendix of monthly reports; "Hashimoto Mure chūjō Takeda no miya kaisō ōtōroku" (Discussion between Lieutenant General Hashimoto Mure and Prince Takeda), *GS,* Vol. 9; and Hora Tomio, "Rokōkyō jiken no hottan" (Start of the Marco Polo Bridge Incident), in *Kindai senshi no nazo* (Riddles of Modern Wars).

33. "Ishiwara Kanji chūjō kaisō ōtōroku" (Interview with Lieutenant General Ishiwara Kanji), *GS,* Vol. 9.

34. Horiba, *Shina jihen senso shidō-shi;* and "Nishimura Toshio kaisō-roku" (Reminiscenses of Nishimura Toshio), *GS,* Vol. 12.

35. Horiba, *Shina jihen senso shidō-shi.*

36. *Ibid.*

37. "Shina jihen shori konpon hōshin" (A Fundamental Policy toward the China Incident), in *Nihon gaikō nenpyō narabi ni shuyō monjo,* Vol. 2.

38. "Watanabe kōsaku no genjō" (Current Status of the Watanabe Operation), in Imai, *Nisshi jihen no kaisō.*

39. Imai, *Nisshi jihen no kaisō.* Even as late as September 5, 1944, when the war had gone irretrievably against Japan, the Supreme Council for the Direction of the War insisted that "There will be no change in the status of Manchukuo." See "Tai Jūkei seiji kōsaku jisshi ni kansuru ken" (Political Strategy toward Chungking), in Sanbō Honbu, *Haisen no kiroku* (Record of Defeat).

CHAPTER 5. THE WAR IN CHINA: A CLASH OF POLITICAL VALUES

1. "Manmō mondai ni tsuite" (Concerning Manchuria and Mongolia) *TSM, Bekkan.*

2. *Kido Kōichi nikki,* April 18, 1939.

3. "Seijiteki hijō jihen boppatsu ni shosuru taisaku yōkō" (Countermeasures against Political Emergencies); Hata, *Gun Fashizumu undō-shi,* materials appendix.

4. "Hokushi mondai ni tsuite" (The Problem of North China), in *Nihon gaikō nenpyō narabi ni shuyō monjo,* Vol. 2.

5. "Nitka kihon jōyaku ni kansuru sūmitsuin dai ikkai shinsa iinkai kiroku" (Records of the First Session of the Privy Council's Review Committee on a Basic Japan-China Treaty), *GS,* Vol. 9.

6. Ogoshi Chihaya, "Tozasareta shōnen no hitomi" (The Murdered Young Man), in *Chichi no senki.*

7. *TSM,* Vol. 3.

8. Statement by Morishima Morito in "Manshū jihen zengo" (At the Time of the Manchurian Incident), in Ikejima Shinpei, ed., *Rekishi yomoyama banashi, Nihonhen ge* (Conversations on History, Japan), Vol. 2.

9. Imai, *Nisshi jihen no kaiso.*

10. Statement by Ho Kuei-kuo on July 9, 1945, quoted in Imai, *Nisshi jihen no kaiso.*

11. Theodore H. White, ed., *The Stilwell Papers.*

12. Oka, *Kokusai seiji-shi.*

13. Hugh Thomas, *The Spanish Civil War;* Franz Borkenau, *The Spanish Cockpit;* Saitō Takashi, *Supein Sensō* (The Spanish Civil War), etc.

14. "Saikin Beikoku zaikai no ken'isha bōshi no raichō o ki to shi Nihon zaikai bō yūryokusha to no kaidan yōryō" (Summary of Conversation between an Influential American Businessman Visiting Japan and an Important Japanese Business Leader), in *Kido Kōichi kankei bunsho* (Documents Concerning Kido Kōichi). See also Chapter 4, note 23.

15. For example, Inada Masazumi, who in 1938 became chief, Operations Section, Army General Staff. He reportedly said to Nakada Makoto: "I had in mind to wrap up the China Incident, or even before it was settled, assign most of our strength to Manchuria and switch to an operation to reach all the way to Lake Baikal." Nakada Makoto, "Manshū jihen no shinsō" (The Truth about the Manchurian Incident), *Rekishi Kenkyū,* September 1966. At the June 1939 meeting between Itagaki Seishirō and Wang Ching-wei, the former said, "With regard to anti-communism, it is not just the Chinese Communist party. There is also the problem of the Russian threat to Manchukuo and to China's northern border. Unified and determined, Japan is now preparing to eradicate communism at home and to the north of Manchuria. It is opposition to communism that has led us to have this determination and to make these preparations." "Itagaki rikushō-O kaidan yōryō" (Summary of Discussions between Army Minister Itagaki and Wang [Ching-wei]), *GS,* Vol. 9. Before the Mukden Incident, Itagaki said publicly that when Japan occupied Manchuria, "Our first line of defense will run from the Amur River to Tahsing and Anling," and "Areas like the Maritime Provinces will naturally have to come under our power and influence." Nakada, "Manshū jihen no shinsō."

16. "Nishimura Toshio kaisōroku" (Recollections of Nishimura Toshio), *GS,* Vol. 12.

17. *TSM,* Vol. 4.

18. *GS, Vol. 10, Nitchū sensō,* Vol. 3; *TSM,* Vol. 4; Hayashi Katsuya, "Nomonhan senshi" (History of the Nomonhan Fighting, an essay in the translation of A. B. (The Air War at Nomonhan); USSR Research Institute on Marxism-Leninism, *History of the Second World War, 1941–1945,* Vol. 2; and Hora Tomio, "Nomonhan jiken no hottan" (Outbreak of the Nomonhan Incident), in *Kindai senshi no nazo.*

19. *TSM,* Vol. 5.

20. "Shōwa jūrokunen shichigatsu futsuka gozenkaigi" (Imperial Conference, July 2, 1941), *TSM, Bekkan.*

21. *Ibid.,* and *Nihon gaikō nenpyō narabi ni shuyō monjo,* Vol. 2.

22. Ianemura, *Daihon'ei kimitsu nisshi.*

23. Shimada, *Kantōgun; TSM,* Vol. 5; and Hattori Takushirō, *Dai Tōa sens ō zenshi* (Complete History of the Greater East Asian War).

24. Hayashi, *Taiheiyō sensō rikusen gaishi;* Takaki Sōkichi, *Taiheiyō kaisen-shi,* revised edition, 1959.

25. *Saionji-kō to seikyoku*, supplementary volume, memorandum dated July 12, 1937.

26. "Kawabe Torashirō shōshō kaisō ōtōroku."

27. "Shimomura Sadamu taishō kaisō ōtōroku" (Interview with General Shimomura Sadamu), *GS*, Vol. 9.

28. "Kawabe Torashirō shōshō kaisō ōtōroku."

29. Remarks by Hoshino Naoki in "Manshū jihen zengo."

30. Nishi Haruhiko, *Kaisō no Nihon gaikō* (Memories of Japan's Diplomacy).

31. "Minzoku to heiwa to no tame ni" (For the Nation and Peace), *Tsūshin*, January 1937; and *Yanaihara Tadao zenshū* (Complete Works of Yanaihara Tadao), Vol. 18.

32. "Shina mondai no shozai" (The Locus of the China Problem), in *Yanaihara Tadao zenshū*, Vol. 4.

33. "Shōkyokuteki ni idai naru Shina" (China, The Quiet Power); Kiryū Yūyū, *Chikushōdō no chikyū* (A Bestial World), published posthumously.

34. *Ibid.*, "Mō Taku-tō no yōgen" (Mao Tse-tung Speaks Out).

35. *Nakae Ushikichi shokanshū* (The Collected Letters of Nakae Ushikichi).

36. Iwamura Michio and Nohara Shirō, *Chūgoku gendai-shi* (History of Modern China); Takeuchi Yoshimi et al., *Chūgoku kakumei no shisō;* Hidaka Rokurō, "Sensō kakudai no kiken to hansen heiwa no genri" (The Danger of an Expanded War and Pacifism"), *Shin Nihon Bungaku*, October 1966; Ubukata Naokichi, "Kaisō no kokusai kaigi—Shanhai hansen kaigi (1933) ni tsuite" (Memories of an International Conference—The 1933 Shanghai Antiwar Conference), *Chūgoku Kenkyūjo Kiyō*, No. 1.

37. "Rinji dokuritsu hikōtai hensei hakken ni kansuru meirei shiji" (Orders and Directives Concerning the Formation and Transfer of the Provisional Independent Squadron), *GS*, Vol. 12, and *TSM*, Vol. 3.

38. Imai, *Nisshi jihen no kaiso.*

39. My description of anti-Japanese resistance in Manchukuo is based mainly on Manshūkoku Gunseibu Komon, *Manshū kyōsanhi no kenkyū* (Research on the Communist Bandits of Manchuria). Other sources used included the following: "Manshūkokugun no hanran" (The Revolt of the Manchukuo Army), in *Kido Kōichi kankei bunsho;* "Manshū nōgyō imin zadankai kiroku" (A Roundtable Discussion of Agricultural Settlers in Manchuria), quoted in Yamada Gōichi, "Manshū ni okeru hanman kōnichi undō to nōgyō imin" (Agricultural Settlers and the Anti-Manchukuo and Anti-Japan Movement), Part 2, *Rekishi Hyōron*, July 1962; *Manshū nenkan* (Manchuria Yearbook, 1941 edition); and Manshū Teikoku Kyōkai Chūō Honbu Chōsakyoku, ed., *Kyōwakai soshiki undō* (Organizing the Harmony Association), Vol. 2, Part 1, quoted in Andō, *Mantetsu*. The deep impression these activities made on the Chinese is apparent from publications at the time. The *Tung-pei chih-shih* (Information on the Northeast, Vol. 1), published in North China, carried articles on "Tung-pei jen-min tan-ch'ien-te yao-ch'iu" (The Just Demands of the People of the Northeast), and "Tung-pei i-yung-chun chan-cheng-shih" (Battle Record of the Northeast Volunteer Army). The *Tung-pei k'ang-jih lieh-shih-chuan* (The Patriotic

Resistance to Japan in the Northeast) was published in Paris. Similar publications appeared in America and elsewhere. See Cabinet Information Department, *Shisōsen tenrankai kiroku zukan* (Illustrated Record of an Exhibition on the Ideological War), and *Shōwa hakkin nenpyō.*

40. Lu Chi-t'uan, "Shōwa jūyonen tōki sakusen keika no gaiyō" (Summary of Operations, Winter 1939), *GS,* Vol. 9.

41. Unless otherwise noted, descriptions of the Communist forces are drawn from the following sources: Edgar Snow, *China Record, The Battle for Asia,* and *Red Star Over China;* Agnes Smedley, *China Fights Back, Battle Hymn of China,* and *The Great Road—The Life and Times of Chu Teh;* Guenther Stein, *The Challenge of Red China;* White, *The Stilwell Papers;* and Jack Belden, *China Shakes the World.* Jōno Hiroshi's *Sansei dokuritsu senki* (The War for Independence in Shansi) substantiates the descriptions by Western writers of Communist military units. Jōno fought against Communist forces in Shanghai after 1945. His perspective was very different from that of foreign journalists, yet his account parallels theirs.

42. Mao Tse-tung, "The Course, Strategy and Future of the Fight against the Japanese Advance," and "On Protracted War," in *Collected Works of Mao Tse-tung,* Vol. 3; Takeuchi Yoshimi, "Chūgoku no jinmin kaku mei" (The People's Revolution of China); and *Hyōden Mō Taku-tō* (A Critical Biography of Mao Tse-tung), in *Shinpen gendai chūkokuron* (Modern China).

43. Mao Tse-tung, *The New Democracy.*

44. For example, when the garrison on Mereyon Island was cut off from supplies and faced starvation, the remaining rations were allocated strictly on the basis of rank. The brigade staff got more than the subordinate unit staffs; officers got more than enlisted men (Asahi Shimbunsha, *Mereyontō* (Mereyon Island), "Kuwae chūtaichō no kiroku" (Record of Company Commander Kuwae). Rank had its privileges even in death. The fatality rate on Mereyon was 38 percent for officers and 74 percent for enlisted men and noncommissioned officers (*Sekai,* June 1946).

45. "Hachirogun jōhō" (Intelligence report on the Eighth Route Army), *Jinbutsu Orai,* October 1966.

46. Morishige Hisaya, "Morishige kokyo ni kaeru" (Morishige Returns Home), in *Shōwa sensō bungaku zenshū* (Complete Collection of Shōwa War Literature), Vol. 12.

47. Fukuzawa Usuke, "Rekishi no ashioto" (Footsteps of History) *Hiroku dai Tōa senshi,* Vol. 2, 1954 edition; Izumi no Kai, ed., *Shufu no sensō taikenki* (Wives' War Experiences), Horiuchi Komako, "Harubin no ichi nenkan" (A Year in Harbin); and comments by Nattori Sadaichi and Nishiyama Atsushi, former agricultural settlers in Manchuria, on the Tokyo Channel 12 program "Watakushi no Shōwa-shi" (My History of the Shōwa Era), September 16, 1966.

48. Mikasa no miya Takahito, *Teiō to haka to minshu* (Rulers, Tombs, and the People), "Waga omoide no ki" (My Recollections).

49. Matsumoto Sōkichi, *Shina no shinshi* (The New China), 1942 edition, in *TSM,* Vol. 4.

50. Satō Takeo, "Watakushi mo Batsūn ni mannada—Hachirogun iryō

kōsaku ni sanka shita ichi Nihonjin ishi no kiroku (I Also Learned from Bethune—The Record of a Japanese Doctor Who Served with the Medical Staff of the Eighth Route Army), in Chou Erh-fu, *Pai-chiu-en tai-fu Doctor Bethune.*
51. Stein, *The Challenge of Red China.*
52. Hayashi, *Taiheiyō sensō rikusen gaishi;* Hattori Takushirō, *Dai Tōa sensō zenshi;* Horiba, *Shina jihen sensō shidōshi;* Imai Takeo, *Kindai no sensō,* Vol. 5, *Chūgoku to no tatakai* (Modern Wars, The Battle with China), Vol. 5.
53. Some of the comments made by the "man in the street" on August 15, 1945, when Japan's surrender was announced reflect this attitude. For example, "Well, even if we couldn't beat America and England, it's humiliating to surrender to the Chinese"; or "To be lorded over by the Chinese and Koreans is such a disgrace that it might be better to kill ourselves and the children and get it over with." (Hayashi, *Nihon shūsen-shi.*) That attitude, unfortunately, is still very much alive in Japan today.

CHAPTER 6. THE WAR AT HOME: DEMOCRACY DESTROYED

1. "Araki rikushō no Saitō sōri e no shokan oyobi kinkyū shisaku kisōan (Army Minister Araki's Letter and Proposal for Emergency Measures Sent to Premier Saitō) in Hata, *Gun fashizumu undō-shi.*
2. Lawyers repeatedly protested these actions (See Nihon Bengoshi Rengōkai, ed., *Nihon bengoshi enkaku-shi* (History of Japanese Lawyers). However, stripped of freedom of expression, the Japanese people already lacked the power to build a mass protest movement.
3. Uchikawa Yoshimi and Kōuchi Saburō, "Nihon fashizumu keiseiki no masūmedia tōsei" (Control of the Mass Media during the Formative Period of Japanese Fascism), *Shisō,* July 1961; Kōuchi Saburō, "Jōhōyoku no kikō to sono henyō" (Structure and Changes in the Cabinet Information Bureau), *Bungaku,* May 1961; Nunokawa Kakuzaemon, "Senji no shuppan tōsei" (Wartime Controls on Publications), *Bungaku,* May 1961; Nunokawa Kakuzaemon, "Senjichū no shuppan jijō" (Conditions in the Publishing World during the War), *Bungaku,* December 1961; Hatanaka Shigeo et al., *Genron dan'atsu-shi* (A History of Suppression of Speech and Expression); Hatanaka Shigeo, *Oboegaki Shōwa shuppan dan'atsu shōshi* (Short History of Restrictions on Publications in the Shōwa Period); Saigusa Shigeo, *Genron Shōwa-shi* (History of Speech and Expression in the Shōwa Period); Matsuura Sōzō, "GHQ ni kinjirareta kotoba" (Words Prohibited by General Headquarters), *Bungei Shunjū,* August 1966. While not used in the present work, Okudaira Yasuhiro, "Ken'etsu seido" (The Censorship System), in *Nihon kindaihō hattatsu-shi* (History of the Development of Modern Japanese Law), Vol. 11, is the most comprehensive and detailed study of the controls on publications.

4. Kiryū Yūyū, "Genron hōdō no fūsa" (Freeze on Information), *Tazan no Ishi* (Stones from Other Mountains), August 5, 1937, as quoted in Maeda Yūji, *Pen wa shinazu* (The Pen That Would Not Die).

5. Hatanaka, *Oboegaki Shōwa shuppan dan'atsu shōshi.*

6. Jō Ichirō, *Hakkinbon* (Banned Books).

7. Takeuchi Yoshimi, "Chūgokujin no kōsen ishiki to Nihonjin no dōtoku ishiki" (The Chinese Spirit of Resistance and the Japanese Sense of Morality), in *Shinpen gendai Chūgoku-ron,* new edition.

8. Captain Suzuki Hideo, an army doctor, wrote down many observations while serving at the front in China. Among his comments were these: "The press lies. They deceive the people back home. They don't tell them about the hard fighting, the casualties on the Hankow front." Quoted in Okamura Toshihiko, *Hodabi* (A Wood Fire).

9. Katō Hidetoshi, "Bidan no genkei—bakudan sanyūshi" (The Prototype of the "Heroic Exploits"—The Three Human Bombs of Shanghai) *Asahi Janaru,* April 11, 1965; and remarks by Tanaka Ryūkichi quoted in Kijima Takeshi, "Tsukurareta bidan" (Fabricated Heroics), letter to the editor, *Asahi Janaru,* April 18, 1965.

10. Kaikō Takeshi, "Nihonjin ga shiranakatta Nihon no sensō" (The War the Japanese Didn't Know About) *Sande Mainichi,* July 18, 1965; Suga Fuminao, "Chōkohō de" (At Changkufeng), *Sande Mainichi,* August 25, 1965; Otake Yasuko, *Byōinsen* (Hospital Ship), in *Shōwa sensō bungaku zenshū,* Vol. 9 (1939 edition); Hokama Moriyoshi, "Higeki no shima" (Island of Tragedy), *ibid.,* Vol. 11; Hayashi Hiroichirō, "Tōbōhei to shōnen heiho" (Deserters and Young Replacements) in *Chichi no senki;* Moriya Tadashi, *Ragunako no kita, watashi no Hitō senki* (North of Lake Laguna, My War in the Philippines); Sugano Shizuko, *Saipantō no saigo* (The Death of Saipan); Miyazaki Shūichi, "Jigoku sensen yori no dasshutsu" (Escape from a Battlefield Hell), in *Taiheiyō sensō no zenbō* (The Whole Story of the Pacific War); and Funasaka Hiroshi, *Eirei no zekkyō* (Screams of the War Dead).

11. Sakisaka Itsurō, ed., *Arashi no naka no hyakunen, gakumon dan'atsu shōshi* (Stormy Century: A Short History of the Suppression of Academic Freedom); Sasaki Sōichi et al., eds., *Kyōdai jiken* (The Kyoto University Incident); Tanaka Kōtarō, Suekawa Hiroshi, Ouchi Hyōe, and Miyazawa Toshiyoshi, *Daigaku no jichi* (University Autonomy); Minobe Ryōkichi, *Kumon suru demokurashii* (The Agony of Democracy); and Ienaga Saburō, *Daigaku no jiyū no rekishi* (The History of University Freedom).

12. Hatanaka, *Oboegaki Shōwa shuppan dan'atsu shōshi.*

13. "Jiyū ni shisu, Kawai Eijirō hōtei tōsōki" (He Fought for Freedom: The Legal Battle of Kawai Eijirō), *Chūō Kōron,* January 1950, appendix.

14. Hatanaka, *Oboegaki Shōwa shuppan dan'atsu shōshi; Chūō Kōronsha nanajūnen-shi* (Seventy Year History of the Chūō Kōron Company); and Kuroda Hidetoshi, *Shōwa genron-shi e no shōgen* (Freedom of Speech in the Shōwa Period).

15. Jōno, *Sansei dokuritsu senki.*

16. *Iwanami Shōten gojūnen* (Fifty Years of Iwanami Shoten). The most comprehensive list of books banned in this period is the four-volume work by Odagiri Hideo and Fukuoka Ikichi, *Shōwa shoseki, shimbun, zasshi hakkin nenpyō* (Chronology of Banned Books, Newspapers, and Magazines).

17. Moriguchi Tari, *Bijutsu hachijūnen-shi* (Eighty-Year History of Fine Arts).

18. Sonobe Saburō, *Nijūseiki Nihon bunmei-shi, ongaku gojūnen* (History of Twentieth-Century Japanese Civilization, Fifty Years of Music).

19. *Akita ujaku nikki;* Saitō Shōzō, "Shingeki" (New Theater), in *Zusetsu Nihon bunka-shi taikei* (Illustrated Outline of Japanese Cultural History), Vol. 12; Ishikawa Hiroyoshi, "Dainiji taisenchū no goraku" (Entertainment during the Second World War), *TBS chōsa jōhō* (TBS Investigative Report), July 1967. For motion pictures, see Itoya Hisao, "Eiga ken'etsu seido no keifu" (Genesis of the Censorship System for Motion Pictures), *Hōritsu Jihō,* August 1965.

20. Kokubu Ichitarō, ed., *Ishi o mote owareru gotoku* (The Purged Teachers).

21. Mombushō, Futsu Gakumukyoku (Ministry of Education, Middle and Elementary School Bureau), *Kokumin gakkō-rei oyobi kokumin gakkō-rei shikō kisoku* (The National School Ordinances and Enforcement Regulations).

22. As related by the young victim in Karasawa Timitarō, *Kyōkasho no rekishi* (The History of Textbooks).

23. *Yamagata no kyōiku* (Education in Yamagata Prefecture), in *Gendai kyōiku,* Vol. 5, *Nihon kindai kyōiku-shi.*

24. *Maebashi kōkō hachijūshichinen-shi* (Eighty-seven Year History of the Maebashi Higher School). Similar accounts may also be found in *Miyagi ken dai-ichi josei kōtō gakkō rokujūnen-shi* (Sixty Year History of the Miyagi Prefecture First Girls' High School).

25. Bessho Makiko, "Kusa ikire" (Fragrant Country Grass), *Shufu no sensō taikenki.*

26. Nakane Mihoko, *Sokai gakudō no nikki* (Diary of an Evacuated Schoolgirl).

27. Nakane Mihoko, *Nihon Dokusho Shimbun,* May 16, 1966.

28. Ienaga, *Daigaku no jiyū no rekishi.*

29. Hakuō Izoku-kai, ed., *Kumo nagaruru hate ni, senbotsu hikō yobi gakusei no shuki* (Behind the Clouds: Notes of Student Cadet Pilots Killed in the War). (This book is partly a response to *Kike, Wadatsumi no koe,* which, while also a collection of the writings of student volunteers killed in the conflict, included only documents that expressed antiwar feelings. According to the preface, the Hakuō Izoku-kai compilers regarded this approach as "catering to the times," i.e., the pacifist mood of postwar Japan. They "believed that [the student pilots'] emotions were much more pure and wanted to present them to the world.") Hōsei University professor Honda Akira used to write in letters to his drafted students, "Take care of yourself." One student wrote back that Honda should add "For the sake of the Empire." See Honda Akira, *Shidōsha* (The Opinion Makers). Ikeda Kōhei's *Unmei to setsuri, ichi senbotsu gakuto no shuki* (Fate and Providence, The Writings of a Student Draftee Killed in Battle) was the earliest of these

collections. It shows the excellent academic training he received in the prewar high schools. Yet he evinced no doubts or criticism about the war. The contrast between his impressive grasp of abstract philosophical concepts and the absence of a critical consciousness toward reality is striking.

30. Yoneda Yutaka and Takayama Keiki, *Shōwa no shukyō dan'atsu* (Religious Repression); Yoneda Yutaka, *Shōwa no junkyōsha* (The Shōwa Martyrs); and Otani, *Shōwa Kenpei-shi.*

31. Asami Sensaku, *Shōjujika* (The Little Cross), and Takeda Kiyoko, "Asami Sensaku no heiwa shisō" (The Pacifist Thought of Asami Sensaku), in *Dochaku to haikyō* (Christianity in Japan, Apostasy and Drift).

32. Wada Yōichi, "Sen kyūhyaku sanjūshichinen natsu no Dōshisha chaperu rōjō jiken" (The Confinement Incident at the Dōshisha University Chapel in the Summer of 1937), *Kirisutokyō Shakai Mondai Kenkyū,* No. 8; and *Seinan jogakuin sanjūnen-shi* (Thirty-Year History of Seinan Girls Academy).

33. Naimushō, Keimukyoku, *Shakai undō no jōkyō* (The Current State of Social Movements), 1936 through 1943; and Ohara Shakai Mondai Kenkyūjo, *Taiheiyō sensōka no rōdō undō* (The Labor Movement during the Pacific War).

34. *Shakai undō no Jōkyō,* 1936 through 1943; and *Taiheiyō sensōka no rōdō undō.*

35. Saitō's speech was deleted from the stenographic record; a correct version was not available until after the war. The full text is in *GS,* Vol. 13, *Nitchū sensō,* Vol. 5. In addition to a few Diet members from the proletarian parties, Tazawa Yoshiharu strongly opposed Saitō's expulsion. (Tazawa Yoshiharu Kinenkai, *Tazawa Yoshiharu*).

36. Yokusan Undō-shi Kankōkai, *Yokusan kokumin undō-shi* (History of the Imperial Assistance Movement).

37. The Supreme Court declared the Diet election in Kagoshima Prefecture invalid on March 1, 1945. See Saitō Hideo, *Saibankan-ron* (Judges).

38. Ari Makuji, "Chihō seido—burakukai, chōnaikai seido" (Local System —The Hamlet Associations and Neighborhood Associations), in *Nihon kindaihō hattatsu-shi,* Vol. 6; "Machi no shintaisei" (The New Block System), *Asahi Gurafu,* September 4, 1940; "Tontonton karari no tonarigumi jōkai fūkei" (Knock, knock, knock—The Neighborhood Association Is Meeting), *Asahi Gurafu,* October 23, 1940; and "Susume tonarigumi" (The Association Carries On), *Asahi Gurafu,* November 25, 1942.

39. "Machi o uzumeru kokusaku hyōgo" (Government Slogans Everywhere), *Asahi Gurafu,* February 26, 1941. Visible in the photographs are the slogans "Don't complain" and "Christians, join a Japanese religion!"

40. Wada Yōichi, *Haiiro no yūmoa* (Prison and Other Funny Things); Kozai Yoshishige, "Ryūchijo no omoide" (Memories of the Lockup), *Ekonomisuto,* August 2, 1966.

41. Eguchi Kiyoshi, *Mittsu no shi* (Three Deaths); and Tezuka Hidetaka, *Kobayashi Takiji.*

42. Kuroda, *Shōwa genron-shi e no shōgen;* Mimasaka Tarō, Fujita Chikamasa, and Watanabe Kiyoshi, *Genron no haiboku* (Freedom of

Speech Defeated); and Aoyama Kenzō, *Yokohama jiken* (The Yokohama Incident).

43. Hani Goro, "Tetsugakusha no gokushi" (A Philosopher Dies in Prison), *Tokushū Bungei Shunjū, watakushi wa soko ni ita* (Bungei Shunjū Special Issue: I Was There).

44. For example, see "Tokkō kyōhan" (Special Higher Police Textbook), compiled by the Special Higher Police Section, Shizuoka Prefecture, in "Gendai-shi no dokyumentari suketchi" (Documentary Sketch of Modern History), Vol. 1, *Misuzu,* April 1961.

45. "When I said, I'm keeping a diary, Shimanaka replied, 'That's dangerous!' " Kiyosawa, *Ankoku nikki,* August 1, 1943. Kiyosawa also wrote, "I'll leave my diary in Karuizawa when I go back to Tokyo. I'm worried that it might be discovered. I have to be careful and disguise my real meaning even when writing in it." *Ibid.,* July 9, 1944. The same apprehension is expressed in *Takami Jun nikki,* January 8, 1944.

46. Haruno Yoshie, "Sensōchū no keiken kara" (From a Wartime Experience), letter to the editor, *Asahi Shimbun,* November 20, 1958; and roundtable discussion, "Katenai sensō no naka de" (In the Middle of a Hopeless War), *Asahi Janaru,* January 23, 1966.

47. Matsumoto Chizuko, "Rākunparushita to A-san no omoide" NET Terebi Shakai Kyōyōbu, ed., *Hachigatsu jūgonichi to watakushi.*

48. Victor Frankel, *Ein Psycholog Erlebt Das Konzentrationslager;* and Olga Lengyel, *Five Chimneys.*

49. Ienaga, *Shihōken dokuritsu no rekishiteki kōsatsu;* Aoki Eigorō, *Saibankan no sensō sekinin* (The War Responsibility of Judges); and Aoki Eigorō, *Keiji saiban no ronri* (The Logic of Criminal Courts).

50. Horiba, *Shina jihen sensō shidō-shi.*

51. Ogata, *Ichi gunjin no shōgai.*

52. Ueda Mannen and Matsui Kanji, *Dai Nihon kokugo jiten* (Encyclopedia of the Japanese Language).

53. Rikugunshō, *Gakkō kyōren hikkei* (School Training Manual).

54. "Manshū jihen to kokusai renmei" (The Manchurian Incident and the League of Nations), *GS,* Vol. 11.

55. Quoted in Watanabe Toru, *Nihon rōdō kumiai undō-shi* (History of the Japanese Labor Union Movement).

56. "Han-teikokushugi sensō teze" (The Thesis on Opposing the Imperialist War), *GS,* Vol. 14, *Shakaishugi undō* (The Socialist Movement), Vol. 1.

57. "Nihon kyōsantō kōhan tōsō daihyō chinjutsu sokkiroku" (Stenographic Record of Statements by Representative Defendants in the Japan Communist Party's Public Trial Struggle), *GS,* Vol. 17, *Shakaishugi undō,* Vol. 4.

58. "Suzuki memo" (Suzuki memorandum), in *Musan seitō-shi shiryō (senzen) kōki* (Historical Materials on the History of the [prewar] Proletarian Parties, Later Period); and Suzuki Mosaburō, *Aru shakaishugisha no hansei* (My Life as a Socialist).

59. A part of *Deinamikku* is included in Ishikawa Sanshirō, *Waga hisenron-shi* (My Pacifism).

60. Quoted in Watanabe, *Nihon rōdō kumiai undō-shi.*

61. After the war even those who had used the slogan "From War to Revolution" admitted that it lacked concrete meaning. The delusion that "the revolution was at hand" was an erroneous estimate of the political situation. See "Shōwa shisō-shi e no shōgen" (Testimony regarding Shōwa Intellectual History), *Ekonomisuto,* June 28, 1966.

62. Matsuzawa Hiroaki, "Marukusushugi ni okeru shisō to shūdan" (Marxist Thought and Organization in Japan), in *Kindai Nihon shisō-shi kōza* (Lectures on the History of Modern Japanese Thought), Vol. 5; Odagiri Hideo, "Senji taiseika no bunka" (Culture under the Wartime Restrictions), in *Iwanami kōza Nihon rekishi,* Vol. 20; Odagiri Hideo, "Shōwa bungaku-shi ni okeru jūnendai" (The History of Shōwa Literature, the First Decades), *Kokubungaku Kaishaku to Kanshō,* June 1966; and Takeuchi Yoshitomo, "Nihon no Marukusushugi" (Japanese Marxism), in *Gendai Nihon shisō taikei, Marukushizumu* (Modern Japanese Thought, Marxism), Vol. 2.

63. Mashita Shin'ichi and Shinmura Takeshi, "Kurai jidai no teikō no rekishi—zasshi 'Sekai Bunka' o megutte" (Resistance during the Fascist Years, the magazine *World Culture*), *Meidai Hyōron,* May 1965; and Wada Yōichi, *Haiiro no yūmoa.*

64. Dimitrov, G. (The Anti-fascist United Front).

65. *GS,* Vol. 14.

66. Yamabe Kentarō, "Kaisetsu" (Introduction), *Kominterun Nihon ni kansuru tezashū* (Comintern Theses Related to Japan). It was not just bad timing, a correct position established too late. The Comintern's tactical shift lacked a careful analysis of the relationship between communism and democracy. As a result, not only in Japan but in many other countries as well, it was impossible for "bourgeois democracy" and communism to wage an anti-Fascist struggle. This aspect is discussed in Saitō Takashi, "Senkyūhyaku sanjūnendai" (The 1930s), *Gakutō,* June and July 1967.

67. Shihōshō, Keijikyoku (Ministry of Justice, Criminal Investigation Bureau), "Shōwa jūsannen rokugatsu shisō jitsumuka kaidō giji sokkiroku" (Stenographic Record of Meeting of Officials Working on Thought Problems, June 1938); *Shisō Kenkyū Shiryō* (Research Materials on Thought), No. 45; and Naimushō, Keihokyoku, *Shakai undō no jōkyō.*

68. Otani, *Shōwa kenpei-shi;* Radio TBS Special Program, "Futatsu no hansen undō" (Two Antiwar Movements), August 12, 1963.

69. *Tōyō keizai shinpō genron rokujūnen* (Sixty Years of the Magazine Tōyō Keizai Shinpō); and Chō Yukio, "Nihon shihonshugi ni okeru riberarizumu no saihyōka—Ishibashi Tanzan-ron" (Ishibashi Tanzan and a Reevaluation of Liberalism in Japanese Capitalism), in *Nihon keizai shisō-shi kenkyū* (Research on the History of Japanese Economic Thought).

70. Ienaga Saburō, "Senjika no kojin zasshi" (Private Magazines during the War), *Shisō,* January 1964; Ienaga Saburō, *Kenryokuaku to no tatakai, Masaki Hiroshi no shisō katsudō* (The Struggle against Authoritarianism— The Activities of Masaki Hiroshi). Parts of *Tazan no Ishi* are in *Chikushōdō no chikyū,* and Maeda, *Pen wa shinazu.* Parts of *Chikaki Yori* are collected in the single-volume work of that title. Writings from *Tsūshin* and *Kashin* are scattered in *Yanaihara Tadao zenshū,* Vols. 6–15, 17–18,

and elsewhere. Complete editions of the publications have also been reprinted.

71. Shakai Minshutō, "Nihon musan kaikyū wa Manmō mondai o dō miru" (How Do the Japanese Proletariat View the Problem of Manchuria and Mongolia), in *Musan seitō-shi shiryō (senzen) kōki.*

72. Sources on ideological conversions are too numerous to list in detail. For one outstanding example, see Nakamura Yoshiaki, *Kyōsantō bōhikoku no tenkō kiroku—seika seinen kyōka tokuhon* (A Record of the Ideological Conversion of a Communist Party Defendant—A Textbook on Radical Youth). The best collection of materials showing the prosecutor's techniques is Ikeda Masaru, *Bōhan kagaku zenshū dai rokukan, shisōhan-hen* (Complete Collection of Criminology, Vol. 6, Thought Crimes). For a perspective on the conversion process from an individual who recanted during the war and then reverted to his earlier beliefs after Japan's defeat, see the personal account of Yamada Seizaburō, *Tenkōki, kiri no jidai* (Conversion, The Cloudy Years), and *Tenkōki, arashi no jidai* (Conversion, The Stormy Years).

73. Honda Shūgo, *Tenkō bungakuron* (The Literature of Ideological Conversion); Takami Jun, "Tenkō ni tsuite" (On Ideological Conversion), in *Shōwa bungaku seisui-shi* (The Vicissitudes of Shōwa Literature); Yoshimoto Takaaki, *Geijutsuteki teikō to zasetsu* (Artistic Resistance and Failure); Shisō no Kagaku Kenkyūkai Kyōdō Kenkyū, *Tenkō* (Ideological Conversion), Vols. 1, 2.

74. Fujikake Shizuya, "Jobun" (Preface, dated July 1943), in *Ukiyoe no kenkyū* (Research on Ukiyoe).

75. Kawakami Hajime, *Bannen no seikatsu kiroku* (My Later Years), December 27, 1943.

76. For example, see "Nihon kirisutokyō-dan yori dai Tōa kyōeiken ni aru kirisutokyōto ni okuru shokan" (Letters from the United Church of Christ in Japan to Christians in the Greater East Asia Co-Prosperity Sphere), in *Fukuin to Sekai,* May 1967. For a Christian's reflections on war responsibility, see Andō Hajime, *Fukaki fuchi yori—Kirisutosha no sensō keiken* (From the Abyss; A Christian's War Experience).

77. *Takami Jun nikki; Akita Ujaku nikki* (Diary of Akita Ujaku); Nakajima Kenzō, *Shōwa jidai* (The Shōwa Era); and Hirotsu Kazurō, *Zokunendai no ashi-ato* (Traces of The Age, Continued).

78. Moriguchi Tari, *Bijutsu hachijūnen-shi* (History of Eighty Years of Art); and "Taiheiyō sensō meigashū" (Masterpieces of the Pacific War), a special issue of the *Mainichi Gurafu,* November 3, 1967. Many excellent articles on literature and the arts during the war are in "Senjika no bungaku, geijutsu" (Literature and the Arts during the War), special issues of *Bungaku,* May, August, and December 1961, and April 1962.

79. For accounts of frequent visits by the Special Higher Police, see *Akita Ujaku nikki; Takami Jun nikki;* and Shimaki Kensaku, *Ogigayatsu nikki* (Ogigayatsu Diary), in *Shōwa sensō bungaku zenshū,* Vol. 14.

80. The Shōwa Kenkyūkai (Shōwa Research Society) under Konoe Fumimaro purportedly intended to check the military by popular-based organized political power. I cannot, however, regard such a group and its activities as really opposed to the hawks. Giving them the benefit of the doubt regarding intentions, it is a good example of intellectual cooptation. They ended up supporting the very forces they hoped to control. Sakai Saburō, "Shōwa kenkyūkai no higeki" (The Tragedy of the Shōwa Research Society), *Bungei Shunjū,* October 1964; and Suda Teiichi, *Kazami Akira to sono jidai* (Kazami Akira and His Time). The same intention was also present to a slight degree in the formation of the IRAA.

81. The most outstanding example is the wartime writing of Ozaki Hotsumi.

82. Minobe, *Kumon suru demokurashi.* According to Minobe, "About the spring of 1937 Assistant Professor Hashizumi Akio of the economics department was appointed an adviser to the Police Bureau, Home Ministry, and became a kind of assistant to bureau chief Tomita Kenji. In other words, a police agent was openly placed in the professorial ranks."

83. Kiyosawa, *Ankoku nikki.*

84. Specific instances are recorded in *Akita Ujaku nikki,* September 15, 1938, January 1, 1943, and elsewhere.

85. Maruyama Masao, "Nihon fashizumu no shisō to undō" (The Ideology and Dynamics of Japanese Fascism), in *Gendai seiji no shisō to kōdō* (Thought and Behavior in Modern Japanese Politics).

86. Mori Isao, *Shōwa ni ikiru* (A Life in Shōwa).

87. Kurita Sadako, "Nagai nagai sensō" (The Long, Long War), in *Shufu no sensō taikenki.*

88. Yoshioka Yukio, "Tatakai no naka de" (In the Battle), in Hiroshima-ken Hibakusha no Shuki Henshū Iinkai, ed., *Genbaku yurusumaji* (Don't Allow the Bomb).

89. Imai Haru, "Sōmato" (Light on the Past), in *Shufu no sensō taikenki.* Similar accounts are in Tsuyama, *Sensō dorei.*

90. Imai Takajirō, "Otō-san" (Father), in *Kaeranu oshiego* (My Students Who Never Came Back).

91. Watanabe Kiyoshi, "Mura no senchū nikki (zoku)" (Village War Diary, Continued), in *Wadatsumi no koe,* January 1967.

92. Correspondence with the author.

93. Even persons like myself who were in Japan and resigned to being drafted and bombed felt this way. This attitude was much stronger, I believe, among the student draftees and others who knew they were facing certain death. An account of a typical experience is in Hayashi Tadao's diary, *Waga inochi getsumei ni moyu* (My Life Flared in a Moonbeam).

CHAPTER 7. JAPAN EXTENDS THE WAR TO THE PACIFIC

1. *TSM,* Vol. 6.

2. "Hokkai jiken keika gaiyō" (Summary of the Peihai Incident), in *GS,* Vol. 8, *Nitchū sensō,* Vol. 1.

3. "Kokusai jōsei to teikoku no tachiba" (The International Situation and the Empire's Position), in *Nihon gaikō nenpyō narabi ni shuyō monjo,* Vol. 1.

4. *TSM,* Vol. 6.

5. "Tai Futsuin, Tai shisaku yōkō" (General Policy Regarding French Indochina and Thailand), in *Nihon gaikō nenpyō narabi ni shuyō monjo,* Vol. 2.

6. "Tai Ranin keizai hatten no tame no shisaku" (Measures for the Economic Development of the Dutch East Indies), *ibid.*

7. "Ishizawa sōryōji teishutsu no tai Ranin yōkyū narabi ni kaitō" (Demands Presented by Counsel General Ishizawa to the Dutch East Indies and the Dutch Replies), "Batavia nite Yoshizawa daihyō teishutsu no wagahō dainiji yōkyū oyobi Ranin kaitō" (Our Second Demands Presented in Batavia by Representative Yoshizawa and the Dutch Replies), and "Nichi-Ranin kōshō uchikiri ni kansuru jōhōkyoku happyō" (Cabinet Information Bureau Announcement Regarding the Termination of the Japan–Dutch East Indies Negotiations), *ibid.*

8. *TSM,* Vol. 8.

9. Suzuki Teiichi, "Kaisen kettei no shunkan" (The Moment When War Was Decided), in Andō, *Shōwa keizai-shi e no shōgen,* Vol. 2.

10. Okazaki Ayakoto, "Gunju seisan no hōkai" (Armament Production Collapses), in *ibid.* Kido Kōichi's diary has the following entry on August 7, 1941: "From another angle, the problem has become extremely simple, i.e., the question is oil."

11. Arthur Schlesinger, *The Age of Roosevelt,* Vol. II, *The Coming of the New Deal;* and Robert E. Sherwood, *Roosevelt and Hopkins.*

12. Mainichi Shimbunsha, *Taiheiyō sensō hishi, Bei senji shidōsha no kaisō* (Secret History of the Pacific War, Recollections of America's Wartime Leaders); Herbert Feis, *The Road to Pearl Harbor,* and *TSM,* Vol. 6.

13. *TSM,* Vol. 7.

14. "Shōwa jūrokunen jūgatsu jūyokka gozen kakugi ni okeru rikugun daijin setsumei no yōshi" (Summary of the Army Minister's Explanation at the Cabinet Meeting on the Morning of October 14, 1941), *TSM, Bekkan.*

15. "Konoe shushō jishoku jōsōbun" (Premier Konoe's Resignation Report to the Emperor), from "Heiwa e no doryoku," in *Sekai Bunka,* February 1946.

16. Tōgō, *Jidai no ichimen.*

17. Tanemura, *Daihon'ei kimitsu nisshi,* October 6, 1941, and "Senshishitsu shiryō" (Materials in the War History Room), quoted in *TSM,* Vol. 7.

18. Konoe, "Heiwa e no doryoku," and "Senshishitsu shiryō." According to Yamamoto Kumaichi, during a break in the Liaison Conference on November 1, 1941, Admiral Nagano approached him with a proposal to leave everything up to the Foreign Ministry. It was a bid by the navy to avoid responsibility for the decision to go to war. See Yamamoto, "Dai Tōa sensō hishi" (Secret History of the Greater East Asian War), in Nihon Kokusai Seiji Gakkai, *Nihon gaikō-shi no shomondai* (Problems in the History of Japanese Foreign Relations), Vol. 1.

19. Statement by Fukudome Shigeru in "Teitoku zadankai" (Roundtable Discussion by the Admirals), and Tomioka Sadatoshi, "Taiheiyō senmetsu sensō" (War of Annihilation in the Pacific), *Tokushū Bungei Shunjū, Nihon rikukaigun no sōkessan* (Bungei Shunjū Special Issue, Closing the Books on the Japanese Army and Navy). Premier Konoe asked Suzuki Teiichi, director of the planning board, "if it is not foolish to incur the enormous sacrifices of a war against America and England" because of a shortage of resources for armaments production. Suzuki replied, "It is, but going to war is a matter of domestic politics." "Heiwa e no doryoku." Foreign Minister Tōgō instructed Ambassador Nomura on November 4, 1941, that it was "domestically impossible" to accede to American wishes and added, "Because of domestic politics, further concessions are utterly impossible." *Nihon gaikō nenpyō oyobi ni shuyō monjo,* Vol. 2. By these remarks, Japan's leaders acknowledged that the most important consideration was not pressure from the international environment but domestic politics. The crucial factor was that prowar elements, the military and their allies, could not be restrained. This admission by the elite who took the country to war is highly significant in assessing causation.
20. Fukutomi Shigeru, *Shikan Shinjuwan kōgeki* (The Pearl Harbor Attack).
21. "Nichibei kōshō jūichigatsu nijūrokunichi Bei-gawa teian" (U.S. Proposal of November 26, 1941, in the Japan–U.S. Negotiations), in *Nihon gaikō nenpyō narabi ni shuyō monjo,* Vol. 2.
22. "Tai Bei tsūchō (Jūnigatsu muikkazuke)" (Notification to the U.S. dated December 6), *ibid.*
23. *TSM,* Vol. 7.
24. Sherwood, *Roosevelt and Hopkins;* Feis, *The Road to Pearl Harbor;* and *Taiheiyō sensō hishi, Bei senji shidōsha no kaisō.*
25. Mainichi Shimbunsha, ed., *Nihon no shōri to higeki, Uinsuton Chachiru 'Dainiji sekai taisen kaikoroku' Nihonban* (Japan's Victory and Tragedy, Winston Churchill 'Recollections of World War II,' Japan edition).
26. Mao Tse-tung, "On Protracted War," *Selected Writings of Mao Tse-tung,* Vol. 3.
27. Immediately after Ikezaki's *Beikoku osoruru ni tarazu* appeared, Mizuno Hironori wrote a devastating criticism of its "easy victory" thesis. *Tokyo Asahi Shimbun,* November 8, 1929. In 1932 Mizuno published *Nichibei kōbō no issen* (Battle for Survival: Japan versus America). Written in novel form to avoid censors and fanatics, Mizuno warned that if Japan went to war with the U.S., it would probably lose. The book was an accurate forecast of what happened in the 1940s. Mizuno's work deserves further study. See Ienaga Saburō, "Mizuno Hironori no hansen heiwa shisō" (The Antiwar and Pacifist Thought of Mizuno Hironori), *Shisō,* September 1967.
28. "Jūichigatsu tsuitachi dairokujūrokkai renraku kaigi" (The Sixty-sixth Liaison Conference, November 1 [1941]), in *TSM, Bekkan.*
29. Yamamoto, "Dai Tōa sensō hishi."
30. *Ibid.*
31. Oi Atsushi, *Kaijō goeisen* (Escort Duty).

32. Memorandum quoted in *ibid.*

33. Hayashi Saburō, *Taiheiyō sensō rikusen gaishi,* and Morishima Morito, *Shinjuwan, Risubon, Tokyo* (Pearl Harbor, Lisbon, Tokyo).

34. "Senshishitsu shiryō," quoted in *TSM,* Vol. 6.

35. Such views were not confined to the army. Foreign Minister Tani Masayuki, a career diplomat with long overseas experience, could still say in 1943: "America has spiritual deficiencies. There are other problems like organized labor and elections. The U.S. has extraordinary weaknesses, so our judgment is that the U.S. might lose the will to fight." Sanbō Honbu, *Sugiyama memo* (Sugiyama Memorandums), Vol. 2.

36. Nambara Shigeru, *Onozuka Kiheiji.*

37. Muyahara Noriko, "Watakushi no sensō taiken" (My War Experiences), in Funabashi Seibu Fujin kai, *Kurushikatta sensō no omoide* (Memories of a Bitter War).

38. *Kido Kōichi nikki,* November 29, 1941.

39. Yamamoto, "Dai Tōa sensō hishi." Tōjō's pet phrase to cut off discussion was, "We want you to have faith in the government." He used it over and over again in Privy Council meetings. See Fukai Eigo, *Sūmitsuin jūyō giji oboegaki* (Notes on Important Privy Council Deliberations).

40. In addition to works cited, this description is based on the following: Hattori, *Dai Tōa sensō zenshi;* Takagi, *Taiheiyō kaisen-shi;* Hayashi, *Taiheiyō sensō rikusen gaishi;* Kojima Noboru, *Taiheiyō sensō* (The Pacific War), Vols. 1–2; and Itō Masanori, *Rengō kantai no saigo* (The End of the Combined Fleet).

41. *Nihon Hyōron,* January 1942.

42. Odagiri Susumu, "Jūnigatsu yōka no kiroku" (The Record of December 8 [1941]), *Bungaku,* December 1961 and April 1962; and Murakami Hyōe, "Shōwa jūrokunen jūnigatsu yōka, sono hi . . ." (That Day, December 8, 1941), *Gendai no Me,* December 1967.

43. Fuchida Mitsuo and Okumiya Masatake, *Middoue* (Midway).

44. In *Shōwa sensō bungaku zenshū,* Vol. 6.

45. Sherwood, *Roosevelt and Hopkins; Taiheiyō sensō hishi, Bei senji shidōsha no kaisō;* and Oka, *Kokusai seiji-shi.* There was also friction among the Allies, between the Allied governments and the various anti-Japan resistance groups, and among the different factions in the resistance movements (see Chapter 8). These were a source of the Cold War.

46. Matsumoto Zentarō, *Senkan Yamato, Musashi—sekkei to kenzō* (The Battleships *Yamato* and *Musashi*—Their Design and Construction); and Yoshimura Akira, *Senkan Musashi* (The Battleship *Musashi*).

47. "Himitsu kūbo Taihō, Shinano" (The Secret Aircraft Carriers *Taihō* and *Shinano*), *Maru,* special issue, November 1960.

48. In addition to the works by Hattori and Hayashi Saburō previously cited, the following have detailed accounts: Takagi, *Imparu;* Takagi Toshirō, *Kōmei* (Disobedience); *Hiroku Dai Tōa senshi,* Vol. 3; and Maruyama Shizuo, "Imparu shi no haitō" (Imphal: Debacle of Death), *Chūō Kōron,* August 1964.

49. In addition to Hattori and Hayashi, see the following: Kon Hidemi,

"Sanchū hōrō" (Wandering in the Mountains), *Shōwa bungaku sensō zenshū,* Vol. 6; Ezaki Seichi, "Ruson no tanima" (The Valleys of Luzon), *ibid.;* Kamiko, *Ware Reite ni shisezu;* and Moriya, *Ragunako no kita.* Ooka Shōhei's *Nobi* (Fires on the Plain) is a work of fiction but very interesting.

50. Robert Sherrod's *Saipan* has detailed accounts of the fierce battle for the island.

51. *Kido Kōichi nikki; Okada Keisuke kaikoroku* (Memoirs of Okada Keisuke); and "Seihen Keii" (Details on the Change of Cabinets), in Sanbō Honbu, *Haisen no kiroku,* introduction to materials.

52. The savage fighting is written in the casualty figures. The 20,000-man Japanese garrison was virtually annihilated. U.S. forces suffered 6,800 killed and 20,000 wounded. See Richard F. Newcomb, *Iwo Jima.*

53. In addition to the works by Takagi Sōkichi and Itō Masanori previously cited, see Yoshida Mitsuru, *Senkan Yamato no saigo*; and Nomura Jirō, *Dōkoku no umi Senkan Yamato shitō no kiroku* (The Sea Screams: The Death Struggle of the Battleship *Yamato*).

54. See previously cited works by Hattori, Hayashi, and Kojima. Among the many detailed accounts are the following: Kamichi Isshi, *Okinawa senshi* (The Battle for Okinawa); Urasaki Jun, *Kieta Okinawa-ken* (Okinawa Prefecture Is Gone); Okinawa Taimusu-sha, *Tetsu no bōfū* (Storm of Steel); and Yoshikawa Seibi, *Okinawa no saigo* (The Last of Okinawa).

55. Gaimushō, *Shūsen shiroku.*

56. Fletcher Knebel and Charles W. Bailey II, *No High Ground;* Len Giovannitti and Fred Freed, *The Decision to Drop the Bomb;* and *Taiheiyō sensō hishi, Beisenji shidōsha no kaisō.*

57. See Hattori and Hayashi Saburō. Other useful sources include *The History of World War II* (published in Russian, Marxism-Leninism Research Institute); and Gomikawa Junpei, "Kaimetsu no hi" (Day of Destruction), *Shūkan Yomiuri,* November 4, 1967.

58. Oi, *Kaijō goeisen;* and Tamura Kyūzō, "Ikiteiru kaigun, sōkai butai" (The Surviving Navy, A Minesweeping Unit), *Tokushū Bungei Shunjū, Nihon rikukaigun no sōkessan.*

59. United States, Strategic Bombing Survey, *The Destruction of Japan's War Economy;* Jerome B. Cohen, *Japan's Economy in War and Reconstruction;* and Okazaki, "Gunju seisan no hōkai."

60. *Asahi Gurafu,* December 1, 1943.

61. "Shijō saidai no sensuikan i-go yonhyaku" (The Largest Submarine in the World, I–400), *Sande Mainichi,* August 18, 1963.

62. Horikoshi and Okumiya, *Zerosen.*

63. Itō, *Rengō kantai no saigo.*

64. *Shōwa sangyō-shi,* Vol. 1; Fuchida and Okumiya, *Middoue;* Nomura Ryōsuke, "Taiwan kōkū senki" (Air War over Taiwan), *Taiheiyō sensō no zenbō, bessatsu.*

65. See Chapter 9.

66. *Asahi Shimbun,* March 15, 1956.

CHAPTER 8. THE GREATER EAST ASIA CO-PROSPERITY SPHERE: LIBERATION OR EXPLOITATION?

1. "Tai Doku-I-So kōshōkan yōkō" (Summary of Proposals for Negotiations with Germany, Italy, and the Soviet Union), decisions at the Liaison Conference, February 3, 1941, in *Nihon gaikō nenpyō narabi ni shuyō monjo,* Vol. 2.
2. Kaneko Mitsuharu, *Zetsubō no seishin-shi* (The Depths of Despair).
3. "Shōwa jūrokunen jūichigatsu itsuka gozen kaigi" (Imperial Conference, November 5, 1941), in *TSM, Bekkan.*
4. *Ibid.*
5. Waseda Daigaku Shakai Kagaku Kenkyūjo, *Indonesia ni okeru Nihon gunsei no kenkyū* (Research on Japanese Military Administration in Indonesia).
6. *Sugiyama memo,* Vol. 2.
7. *Indonesia ni okeru Nihon gunsei no kenkyū.*
8. *Ibid.,* and *Sugiyama memo,* Vol. 2.
9. "Shina dendō yōkō" (Summary of Japan's Christian Proselytizing Mission in China), in *Yanaihara Tadao zenshū.*
10. Hanaya, "Manshū jihen wa kōshite keikaku sareta"; Kanda, *Oryokkō;* and Toyoshima, "Chōsengun ekkyō shingekisu."
11. "Shōwa jūrokunen nigatsu mikka daihachikai renraku kondankai" (The Eighth Informal Liaison Meeting, February 3, 1941), army statement, in *TSM, Bekkan.*
12. Fujimura Yoshirō, "Daresu Kōsaku" (The Dulles Operation), quoted in *Shūsen shiroku,* Vol. 2.
13. Tanaka Jirō, ed., *Gyōsei hōkishū* (Administrative Laws and Regulations), Vol. 1; and Hosokawa, *Gendai Nihon bunmei-shi,* Vol. 10, *Shokumin-shi.*
14. "It is anachronistic to have a system of special allowances for Japanese officials but not for Korean officials. It is because Japan regards Korea as a colony." "Chihō gikai ni okeru giin no yōchūi gendō ichiranhyō" (List of Significant Remarks by Members of Local Assemblies), in Chōsen Sōtokufu, Keimukyoku (Korea Government-General, Police Affairs Bureau), *Saikin ni okeru Chōsen chian jōkyō, Shōwa jūsannen* (The Recent State of Public Order in Korea, 1938).
15. Morita Yoshio, "Chōsen ni okeru Nihon tōchi no shūen" (The End of Japanese Rule in Korea), in Nihon Kokusai Seiji Gakkai, *Nikkan kankei no tenkai* (The Development of Japan-Korea Relations). Draft proposal, "Kongo torubeki sensō shidō no taikō ni motozuku taigai seisaku shidō yōryō" (Summary of Policy Guidance Toward Overseas Areas Based on the General Outline of War Measures to Be Adopted), dated August 8, 1944, states: "Plan to intensify policies to make residents of the Korean peninsula and Taiwan loyal subjects. While they should be given the rights and duties of subjects, independence activities must be stringently controlled."
16. Ministry of Home Affairs, *Chōsen oyobi Taiwan no genkyō* (Present

Situation in Korea and Taiwan), in *Gendai kyōikugaku,* Vol. 5, *Nihon kindai kyōiku-shi* (Modern Pedagogy, Vol. 5, History of Modern Education in Japan).

17. Hosokawa, *Gendai Nihon bunmei-shi,* Vol. 10, *Shokumin-shi.*

18. Komatsu Shigeo, "Watakushi no taiken ni okeru Chōsen mondai" (My Experience with the Korean Problem), *Tenbō,* November 1965. Although Kim Tal-su's *Genkainada* is a literary work, its factual basis makes the book of interest to historians.

19. Kim Ki-song's notes, in "Sugamo BC-kyū senpan no shuki" (The Notes of B and C Class War Criminals in Sugamo Prison); and Izumi Jun, "Shikeishu ga nokoshita techō" (The Pocket Notebook of an Executed Prisoner), in *Chichi no senki.*

20. Kamata Shōji, "Kita Chōsen Nihonjin kunanki" (The Hardships of Japanese in Northern Korea), in *Shōwa sensō bungaku zenshū,* Vol. 12.

21. Nihon Dokusho Shimbun, ed., *Dokyumento Chōsenjin* (Facts about Koreans).

22. Hosokawa, *Gendai Nihon bunmei-shi,* Vol. 10, *Shokumin-shi;* "Shokuminchi no kyōiku" (Education in the Colonies), *Gendai kyōikugaku,* Vol. 5, *Nihon kindai kyōiku-shi,* VIII; and "Warera wa Kōkoku shinmin nari" (We Are Subjects of the Empire), *Asahi Gurafu,* March 6, 1940.

23. *Dokyumento Chōsenjin.*

24. Miyauchi Akira, "Sensōchū no Chōsen kirisutokyōkai" (The Christian Church in Korea during the War), in Satō Kōichirō's private magazine *Mugi,* November 15, 1965; Letter by Yanaihara Tadao, June 18, 1940, in *Yanaihara Tadao zenshū,* Vol. 29; and Yanaihara Tadao, "Chōsen raishin" (Letter from Korea), in *ibid.,* Vol. 23.

25. Morita Yoshio, *Chōsen shūsen no kiroku* (Korea at the End of the War).

26. Pak Kyong-sik, *Chōsenjin kyōsei renkō no kiroku* (Korean Slave Laborers).

27. Sakai Manabu, "Dokata gakkō" (A Laborer's Life), from "Sensō no kioku, dokusha no taiken kiroku kara" (Recollections of the War, From Readers' Experiences), in *Nihon Dokusho Shimbun,* August 13, 1956.

28. For a description of the fate of Korean students who unwillingly volunteered for the Japanese army, see "Chōsen gakutohei no saigo" (The Fate of the Korean Student Soldiers), *Bungei Shunjū,* October 1964.

29. Pak Kyong-sik, *Chōsenjin kyōsei renkō no kiroku.*

30. Comments by an elderly Korean ship captain, quoted in Okamura Akihiko, *Minami Betonamu sensō jugunki* (With the Army in Southern Vietnam); "Toka" (River Crossing), in *Mainichi Gurafu bessatsu, Nihon no senreki;* and Tsuyama, *Sensō dorei.* Tamura Taijirō's novel *Inago* (Locust) cannot be taken literally (correspondence with the author). However, it is a valuable source about the plight of Korean prostitutes with the army.

31. *Manshū kyōsanhi no kenkyū,* and *Saikin ni okeru Chōsen chian jōkyō, Shōwa hachinen, Shōwa jūsannen* (The Recent State of Public Order in Korea, 1933, 1938).

32. Tanaka, *Gyōsei hōkishū;* and Hosokawa, *Gendai Nihon bunmei-shi,* Vol. 10, *Shokumin-shi.*

33. Taketani Mitsuo, "Taiwan ni okeru kokugo kokuji mondai" (The Problem of National Language and a National Script in Taiwan), *Kagaku Hyōron,* May 1926; *Benshōhō no shomondai* (Problems in Dialectics) and "Shokuminchi no kyōiku."

34. "Kankokujin ni kokoro kara wabi yo" (My Deepest Apology to Koreans), letter to the editor, *Asahi Shimbun,* July 28, 1966.

35. Cheng Haruko, "Dairen ni aru watakushi no bokō" (My Alma Mater in Dairen), in "Watakushi to Chūgoku" (China and I), *Sekai,* September 1960.

36. Ienaga Miyako. My wife was a student at the same school.

37. *Ibid.*

38. "Shin no yūjō de musubu hi made" (Till the Day of True Friendship), in "Watakushi to Chūgoku."

39. "Manmō mondai shori hōshi yōkō" (Summary of Policy toward Manchuria-Mongolia), in *Nihon gaikō nenpyō narabi ni shuyō monjo,* Vol. 2; and "Manmō shinkoka seiritsu ni tomonau taigai kankei shori yōkō" (Summary of Measures toward Foreign Countries in Conjunction with the Establishment of the New States of Manchukuo and Mongolia), *TSM, Bekkan.*

40. *GS,* Vol. 7.

41. *Ibid.,* Vol. 9.

42. *Nihon gaikō nenpyō narabi ni shuyō monjo,* Vol. 2.

43. Henry Pu-yi, *Ai-ch'in chueh-luo* (From Emperor to Citizen).

44. Hosokawa, *Gendai Nihon bunmei-shi,* Vol. 10, *Shokumin-shi.*

45. Ida Rintarō, "Manshū sodachi no jukkai" (Growing up in Manchuria), Chūgoku no Kai, *Chūgoku,* Vol. 13.

46. *Takami Jun nikki,* November 29, 1944. Defeat and imprisonment did not change attitudes. Taken prisoner by the Russians in Siberia, a Kempeitai officer got into an argument with a fellow prisoner, an officer from the Manchukuo army. The Japanese chewed out his erstwhile ally: "What did you say? You Chink! You're an insolent bastard. Let's go outside and I'll take care of you." Takasugi Ichirō, *Kyokkō no kage ni* (The Aurora Borealis in Siberia).

47. Tokuma Mitsuko and Kiribuchi Kiku both went to Manchuria as brides of agricultural immigrants, known at the time as "continental brides." Reflecting back on the experience, they thought: "The policy of sending farmers to settle and develop Manchuria was really rough on the local people. The land that Chinese and Koreans had improved and lived on was purchased and became ours. 'Purchased' was the word used but actually the Chinese and Koreans got only one-tenth the real value of their property. It was a kind of robbery. The Chinese had every right to be furious." "Tairiku no hanayome no sanjūnen" (Thirty Years as a Continental Bride), *Asahi Shimbun,* July 6, 1967.

48. Kamura Mitsuo, *Manshūkoku kaimetsu hiki* (Secret Account of the Destruction of Manchukuo), quoted in Hayashi Shigeru, ed., *Nihon shūsen-shi.*

49. Kitasaki Manabu, "Tatakawazaru fukumengun" (The Secret Forces That Never Fought), in *Hiroku dai Tōa senshi,* Vol. 2.

50. Sugawara Tokio, "Kotōsanroku no kiroku" (Record of Hu-t'ou shan-lu), "Sensō no kioku, dokusha no taiken kiroku kara."

51. Sanbō Honbu, "Manshū jihen-shi daigokan an."

52. A warning order by the chief of staff, Kwantung Army, in Kantōgun, "Manshū jihen kimitsu seiryaku nisshi."

53. Kōzuma Hitoshi, "Bujun hiwa" (Secret Account of Fushun), in *Hiroku dai Tōa senshi,* Vol. 2; Morishima, *Inbō, ansatsu, guntō;* and comments by Shang Ch'i-chi in Yokoyama Teruhiko, "Soren, Chōkyo ni yokuryū jūgonen no omoide" (Memories of Fifteen Years' Internment by the Russians and the Chinese Communists), *Asahi Shimbun,* February 17, 1962. Many Chinese publications reported this incident, but they were suppressed. (Odagiri and Fukuoka, *Shōwa shoseki shimbun zasshi hakkin nenpyō).*

54. Itō, *Mantetsu ni ikite.*

55. Inuma Jirō, ed., *Nekka senkyō no kiroku* (Proselytizing in Jehol).

56. *Kido Kōichi kankei bunsho,* "Okura Kinmochi-shi ni Saikin no Manshu jijō o kiku" (An Account by Okura Kinmochi of the Current Situation in Manchuria).

57. Okuse Heishichirō, "Zaiman nikkeijin o kinmu hyōtei suru" (Evaluating the Japanese Record in Manchuria), *Jinbutsu Orai,* March 1966; and statement by Ashida Akiko in roundtable discussion, *Shūkan Yomiuri,* November 24, 1967.

58. "Watakushi wa shōgen suru, mayaku to sensō, Nitchū sensō no himitsu heiki" (I Testify: Drugs and The War, Japan's Secret Weapon in China), *Jinbutsu Orai,* September 1965. See also Itō Keiichi, "Katana o nukanu sanbō" (The Staff That Never Unsheathed Their Swords), *Bessatsu, Bungei Shunjū,* Vol. 93.

59. Suzuki Teiichi, "Kaisen kettei no shunkan"; and Horiba, *Shina jihen sensō shidō-shi.*

60. Endō Saburō, "Teikoku rikugun to kōkūki kōgyō no hōkai" (The Imperial Army and the Destruction of the Aircraft Industry), in Andō, *Shōwa keizai-shi e no shōgen.*

61. Cheng Chen-tuo,

62. Tamura Masao, "Meifuazu na ushi no hanashi" (The Stolen Cow), in *Chichi no senki.*

63. Gomi Yasusuke, "Tairiku sensen o yuku" (At the Front in China), in *Tokushū Bungei Shunjū, akagami ichimai.*

64. In Tamura, *Inago.* Correspondence with the author.

65. Kuang Chun-ming, *Nanasai no horyo* (The Seven-Year-Old Prisoner).

66. Kanki Haruo, ed., Sankō, *Nihonjin no Chūgoku ni okeru sensō hanzai no kokuhaku* (Confessions of War Crimes Committed in China).

67. Watanabe Kiyoshi, "Mura no senchū nikki," February 17, 1942, in *Wadatsumi no koe,* August 1966.

68. Quoted in diary entry of January 31, 1943, *Kike, Wadatsumi no koe.*

69. Hirata, "Ippatsu no jūsei," *Sekai* (September 1960).

70. Isoda Osamu, "Munashiki tairiku jūdan sakusen" (The Futile Strategy of Cutting China in Half), in *Hiroku dai Tōa senshi,* Vol. 4. See also Okubo Masanobu, "Seishun o kaketa tatakai no kizu" (An Embittered Veteran), in *Chichi no senki.*

71. Chūgokujin Kyōsei Renkō Jiken Shiryō Hensan Iinkai, ed., *Kusa no bohyō, Chūgokujin kyōsei renkō jiken no kiroku* (Tombstones of Grass, Chinese Slave Laborers); Ou-yang and Wen Pin, (Fourteen Years in Hiding, Chinese Prisoner Liu Lien-jen); and *Nitchū fusen no tsukai, Chūgokujin horyo junnansha meibō hoji daihyōdan hōkokusho* (Mission for Japan-China Peace, Report of the Delegation to Present the Name List of Martyred Chinese Prisoners).

72. Kosaka Toshikame, "Anya ni kieta kōsakuin" (The Agent Who Disappeared at Night), in *Chichi no senki.*

73. Ogoshi, "Tozasareta shōnen no hitomi."

74. *Hasegawa Makoto nikki* (Diary of Hasegawa Makoto), January 18, 1945, in *Kike, Wadatsumi no koe.*

75. Shinobu Junpei, *Senji kokusaihō kōgi* (Lectures on International Law in Wartime), Vol. 2.

76. Okamura, *Hodabi.*

77. Mikasa no miya, "Waga omoide no ki."

78. Tamura Taijirō, "Rajo no iru tairetsu" (The Formation with Naked Women), and "Sanjo jinchi" (Mountain Encampment), in *Inago;* and Jōno, *Sansei dokuritsu senki.*

79. Itō, *Zoku kanashiki senki.*

80. Imai, *Nisshi jihen no kaiso,* and "Itagaki-O kaidan yōryō." For the Wang Ching-wei regime's attempts to resist excessive Japanese demands, see "Nisshi kokkyō chōsei gensoku ni kansuru kyōgikai giji yōroku" (Digest of Proceedings of the Conference on the Adjustment of Relations between Japan and China), *GS,* Vol. 13.

81. Tsukui Tatsuo, *Watakushi no Shōwa-shi* (My History of Shōwa).

82. Nakamura Yasuji, "Firipin seifu no yokogao" (A Profile of the Philippine Government), in *Hiroku dai Tōa senshi,* Vol. 5.

83. Asahi Hōtei Kishadan, *Tōkyō saiban* (The Tokyo Trial).

84. "America treated the high officials and landlord class which had collaborated with Japan very leniently so that they could be used later. The anti-imperialist, anticolonial activists from the labor and peasant classes, like the Huks who fought guerrilla warfare against the Japanese, constituted a postwar threat and were repaid for their efforts by suppression and death." From Ohata Tokushirō, *Kindai no sensō,* Vol. 7, *Taiheiyō sensō,* Vol. 2. (Modern Wars, Vol. 7, The Pacific War, Vol. 2).

85. *Asahi Tōa nenpō, Shōwa jūshichinen ban* (Asahi East Asian Yearbook 1942).

86. Tsuyoshi Hideo, "Maregun tsuihō" (Removing the Malay Army), in *Hiroku dai Tōa senshi,* Vol. 3; and "Koheibō no hanashi" (A Veteran's Story), in *Ayukawa Nobuo senchū shuki* (Wartime Notes of Ayukawa Nobuo).

87. Yokota Yasuo, "Shingapōru no yūhi" (Singapore Sunset), in *Hiroku dai Tōa senshi,* Vol. 3.

88. "Heishi no hanashi" (A Soldier's Story), in *Ayukawa Nobuo senchū shuki;* and Kuroda Hidetoshi, *Gunsei* (Military Administration).

89. Yokota, "Shingapōru no yūhi."

90. Kuroda, *Gunsei.*

91. U Nu, "Nihon senryōka no Biruma" (Burma under Japanese Occupation), *Chūō Kōron,* April and May 1955; Maruyama Shizuo, *Nakano gakkō* (The Nakano School); Tsuboya Shōgo, "Kenkoku hiwa" (The Secret Story of Building a Nation), in *Hiroku dai Tōa sensō-shi,* Vol. 3; and Sawayama Yūzō, "Shirohata o kakagete" (Hoisting the White Flag), in *ibid.* Even those works that defend Japanese military rule acknowledge the "suffering and popular disaffection" and that "the anti-Japanese resistance movement spread." See, for example, Ota Tsunezō, *Biruma ni okeru Nihon gunsei no kenkyū* (Research on Japanese Military Administration in Burma).

92. Maruyama Shizuo, "Himitsu no tatakai" (The Secret Battle), in *Hiroku dai Tōa senshi,* Vol. 3.

93. Smedley, *Battle Hymn of China.*

94. "Dai Tōa seiryaku shidō taikō" (Outline of Strategy to Lead Greater East Asia), in *Nihon gaikō nenpyō narabi ni shuyō monjo,* Vol. 2.

95. Unless otherwise noted, the discussion of the Dutch East Indies is based on *Indonesia ni okeru Nihon gunsei no kenkyū.*

96. Muno Takeji, *Taimatsu jūrokunen* (Sixteen Years of Publishing the *Taimatsu*).

97. Kuroda, *Gunsei.*

98. Herawateideia, "Jūnen no nikushimi o koete, Nihongun senryō tōji yori Indonesia dokuritsu made no chi to namida no kiroku" (Blood and Tears, A Decade of Hatred from the Japanese Occupation to Indonesia's Independence). The outrages against Indonesians by the Japanese military are also described in Aoki, *Saibankan no sensō sekinin.*

99. Notes of Yonekawa Kingo and Fukushima Kan'ichi, "Sugamo BC-kyū senpan no shuki."

100. Masuda Atou, "Taiheiyō sensōki no Indonesia minzoku undō" (The Indonesian Nationalist Movement during the War), *Rekishigaku Kenkyū,* 289.

101. Tominagu Toyofumi, "Ochō ruten" (Vicissitudes of a Dynasty), in *Hiroku dai Tōa senshi,* Vol. 3; and "Genchi de miru bakugekika no kita Betonamu, Daiichi Tsūshō no Nomura (Yoshihiko) shi ni kiku" (Eyewitness to the Bombing of North Vietnam, Interview with Nomura (Yoshihiko) of Daiichi Tsūshō), *Mainichi Shimbun,* May 28, 1965.

102. This description is based mainly on Vietnam Labor Party Central Committee Information Section, Party History Research Association, *History of the Thirty-Year Struggle of the Vietnamese Labor Party.* This work lacks details, but no other materials are presently available.

103. Tominaga, "Ochō ruten."

104. Statement by State Minister Aoki on Station QR program "Minzoku undō" (Nationalist Movement), August 2, 1958, as quoted in "Dokusha no rajio-hyō" (Readers Comment on Radio Programs). *Asahi Shimbun,* August 5, 1958. A similar story is in comments by Tsuji Masanobu, "Minna naita, '*Nijūshi no hitomi*' " (Everyone Cried, *Twelve Pairs of Eyes*), *Shūkan Asahi,* October 3, 1954; and an account by Kawauchi Yasunori in *Shūkan Shinchō,* September 2, 1963.

CHAPTER 9. THE HORRORS OF WAR

1. Tamura, "Senjō to watakushi, sensō bungaku no mō hitotsu no me."
2. Remarks by chief, Police Bureau, Osaka, in Hosokawa, *Jōhō tennō ni tassezu,* June 21, 1945.
3. Kamiko, *Ware Retei ni shisezu.*
4. Takagi Toshirō, *Senshi* (Killed in Battle).
5. A tragic byproduct of the stupid campaign in Burma was the construction of the Thai-Burma Railroad, made famous by the movie *Bridge on the River Kwai.* Needed as a supply route for Japanese forces, the railroad was built from January to May 1945 by forced labor under pitiful conditions. The death toll shows the utter disregard for human life; approximately 10,000 prisoners of war, 30,000 Burmese, and 1,000 Japanese died on the project. See Mizutani Chieko, " 'Senja ni kakeru hashi' ni shisu" (Death on the Bridge to the Battlefield), *Bungei Shunjū,* March 1965; Fukuda Tsuneo, "Taimen tetsudō jiken" (The Thai-Burma Railroad); Sugamo Hōmu Iinkai, "Harukanaru minami jūjisei" (The Distant Southern Cross); and *Shijitsu kiroku, sensō saiban, Eiryō chiku* (The Factual Record, War Crimes Trials, British Territory).
6. Iguchi Rikihei and Nakajima Tadashi, *Kamikaze tokubetsu kōgekitai* (The Divine Wind Special Attack Units), 1951 and 1964 editions.
7. Takagi, *Chiran.* Information on the compulsory aspect of the Special Attack units may also be found in Tominaga Toshimi, "Kaerazaru kyūkōka" (Nose Dive to Oblivion), in *Chichi no senki;* Honda, *Shidōsha;* Mizuki Hitoshi, "Kishū sentei" (Choosing a Plane), in Kaigun Hikō Yobi Gakusei Daijūyonkikai, ed., *Aa, dōki no sakura* (A Navy Pilot Classmate), appendix, "Dōkisei no shuki" (A Classmate's Notes). For a point of view diametrically opposite to the interpretation of Iguchi and Nakajima cited in note 6, see the self-criticism of professional navy officer Yokoi Toshiyuki, "Kikusui sakusen tsui ni narazu" (The *Kikusui* Strategy Failed), *Taiheiyō sensō no zenbō, bessatsu chisei.*
8. "Kongo torubeki sensō shidō taikō" (Summary of War Measures to Be Adopted), in Takagi, *Taiheiyō kaisen-shi,* appendix.
9. *Shōwa sangyō-shi,* Vol. 1; Torisu Kennosuki, "Suichū tokkō kaiten" (Human Torpedoes), *Tokushū Bungei Shunjū Nihon rikukaigun no sōkessan;* "Saikai hachinin no 'kaiten' tokkō taiin" (Reunion of Eight Human Torpedo Kaiten Special Attack Unit Members), *Asahi Gurafu,* August 20, 1965; and Mainichi Shimbunsha, *Ningen gyorai kaiten tokubetsu taiin no shuki* (Human Torpedoes: Diaries of Kaiten Special Attack Unit Members).
10. "Kongo torubeki sensō shidō taikō."
11. See Chapter 3.
12. Fujii Shigeo, *Hi no maru butai* (The Rising Sun Unit). Nishiguchi Katsumi's *Kuruwa* (The Brothels) is a work of fiction generally based on fact. Correspondence with the author.
13. Chihaya Masataka, "Norowareta Awa-maru" (The Doomed Awa-maru); Chihaya Masataka, "Awa-maru gekichin no fuhō o tsuku" (The Illegal Sinking of the Awa-maru), *Jinbutsu Orai,* August 1965; and Arima Yoriyoshi, *Seizonsha no chinmoku* (The Survivor Is Silent).

14. Sherrod, *Saipan*. The Japanese army not only seized food and drinking water from Japanese civilians, but also murdered them. See Okuyama Yoshiko, *Gyokusai no shima ni ikinokotte* (Survivor from the Island of Honorable Death).

15. Kamichi, *Okinawa senshi;* Urasaki, *Kieta Okinawa-ken;* Matsumoto Katsumi, "Nihonhei ga Okinawajin o koroshita" (Japanese Soldiers Killed Okinawans), *Gendai no Me*, November 1964; Yoshikawa, *Okinawa no saigo;* Ishida Ikuo, "Okinawa to Nippon" (Okinawa and Japan), *Bungei,* October 1967; and Ishida Ikuo, "Okinawa no dansō" (Okinawan Escarpment), *Tenbō,* November 1967.

16. Snow, *The Battle for Asia;* and Hora Tomio "Nankyō jiken" (Nanking Incident), in *Kindai senshi no nazo.*

17. Imai Masatake, "Nankinjō nai no dairyō satsujin" (Mass Murder in Nanking), in *Tokushū Bungei Shunjū, watakushi wa soko ni ita.*

18. Sasaki, *Aru gunjin no jiden,* revised edition. This is substantiated by Ishii Itarō's diary entry for January 6, 1938, in *Gaikōkan no isshō* (The Life of a Diplomat).

19. Horiba, *Shina jihen sensō shidō-shi.*

20. Sasaki Ayao, "Ningen kara mita seiji" (A Human View of Politics), in Maruyama Masao, ed., *Ningen to seiji* (Man and Politics).

21. "Hashimoto Mure chūjō Takeda no miya kaisō ōtōroku." According to sources quoted in note 23 below, bacteriological warfare was used in the campaign in the lake T'ung-t'ing area.

22. "Kanashiki dokugasu kanjatachi" (The Wretched Victims, Poison Gas Casualties), *Asahi Janaru,* January 9, 1966; and "Nihon ni atta dokugasutō" (The Poison Gas Island in Japan), *Mainichi Gurafu rinji zōkan, zoku Nihon no senshi* (Mainichi Gurafu Special Issue, Japan's War History, Continued).

23. Akiyama Hiroshi (pseudonym), "Saikinsen wa junbi sareteita" (Biological Warfare Was Ready), *Bungei Shunjū,* August 8, 1955; Akiyama Hiroshi, *Tokushū butai nanasanichi* (Special Unit 731); and Japanese army documents and court records quoted in USSR Foreign Language Press. *Saikinsenyō heiki no junbi oyobi shiyō no kado de kisō sareta moto-Nihongun gunjin no jiken ni kansuru kōhan shorui* (Public Trial Documents of Former Japanese Military Personnel Tried on Suspicion of Preparation and Use of Germ Warfare Weapons); Naruchi Hideo, "Hirasawa Sadamichi wa de wa nai" (Hirasawa Sadamichi Didn't Do It), *Nippon,* April 1963; and Morita Hiroshi, "Teigin jiken to saikin butai" (The Teikoku Bank Incident and the Biological Warfare Unit), *Bungei Shunjū,* June 1955.

24. Senba Yoshikiyo, *Seitai kaibō jiken* (The Human Vivisection Incident); and Hirako Goichi, "Sensō igaku no ojoku ni furete, seitai kaibō jiken shimatsuki" (The Degradation of Wartime Medicine: the Complete Story on Human Vivisection), *Bungei Shunjū,* December 1957.

25. Systematic deception and covert operations were also ways that war destroyed man's humanity. Espionage and covert political action are essentially acts of betrayal; they require the destruction of moral values and inevitably lead to crude and savage methods like assassination and murder. (See Kusakabe Ichirō, *Bōryaku Taiheiyō sensō, rikugun Nakano gakkō* *hiroku* (Covert Operations in the Pacific War, Secret Records of the Army Nakano School).

26. Hirata, "Ippatsu no jūsei."

27. Kaneyama Makoto, "Minamitorishima no higeki" (The Tragedy of Minamitorishima), *Sekai,* August 1955.

28. Miyamoto Masayuki, "Yonin no horyo to supūn" (Four Prisoners of War and Their Spoons), in *Chichi no senki;* and Maeoka Akira, "Seito no inochi" (The Student's Life), in "Sensō no kioku, dokusha no taiken kiroku kara," *Nihon Dokusho Shimbun,* August 13, 1956. There are many similar examples.

29. Kuroda, *Gunsei.*

30. Takagi, *Imparu.* There is a similar account in Ishii, *Gaikōkan no isshō.*

31. Kamichi, *Okinawa senshi.*

32. Kuzumi Teishi, "Hiklage no hi made" (Till the Day of Repatriation), in *Hiroku dai senshi,* Vol. 2; and Hasegawa Uichi, "Muteki Kantōgun no kaimetsu" (The Kwantung Army Collapses Without a Fight), *Tokushū Bungei Shunjū, Nihon rikukaigun no sōkessan.*

33. Yamada Ichirō, "Shinkirō no kuni ni ikite" (Living in a Mirage), in *Hiroku dai Tōa senshi,* Vol. 2.

34. Kamata Shōji, "Kita Chōsen Nihonjin kunanki" (The Japanese Ordeal in Northern Korea), in *Shōwa sensō bungaku zenshū,* Vol. 12.

35. Fujii, *Hinomaru butai.*

36. Kamiko, *Ware Reite ni shisezu;* Sumi Takeyuki, "Jigoku sensen no Nihonhei" (Japanese Soldiers in a Battlefield Hell); and "Reite sanchū ni kieta Kaki heidan" (The Kaki Army Corps That Disappeared in the Mountains of Leyte), *Shūkan Bunjū,* August 3, 1959.

37. Otani, *Shōwa kenpei-shi.*

38. Hayashi, *Nihon shūsen-shi.*

39. Kajinishi Mitsuhaya, *Shōwa keizai-shi* (An Economic History of Shōwa).

40. Ohara Shakai Mondai Kenkyūjo, *Taiheiyō sensōka no rōdōsha jōtai* (The Situation of Laborers during the Pacific War).

41. *Ibid.* See Watanabe, "Mura no senchū nikki (zoku)." Because of inadequate food and other hardships, many people who would ordinarily have recovered died of illnesses. Hashimoto Noriko was a mobilized student who died from a catarrh of the colon caused by fatigue, cold, and a diet of beans. See "Hateshinaki rōdō" (Work Never Ends), in *Wadatsumi no koe,* December 1961.

42. "Ordinary people were surviving on millet, wheat, and potatoes, while the town officials were getting a special ration of sugar. When the mayor held a party at his house for military officers and people connected with the government, there was plenty of white rice. My brother-in-law was an army major. His family never lacked for anything. It was just as if there was no war on." Itō Kayo, "Ikusa wa iya" (War Is Lousy), *Shufu no sensō taikenki.* "It was about the time we had been reduced to eating bread made of bran flour and squash leaves. I was invited to a party to celebrate the birth of a second son to the owner of an armaments factory. I couldn't believe it. There was a sumptuous feast laid out for us. Every kind of food. I thought perhaps I had wandered into a fairyland. I just stared in astonishment." Haraguchi Kiyoko, "Sono koro no koto" (Things That Happened Then), in Kusa no Mi Kai Dainana Gurupu, ed., *Sensō to watakushi* (The War and I). "We couldn't get enough food to live on, yet a family in our neighborhood whose father was in the Kempeitai had sugared candy, canned goods, everything. They were very ostentatious about it." Responses to a survey entitled "Kore dake wa doshitemo iitai" (I Must Say This), in *Kurushikatta sensō no omoide.*

43. Kiyosawa, *Ankoku nikki.*

44. According to Mita Munesuke, "Imeji no kindai Nihon-shi" (Impressions of Modern Japan), *Gendai Nihon no seishin kōzō* (Spiritual Structure of Modern Japan), a television poll by NTV in 1963 asked "What was the best time of your life?" The wartime period was picked by 0.8 percent of the respondents, or approximately 480,000 persons.

45. Watanabe, "Mura no senchū nikki."

46. A work on the Balkan War by J. W. Martel, *Barkan Krieg,* was banned by the authorities as "pornography" because it described the sadistic treatment of enemy women. It was an extreme example of how war perverted sexual relationships, a phenomenon demonstrated over and over again in the Pacific War. Japanese can no longer scoff at *Barkan Krieg* as absurd sensationalism.

47. Accounts of labor mobilization are in comments by Hashimoto Noriko in "Hateshinaki rōdō"; Tsuji Toyoji, *Aa, Toyokawa joshi teishintai* (Ah, The Toyokawa Women's Volunteer Corps); and Miyano Hideya, *Pen o ubawareta seishun* (Young People Who Will Never Write).

48. For collections of notes and writings by students killed in the war, see the following: *Harukanaru sanga ni, Tōdai senbotsu gakusei no shuki; Kike, wadatsumi no koe; Kumo nagururu hate ni; Aa, dōki no sakura;* Hayashi, *Waga inochi getsumei ni moyu;* Wadatsumikai, ed., *Senbotsu gakusei no isho ni yoru jūgonen sensō* (The Fifteen-Year War Through the Writings of Students Killed in Battle); Takujima Norimitsu, *Kuchinashi no hana* (A Cape Jasmine); and Wada Minoru, *Wadatsumi no koe kieru koto naku* (Unstilled Voices). For an account by a survivor, see Yasuda Takeshi, *Gakuto shutsujin* (Students to the Front).

49. *Yamagata no kyōiku; Shizuoka no kyōiku* (Education in Shizuoka), quoted in *Gendai kyōikugaku,* Vol. 5, *Nihon kindai kyōiku-shi;* and "Zadankai, dai Tōa sensō to bokura" (The Greater East Asian War and Us), *Chisei,* August 1956; "Warera wa shōnen senshahei" (We Are Young Tankers), *Asahi Gurafu,* February 7, 1940; "Shōnen hikōhei, shōnen senshahei, sono ta" (Young Pilots, Young Tankers and Others), *Asahi Gurafu,* November 10, 1943; "Tsuzuke shōnenhei ni, shōkokumin sōkekki taikai hiraku" (More Young Soldiers, A National Youth Rally Opens), *Asahi Gurafu,* December 29, 1943; and "Hinawashi wa kitaeru" (Young Eagles Train). There are pictures in "Kokumin gakkō mo gun no yobikō e" (National Schools Also Turn into Army Prep Schools), *Asahi Gurafu,* November 7, 1943.

50. Hamada Kikuo, *Gakudō shūdan sokai no kiroku, ukigumo kyōshitsu*

(Group Evacuation of Children, A Classroom Adrift); Gekkogahara Shōgakkō, *Gakudō sokai no kiroku* (Student Evacuation); Nakane, *Sokai gakudō no nikki;* and Sawada Kazuya, *Sokaikko* (Child Evacuee).

51. Matsushita Motoko, "Shūdan sokai" (Group Evacuation), in *Shufu no sensō taikenki.*

52. Both statements are in *Sensō to watakushi.* Many similar accounts are in Tsurumi Kazuko and Makise Kikue, eds., *Hikisakarete, haha no sensō taiken* (Separated: Mothers' War Experiences).

53. See Chapter 7.

54. Sasaki Nobutsuna and Itō Yoshio, eds., *Shōi gunjin seisen kashū* (Songs of Soldiers Disabled in the Holy War).

55. "A widow whose husband was killed during the war told this story. The day the official death report arrived, his mother and father went deep into the mountains and stayed there till dusk. They had cried so hard their voices were almost gone. One said, 'We went into the mountains and cried all day.' To sob loudly or be seen crying marked a person as a traitor. No wonder that grieving relatives would console each other late at night in the privacy of their own homes, but they could not tell others." Kikuchi Keiichi and Omura Ryō, eds., *Ano hito wa kaette konakata* (They Never Came Back), Part II, "Sakebazuni kita nijūnen" (Twenty Years without a Scream).

56. Sherrod, *Saipan.* For Japanese accounts, see Kanno, *Saipantō no saigo,* and Okuyama, *Gyokusai no shima ni ikinokotte.* According to Nakajima Fumihiko, "Tenian kichi no gyokusai" (The Tinian Garrison Dies), *Taiheiyō sensō no zenbō, bessatsu chisei,* women and children on Tinian also committed collective suicide.

57. Kinjō Kazuhiko, *Minami no iwao no hate ni* (On the Edge of the Southern Cliff) and *Ai to senchi no kiroku* (Love and Blood).

58. Kamichi, *Okinawa senshi;* Urasaki, *Kieta Okinawa-ken;* "Watakushitachi no sensō taiken, Okinawa kenritsu daiichi kōjo sotsugyōsei no zadankai" (Our War Experiences, A Roundtable Discussion by Female Graduates of Okinawa Prefecture First High School), in *Okinawa no fujin* (Women of Okinawa), August 30, 1966. According to one study, Okinawans cooperated in the defense of the islands because for many years other Japanese had treated them "as if they were a different nationality." That "sense of prejudice" drove many Okinawans to "martyrdom for the nation." They saw the battle as a good opportunity to prove with their lives that they were loyal subjects of the empire. (Ota Masahide, *Okinawa no minshū ishiki* (Okinawan Consciousness). If this is correct, handing Okinawa over to the U.S. in 1952 was a barbarous betrayal.

59. Kinjō, *Minami no iwao no hate ni.*

60. Kamichi, *Okinawa senshi;* Urasaki, *Kieta Okinawa-ken;* and *Okinawa no fujin.*

61. "Shōidan o abite" (Incendiaries Fall Like Rain), *Sensō to watakushi;* "Kūshū" (Air Raid), in *Shufu no sensō taikenki;* and NET Shakai Kyōyōbu, ed., "Kūshū" (Air Raid), in *Hachigatsu jūgonichi to watakushi; Hiroku dai Tōa senshi,* Vol. 6; Oya Ten'ichi (Isshiki Jirō), *Tōkyō kūshū* (Tokyo Air Raid); and Miyano, *Pen o ubawareta seishun.*

62. Ishikawa Kōyō, *Tōkyō daikūshū hiroku shashinshū* (Photographs of the Great Tokyo Air Raid); Kageyama Kōyō, *Aru hōdō shashinka no mita Shōwa sanjūnen-shi* (A News Photographer's Record of Three Decades); and *Mainichi Gurafu rinji zōkan, zoku Nihon no senreki* (Mainichi Gurafu Special Issue, Japan's War Record, Continued).

63. Sugawara Kiyoe, "Ikiteita" (I Was Alive), in *Kurushikatta sensō no omoide;* "Sangatsu tōka, Tōkyō daikūshū" (That March 10, The Great Tokyo Air Raid), *Shūkan Yomiuri,* March 17, 1967; and Matsuura Sōzō, "Kakarezaru Tōkyō daikūshū" (It Could Not Be Written: The Great Tokyo Air Raid), *Bungei Shunjū,* March 1968.

64. Chino Toshiko, *Ashi orenu* (The Reed Dies). She wrote the comment early in the summer of 1945.

65. Tsuji, *Toyokawa joshi teishintai;* and *Mainichi Shimbun,* March 26, 1966.

66. Osada Arata, ed., *Genbaku no ko, Hiroshima no shōnen shōjo no uttae* (Children of the A Bomb); Ogura Toyofumi, *Zetsugo no kiroku* (Never Before, Never Again); Hachiya Michiko, *Hiroshima nikki* (Hiroshima Dairy); Ota Yōko, *Shikabane no machi* (Street of Corpses); Hiroshima-shi Genbaku Taikenki Kankōkai, *Genbaku taikenki* (We Experienced the Atomic Bomb); *Genbaku yurusumaji;* "Genbaku higai no hatsu kōkai" (First Public Display of the Casualties and Damage Caused by the Atomic Bombings), Special Issue of the *Asahi Gurafu,* August 6, 1952; and Iwanami Photograph Collection, 72, Hiroshima.

67. Knebel and Bailey, *No High Ground;* and Giovannitti and Freed, *The Decision to Drop the Bomb.*

68. P. M. S. Blackette, *Fear, War and the Bomb: Military and Political Consequences of the Bomb.*

69. Nihon Shobō, ed., *Zenyaku, Nihon muzairon* (Japan Is Not Guilty); Tokyo Saiban Kenkyūkai, *Kyōdō kenkyū, Paru hanketsusho* (The Pal Dissent); and Ienaga, "Jūgonen sensō to Paru hanketsusho" (The Pacific War and the Pal Dissent), *Misuzu,* February 1967.

70. In *Hanrei jihō* (Case Review), 355.

71. Condemnation of atrocities committed by the Japanese military must be accompanied by equally strong censure of Allied excesses. The Japanese army indiscriminately killed and mistreated enemy prisoners. By contrast, U.S. treatment of Japanese prisoners appears to have been generally humane. Ooka Shōhei, *Furyoki* (A POW's Record); Moriya, *Ragunako no kita,* and so on. According to *Shijitsu kiroku, sensō saiban, Eiryō chiku,* and other sources, an exception was Allied treatment of suspected Japanese war criminals in the southern area, which appears to have been extremely callous. However, we must also note the internment of Japanese-Americans in the U.S., which resulted in great personal hardships and financial loss. See Ishigaki Ayako, "Kaisō no Sumedore (Recollections of Smedley), *Misuzu,* September 1966; and Fujishima Taisuke, *Chūsei toroku* (Loyalty Oath).

72. Nihon Gensuikyō, Senmon Iinkai, *Gensuibaku hakusho* (White Paper on the Atomic Bombings).

73. Keizai Antei Honbu, *Taiheiyō sensō ni yoru waga kuni no higai sōgō* *hōkokusho* (Comprehensive Report on Damages Suffered by Japan in the Pacific War).

74. Japanese merchant seamen were not military personnel and should have been engaged in peaceful commercial shipping. However, 30,593 merchant seamen and officers were killed in the war. The merchant marine casualty rate was 43 percent compared to casualty rates for the Japanese army and navy, respectively, of 20 percent and 16 percent. Kaijō Rōdō Kyōkai, *Nihon shōsentai senji sōnan-shi* (Japan's Merchant Marine Losses in the War).

CHAPTER 10. DISSENT AND RESISTANCE: CHANGE FROM WITHIN

1. Arahata Kanson, "Taiheiyō sensō no yonenkan" (The Four Years of the Pacific War), *Kanson jiden* (Autobiography of Arahata Kanson), Vol. 2.

2. Tsurami Shunsuke's introduction to Ishikawa Sanshirō, *Ishikawa Sanshirō jijoden* (Autobiography of Ishikawa Sanshirō).

3. Ooka Shōhei, "Shussei" (At the Front), in *Furyoki.*

4. It is difficult to evaluate the Omoto's prewar ideology. From the third wave of repression in 1935 till the end of the war, Deguchi and other staff members passively resisted the conflict. According to church sources, after Deguchi Onisaburō was released from prison in August 1942, he instructed men going off to the front to "Fire your weapons in the air" and gave them good luck amulets with the message "A great victory for us and the enemy." Omoto Nanajūnen-shi Hensankai, ed., *Omoto nanjūnen-shi* (Seventy-Year History of the Omoto), Vol. 2; Deguchi Kyōtaro, *Kyojin Deguchi Onisaburō* (The Great Deguchi Onisaburō); and Murakami Shigeyoshi, *Kindai minshū shukyōshi no kenkyū* (Research on the History of Modern Popular Religions).

5. *Mainichi Shimbun,* August 10, 1967.

6. Odagiri Hideo, *Kōza Nihon kindai bungaku-shi* (Lectures on the History of Modern Japanese Literature), Vol. 5; Ara Masato, "Senjika no geijutsuteki teikōha" (Wartime Resistance in the Arts), *Kokubungaku Kaisetsu to Kanshō,* special issue on writings of the 1930s and 1940s.

7. Nagai Kafū, *Danchōtei nichijō* (Dyspepsia House Days); *Nagai Kafū zenshū* (Complete Works of Nagai Kafū).

8. "Sakka no sugao" (The Novelist at Ease), *Shōsetsu Gendai,* July 1967.

9. Statements by Funabashi Seiichi in commentary by Yoshiyuki Junnosuke, *Gendai no bungaku, Funabashi Seiichi-shū* (Modern Literature, Collected Works of Funabashi Seiichi).

10. There are problems with this book. This is always the case to a greater or lesser degree with the wartime statements of individuals with a previous record of leftist political activity.

11. *Bi to shūdan no ronri* (The Logic of Beauty and the Group).

12. *Katō Tadashi zenshū* (Complete Works of Katō Tadashi), Vol. 2.

13. *Meiji ishin* (The Meiji Restoration).

14. *Nihon seiji shisō-shi kenkyū* (Research on the History of Japanese Political Thought).

15. *Ibid.*

16. *Kindai shihonshugi no keifu* (The Genesis of Modern Capitalism).

17. Ienaga, *Minobe Tatsukichi no shisō shiteki kenkyū*.

18. *Ishimoda Shō, Chūseiteki sekai no keisei* (The Formation of the Medieval World), epilogue; Matsumoto Shinpachirō, *Hōkenteki tochi shoyū no seiritsu katei* (The Formative Process of Feudal Landownership), preface.

19. *Nakae Ushikichi shokanshū.*

20. Nagai Kafū, *Danchōtei nichijō.*

21. Correspondence quoted in Matsushita Yoshio, *Mizuno Hironori.*

22. Kiyosawa, *Ankoku nikki.*

23. "Senjika nikki" (Wartime Diary), *Tenbō,* August 1966.

24. There are excellent examples in the following: Miyamoto Kenji and Miyamoto Yuriko, *Jūninen no tegami* (Twelve Years of Letters), 3 vols.; Yanaihara Tadao's correspondence in *Yanaihara Tadao zenshū,* Vol. 29; Kawakami Hajime, *Kawakami Hajime jijoden* (Autobiography of Kawakami Hajime); Kawakami Hajime, *Gokuchū nikki* (Prison Diary); Kawakami, *Bannen seikatsu kiroku;* Kawakami Hide, *Rusu nikki* (While He Was Away); Kaneko Mitsuharu's poems published later in *Kaneko Mitsuharu zenshū* (Complete Works of Kaneko Mitsuharu), Vol. 2; and Kozai Yoshishige, *Senchū nikki* (Wartime Diary).

25. *Taiheiyō sensōka no rōdō undō.*

26. See Chapter 6, note 70.

27. *Ibid.*

28. *Chikaki Yori,* September–October 1944; Masaki Hiroshi, *Bengoshi, watakushi no jinsei o kaeta kubinashi jiken* (The Headless Corpse Case).

29. Chono Toshiharu, "Watakushi no ayanda michi" (The Path I Walked); Chono Sensei Kanreki Kinenkai, ed., *Chono-san to watakushi* (Mr. Chono and I); Ienaga, *Shihōken dokuritsu no rekishiteki kōsatsu.*

30. Saitō, *Saibankanron;* and Yoshida Hisashi's remarks in Nomura Masao, *Hōsō fūunroku* (Judges, Prosecutors, and Lawyers).

31. Ienaga Saburō, "Ankoku jidai no shisōteki teikō" (Intellectual Resistance During the War), *Bunkō,* July 1959.

32. Suzuki Ken'ichi, "Hōkaiki no rikugun naibu gunki" (Army Discipline at the End of the Pacific War), *Rekishigaku Kenkyū,* No. 174.

33. "Tōbōhei to shonen heiho" (Deserters and Young Replacements), in *Chichi no senki.*

34. Kaneko, *Zetsubō no seishin-shi;* statement by Kinoshita Junji, "Zadankai, katenai sensō no naka de"; Shirai Kenzaburō, "Chōhei kihisha no kaisō" (Recollections of Draft Dodgers), in *Wadatsumi no koe,* December 1965.

35. Kaneko, *Zetsubō no seishin-shi;* Kinoshita, "Zadankai, katenai sensō no naka de"; and Shirai, "Chōhei kihisha no kaisō."

36. Soeda Tomomichi, *Nihon shunkakō* (On Obscene Japanese Songs). Details about the song may be found in Police Bureau, Ministry of Home Affairs, "Shakai undō no genjō" (Current Status of Social Movements).

37. Ishiga Osamu, "Kenpei to heieki kyōhi no aida" (Between the

Kempeitai and Refusal of Military Service), *Bungei Shunjū,* March 1966; Takada Tetsuo, " 'Ryōshinteki heieki kyōhi' ni tsuite" (On Refusal to Perform Military Service for Reasons of Conscience), in *Wadatsumi no koe,* August 1965.

38. Tokuda Kyūichi and Shiga Yoshio, *Gokuchū jūhachinen* (Eighteen Years in Prison); Sugimori Hisahide, *Tokuda Kyūichi* (Tokuda Kyūichi); and Nuyama Hiroshi, *Amigasa* (The Braided Hat), and others.

39. Uchida Jōkichi, "Sugiyuku jidai no gunzō" (The Last Generation), *Nihon Dokusho Shimbun,* June 30, 1958.

40. Sasaki Binji, "Chian ijihō kaiaku to Kirisutokyokai" (Additional Restrictions in the Peace Preservation Law and the Christian Church), *Kirisutokyō Shakai Mondai Kenkyū,* No. 10.

41. Kaji Wataru, *Nihon heishi no hansen undō* (The Antiwar Activities of Japanese Troops), 2 vols.; Kaji Wataru, *Hi no gotoku, kaze no gotoku* (Like the Fire, Like the Wind), 2 vols; and "Hansen no kinen arubamu" (Photographs to Commemorate the Antiwar Movement), *Asahi Gurafu,* June 15, 1946. Kaji Wataru's documentation has been criticized by Niijima Atsuyoshi in the *Nihon Dokusho Shimbun,* February 16, 1959, and by Komada Shinji, *Asahi Janaru,* April 12, 1964. In contrast with the very few conscientious objectors in Japan, 6,000 men were imprisoned in the U.S. for refusing military service on grounds of conscience. These statistics alone show the vast ideological difference between Japan and America. Nihon Yūwakai, ed., *Ryōshinteki heieki kyōhi* (Conscientious Objection to Military Service).

42. Nihon Kyōsantō Chūō Iinkai, *Hansen heishi monogatari, Zai-Ka Nihonjin hansen domeiin no kiroku* (Accounts of Antiwar Soldiers, Records of the Japanese Antiwar Federation in China); *Nozaka Sanzō senshū, senjihen* (Selected Writings of Nozaka Sanzō, The Wartime Period); and Stein, *The Challenge of Red China.*

43. Satō Takeo, "Hachirogun iryō kōsaku ni sankashita ichi Nihonjin ishi no kiroku" (Record of a Japanese Doctor in Service with the Eighth Route Army), postscript in *Ishi Batsūn* (Doctor Bethune) epilogue.

44. Oka Naoki, Shioda Shōbei, and Fujiwara Akira, eds., *Sokoku o teki toshite—ichi zai-Bei Nihonjin no hansen undō* (The Fight against the Fatherland—The Antiwar Activities of a Japanese in America).

45. Yashima Tarō, "Nihon kōfuku kankoku no senpei toshite" (I Urged Japan to Surrender), *Bungei Shunjū,* December 1957. For information on Furuhata Yoshikazu, see Uchida, "Sugiyuku jidai no gunzō, " *Nihon Dokusho Shimbun,* June 16, 1958.

46. Henri, Michel *Les Mouvements Clandestins en Europe.* The idea that when the fatherland was in evil hands, it would be destroyed in order to restore righteousness (of course, destruction meant only those evil men who had seized control of the country) was suggested long ago in Japan. Nichiren accepted Japan's destruction by the twelfth-century Mongol invaders in his public pronouncement that "Even if the country perishes, the law will not fade away." *Itai dōshinji* (Many in Body, One in Spirit). For a similar comment by Uchimura Kanzō, see Conclusion, note 2.

47. *GS, Vol. 2, Zoruge jiken* (The Sorge Incident), Vol. 2; Ozaki Hotsumi, *Aijō wa furu hoshi no gotoku* (Love Is a Falling Star); Kazama

Michitarō, *Aru hangyaku, Ozaki Hotsumi no shōgai* (A Case of Treason, The Life of Ozaki Hotsumi); and Ozaki Hideki, *Zoruge jiken* (The Sorge Incident).

48. Quoted in Hayashi Shigeru, ed., *Nihon Shūsenshi* (Termination of the War).

49. That popular dissatisfaction was known to the ruling elite is clear from the following: *Kido Kōichi nikki,* July 18, 1944, and April 5, 1945; "Kokuryoku no genjō 2. Minshin no dōkō" (Present National Strength 2. Popular Morale), a document prepared for the Imperial Conference of June 8, 1945, in Sanbō Honbu, *Haisen no kiroku* (Records of the Termination of the War); and Shimomura Kainan, *Shūsenki* (The End of the War).

50. Kawana Shōichi, letter to the editor, "Okami-san no kotoba" (A Housewife Speaks Out), *Asahi Janaru,* October 3, 1965.

51. Otani, *Shōwa kenpei-shi.* It was a miniature version of the July 1944 plot by German army officers to assassinate Hitler.

53. Hibi Tatsusaburō, *Haisen gojitsu monogatari* (Tales from Defeat); and Ienaga Saburō, "Taiheiyō sensōka no shisōteki teikō" (Intellectual Resistance during the Pacific War), in *Rekishi to Kyōiku* (History and Education).

54. Günther Weisenborn, *Der Lautlose Aufstand;* Hans Rothfels, *Der Deutsche Opposittion gegen Hitler;* Inge Scholl, *Die weisse Rose;* and Kanbashi Teijirō, "Doitsu ni okeru han-fuashizumu teikō tōsō" (The Anti-Fascist Resistance Struggle in Germany), *Shisō,* November 1964 and February 1965.

55. Yamazaki Isao, *Itaria toiu kuni V, Teikō undō* (A Country Called Italy: V, The Resistance Movement).

56. Michel, *Les Mouvements Clandestins en Europe.*

57. Dominique Lapierre and Larry Collins, *Is Paris Burning?* and Simone de Beauvoir, *The Prime of Life.*

58. Stein, *The Challenge of Red China.* For Nozaka's ideas on postwar reforms, see *Nozaka Sanzō senshū, senjihen* (Selected Writings of Nozaka Sanzō, Wartime Period).

59. Kiyosawa, *Ankoku nikki.*

60. *Morita Sōhei senshū* (Selected Writings of Morita Sōhei), Vol. 5.

61. *Senbotsu gakusei no isho ni yoru jūgonen sensō.*

62. *Ibid.*

63. *Kike, wadatsumi no koe.*

64. Chino, *Ashi orenu.*

65. *Shakai undō no jōkyō, Shōwa jūsannen.*

66. Cohen, *Japan's Economy in War and Reconstruction; Taiheiyō sensōka no rōdōsha jōkyō;* and Usami Seijirō, "Sensō keizai no isan" (Legacy of the Wartime Economy), in Chōryū Editorial Staff, ed., *Nihon fashizumu to sono teikōsen, ankoku jidai no umidashita mono* (Japanese Fascism and the Resistance, The Dissenters).

67. "Senshu ni mamoru sangyō sensen" (The Production Front Defended by Women's Hands), *Asahi Gurafu,* July 12, 1939; "Sangyō senshi no ikusei, Kandabashi joshi tengyō hodōsho" (Training Industrial Warriors, The Kandabashi Women's Employment Center), *Asahi Gurafu,* December 4,

1940; "Sensen no danshi ni kawatte" (Replacing the Men at the Battlefront), *Asahi Gurafu,* December 18, 1940; "Otome seisan sensen e" (Maidens to the Production Front), *Asahi Gurafu,* February 17, 1943; "Kunrō josei wa hogarakani" (The Girls Work Cheerfully), *Asahi Gurafu,* November 24, 1943; "Joshi zōsen senshi" (Women Shipyard Workers), *Asahi Gurafu,* March 1, 1944; "Shufu mo minato no heikisho e" (Housewives Also Work at the Harbor Weapons Plant), *Asahi Gurafu,* March 8, 1944; and Cohen, *Japan's Economy in War and Reconstruction.*

68. Inoue Harumaru, "Senji keizai no isan" (Legacy of the Wartime Economy), in *Nihon fuashizumu no teikōsen, ankoku jidai no umidashita mono;* Katō Ichirō, "Senjika no nōchi rippō" (Wartime Agricultural Legislation), in *Nihon kindaihō hattatsu-shi,* Vol. 6; and Yamazaki Harunari, "Senji shokuryō seisaku to jinushisei" (Wartime Food Production Policy and the Landlord System), in Rekishigaku Kenkyūkai, ed., *Sengo Nihon-shi* (History of Postwar Japan), Vol. 5.

69. Shigeta Nobuichi, "Senjika ni okeru kōteki fujo no dōkō" (Changes in Public Assistance during the War), in Nihon Shakai Jigyō Daigaku Kyūhin Seido Kenkyūkai, *Nihon no kyūhin seido* (Japan's Public Relief System); and Kawakami Takeshi, Gendai Nihon Iryō-shi (History of Medical Service in Modern Japan).

CHAPTER 11. DEFEAT

1. *Shūsen shiroku;* Nihon Gaikō Gakkai, ed., *Taiheiyō sensō shūketsu-ron* (Ending the Pacific War); Hayashi, *Nihon shūsen-shi;* Imai, *Nisshi jihen no kaiso;* Arita Hachirō, "Tennō e no tegami, dai Tōa sensō shūketsu ni kansuru jōsōbun" (A Letter to the Emperor, A Report to the Throne on Ending the Greater East Asia War), *Heiwa,* September, 1955; and Ienaga, *Kenryokuaku to no tatakai, Masaki Hiroshi no shisō katsudō,* Chap. 4, sec. 3.

2. Hayashi, *Taiheiyō sensō rikusen gaishi;* Hattori, *Dai Tōa sensō zenshi;* "Shōwa-shi no tennō" (The Emperor in the History of the Shōwa Period), *Yomiuri Shimbun,* September 19 through October 2, 1967.

3. Tanemura, *Daihon'ei kimitsu nisshi,* June 4, 1945.

4. This interpretation is based on *Saionji-kō to seikyoku; Kido Kōichi nikki;* Hosokawa, *Jōhō tennō ni tassezu;* and Ogata, *Ichi gunjin no shōgai.*

5. *Kido Kōichi nikki,* July 18, 1944.

6. Hosokawa, *Jōhō tennō ni tassezu* and *Nihon gaikō nenpyō narabi ni shuyō monjo,* Vol. 2.

7. "Takagi Sōkichi hiroku" (Secret Records of Takagi Sōkichi), in *Shūsen shiroku.*

8. According to "Konoe-kō to watakushi" (Prince Konoe and I), in *Oyama Kango nikki* (Oyama Kango Diary), appendix. In view of Japan's past relations with the Soviet Union, Oyama thought it ridiculous to expect assistance from the USSR, and he warned Konoe against the initiative.

9. On the course of events until surrender, see *Shūsen shiroku; Taiheiyō sensō shūketsu-ron;* Shimomura Kainan, *Shūsenki* (Ending the War); *Kido Kōichi nikki;* Fukui, *Sūmitsuin jūyō giji oboegaki;* Takagi Sōkichi, *Shūsen oboegaki* (Notes on Ending the War); Fujita Hisanori, *Jijūchō no kaisō* (Recollections of the Grand Chamberlain); and Niwa Fumio, *Nihon yaburetari* (Japan Was Defeated).

10. Shimomura Kainan, *Hachi-ichi-go jiken* (August 15th Incident); Hayashi, *Nihon shūsen-shi;* Otani, *Shōwa kempeitai-shi;* and Hino Ashihei, *Kakumei zengo* (Time of Change).

11. *Shūsen shiroku,* Vol. 2; and Sanbō Honbu, *Haisen no kiroku,* essay on materials.

12. "Watakushi no hachigatsu jūgonichi" (My August 15), *Nihon shūsenshi;* "Watakushi no hachigatsu jūgonichi" (My August 15), *Sekai,* August 15, 1955; *Shufu no sensō taikenki; Sensō to watakushi; Hachigatsu jūgonichi to watakushi;* Shiraishi Toku, *Onna no rokujūroku nenkan nikki yasuminaku* (A Woman's Diary, Every Day for Sixty-six Years), *Mainichi Shimbun,* January 3, 1966; Hachiya, *Hiroshima nikki;* Moriya Misa, "Watakushi no Hiroshima nōto" (My Notes on Hiroshima), in *Wadatsumi no koe,* August 1966: Mori, *Shōwa ni ikiru; Takami Jun nikki,* Vol. 5; Kawakami, *Bannen no seikatsu kiroku,* Vol. 2; Katō Shūichi, "Hitsuji no uta" (Sheep's Song), *Asahi Janaru,* April 9, 1967; Sugawara Kiyoe, "Yurusarete akaritomo seshi yorokobi wa yabureshi kuni no kanashimi yori wa" (My Joy at Being Alive Is Greater Than My Sorrow at Our Defeat), in *Kurushikatta sensō no omoide;* Matsushita Kōnosuke, "Kukyō o koete" (The Crisis), *Asahi Shimbun,* August 13, 1962; Nishiguchi Seiichi, "Sobo no kataru shūsen no hi" (My Grandmother's Account of August 15), letter to the editor, *Asahi Shimbun,* August 14, 1965; "Watakushi no naka no 'sensō' " (What the War Meant to Me), *Shuppan Rōkyō,* August 15, 1967: "I was in second grade in 1945. . . . My most vivid experience of the war . . . was my father crying loudly after hearing the emperor's broadcast." And Odagiri Susumu, "Hachi ichi go no kiroku" (A Record of August 15), *Bungaku,* August 1965.

13. Letter by Okajima Sueko describing the final remarks by "Mr. Ejima" to the students, quoted in Takagi, *Chiran.*

14. Masuko Jun'ichi, " 'Idainaru ōja'o mune ni" (On Seeing a German Movie), in *Chichi no senki.* According to Shiratori Kunio, in his final speech to the students the superintendent of the Navy Accounting School said, "Keep in touch with each other secretly. We'll rise up in twenty years. You're being given a twenty-year break from your duties." See Shiratori Kunio, *Watakushi no haisen nikki* (My Diary of Defeat).

15. In addition to the works cited, the following were useful: *Hiroku dai Tōa senshi,* Vol. 2; *Shufu no sensō taikenki; Sensō to watakushi; Shōwa sensō bungaku zenshū,* Vol. 12; Iinuma, *Nekka senkyō no kiroku;* Morita, *Chōsen shūsen no kiroku;* "Fubo no sensō taiken" (My Parents' War Experiences), in *Gakushū shidō shiryō jiten* (Reference Encyclopedia), appendix, "Shakaika no geppō" (Monthly Bulletin on Social Study); Fujiwara Tei, *Nagareru hoshi wa ikiteiru* (Escape with the Stars); *Chichi no senki;*

Yamada, *Tenkōki, arashi no jidai.* Gomikawa's *Ningen no jōken* is also valuable.

16. Takeda, "Haikyōsha Katō Kanji no nōmin kyōiku shisō" (Katō Kanji's Views on Education for Farmers), in *Dochaku to haikyō;* Tsunoda Fusako, *Bohyō naki hachiman no shisha, Manmō kaitakudan no kaimetsu* (Eighty Thousand Unmarked Graves, The Agricultural Settlers in Manchuria and Mongolia).

17. "Oyama Ginza kaitakudan no saigo" (The End of the Oyama Ginza Agricultural Settlers Group), *Yomiuri Shimbun,* April 30, 1948.

18. "Roba ni sareta watakushi" (Doing a Donkey's Job), *Asahi Shimbun,* September 13, 1948, and "Hōsō ura-omote" (The Broadcasting World), *Asahi Shimbun,* December 7, 1965.

19. Nakamura Taisuke, *Shiberia yo sayōnara, Shiberia yokuryū ninenkan no kiroku* (Farewell to Siberia, A Record of Two Years' Internment); Hasegawa Shirō, *Shiberia monogatari* (Tales of Siberia); Yamada, *Tenkōki, hyōsetsu no jidai;* Uchimura Gōsuke, *Ikiisogu Sutarin goku no Nihonjin* (Getting By, The Japanese in Stalin's Prisons). However, unit commander Yoshimura's "Akatsuki ni inoru" (Brutality in the Barracks) and other incidents indicate that the ruthless behavior of some Japanese prisoners who collaborated with the Soviet authorities caused a great many of the prison camp deaths.

20. Yoneno Toyomi, "Hishū no minato, Tairen" (Harbor of Pathos, Dairen), in *Hiroku dai Tōa senshi,* Vol. 2; " 'Shō Kai-seki ongi-ron' no shinsō" (The Reality of Our "Indebtedness to Chiang Kai-shek"), *Nihon to Chūgoku,* special issue, March 1, 1964; Nakazono Eisuke, "Kokkyō naisen, Nihonhei made kachūni" (The Nationalist-Communist Civil War, Japanese Soldiers Caught in the Middle), *Mainichi Shimbun,* August 15, 1965, and Jōno, *Sansei dokuritsu senki.*

21. Wada Sanae, "Tokke wa itsutsu naita" (The Lizard Cried Five Times), in *Chichi no senki;* "Senshisha o shiraberu, Indonesia seifu ga yakusoku" (Indonesian Government Promises to Search for Bodies), *Asahi Shimbun,* May 20, 1965; and Fuji Terebi, "Dokyumentari gekijō, 'Raosu no Nihonjin' " (Documentary Theater, "The Japanese in Laos"), September 19, 1965.

22. Kamiko, *Ware Reite ni shisezu.*

23. Masutomi Oko, "Koji o sodatete" (Raising an Orphan), *Fujin Gahō,* April 1948.

24. "Masa-chyan, nijūnen mae no nesan o yurushite" (Little Akira, Please Forgive Me for Twenty Years Ago), *Sande Mainichi,* April 3, 1966.

25. "Sōnan shita Karafuto hikiagesen" (The Karafuto Repatriation Ship That Sank), *Mainichi Shimbun,* August 22, 1965.

26. Many of the most bellicose prowar people seemed to forget that until August 14 they had been screaming about the "American and British beasts." They neatly doffed their jingoism, cooperated with America, and skillfully adjusted to the postwar realities. Some Japanese overseas could not switch gears so quickly. In August and September 1945, 86 percent of the Japanese in Brazil reportedly still believed that Japan would win the war. Even when it gradually became known that Japan had lost, one group called the Victory Organization insisted that Japan would win the war. Anyone who said Japan had lost was called a traitor; a number of persons were reportedly killed or ostracized. See Takagi Toshirō, "Burajiru no katchigumi, makegumi" (Japan Will Win, Japan Has Lost Groups in Brazil), *Asahi Shimbun,* August 11–15, 1964; "Inochigake no haisen hōdō" (Dangerous Report: Japan Is Defeated), *Asahi Shimbun,* November 12–13. 1964; and *Coronia bungaku,* No. 3, as quoted in *Mainichi Shimbun,* July 3, 1967.

27. Kikuchi and Omura, *Ano hito wa kaette konakatta;* "Otōsan ga inai" (No Father), *Asahi Shimbun,* July 28, 1965; Saga-ken Izoku-kai Seinen-bu, ed., *Otō-san* (Father!) and Nihon Izoku Kai, ed., *Ishizue* (Foundation).

28. "Genbakubyō de musume-san shinu, nijūsai de totsuzen hatsubyō" (Woman Dies of Radiation Disease, Struck Suddenly at Age Twenty), *Yomiuri Shimbun,* July 29, 1965; "Hannen no shisha nijūkyūnin, Hiroshima no hibakusha" (Twenty-nine Die in Half Year, Hiroshima Radiation Victims), *Asahi Shimbun,* August 3, 1965; "Genbakuki mae ni mata gisei, Nagasaki no rōnin futari" (More Die before the Anniversary of the Bombing, Two Elderly Persons in Nagasaki), *Yomiuri Shimbun,* August 8, 1965; and "Hibakusha futari mata shinu" (Two More A-Bomb Victims Die), *Mainichi Shimbun,* August 5, 1967.

29. Ministry of Health and Welfare report, *Asahi Shimbun,* February 5, 1967.

30. Chūgoku Shimbunsha, *Hiroshima no kiroku* (A Record of Hiroshima); 3 vols; Yamashiro Tomoe, *Kono sekai no katasumi de* (A Corner of the World); Oe Kenzaburō, *Hiroshima nōto* (A Note on Hiroshima); *Nagata Tōzō shashinshū, Hiroshima 1960* (Photographs by Nagata Tōzō, Hiroshima 1960); Domon Ken, *Hiroshima;* "Jūyonnenme no tsumeato, genbakubyō wa mada tsuzuiteru" (Scars Fourteen Years Later, The Atomic Disease Lingers On), *Shūkan Asahi,* August 16, 1959; "Wasurezaru genbaku, ima mo tsuzuku jūgonenme no kizuato" (The Unforgettable Atomic Bomb, More Scars Fifteen Years Later), *Shūkan Asahi,* August 14, 1960; "Genbakushō no omoni chikaratsuki musume-san no jisatsu" (The Burden of the Radiation Disease, Suicide of a Young Woman), *Yomiuri Shimbun,* January 19, 1965; "Nagasaki de genbakushō kanja ga jisatsu" (Suicide of a Radiation Disease Sufferer in Nagasaki), *Yomiuri Shimbun,* March 30, 1965; NHK Terebi, "Aru jinsei, 'Miminari' " (One Life, "Buzzing in the Ears"), April 25, 1965; "Hiroshima 65nen (1), tsuzuki genbaku suramugai, hankagai no kakki no kage ni" (Hiroshima 1965 [1] The Atomic Slum Street, Surrounded by Prosperity), *Asahi Shimbun,* August 4, 1965; "Genbaku hibakusha seikatsu hogo nisshi" (Radiation Disease Sufferer's Public Relief Record), *Gendai no Me* (October–November 1965); "Soredemo ikitekita nijūnen, Nagasaki nimo genbaku shōtōji ga ita" (Two Decades of Dedication: There Were Microcephalic Babies in Nagasaki Too), *Shūkan Asahi,* August 12, 1966; "Genbaku shōtōbyō" (Radiation Microcephalism), *Asahi Shimbun,* April 3, 1967; "Gonin ni hitori ga ijō, hibaku nise no kenkō chōsa" (One Out of Five Affected, Health Survey of Second-Generation Radiation Disease Victims), *Asahi Shimbun,* August 4, 1967; "Ima mo nokoru shi no kage" (The Shadow of Death Still Hovers), *Asahi Shimbun,* August 5, 1967; "Hibakusha no kono koe o kike" (Hear the Call of the Atomic Bomb Victims), *Asahi Shimbun,* August 8, 1967. There are innumerable additional accounts.

31. "Beigun seiteki shinchū-shi" (History of the Sexual Activities of the U.S. Occupation Forces), in Kanzaki Kiyoshi, *Yoru no kichi* (Night Life around the Bases), Chap. 1; Mark Gayn, *Japan Diary,* May 10, 21, 1946; "DDT to onna" (DDT and Women), in Sumimoto Toshio, ed., *Senryō hiroku* (Secret Record of the Occupation); *Takami Jun nikki,* November 13, 1945; "Teisō no bōhatei ni natta onnatachi" (The Prostitutes, Protectors of Chastity), *Shūkan Bunshun,* August 16, 1965; and "Sensō to sei, kono ijō taiken ga motarashita kizuato" (War and Sex, Afflicted by a Strange Experience), *Asahi Gurafu,* August 20, 1967.

32. Mizuno Hiroshi, *Nihon no teisō, gaikokuhei ni okasareta josei no shuki* (Japanese Chastity, Notes of Women Assaulted by Foreign Soldiers); Gotō Tsutomu, *Zoku Nihon no teisō* (More on Japanese Chastity); Gotō Tsutomu, *Sengo zankoku monogatari* (Tales of Postwar Cruelty); Tanabe Tamiko, "Gake no ue no omoide" (Memories of the Cliff), in *Sensō to watakushi;* and Ishizuka Mieko, "Tenkei" (Background), in *ibid.* An American woman soldier reportedly drugged a Japanese male student and used him as a sexual plaything. Kaneko, *Zetsubō no seishin-shi.*

33. One of the mixed-blood children followed exactly in her mother's footsteps by becoming a prostitute for American servicemen stationed in Japan in connection with the Vietnam war. The stigma of her birth persisted through an unhappy childhood: "No matter how good I tried to be, I was taunted. They said 'You're the daughter of a slut.' " "Kamera wa mita! Yokosuka no aibito" (The Camera Saw Her! Sweetheart of Yokosuka), *Asahi Gurafu,* May 12, 1967.

34. "Tōnan A no sensō iji konketsujitachi" (Mixed-blood orphans of Southeast Asia), *Mainichi Shimbun,* July 19, 1966; and "Hisanna Hikoku nikkei koji jitsjujō" (The Wretched Plight of Japanese-Filipino Mixed-Blood Orphans), *ibid.,* May 10, 1966.

35. Shinchūgun Higaisha Renmei, *Wasurerareta hitobito, Senryōka ni atta Jirado jiken* (The Forgotton Ones, The Girard Case during the Occupation), and directives regarding "Criminals Acts by the Allied Forces," in Shūsen Renraku Chūō Jimukyoku, *Keisatsu ni kansuru rengōkoku shireishū* (Allied Directives Concerning the Police), Vol. 2.

36. "Sugamo BC kaikyū senpan no shuki"; Satō Ryōichi, "Pekin shūyōsho" (Peking Detention Center), in *Shōwa sensō bungaku zenshū,* Vol. 12; *Shijitsu kiroku, senpan saiban, Eiryō chiku;* and Tsukuba Hisaharu, "BC kyū senpan to sengo shisō" (B and C Class War Criminals and Postwar Thought), *Shisō no Kagaku,* August 1960.

37. "Urareta Ogasawaratō" (Sold Out, The Bonin Islands) *Shūkan Yomiuri,* August 18, 1960.

38. Okinawa-ken Gakusei-kai, *Sokoku naki Okinawa* (Okinawa, Prefecture without a Country); Senaga Kamejirō, *Minzoku no higeki* (Tragedy of a Nation); Senaga Kamejirō, *Okinawa kara no hōkoku* (Report from Okinawa); Nakano Yoshio and Arasaki Moriteru, *Okinawa mondai nijūnen* (Twenty Years of the Okinawan Problem); Nikkyōso Okinawa Kyōshokuinkai, *Sakubun wa uttaeru, Okinawa no kora* (Their Compositions Beseech, The Children of Okinawa); "Fuan tsunoru kichi Okinawa" (Okinawa, Anxious Outpost), *Yomiuri Shimbun,* March 30, 1965; and "Betonamu sensō hokyū kichi Okinawa o miru" (A Look at Okinawa,

Supply Base for the Vietnam War), *Asahi Shimbun,* May 4, 1966. A convincing argument has been made that article 3 of the Peace Treaty, which permits the continued occupation of Okinawa, and the way the islands are used by the U.S. military are unconstitutional. See Diet debate in *Asahi Shimbun,* February 25, 1961; the Japan Socialist party's interpretation, *Yomiuri Shimbun,* February 10, 1965; plaintiff's argument in the Okinawa suit, *Asahi Shimbun,* September 9, 1965; and the report by the Nihon Bengoshi Rengōkai in *Asahi Shimbun,* November 8, 1967.

39. "Sensai koji, jūhachinen no ayumi" (War Orphans, Eighteen Years of Effort), *Mainichi Shimbun,* May 17, 1964.

40. NHK Terebi, "Gendai no eizo, 'Nao byōshō ni fusu shōbyōhei'" (Contemporary Images, "Wounded Soldiers Still Bedridden"), August 12, 1966; and TBS Terebi, "Yameru akagami" (The Sick Draftee), November 22, 1966.

41. "Kanashiki dokugasu kanjatachi"; "Nihon ni atta dokugasutō"; TBS Rajio, "Jūkyūnenme no dokugasubyō kanja" (The Poison Gas Victims Nineteen Years Later), August 15, 1964.

42. Nihon Terebi, "Non-fuikushon gekijō, 'Wasurerareta kōgun' " (Nonfiction Theater, "The Forgotten Imperial Military Forces"), August 16, 1963; Pak, *Chōsenjin kyōsei renkō no kiroku;* and Karashima Akatsuki, "Kono Chōsenjin o dare ga sukuu no ka" (Who Will Help This Korean), *Toki no Kadai,* January 1966.

43. "Kankoku no genbaku hisaisha o tazunete" (A Visit with Korean Atomic Bomb Victims), *Hiroshima no kiroku,* Vol. 1; "Hiroshima no Ubasuteyama, Chōsenjin hibakusha buraku" (The Ubasuteyama Section of Hiroshima, Korean A-Bomb Victims' Ghetto), *Asahi Janaru,* August 20, 1967; and Pak Su-nam, "Ubawareta Chōsenjin hibakusha no ningensei" (Stripped of Humanity, The Korean Atomic Bomb Victims), *Asahi Gurafu,* November 26, 1967.

CONCLUSION

1. Minobe Tatsukichi, *Shinkenpō chikujō kaisetsu* (Explanation of the New Constitution by Articles), and Yokota Kisaburō, *Tennōsei* (The Emperor System).

2. *Uchimura Kanzō zenshū* (Complete Works of Uchimura Kanzō), Vol. 16; *Uchimura Kanzō chosakushū* (Collected Works of Uchimura Kanzō), Vol. 3.

3. Ienaga, "Rekishika no tachiba kara mita kenpō mondai" (A Historian Looks at the Constitution), in *Rekishika no mita kenpō, kyōiku mondai* (A Historian Looks at Problems of the Constitution and Education).

4. Kenpō Chōsakai (Commission on the Constitution), *Kenpō seitei no keika ni kansuru shōiinkai hōkokusho* (Subcommittee Report on the Process of Enacting the Constitution), and Satō Tatsuo, *Nihonkoku kenpō seiritsu-shi* (History of the Establishment of the Constitution of Japan), Vol. 2.

5. At the San Francisco peace conference, Egypt opposed the continued stationing of U.S. troops in Japan. India refused to participate in the conference for the same reason. The actions of these non-Communist Third World nations are of renewed interest.

6. A Channel 12 program on "Nihon no gunjiryoku" (Japan's Military Power) broadcast on August 12, 1965, brought a reaction from viewers. On the program Self-Defense Force pilots gave orders and reports in English. One startled viewer wrote to a newspaper: "I wondered what country's air force I was watching. Then I saw their faces and no question about it, they were Japanese pilots" (*Asahi Shimbun,* August 14, 1965). The writer had every reason to be surprised.

7. "Mitsuya kenkyū" (Three Arrows Research) *Gendai no Me* (May 1965). The article includes classified documents from the Self-Defense Forces made available by Diet member Okada Haruo. In the materials is the statement: "With regard to initial preparatory operations for the defense of Japan, the control of the U.S. military commander in Japan has already [i.e., under previously specified conditions] been acknowledged; with regard to operations for the direct defense of Japan, except for special matters, the U.S. military in Japan will be in command."

8. Ienaga, "Shisō no jiyū to sono genkai" (Encroachments on Intellectual Freedom), in *Zusetsu Nihon bunka-shi, gendai* (Illustrated History of Japanese Culture, Modern Period), first edition.

9. Nakano Yoshio, "Nihonjin no kenpō ishiki" (Japanese Understanding of the Constitution), in Kenpō Mondai Kenkyūkai, ed., *Kenpō o ikasu mono* (Making the Constitution Live); Kobayashi Naoki, *Nihonkoku kenpō no mondai jōkyō* (Problems of the Japanese Constitution); Kobayashi Naoki, *Nihon ni okeru kenpō dōtai no bunseki* (An Analysis of Constitutional Dynamics); and Nihon Hōshakai Gakkai, ed., *Kenpō ishiki no teichaku* (Acceptance of the Constitution).

10. Hidaka Rokurō, ed., *Senkyūhyaku rokujūnen gogatsu jūku nichi*, May 19, 1960.

11. A few examples are the numerous coordinated antiwar demonstrations held in Japan and America from May 22, 1965, on; the conference of Japanese and American antiwar activists held in Tokyo in August 1966; and the desertion of crewmen from a U.S. aircraft carrier with Japanese assistance in November 1967.

NOTE: CHANGING JAPANESE VIEWS OF THE WAR

1. "Kawabe Torashirō shōshō kaisō ōtōroku (Statement by Major General Kawabe Torashirō), *Gendaishi shiryō* (12) *Nitchū sensō (4)* (Source Materials on Contemporary History, Vol. 12, Japan-China War, Vol. 4). (Hereafter cited as *GS.* Succeeding information indicates volume number in series, individual volume title, and volume number under individual title).

2. Takagi Toshirō, *Imuparu* (Imphal).

3. Hosokawa Morisada, *Jōhō tennō ni tassezu* (What the Emperor Was *Not Told*), March 4, 1945.

4. Gaimushō (Foreign Ministry), *Nihon gaikō nenpyō narabi ni shuyō monjo* (Chronology and Major Documents of Japan's Foreign Policy), Vol. 2.

5. "Kokka Shintō ni tsuite no shirei" (Directives on State Shintō); Mombushō (Ministry of Education), *Shinkyōiku shishin* (Guidelines for the New Education).

6. Tanemura Suketaka, *Daihon'ei kimitsu nisshi* (Secret Record of Imperial Headquarters), December 10, 1941.

7. Yokota Kisaburō, *Sensō hanzairon* (On War Crimes), and Dandō Shigemitsu, "Sensō hanzai no rironteki kaibō" (A Theoretical Analysis on War Crimes), in *Keihō no kindaiteki tenkai* (The Modern Evolution of Criminal Law).

8. "Kokkai ni hana hiraku bunkyōron" (An Interpretation Blooms in the Diet), *Tosho Shimbun,* February 21, 1953.

9. Kamikawa Hikomatsu, "Taiheiyō sensō e no michi (Japan's Road to the Pacific War), in *Nihon Gakushiin Kiyō,* Vol. 23, No. 1; and Kamikawa Hikomatsu, "Kankō kanryō ni atatte" (As We Finish Publication), in *Taiheiyō sensō e no michi* (Japan's Road to the Pacific War, hereafter cited as TSM), Vol. 7, postscript.

10. Agawa Hiroyuki, "Watakushi no sensō bungaku" (My War Writing), *Yomiuri Shimbun,* August 17, 1964.

11. *Shūkan Dokushojin,* September 14, 1964.

12. Tamura Taijirō, "Senjō to watakushi, sensō bungaku no mō hitotsu no me" (I Saw the Battlefield; Another Side of War Literature), *Asahi Shimbun,* February 24, 1965; Gomikawa Junpei, "Seishin no gan—Nihonjin to tai Chūgoku sensō" (A Spiritual Cancer—Japanese and the War in China), in *Gendai no hakken, Watakushi to sensō* (Discovering Our Time, The War and I), Vol. 1.

13. Ienaga Saburō, "Sengo no rekishi kyōiku" (Postwar Historical Education), in *Iwanami kōza Nihon rekishi* (Iwanami Lectures, Japanese History), Vol. 23.

14. Ienaga Saburō, *Kyōkasho kentei* (Government Textbook Certification).

15. Murakami Hyoe, "Dai Tōa sensō shikan" (An Interpretation of the Greater East Asian War), *Chūō Kōron,* March 1958.

Index

Abe Isoo, 16, 110
Abe Nobuyuki, 82
Abe Tomoji, 205
Adachi Kenzō, 64, 121
Agawa Hiroyuki, 254
air force (Japan), 142, 151, 251; special attack units (Kamikaze), 108, 148, 151, 183
air raids (Japan), 140–1, 147, 148, 156, 189, 196–7, 199–200, 202, 206, 208, 209, 221; *see also* atomic bomb/bombings
Akamatsu Katsumarō, 121
Akamatsu Yoshitsugu, 185
Akashi Junzō, 217
Akashi Mahito, 217
Aleutians, 144
Amakasu Masahiko, 60
Anami, 232
Anti-Comintern Pact, 80
Aoto Minso, 215
Arahata Kanson, 204
Araki Sadao, 40, 45, 97–8
Arita Hachirō, 130
army (Japan): antiwar front-line propaganda aimed at, 218, 219; codes of behavior, 48, 49–50, 61, 81; dead, 30, 49–50, 102, 126–7, 147, 149, 152, 182, 184, 197, 198, 214 (*see also* casualties; special attack [suicide] units); discipline and discipline problems (plots and insubordination), 30, 33, 37–8, 39, 41–7 *passim*, 51, 52–3, 54, 70, 81, 82, 131, 213, 214, 215, 232; draft, 47, 51, 125, 126, 150, 157, 158, 193, 195, 198, 214–15; draft, and refusal to serve, 30, 213, 214, 215; drug

trade, protection for, 69, 73, 101, 165; fighting spirit and toughness emphasized, 48–54 *passim;* food supply, 51, 143, 146, 147, 166, 192; and Indian National Army, 175; Koreans in, 157, 158, 239; looting by, 95, 166, 186, 187; military police, *see* Kempeitai; and navy, relationship, 39, 72; postwar disbanding of, 192, 241; and prisoners of war, 53, 168, 169, 186; as prisoners of war, 49–50, 184, 218, 234; reservists/reservist associations, 98, 112, 124, 191; sexual debauchery, 187, 190–1, 194 (*see also* rape); structure, 33, 34–5, 36, 46–54; structure, common soldiers, 47, 50–4 *passim,* 124, 254; structure, NCOs, 51, 53, 54, 124; structure, officers, 41, 47, 48, 49, 194, 254; weapons and equipment, 48, 51, 52, 82, 145, 146, 150, 151 (*see also* special attack [suicide] units); Western forces as model, 48; wounded, 147, 182, 192, 197, 235, 239; *see also* atrocities; Korea Army; Kwantung Army; Manchukuo Army; military forces/militarism; individual conflicts
art, 105, 123, 202
Asahi Gurafu, 29, 103, 125, 140–1, 170, 193
Asami Sensaku, 109
Asō Fumiko, 160
atomic bomb/bombings, 97, 101, 126, 150, 151, 188, 200–2, 231; after-effects (A-bomb disease), 236, 236*n.*, 239

305

About the Author

Saburō Ienaga was born in Nagoya in 1913. He taught at the Tokyo University of Education from 1949 to 1977, and is now a professor emeritus of that institution. He is the author of fifty books; his major works include *The Development of the Logic of Negation in the History of Japanese Thought; Research on Ueki Emori; Minobe Tatsukichi, His Life and Thought;* and *Tanabe Hajime, War and a Philosopher.* Professor Ienaga's lengthy legal campaign against textbook certification by the government is currently before the Japanese Supreme Court.

Ex-Libris- Branch of
Lake County Public Library

ULISYS

10816700

Ex-Library: Friends of
Lake County Public Library

940.5352 IENA
Ienaga, Saburo, 1913-
The Pacific War : World
War II and the Japanese, 19
1931-1945

LAKE COUNTY PUBLIC LIBRARY
INDIANA

AD	FF	MU
AV	GR	NC
BO	HI	SJ
CL	HO	CNL
DS	LS	

10-78

Some materials may be renewable by phone or in person if there a
no reserves or fines due.   www.lakeco.lib.in.us   LCP#03